FOR A NEW AMERICA Essays in History and Politics from *Studies on the Left,* 1959–1967

FOR A NEW AMERICA Essays in History and Politics from *Studies on the Left,* 1959–1967

EDITED BY James Weinstein AND David W. Eakins

RANDOM HOUSE   New York

FIRST PRINTING
9 8 7 6 5 4 3 2

Library of Congress Catalog Card Number: 73-85618

Manufactured in the United States of America
by The Haddon Craftsmen, Inc.

Designed by Vincent Torre

Preface

Studies on the Left began publishing in Madison, Wisconsin, in the fall of 1959 and ceased publication in New York City in the summer of 1967. During those seven and a half years, twenty-eight editors served as board members, some for less than a year, others for almost the entire time. Although all the editors were leftists they represented a wide range of views and tendencies and many professional concerns and interests. *Studies* was many things to its editors and to its readers, and several very different anthologies could be made from its pages. This volume brings together the articles and reviews that we think are most important to the historical and theoretical development of a revolutionary movement in the United States.

The emphasis in these selections is on an historical examination of the American political economy in the twentieth century, and on the histories of the socialist and Afro-American movements. Consequently, many articles— on early American history, Cuba and Latin America, literary criticism, reports of movement activities—have been omitted, some because they clearly do not fit into the framework of this collection, others because their interest, in our opinion, was short-lived. Other articles, such as William A. Williams' essays on "American Intervention in Russia, 1917-1919," have been omitted because they have been reprinted elsewhere.[1]

We believe that *Studies on the Left* was important in

[1] Williams' articles appear in *Containment and Revolution,* David Horowitz, ed. (Boston, Beacon Press, 1967).

two ways. First, it helped to revive radical scholarship in the United States and to create a new radical understanding of the American political economy. Second, *Studies* contributed to the consciousness and ideological development of the New Left.

We think it is important to discuss the political history of *Studies* itself, and we have therefore written our own essay on the journal's development in place of a general introduction to this anthology. Such a history is unavoidably both internal and partisan, and we realize that ours is only one of several possible treatments of the basic direction of the journal and its contents. Of necessity also, our essay touches only on several aspects of the journal's contents and skips entirely over much more. A comprehensive review of *Studies'* content, however, would be impossibly long, boring, and unnecessary in any event— complete runs of the journal are available in many libraries and all seven volumes are being reprinted.[2] We hope this selection will stimulate readers to look at the complete volumes.

D.W.E.

J.W.

[2] A.M.S. Press, New York, 1969.

Editors of
Studies On The Left

(Editors are listed in chronological order. Only resident editorial board members are listed. The many non-resident and associate editors are not included.)

Joan Bromberg	1959-1961
David W. Eakins	1959-1963
Lloyd Gardner	1959-1960
Saul Landau	1959-1963
Nancy O'Connor	1959-1960
William Rouff	1959-1961
Dena Samberg	1959-1961
Stephen Scheinberg	1959-1963
Martin J. Sklar	1959-1965
Carl Weiner	1959-1961
Lee Baxandall	1960-1967
Matthew Chapperon	1960-1963
Arthur Hack	1960-1963
Eleanor Hakim	1960-1963
James Weinstein	1960-1967
Helen M. Kramer	1961-1967
Michael A. Lebowitz	1961-1963
Alan Cheuse	1964-1965
Norman Fruchter	1964-1966
James O'Connor	1964-1964
Stanley Aronowitz	1964-1967
Eugene D. Genovese	1964-1967
Tom Hayden	1965-1966
Staughton Lynd	1965-1966
Ronald Aronson	1966-1967
Shin'ya Ono	1966-1967
Robert D. Wolfe	1966-1967

Contents

PART II

AN AMERICAN SOCIALISM

PART III

BLACK NATIONALISM

Contents

PART IV

JEWISH IDENTITY

FOR A NEW AMERICA Essays in History and Politics from *Studies on the Left,* 1959–1967

Introduction

The late 1950's was a period of profound crisis for the old left, particularly for the Communist Party, which had been the major socialist party in the United States since the middle 1920's. The Party had reached its high point during the wartime alliance between the United States and the Soviet Union, gaining the greatest respectability and largest popular following in its history; however, its successes were achieved by a surrender to liberalism on the ideological front—by a cessation of serious thought about the attainment of socialism in the United States, and the ending of public agitation for a socialist alternative to the corporate liberal state.

After the war, when the temporary alliance of the Western imperial powers and the Soviet Union against Germany, Italy, and Japan ended, Communists in the United States, as elsewhere, once again came under attack as agents for the Soviet Union. These attacks were the domestic Cold War counterpart of an aggressively expansionist American foreign policy. In the years 1946 to 1948 the government instituted a purge of federally employed "potential subversives" and established a list of subversive organizations as a basis for similar action in private industry. In the labor movement action was initiated to expel pro-communist leaders and unions from the CIO. State and federal un-American activities committees worked successfully to isolate left wing unions and to drive radicals from the nation's colleges and universities. The Communist Party leadership was indicted under the Smith Act, and a number of spy trials molded public opinion.

As the left-liberal coalition disintegrated and Communists were losing their influence in the unions, the Party helped make possible Henry A. Wallace's independent candidacy in 1948 and the organization of the short-lived Progressive Party. Wallace's small vote (he won only 1,156,000 in a total of over 50,000,000), and then his split with the Communists over his support for the Korean war completed the Party's isolation. By 1950 the party had lost almost all of its support, as well as the remnants of its identification with American socialism.

The years immediately following the collapse of the Progressive Party were years of defensiveness and disintegration for the left. The old left had relied heavily on liberal-left coalitions, and by 1950 these had all but disappeared. This was true even before the accelerated onslaught of such demagogues as Senator Joseph R. McCarthy and Representative Richard M. Nixon, who simply built upon the existing premises of Cold War liberalism and the oppressive climate it had already created. As domestic hysteria increased, virtually none of those Democrats and liberals who had once participated with the left in the New Deal or the wartime alliance were willing to defend their former activities and associations. Now, in an effort not only to prove themselves loyal, but also as a consequence of the logic of their own Cold War, liberals frequently exceeded the right wing in their attacks on Communists and other critics of post-war policies.

By this time, the Communist Party itself had no sense of direction, no means of defense other than an appeal—to the very liberals who were attacking it—to uphold traditional civil liberties. These appeals were fruitless monologues and gained very little support outside the ranks of the dwindling left. The Cold War at home succeeded in creating a cowed and passive population in large part because the left had built its strategy on a popular front alliance with liberal leaders and union bureaucrats. When these groups abandoned the left the limited accomplishments of the Communists during the 1930's "Red Decade" became clear.

Ironically, despite McCarthy's success in terrorizing liberals, conservatives, and leftists alike, the domestic repression symbolized by his attacks actually delayed the ultimate crisis within the Party. Defense of the Party and resistance to McCarthyism occupied the thoughts and actions of Party members during these years. In a period of contraction and defense there is little time or apparent need for thinking about a positive program or a new society. The defense against McCarthyism became an end in itself—a defense for the Party's survival—and coincidentally one of the liberal social order, rather than an opportunity to expose corporate liberalism in the name of a better way of life. Only with the end of McCarthyism did recognition of the real nature of the crisis become unavoidable.

By 1955, Communists and those close to the Party's various front-organizations became increasingly aware that they had no direction—no vision of a socialist United States other than the example offered by Soviet life, and no long-range strategy aimed toward social transformation. This had been true for a long time, of course, but now with the anti-fascist alliance broken, many Party members and followers acutely perceived their lack of perspective.

This growing consciousness was well advanced by 1956, when the left was struck by Nikita Khrushchev's revelations about Stalinist terror (at the Twentieth Congress of the Communist Party of the Soviet Union), and by the Russian Army's invasion of socialist Hungary. Now, not only did the Communist left have no publicly articulated socialist program, but its private vision of a Soviet America was also shattered. The combination of the steady decline of Party influence, post-McCarthy aimlessness, and the disillusionment caused by events in Russia and Hungary reduced the Communist left to the impotence of other socialist sects; events had cleared the ground for a new

kind of left politics. For the first time since 1900 American
left-wing socialists were on their own—not only without
a coherent theory or a vision, but also without an organized
movement.

Studies on the Left came into being in this situation.
It was both a product of the disenchantment with the old
left and a forerunner and participant in the new. The
journal was the creation of a group of graduate students
at the University of Wisconsin, many of whom were members of the Wisconsin Socialist Club, and most of whom
were historians. Several of the initial editors had been
members of the Communist Party or of its youth organization, the Labor Youth League. Others had recently
become radicals or Marxists in the course of their studies.
All shared two things: an awareness of the severe failure
of the old left, and a commitment to participate in the
development of a body of theory to stimulate the creation
of a new revolutionary movement in the United States.
Underlying the work of the editors was a loosely shared
consciousness of the need to develop socialist thought comprehending American reality.

That consciousness had a strong influence on the selection of a name for the new journal, as well as upon its
editorial policies. The desire to build an explicitly socialist
movement distinguished the *Studies* group from others
also beginning to stir in the less repressive atmosphere of
1958 and 1959. The first distinction, regarding *Studies'*
public face, became clear when the *Studies* group and
another at the University of Chicago (which later published its own journal, *New University Thought*) attempted to merge. The merger proved impossible because
the Chicago group opposed use of the word "left," and
because the *Studies* group intended explicitly to advance
the development of theory for a new *radical* movement, a
goal not actively shared by the Chicago people. They
argued further, that the name "Studies on the Left" would
alienate potential readers before they could turn the

magazine's cover. They believed the prevailing Cold War ideology of the 1950's had fulfilled one of its purposes all too well. Instead, they proposed a "radical" content, but without fear-inducing labels or an explicit statement of purpose, so that the new magazine might be widely accepted. In their hearts the editors could be radicals or socialists; in the journal they would appear as militant liberals. This was viewed by the *Studies* group as a perpetuation of the worst habits of the old left; they rejected the proposal, just as the Chicago people rejected their perspective, and, in the end, two journals appeared.

The greater distinction between *Studies'* underlying purpose and tendencies among other emerging New Left groups was more complex. It concerned disagreement with the original editors' concepts of the nature and function of theory, and their intention to initiate the development of a new American socialism. In the seven and a half years of *Studies'* publication these differences became more sharply defined—particularly over the question of the need for an explicitly socialist politics and the relationship of intellectuals and theory to the rapidly growing student movement. These issues most clearly divided the board in the journal's last three years and led finally to the decision to cease publication.

At first, however, the problem facing the editors was less divisive. The task was simply to define the function of socialist intellectuals in the American political climate, one that denied the legitimacy of radical scholarship, and in which all but a very few Marxist scholars had been purged from higher education. Was there a place for the socialist as scholar, for intellectual work done with the purpose of creating a new and better society? In the prevailing atmosphere of repression and conformity this was no trifling question for students who planned to make academic work their life's activity.

"In academic circles," the editors wrote in their first

editorial, "the term 'objectivity' is generally used to indicate the dispassion, the non-partisanship with which the 'true scholar' approaches his work." But, they continued, "[it is] also frequently used to indicate the prevalent, or 'majority' view." And, in fact, in the currently dominant view in academic circles, "objectivity" was "reducible to the weight of authority, the viewpoint of those who are in a position to enforce standards, the value judgments of the not so metaphorical market place of ideas."

Similarly, the use of "scholarly dispassion" was seen as "a way of justifying acceptance (either active or passive) of the status quo." Thus, "digging up facts to support traditional and accepted interpretations, [with] no interest in the significance of these facts for larger theoretical questions," did not necessarily mean that the "unimpassioned" scholar was any less biased than his neighbor— although it might very well mean that he cared less. "On the other hand, when a scholar arrives at a radical or unconventional interpretation, he may very well become excited by what he is doing. For the act of contradiction involves emotions more tumultuous than those aroused by the state of acceptance. Scholarly dispassion is the true medium of the scholar satisfied with (or browbeaten by) things as they are."

As graduate students committed to understanding "the origins of racism so that we could help stamp it out, [wanting] to know why people suffer, so that we could help to make suffering less," the editors had not been dispassionate in choosing the "intellectual racket." Yet such inquiries were hampered by the prevailing standards of scholarship. They "set up a screen between ourselves and our product," wrote the editors, "an automatic censoring device [that] trims and deflates and confines our work, under the pretext of what is supposed to be 'objective scholarship,' until we no longer know it as our own." Scholarship for them had not meant, and they did not want it to become merely a "means of livelihood and security."

The editors insisted, accordingly, on pursuing their radical purpose. There was, they believed, room for the thinker "committed to the investigation of the origins, purposes, and limitations of institutions and concepts, as well as for the conservative or liberal scholar who is committed to their efficient maintenance and improvement." In short, there was a need in scholarship "for the application of reason to the *reconstruction* of society," as well as for legalistic interpretation and reform. Indeed, the editors suggested, the radical scholar is more likely to be truly objective. His very partisanship gives him a kind of objectivity because of his unconcern with the preservation of established institutions and conventional conceptions. Radical scholars could be truly objective because they would not hesitate "to carry inquiry along paths where so-called 'objective' conservative or liberal scholars would not care to tread."

But the problem of radical scholarship was neither a narrowly intellectual one, nor a personal one. There were, even in the 1950's, men and women both in and out of academic life who pursued their intellectual labor "with a combination of scholarly integrity and commitment to the humanization of society." And there were many others who retained the desire to do so, but were paralyzed by the "forcefully maintained academic standards."

The inhibitory quality of American scholarship therefore defined a two-fold need: to create a radical intellectual community for the then isolated individuals, and for that community to produce work that could initiate the creation of a body of theory for a new radical movement. Extending Woodrow Wilson's assertion that the radicalism of his day consisted not of what was proposed, but of what was disclosed, the editors observed that a relentless disclosure of the nature and causes of social institutions endured as a radical activity. Yet, they concluded, "we hope that the radicalism of what is disclosed, as it increases and matures, may provide knowledge and theory for the future growth of a radicalism of what is proposed."

The development of "a radicalism of what is proposed," however, was still a long way off in 1959. In the meantime, the editors were concerned with immediate developments, and with analyses and criticisms of American society. In the first of several efforts to analyse the increasing activity in the black community, ("Civil Rights and the Birth of Community," 1960) the editors attempted to assess the "revolutionary" developments in the Southern civil rights movement. A later issue (Volume II, No. 3, 1962) examined more deeply the emerging ideological tendencies in black movements with two articles, one by Harold Cruse (reprinted here) and the other an interview with the North Carolina militant, Robert F. Williams.

In the 1962 issue, the editors commented that their earlier statement had "pointed to the growth of the integration struggle in the South as a significant manifestation of the development of self-consciousness and community among Negroes." Yet from 1960 to 1962, they noted, integration had "not been the only program of positive action instituted by Negroes. . . . The rapid growth of black separatist and nationalist organizations, rejection of non-violence and passive resistance, and the espousal of socialism by militant Negroes," had all appeared as reactions to second-class citizenship. "These contrasting trends," the editors wrote, "indicate fundamental differences in the evaluation of the present and raise a question as to whether the Negroes' achievement of human rights (political, economic, and social) is possible through 'integration' into the existing American society, or whether basic changes in social and economic relations must be effected before there can be equal and harmonious relations between the races."

The third issue (Volume I, No. 3, 1960) turned to the Cuban Revolution and reactions of the United States government and among American intellectuals. The Revolution itself was greeted enthusiastically by the editors and played a central role in the development of the

journal. Three editors visited Cuba during the summer
of 1960 and wrote on the Revolution as a new crisis in
Cold War ideology. (The issue included an article on
the Revolution by Jean Paul Sartre and some notes on
the experiences of the revolutionaries by Commandante
Ernesto "Che" Guevara.)

The editorial began by calling on radicals to take the
lead in exposing the sham battle between "freedom" and
"Communism." It then argued that Cuba had presented
the United States with a unique opportunity—to demonstrate that it could accommodate itself to revolution in the
colonial world—but that instead, the State Department
had insisted on attacking what was then clearly a non-
Communist revolution, thereby forcing Cuba to line up on
the Russian side of the Cold War.

The world view promulgated by Cold War ideologues,
and unchallenged by the intellectual community, that all
revolutionary movements were part of a world-wide communist conspiracy made it "impossible to understand,
much less deal with, the changes that have taken place
and are taking place throughout the underdeveloped
countries." The Cuban Revolution, the editors wrote,
"brings this point close to home. Unless the United States
can be freed from its own ideological creation, the American people may find themselves isolated from the world
by the devil theory of communism and popular revolution. While the rest of the world moves forward, the
United States assumes the role of the last haven of reaction."

In another editorial on the Revolution (Volume II, No.
3, 1962), the editors wrote, "at the very time that a world
in upheaval demands that intellectuals directly confront
the problems of man in society," intellectuals in the United
States had, with few exceptions, "marched off in the wrong
direction." In the 50's, in the face of a neo-colonial policy
toward the Cuban Revolution on the part of the Eisen-
hower administration, and in the early 60's despite the

beginnings of important social movements among black and white students, the general intellectual community remained inert. Intellectuals as a group either rationalized and justified the status quo, or ignored the large social questions and concentrated on trivia. The American intellectual had "failed to accept the role of critic and investigator of social institutions" within our society, as well as the relationship of the United States with the rest of the world. Instead, he had "substituted a growing tendency to play the role of scholar as taxonomist, scholar as pragmatic archivist, scholar as specialized technician, concerning himself only with the minute and detailed study and analysis of isolated aspects of our culture, unrelated to the rapid changes occurring in the world at large. Abstracted empiricism, the analysis of non-controversial aspects of society and the reluctance to draw obvious implications from the evidence of research," the editors charged, had "created an intellectual community unable and *unwilling if able* to deal directly with the malfunctionings of our society."

This was true not only of establishment intellectuals, but also of those in the organized left. Radical (socialist) intellectuals, if one could even speak of them as a group, had also "failed almost entirely to pierce their respective myths and dogmas." When thoughtful discussion and rigorous analysis was called for, the vestiges of the organized left had "responded with concerted attempts to force history and ideas into a preconceived mold." Forty-odd years of "fretful history [had] given the many sects on the left little more than a vested interest in defending their past activities and dogmas." Clarifying a theme only touched upon in their first editorial statement, the editors concluded that there was "a pressing need" for the development of "that body of analysis and social theory so necessary to the emergence of a new and meaningful radical movement in this country." While the editors had "few illusions as to the immediate prospects of a major political movement on the left," they firmly believed that such a movement "must be preceded by some genuinely new thinking about American society, and especially about the role of the United States in relation to the rest of the world."

Such thinking was beginning, and a new movement was beginning to form, but in 1962 it was not yet clear what its character would be nor what direction it would take. "*Studies on the Left*," the editors noted, had been "characterized as a theoretical organ for the New Left in this country." Yet they did not yet see "a significant, or even an identifiable movement in the United States that could be characterized as *the* New Left." The journal had not developed any coherent political perspective, nor had the new student groupings. In such a situation, the editors could consider themselves New Leftists only "in the sense that we are striving to free ourselves from the dogmas and myths which have paralyzed the old left, and to put behind us the history of fratricidal warfare on the left."

The job of beginning to assemble a coherent view of American society had begun; the need to formulate an agenda for moving toward a new society was only beginning to enter the editors' consciousness.

By late 1962 several of the original editors had received their degrees at the University of Wisconsin and moved away from Madison. In early 1963, three of the five remaining resident editors moved to New York. They took *Studies* with them and entered a new period. In Madison, although it had published a few articles of sociology, literary criticism and philosophy, *Studies* had been primarily devoted to problems of American history and American imperialism. But in three years' publication in Madison the political climate, especially among students, had changed substantially.

Events in the South, freedom rides and the organization and activities of the Student Non-Violent Coordinating Committee (SNCC), had stimulated northern white students and had acted as a catalyst in the formation of Students for a Democratic Society at the University of Michigan. SDS, in turn, had clearly begun to break with the politics of its parent organization, the League for Industrial Democracy, a Cold War social democratic organization, and to share many of the views expressed in *Studies*. By 1963, SDS had also begun to involve itself deeply in off-campus activities, especially in community organizing in northern ghettoes. All of this was of great interest to the *Studies* group, which saw in the development of SDS the first possibilities for a new kind of socialist politics. In New York, therefore, the remaining editors acted quickly to add new editors who shared an interest in the developing movement, and at the same time to broaden the areas of competence of the board. Within several months two new literary critics and a new economist joined the board, then another historian and a young labor leader, and somewhat later an SDS leader and a prominent activist in civil rights and peace movements. One effect of the board's new diversity was an attempt to publish a series of special issues, two of which appeared—a literature issue, Volume IV, No. 2, and a Latin America issue, Volume IV, No. 4. The more important result, however, was a partial shift in editorial focus from historical, economic, and sociological analysis and theory to more direct reporting and analysis of the student and peace movements, particularly of the community organizing activities of SDS and other groups. This was designed to develop a closer relationship between the theoretical work of the journal and the practical activity of the "movement." The editors hoped such a turn would aid the student movement in developing a comprehensive revolutionary perspective, and at the same time provide a constituency and a more immediate relevance for the theoretical work (still not very highly developed) of the journal.

A substantial basis for working closely with the new student movement already existed in the general critique of American foreign policy and of contemporary American liberalism published in *Studies* during its first three years. The most important statement of the editors' developing view, one that came to be widely shared in the New Left, appeared several months before the journal moved to New York. It was an editorial, "The Ultra-Right and Cold War Liberalism" (Volume II, No. 1, 1962), that postulated the essential responsibility of liberal corporate capitalism for the Cold War, in relation to which the ultra-right assumed a subsidiary role. The editorial was the first distinctive statement and analysis of a political position at odds with both the Communist popular front strategy and the Socialist Party-liberal coalition.

The editorial was a response to the concern expressed on the left in the late 1950's and early 1960's about the danger of a rapid growth of various far-right groups. Radicals and left-liberals alike, the editors observed, viewed the ultra-right as a threat to the existing liberal democratic society, and called "for joint action with the liberal establishment in opposition to the menace from the right." But, the editors suggested, the heavy fire aimed at the ultra-right was misdirected; "these attacks serve more to reveal the ideological confusion on the left than to explain the nature of a possible threat from the right."

Such views were faulty because they all began "by defining the right wing as a menace to an extant liberal society, rather than as a concomitant phenomenon of the increasingly authoritarian liberal mechanism for responsibly waging the Cold War." Power was held by the large corporations and they had no reason in the existing situation to turn to the right for support.

For the past thirty years the corporate élite had been successful in "maintaining its hegemony at home, as well as its ability to extend it abroad," on the basis of including the leadership of organized labor and the middle classes in "a consensus based upon real and apparent concessions to these groups." The adherence, for some fifty years, "to a flexible and developing liberal ideology has been a mark of the sophistication and consciousness of American corporate leadership acting in its own long-range class interest." Since the program of the ultra-right could only destroy the existing consensus and bring various social groups, now passive, into political opposition to the establishment, there was little chance that the ultra-rightists would win the necessary support of big capital.

That did not mean, however, that the editors saw the ultra-right as altogether harmless. On the contrary, the right had "gained attention and deference from working politicians because the rhetoric of the Cold War and the mythology of private enterprise, both of which the irrational right accepts at face value, [were] central to the ideological structure nurtured by the Cold War liberals." In addition, the particular social and policy views of the right were often attractive to "those business groups that are interest-conscious in a narrow sense, as opposed to the more broadly class-conscious leadership of the largest corporations." In many localities, support of narrow interest groups enhanced the ultra-right's political potency.

But the strength of the right seemed to have come from the logical extension of the Cold War and free market rhetoric of the liberals. "The ultras," the editors commented, "may feel more stringent measures are needed to defeat the devil, but they did not concoct the Cold War; nor did they originate the concept that the forces of justice must triumph against Communism or perish—that idea goes back to Woodrow Wilson. Their attitude in this respect is not essentially incompatible with that of such liberals as Rockefeller, Kennedy, Rusk, Stevenson, Rostow, Berle, and their corporate allies." The difference was "that the establishment liberals distinguish between rhetoric and reality, and moreover, are burdened with the responsibilities of actual power which constrain them to take account of the indescribable devastation facing even the 'winner' of a nuclear war."

The relative caution of the establishment liberals, however, provided "no basis for peace of mind," the editors
wrote: "the internal logic of the Cold War drives liberals
and conservatives alike in the direction the rightists would
like to see them go." Because there had been no large-
scale opposition to their policies, establishment liberals
had "thus far adhered to their own programs," but there
was no guarantee this would always be so. "Continuing
setbacks in the Cold War may drive [liberals] to adopt
policies of the right that now appear irrational." If that
occurred, the editors believed, there would be "no need
to call in the ultras, as happened in Germany. The liberal
establishment is itself eminently qualified to institute a
domestic authoritarianism by 'due process,' and to destroy
the world in the bargain." "As the architects and custo-
dians of the warfare state, the liberals have been the primary generators of the anti-democratic trends in American
society. Were they to discard the assumptions and programs of the Cold War, the ground would be cut from
under the ultras. The ideological stream of contemporary
right-wing politics in the United States flows from the
headwaters of corporate, Cold War liberalism. A threat
from a reactionary right has been implicit in the program
of the liberal establishment since the end of World War
II. The mistake of the left," the editors concluded, "has
been to concentrate on the elimination of an admittedly
foul brew, instead of applying itself to the destruction of
the still."

The left, then, if it hoped to play a meaningful role in
American life, was compelled to "cut itself free from the
stifling framework of liberal rhetoric and recognize that
at heart the leaders of the United States are committed to
the warfare state as the last defense of the large-scale corporate system." The editors recognized germinal stirrings
of opposition beyond the new student left, and saw the
possibility of this increasing as the burdens of the warfare
state further impinged on social programs. Also noted was
the steady decline of genuine political debate within the

two-party system. "Under the Kennedy administration," they wrote, the "peculiarities of the Cold War consensus . . . reached their highest stage of development to date: trade union officials lead the hue and cry over military contract cancellations, civil liberties are carefully 'balanced' against national interest and found outmoded, and politics are decreed abolished and replaced by 'techniques.' " Recognition of the "demise of party politics as an arena of policy making" was seen as the cause of movements "outside the traditional channels of political action." "Student demonstrations, peace marches, no less than right wing intrigues, indicate a growing awareness among dissenters that social change cannot be brought about within the framework of the two party system."

But dissident activities had, at that point, involved "only politically marginal groups, and they, insisting on giving exclusive attention to the immediate issues," had "consciously refrained from drawing general conclusions or developing an independent over-view." A "meaningful, cohesive radical opposition" could not develop "without its own ideology." Unfortunately, there was "no radical ideology even potentially available to those workers, farmers, and disaffected middle class persons whose experience might turn them to the left." Indeed, the editors believed, "among the conglomeration of not entirely compatible elements that make up the ultra-right, there are many whose revulsion from liberal politics flows from an ever-narrowing access to the process of political decision-making afforded by the liberal oligarchy." Many of these people might have "turned left were it not for the acceptance by many leftists of the rhetorical framework of liberalism (just as many agrarian radicals in 1936 joined forces with the Coughlinites in the Union party rather than follow the dominant radicalism into coalition with the large corporation-oriented liberalism of the New Deal)." These estranged people, and others who remained passive could not be won to the left, nor could the left itself build a

ing an appeal to conscience.' " Recent history had shown,
the editorial went on, that "radicals who play their cards
of 'immediate demands' while withholding their Ace of
socialism until the 'critical moment' have found that the
critical moment always recedes further into the distance.
Time and again they are shut out of the game to face a
New Deal, while their Ace never reaches the table."

Thus it was no longer enough to be radical in private
theory; and it was not enough to issue calls for "independent politics." A political movement that lacked
fundamentally distinct and richly articulated principles
d objectives, ways and means, as compared with the
minant politics of its time" could not be revolutionary
gardless of its intentions." Neither could it be inde-
dent, "however separate its organizational apparatus."
ory had taught that "if a 'radical' discontent with,
disaffection from the prevailing social system" were
ranslated into a "publicly pronounced program for
eorganization of society," the discontent would re-
radical "only in degree, not in effect, and disaffection
scomfit while remaining politically impotent."
ar, the editorial concluded, mankind had "pro-
o principles that fundamentally differ from those
rialist capitalism, no principles that meet the 'im-
demands' of working people on a foundation of
cy, brotherhood, peace, and individual fulfillment,
n the principles of social ownership and demo-
nning—in one word, Socialism. Shall we not say
nd translate it into the American language and
? The material basis and the historical neces-
gency in this task already exist. Only the will
to make the effort is lacking."
e that only the will to make the effort was lack-
pate within the board in the next three years
rate that; yet, the problem was not quite so
principles of social ownership and planning
ratic planning) had already been tried out in

serious radical movement without developing "a new system of political ideas," one that would be "capable of
serving an effective movement for the good society." The
task of socialist intellectuals, the editors implied, was to
do that work.

In seminal form, and partly obscured by unclear language, the *Studies'* editorial on the ultra-right anticipated
the future political direction of most of the student movements; it also provided the basis of agreement between the
original editors and those who were to join the board in
New York. But in projecting the need to create, or syn-
thesize, a new system of political ideas it also contained
the seeds of difference that would develop into one split in
the board and finally to the decision to cease publication.

At this stage, however, there was clearly a coming together of the thinking of many movement activists and
the *Studies* editorial board. This union was symbolized
by the first explicit discussion of the need for a socialist
perspective, in an article by Staughton Lynd ("Socialism,
the Forbidden Word," Volume II, No. 3, Summer 1963).
Lynd began by noting the New Left's lack of a tradition
around which to orient itself; it had not yet found a
"usable past, nor found a vocabulary with which to express
its inchoate impulses." The "obstacle to intellectual coherence in the New Left," he suggested, was "the taboo on
socialism." By socialism Lynd meant "comprehensive
planning, involving maximum popular participation,
based on public ownership of all major industries." And,
he pointed out, "whichever of the single issues espoused
by the liberals" one took hold of, "a persistent effort to
find a truly adequate solution" would "end at the thresh-
old of comprehensive public ownership and planning."

But public ownership and planning were only "the
technical side of socialism," Lynd wrote. The "deeper purpose of American socialism has always been the completion
of the American Revolution." By that he meant that American socialists had traditionally insisted that "the people

must take into their own hands control of industry if they hoped to retain control of government." And, traditionally, "the essential charge against the capitalist was not what he did to the workingman, but what he did to American democracy."

Lynd's vision of socialism, and his view of the American revolution and its traditions, was abstract and in the end ahistorical. He concluded his article by asserting that "a new American socialism must begin by affirming that an American life is worth no more than any other life," that "the American Revolution is an idea, not a place, and that some other people or peoples may be destined to nurture to maturity the seedling planted here in '76."

At the time the article was published several of the editors found it inadequate, just as later some of the editors would take sharp exception with Lynd's moralism. But Lynd's article was the first by a leading activist to insist on the importance of a socialist perspective for the new student movements, North and South. As such it fit in with the original intention of most of the editors to participate in the development of a new socialist movement in the United States. So far, the *Studies* editors had begun to develop an effective critique of American corporate capitalism—of liberalism, imperialism, and racism—on the structural level, but they had not produced a theory of capitalist development as a continuing historical process. Lynd's article contributed to neither task, but it marked a significant step in the evolution of *Studies'* politics. In the next four years the discussion of socialism—its relationship to the growing student and black movements, the attitude of the journal toward the creation of a new socialist party—came to occupy more and more of the editors' attention. Within the board there was a general consensus that a new socialist organization was desirable, and in the long run necessary, just as there was agreement that the New Left could be evacuated ultimately in terms of its movement toward a revolutionary socialist consciousness.

But, as later became apparent, there were dif the role of the journal and its editors, both theory and in taking the initiative for a n itics. In 1964 and 1965 the editors gene the attention of the journal should be t dent movement, and especially to the nizing projects in which some of the ed But there was disagreement over the various projects and over the quest editors, of initiating a more compreh

The first direct statement suggesti to the developing movements appe devoted to the civil rights mover Summer 1964). In "Civil Ri Ghetto," the editors concluded properly insist that socialism i unemployment, poverty, and But these radicals "delude t sibility if their insistence thinking through an effecti political program." A soci trial capitalism had not cialism meant "many dif [and] virtually nothing "long evaded task of s fore "to provide a po ganizing American cratically planned terms of immediat class in particular

"Failing this," tinue to occupy for the last fo political thoug of their actu absorption b ing to the n

the Soviet Union and Eastern Europe, and were in the early stages of experience in China and Cuba. These experiences offered little to inspire or guide a socialist movement in the United States, other than their long-range intentions and their opposition to Western imperialism. There were specific historical reasons for the irrelevance of these to the American situation—the historical function of socialism in pre-industrial societies was different from what it would be in the industrialized West—but this was not clear to student activists, or even to those long involved in socialist politics. (This point would later be made in "Socialism and the New Left," by Martin J. Sklar and James Weinstein, Volume VI, No. 2, March-April 1966, reprinted here.) Further, American socialist parties over the past fifty years had created no viable body of experience and theory to inspire confidence in the possibility of building a consequential socialist movement in the United States.

The editors' warning, however, so much resembled traditional calls for a "socialist alternative," that they opened themselves to the charge of proposing an empty theory as an antidote to a mindless activism. A few issues later, Ronald Aronson (in "The Movement and Its Critics," Volume VI, No. 1, January-February 1966) so charged. "A strange debate is taking place today on the 'New Left,' " he wrote, "neither side listens to the other, positions are rarely explored and brought nearer; rather they are polarized more sharply." At bottom, Aronson argued, the dispute was "a historical one, between a theory of capitalist society and its possible change that lacks a movement to validate it, and an activism which cannot presently use that theory, yet has no alternative long-range analysis to guide it." Aronson did not see the quality of old left social theory as the problem. Instead, he contended, "American capitalism's success at hiding the roots of current problems at all levels" had succeeded all too well in postponing a widespread confrontation with potential socialist supporters. "The shared experience of most American workers leads them to accept and support the system, because it delivers the goods."

Yet it was obvious that American capitalism still produced antagonists, such as "students outraged by its inhumanity and hypocrisy," poor whites left behind by affluence, and blacks barred from the system and left to do the dirty work. But since all these people were "many levels from the process of production," Aronson argued, Marxian analysis was of no use to them. Yet if the old left analysis were useless, he wrote, it was also true that other than the then current community organizing slogan, "Let the People Decide," there was little in the language of the activists that implied long-range goals. "Participatory democracy has no analysis of society to explain *why* poverty, disfranchisement, concentration of power in elites." Nor did it "offer an analysis of the historical tendencies that may make social change possible." In short, he saw the problem as "a theory without a movement, a movement without a theory."

Aronson's view of the state of things in the New Left posed a fixed and archaic "Marxian" doctrine against a static view of activity in the movement. In place of an analysis within a historical perspective, Aronson offered a reflection of things as they seemed to him. For example, he wrote that in Marx's day "the workers' decisive and immediate problems were transparently those of the system," and that this could be seen in countless immediate ways. But, he added, what was apparent in the 19th century was not so obvious in modern America because "structure upon structure has been added to, has adjusted and modified this system." The problem for SDS organizers of the poor, he observed, was that the primary productive process was all but invisible in the ghetto. Many of these activists had become radicals without thinking about the "legitimacy of capitalism." To them it was an irrelevant question. They were caught up in the day to day problems of the community. Thus it seemed "unlikely that even the most successfully organized project [could make] more than marginal demands." People had to be organized around immediate grievances, and as a "residential group" the poor were likely to be concerned with such things as housing repairs, garbage collection, traffic lights, and the like. Because organizing remained limited to the idea of building local movements, and restricted in its ideas to the immediate problems of these movements, Aronson asserted, a system-wide critique and analysis clearly could not develop.

Aronson also argued that in choosing "poor people organizing" as their realm of activity, the students had opted for a moral, rather than a political, activity. A "political movement conceives its tactics according to concretely defined long-range goals—goals which necessarily include the movement's taking power." In choosing a realm of activity in which ultimate questions of power were perceived as irrelevant, the organizers had, perhaps unwittingly, defined their own limitations. "Moral condemnation of the undemocratic, inhuman system," Aronson wrote, seemed to "fill the place of a long-range political orientation and analysis which could grasp the source of the inhumanity and the conditions for changing it."

And yet, Aronson saw the attitudes of the organizers as outside their control, as "historically determined." Because the movement remained "so remote from any revolutionary political possibilities, its organizers [were said to be] unable to develop" socialist consciousness. Perhaps a "few intellectuals among the organizers may gain a theoretical understanding of the system, but the development of consciousness in the rest seems limited by the narrow prospects for action and the absence of any class whose activity reveals the roots of the system."

Aronson's article was important as a restatement of things as they were in the movement in 1965. Yet, perhaps because it said little that had not repeatedly been said in the previous year, and because it granted so much to those on both sides of the questions, it did not stimulate further serious discussion. In fact, the article took the discussion a step backward in that it took for granted what was at issue. In relation to organizing the issue was whether or not SDS should devote its energies primarily to building community unions, and whether students should define radical activity in terms of organizing the poor. That was at least an open question, but it was taken for granted. Similarly, on the question of theory, Aronson assumed that what passed for Marxist theory in the organized left in the United States was, in fact, all that was possible. Unfortunately, as the editors had already pointed out, it was all that existing socialist sects had to offer. But those who argued for the development of theory and a comprehensive strategy were not proposing the acceptance of what passed for theory in the sects. They were proposing the digestion, synthesis, and creative extension of work already available both in classical Marxist literature and in more recent writings in American history.

Yet another problem in Aronson's article was his misleading statement that there had once been a "social class whose activity reveal[ed] the roots of the system." This implied that the working class had become conscious of the nature of the system simply through its own activity. If that were so, Marxist theory would never have been necessary. Of course, it is true that Marxist analysis starts with the productive process—the source of capital accumulation—just as it is true that industrial workers are the most directly involved in that process and most naturally in conflict with early industrial capitalism. Yet the nature of that conflict and the process of accumulation were not made clear by activity alone. If the relationship of other social groups, such as students and the poor, was less immediately in conflict with the imperatives of capitalism, that did not mean that the nature of these relationships could not be discovered. It simply meant that theoretical work would have to go beyond the earlier work of Marx and his followers. This, of course, has always been the task of serious socialist intellectuals.

In any case, by the time Aronson's article appeared the majority of the editorial board had concluded that community organizing was not the path to new revolutionary politics. The need for a new orientation was sharply expressed by a reader, Evan Stark, who complained about the orientation of the journal toward community organizing ("Theory on the Left," Volume V, No. 4, 1965). If *Studies* were to remain "radical," he warned, it would have to remain critical of the movement and not "turn its pages over to those who dispose of ideology rather than defend its importance and the importance of those intellectuals who depict and formulate it. There is nothing intrinsically wrong," he wrote, "with pen-pushers play-acting as leaders of the proletariat. But when they continually renounce the ideas of the past and pretend to get notions about 'what is needed' from the 'people themselves,' they merely serve to legitimize the strangulation of historical sense and creative thought which the government, the media, and the professional journals have been engaged in for years."

The conclusion was clear: *Studies* was advised to return to its original concept, as a journal designed to stimulate theoretical and analytical work for collective action. Yet, in spite of this decision, the clash of strategists continued; by early 1966 the controversy over *Studies'* direction and function came to a head, and three board members resigned.

The period in which *Studies'* pages had been filled mostly with comments and observations of problems in organizing lasted almost exactly for one volume, Volume V. This was followed by Aronson's article in Volume VI, No. 1. The next issue contained *Studies'* last serious attempt to elevate the problems of community organizing to the level of theory (Robert Kramer and Norm Fruchter,

"An Approach to Community Organizing," Volume VI, No. 2, March-April 1966). The essay concluded that prospects for radical action beyond community organizing were few and hopeless, and that at least, community organizing provided "rallying points" for those who wanted "an entirely new society." At best, such groups could serve as enclaves of resistance in an otherwise bleak landscape.

The black power movement and the anti-war movement (following President Johnson's escalation of the war) were to sweep these particular arguments unceremoniously aside. In 1965 *Studies* had concentrated on the issues of community organizing; in 1966 the emphasis shifted. The editors now unanimously agreed on the need for the movement to turn toward a socialist politics. All supported participation in the movement and the engagement of various sections in discussions about a new socialist perspective. And all agreed on the desirability of developing a comprehensive critique of American corporate capitalism, and on beginning to think through the outlines of a proposed alternative social structure.

Of course, developments in the world and within the movement itself facilitated this shift in political direction, particularly after the beginning of bombing in North Vietnam in February 1965. The escalation of the War fundamentally changed the character of the peace movement, both in its ideology and its social base. The War, and the growing strength of the black power movement forced student activists to orient themselves away from the ghetto and into their own communities, on or off campus. It also made them think much more seriously about questions of power, and to see imperialism as a world-wide system whose center was the United States.

The decisive event in establishing the character and direction of the new peace movement was the SDS March on Washington of 17 April 1965. The March had been planned before the onset of the bombing of North Vietnam. In keeping with its general rejection of red-baiting and with its rejection of old left ideological disputes, SDS decided to invite every group opposed to the War to participate under SDS sponsorship. Various old left youth groups (DuBois Clubs, Young Socialist Alliance, May 2 Movement) accepted the invitations and endorsed the March within a few weeks. But the established liberal peace groups (SANE, Student Peace Union, Women's International League for Peace and Freedom, Turn Toward Peace, Committee for Non-Violent Action, War Resisters' League) ignored the announcement and invitation; some old-line peace leaders raised private objections to having "communist" groups included, and predicted a small and irrelevant turnout in Washington.

The bombing of North Vietnam, followed by a rapid upsurge of support for the March from scores of campuses changed the attitude of the old-line peace groups, which now agreed to support the March. They also asked to become co-sponsors, a proposal that was tentatively accepted by the SDS leadership and then rejected by a vote of the National Council. As support for the March continued to grow, and as it became clear that the demonstration would call for the unconditional withdrawal of United States forces from Vietnam, several old-line peace leaders began privately to red-bait and otherwise attempt to undermine the March. They desired a "responsible" approach, one that condemned "Communist totalitarianism" as well as the American presence in Vietnam. They clearly opposed the view, implicit in SDS literature and attitudes, that the United States was an imperial aggressor against Vietnamese colonials struggling for their independence. In the eyes of most students active in the March the character of the Vietnamese régime was irrelevant—a subject to be decided by the Vietnamese. The old-line peace leaders, however, accepted the underlying assumptions of the Cold War—that "communism" was the devil and had to be exorcised—and therefore

could not take an unequivocal position against intervention in any form.

On April 17 some 25,000 demonstrators, most of them
students, marched on Washington. The outpouring far
exceeded the most sanguine dreams of the organizers.
Most old-line peace groups grudgingly went along, and
took little comfort from the result. The door was now open
to a new kind of anti-war movement, one that did not rely
on moral appeals within the Cold War frame of mind,
but that could fit into a view of the United States as the
leading imperialist power in the world.

The neo-colonialism of the United States had become
more and more difficult to camouflage behind the ideology
of anti-communism. More and more it had become apparent that those who insisted on equating the evils of
communism with the immorality of imperial intervention
on the part of the United States were, knowingly or not,
serving to justify and rationalize intervention and the
suppression of national liberation movements in the colonial countries. Increasingly, the young activists rejected
the sanctimonious hypocrisy of such views and implicitly
or explicitly sided with the anti-imperialist revolutionaries of the Third World.

The growth of a new kind of peace movement, one
that relied on mass participation and direct confrontation
rather than on the accumulation of "respectable" support,
led naturally to a new interest in class alignments and
structures—and to the search for a more comprehensive
view of the nature of American corporate capitalism. This
pushed the movement into a new awareness of its own
potential as a revolutionary force, but unfortunately, it
did not change the community organizers' habit of thought
that their immediate activity was, in itself, the means to
revolutionary change in the United States. If anything,
the tendency to think of the movement as a substitute for
a revolutionary party was momentarily strengthened.

Among radicals in the Vietnam Day Committee at

Berkeley and in various local militant peace groups, the idea that the peace movement *itself* would grow into a revolutionary movement became popular. So, too, did the tendency to measure the success of the peace movement solely in terms of its revolutionary consciousness. This tendency existed within the board of *Studies*. One editor, for example, argued in 1966 that "one of the weaknesses of the American peace movement as presently constituted is that it lacks a clearly defined theory of imperialism." (Robert Wolfe, "American Imperialism and the Peace Movement," Volume VI, No. 3, May-June 1966.)

Yet as it would later become clear, the peace movement *per se* had its own logical demands and its own logical direction, both of which centered on ending the particular war in Vietnam as quickly as possible. That purpose, although it served to educate tens of thousands of Americans about American imperialism, ran counter to the desire of many radicals to establish a theoretically coherent movement for revolutionary change. Since the movement as a whole sought above all an immediate end of the War, it gravitated toward positions offering the best chance of achieving that objective. The movement's popularity depended on support of both new and additional groups, and moved, therefore, toward the least ideological and least divisive forces closest to the existing levers of power. Nevertheless, both within the movement and in the board of *Studies,* many insisted on acting as if the peace movement should be a substitute for an independent socialist movement or party.

Thus, despite agreement in the board—that community organizing could not be a substitute for a new socialist movement, and despite agreement about the importance of the new anti-war movement and its developing anti-imperialist content, the underlying divergence remained as it had been before the split in early 1966. One group still looked to the movement for a spontaneous development of a new socialist politics. It expected, or hoped, that the movement itself would evolve into an organization with a will to power and with an increasingly coherent ideology and strategy to make that will effective. The other group, while appreciating the historic significance of the developing movement, believed that only a self-consciously socialist party could achieve the theoretical and programmatic coherence required for the sustained development of theory and strategy essential to the steady and privileged growth of a revolutionary movement. At some point, they were convinced, a group of people who saw the need for such a political formation would have to take willful action. It was, of course, true that a group prepared to form a party might emerge out of the experience of the movement. But such a group already existed; it perceived the necessity for taking the initial steps. Thus it seemed necessary to act, to begin, in an organized and self-conscious manner, to do the necessary preliminary work.

To the group favoring immediate action toward a new party, this meant that the editors should call for the formation of a preliminary organization, made up mostly of intellectuals, to begin defining the problems of revolution in the advanced industrial society of the United States, and that *Studies* should become the organ of that new grouping. In editorial statements or in various communications and notes published in the journal, the editors had already made clear their belief in the necessity to begin the process that might lead to a new party. Indeed, over the last year or two that position had been stated and restated. Therefore, the time had come to put up—or shut up.

But the other editorial group, while also desiring to see the movement turn toward socialism, believed that to take the initiative in this direction would isolate the journal and its editors from the movement; they insisted that *Studies* should return to its former role of reporting on and analyzing movement activity with the aim of influencing its direction. Because this group was unwilling to participate in the proposed activity of the other group, and since the other group saw no point in continued publication unless the journal were part of a larger group with a specific commitment and common political perspective, a new split was inevitable. This time, however, the board was split almost exactly in half. Neither side could carry on alone. And so, *Studies on the Left* ceased publishing.

In its seven years of publication, along with the new student movement, *Studies* had come a long way. And yet its end marked only the completion of one stage in the intellectual and political development of the New Left— one that is increasingly finding expression as a turn toward revolutionary socialism in the general consciousness of the movement.

PART I

AMERICAN CORPORATE LIBERALISM 1900-1948

The Acquitting Judge

BY *William A. Williams*

Volume III, No. 2
Winter 1963

As a professor at the University of Wisconsin, William A. Williams had a profound influence on many of the original editors of Studies on the Left, and on the journal. He wrote often for Studies. Some of his contributions were of current, and relatively passing, interest; others have been reprinted elsewhere. This selection is one of his briefer pieces, but it is a significant example of his thinking about historical problems.

Ernest R. May* is a young man of uncommon intelligence and industry who is employed at Harvard in the history department.

His first book, *The World War and American Isolation, 1914-1917* (1959), presents a meticulous review of the much written-about story of American entry into The Great War. Though generally following the approach and analysis offered by Charles Seymour in 1934 and 1937, May offers two significant changes in emphasis: he acknowledges more fully the role of economic considerations in establishing the early diplomatic posture of the United States, and he stresses the importance of Wilson's drive to make an American peace settlement in explaining the President's decision to go to war in response to German unrestricted warfare. He does not, however, explore very fully, rigorously, or imaginatively the character of that

*Imperial Democracy, The Emergence of America as a Great Power. New York. Harcourt, Brace and World, Inc. 1961.

image of peace, and for that reason the central question is left hanging in the air. Even so, the book is the best single-volume introduction to the documents.

May has since written occasional articles for professional journals, tried his hand at interpreting current diplomacy (in *The New Republic*), edited a volume on *The Ultimate Decision: The President as Commander in Chief*, and offered over the Voice of America a commentary on the state of American diplomatic history. This last item, now printed under the title of "Emergence to World Power" in John Higham's collection on *The Reconstruction of American History,* offers some insights into what May considers himself to be doing as an historian. He begins by remarking "how odd and improbable a field of study is the diplomatic history of one country." The argument being, of course, that the history of foreign relations has to be investigated (and written about) from the side of all nations involved, and on the basis of multi-archival research.

May then points out that foreign relations should be approached and written about from the point-of-view of asking "What happened? rather than from the angle of asking "What went wrong?" The first he calls history having "Ranke's aim of finding out what actually happened," and describes the second as being Acton's practice "of sitting as a hanging judge." May clearly prefers the combination of multi-archival research and Ranke's goal "of finding out what actually happened," and just as clearly believes he is doing that in his own work. His choices seem at first glance to state and offer an obviously logical and commendable guide for the proper preparation of excellent diplomatic history. But there are at least three fundamental questions to be asked of this apparently satisfactory prescription.

The first concerns the extent to which May's rather narrow emphasis on multi-archival research, and on writing history from several sides, actually produces a dis-

torted story. The point is not to discount or disparage
multi-archival research. It is illuminating and therefore
necessary. But it is *not* the essence of determining why a
given country, say the United States in the decade of the
1890's, chose to embark upon a given foreign policy. The
crucial factors are how and why the given country defined
the situation as it did, how and why it formulated its
alternatives as it did, and how and why it finally chose
the option it did. Some information bearing on those
problems is often discovered in foreign archives. But the
essence of that history is found in deep and wide-ranging
research in the materials of the country in question. In
the specific case in point, his book on the coming of the
war with Spain in 1898, May does not display the results
of that kind of research in the materials bearing on the
American side of the story—from which side he does in
fact write the history of the episode.

The second point involves May's disparagement of asking questions about "What went wrong" He does not
offer any argument for not doing so, and hence any estimate of his reasoning on the point is blocked. The writing
and the study of history are part of the learning process,
however, and that most certainly does include long-run
evaluations of attitudes, ideas, and actions on the basis of
their consequences. And, since any intelligent or relevant
asking of the question involves the work of reconstructing
the events in question in the fullest possible manner,
May's implicit argument that the two approaches contradict each other is a non-sequitur. Furthermore, even if one
assumes that mankind can never become perfect, it still
seems worthwhile to employ the act of reflection in an
effort to inch our way a bit closer to that goal.

The final question in connection with May's remarks
about history arises from his implicit argument that
Ranke's method or approach "of endeavoring merely to
describe what happened" is value free. He never comes
right out and says it is value free, but he does posit an

either-or dichotomy between Ranke's history and Acton's practice "of sitting as a hanging judge." This is a strange position for a man who emphasizes multi-archival research. Even the most casual reading of European intellectual historians, let alone Ranke himself, reveals that very few historians outside the United States any longer believe that Ranke was a purist who simply told what happened.

To mention but three, Ferdinand Schevill, Georg G. Iggers, and H. Stuart Hughes have all documented Ranke's propensity to spiritualize power and the state, and to confuse what happened with either the good *per se*, or with the only thing that could have happened. If one is to term Acton a hanging judge, as May does, then it would seem both more accurate and more in line with reporting what happened to call Ranke the acquitting judge.

The issues raised by these three aspects of May's conception of history bear directly on his most recent book, *Imperial Democracy*. It is a study of American foreign policy during the decade of the 1890's culminating in an account of the coming of war with Spain. The conclusion is the old one that "the United States had greatness thrust upon it." American leaders "were at most only incidentally concerned about real or imagined interests abroad." And, "for the people as for the Government, war with monarchical, Catholic, Latin Spain had no purpose except to relieve emotion." To think otherwise, as some Europeans did, is "a delusion."

May develops this thesis in six broad steps, moving back and forth between the United States, England, Cuba, Europe, and Spain. Part I is called "Tumult in the West," and purports to be an account of the rise of the American movement for imperial expansion. It is twenty-five pages long, and would be sketchy and weak even in a text book. In a book purporting to be a serious history of American expansion centering on the Spanish-American War it is wholly unsatisfactory. Even so, May's summary statement in the section subverts his conclusion for the book. On pages 23-24 he makes the following flat statement: "An imperialist movement had come into being and was not to be demolished. . . . Its leaders had discerned that public opinion could be captured for an imperialist cause, if only that cause could be clothed in the rhetoric of piety. They were stubborn, willful men. . . ." But on page 269 he says: "In the 1890's the United States had not sought a new role in world affairs."

May's efforts in between those two quotations never resolve the contradiction. Most of the evidence he offers from his multi-archival research—and a great deal he seems to have overlooked—supports the first observation about the aggressive movement for imperial expansion and flatly refutes the final conclusion. His second section, which discusses the diplomacy of President Grover Cleveland and the Venezuelan Crisis offers appropriate illustrations of this point. May suggests rather persuasively, for example, that Cleveland was not anti-expansionist so much as he was merely an anti-colonialist who wanted American expansion to employ more moral and subtle methods.

Yet, for all his research, May apparently missed completely the exciting and revealing story of Cleveland's use of the United States Navy to block a revolution in Brazil. As Walter La Feber managed to discover (and in the process wrote a book that won the Beveridge Prize for 1962), this operation was undertaken to preserve the recently negotiated reciprocity treaty with the existing government of Brazil (which favored American exporters), and to forestall further European economic penetration in South America. No one thrust this action upon the United States except American citizens and leaders who defined the issue in such terms. Among those who did so were the President, the Secretary of State, and various

high-powered entrepreneurs who were concerned to preserve and extend their trade.

The simple insufficiency of May's research in American
materials—whatever his findings abroad—is further revealed by his remarks about President William McKinley
and the tariff. One would never learn from this book that
McKinley was the keynote speaker at the founding convention of the National Association of Manufacturers, an
organization which in its early years (1895-1902) largely
concerned itself with the expansion of American exports
through the strategy of reciprocity treaties. Nor would one
find out that McKinley moved from simple protectionism
to a clear understanding of and preference for reciprocity
treaties designed to provide cheap raw materials and export markets. Or, to cite another example, there is no
clear perception of how directly and vigorously the
agrarians pushed for an expansionist policy because of
their desire for ever larger overseas markets.

This kind of oversight and omission would seem to account for the more fundamental failings of May's analysis
and interpretation. These can best be discussed after re-
producing four key propositions advanced by May as his
conclusions:

I. Many Europeans believed that the United States had
deliberately chosen to throw itself into competition for colonies, economic concessions, and the other current gauges and
emblems of international status. . . . They thought they saw
in Washington a government not only commanding great resources but also having the will to use them. This was, of
course, a delusion. The American Government had rarely displayed any purposefulness whatever. (pp. 266-267)

II. Neither the President nor the public had any aim beyond war itself. (p. 268)

III. From first to last, the makers of American policy and
the presumed leaders of American opinion concerned themselves either with abstract morality or with conditions inside
the United States. They scarcely thought of proclaiming to the
world that America was a power. They were at most only incidentally concerned about real or imagined interests abroad.
(p. 269)

IV. In the 1890's the United States had not sought a new
role in world affairs. Issues in Hawaii, China, Turkey, Vene-
zuela, and Cuba had intruded almost of their own accord.
(p. 269)

I would like to suggest that these assertions are mistaken, and to discuss the errors around two aspects of
May's argument.

First. May draws a wholly artificial dichotomy between
policy made with reference to domestic politics and policy
made from an active concern to extend America's participation in world affairs. May's explanation of American
policy in terms of domestic politics is not really an explanation at all. The only way a resort to politics serves in and
of itself as a viable causal explanation is to define politics
as the overt sign of an urge to power *per se*. Otherwise,
politics has to be discussed in terms of the ideas with
which top political leaders interpret pressures exerted by
individuals and groups, and in terms of the economics
and ideas which produce the pressures. Save for the psy-
chotics who see it as an end in itself, people want power
for purposes, and use power for purposes.

Second. May does not interpret McKinley in terms of
a psychotic power drive. It is true that some of his remarks, taken in the context of his failure to explore the
ideas and interests that generated political pressures, can
be read to that conclusion; but that is certainly not May's
intent. The trouble lies rather in May's failure to see that
the domestic political pressures involved and grew out of
very clear and vigorous conceptions of real and imagined
interests abroad, and out of arguments about the intimate
connection between those interests and the situation in
Cuba.

To illustrate this last point in detail would of course
involve writing a book, but the essential points can be
presented in outline form:

A) Throughout the voluminous documents bearing on
the war there is one constantly recurring phrase: "the

prompt and permanent pacification" of Cuba. It was coined by the Cleveland administration, and consequently accepted and used by the McKinley administration, as the basic statement of the American objective. American leaders sought this pacification so that they could deal more effectively and more single-mindedly with domestic and foreign policy matters. Cleveland, for example, had in 1894 stressed the "gravest importance" of the Sino-Japanese conflict because of its bearing on America's commercial expansion into Asia. McKinley put the whole matter as explicitly as anyone could ask in one of his messages to Spain ordering it to settle the Cuban situation: the festering sore of revolution "tends to delay the condition of prosperity to which this country is entitled."

B) The majority of American interest groups, farmers as well as manufacturers, and top political leaders as well as academic theorists, changed their mind between 1892 and 1897 on the question of what had caused the Panic and the ensuing depression. From explaining it as a consequence of dangerous or out-moded *monetary* theories and policies, they came to account for it in terms of overproduction and lack of markets. This crucial change has been brilliantly reconstructed and documented by Thomas McCormick of Ohio University.

C) This shift in ideas served to increase and emphasize ever more pointedly the need to pacify Cuba. This was the case, moreover, in two respects: (1) the need to wind up the Cuban distraction in order to concentrate attention, energy, and effort on the general overseas expansion of the economic system; and (2) the increasing concern in the minds of a good many top leaders with the connection between a show of force against Spain over Cuba and the establishment of an American base of operations in the Philippines. McKinley talked about this relationship with Theodore Roosevelt and others as early as September, 1897 (and perhaps even earlier). And the entire Pacific campaign was planned and readied for immediate action.

It was not necessary—even strategically—to take the Philippines once the Spanish fleet had been bottled up. For that matter, Cuba could have been pacified without Dewey's Asiatic Fleet ever having fired a salvo.

D) Finally, of course, all these considerations were reinforced and dramatized by the progressive heightening of the narrow Cuban crisis. American economic interests were literally being destroyed. High American leaders were rapidly losing their sympathy for the Cuban rebels. And the public reaction to the *Maine* disaster (and to the handling of it by various interested parties) brought all these elements together in an emotional demand to do something.

In the end, that is to say, the United States got the war that the vast majority of its leaders and citizens wanted. Nobody thrust it upon them. They had defined their ideological and economic interests in ways that converged upon a demand for forceful action in the arena of foreign affairs. The overseas interests that they had defined may be considered mistaken by later observers (some citizens considered them such even then), but they were very real at the time.

And so, quite obviously, have been the consequences of acting in that way on those interests. The problem of pacifying Cuba continues to plague American leaders. And it very probably will continue to do so until they leave the island alone to handle that problem in its own way.

Woodrow Wilson and the Political Economy of Modern United States Liberalism

BY *Martin J. Sklar*

Volume I, No. 3
Fall 1960

> . . . Most persons are so thoroughly uninformed as to my opinions that I have concluded that the only things they have not read are my speeches.
> —Woodrow Wilson, 1912

Martin J. Sklar is one of the founding editors of Studies. *His work and his ideas had more influence on the politics and intellectual development of the journal than those of any other individual. This essay is a revision of a chapter from his Master's Thesis at the University of Wisconsin. It is a contribution that has been of seminal importance in the development of a new view of Wilsonian liberalism, one that has been further developed by other historians in recent books on the Progressive Era and Wilsonian imperialism.*

Perhaps the greatest source of historical misconception about Woodrow Wilson is the methodological compartmentalization of his mentality into two distinct components, the "moralistic" and the "realistic" or "commercialistic," as if they were discrete and mutually exclusive. From this point of departure, if one thinks or acts "moralistically," he can not be considered capable at the same time of thinking and acting "realistically," at least not consistently: if one is a "moralist," his political behavior can be considered as deriving only secondarily, if at all, from an understanding of, or a serious concern for, the affairs of political economy.

According to this approach, wherever Wilson is perceived to have spoken or acted for the "little man," "democracy," "liberty," "individual opportunity," and the like, he was "liberal" and moralistic; wherever he is perceived to have spoken or acted for corporate interests, economic expansion abroad, and the like, he was "conservative," "commercialistic," "expedient," or realistic. Where Wilson supported measures promoting large corporate interests at home or abroad, he is considered to have forsaken his moralism, to have been driven by political expediency, personal egoism, or implacable social and economic forces, or to have gathered the unintended consequences of a misdirected moralism. In this view, Wilson the moralist is generally considered the true type, and Wilson the realist, the deviant.

Aside from objections that may be raised against the naïveté and theoretical deficiencies of such an approach to social thought and ideology in general,[1] certain specific objections may be raised against such an approach to Wilson, particularly should the main ideological components generally attributed to Wilson's mentality be granted at the outset, and their implications accorded a modicum of examination.

First, the "Puritan ethic," to which students of Wilson have attached fundamental importance as basic to his mentality, made no such mutually exclusive distinction between a transcendent morality and the world of political economy. Puritanism embraced a morality applicable not

[1] See Karl Mannheim, *Ideology and Utopia* (Harvest Book edition), 59-70. Mannheim here distinguishes between the "particular conception of ideology" and the "total conception of ideology"; it is in terms of the latter that Wilson's world view is comprehended in this essay.

merely to the world beyond, but as well to the living individual and existing society; it sanctioned, indeed posited, capitalist social and economic relations. The affirmation of capitalist society was therefore implicit in Wilson's Protestant morality. From the straightest-laced New England Puritan of the seventeenth century to Poor Richard's Benjamin Franklin, to Gospel-of-Wealth Andrew Carnegie, to New Freedom Woodrow Wilson, religious conviction and "market-place materialism" were each practical, each the uplifting agent of civilization and Providence, each the necessary condition for personal salvation and general human improvement, each a function of the other, mutually interdependent and interwoven like the white and purple threads of the single holy cloth. To the extent, then, that Puritanism entered significantly into Wilson's world view, the affirmation of the capitalist system in the United States (and throughout the world) was a function of his morality, not merely an auxiliary prepossession.

Second, Wilson's moral affirmation of capitalism sanctioned by Puritan conceptions found powerful confirmation in the economic writings of Adam Smith (himself a professor of moral philosophy), John Bright, and Richard Cobden; as student and professor he had become firmly grounded in their theories of political economy which he admired and enthusiastically espoused, and it is not difficult to perceive that such writings would strongly appeal to one reared on Puritanism. In Smith, Bright, and Cobden, Wilson found secular moral sanction for the bourgeois-democratic political economy as well as indefeasible economic principles. Private, competitive enterprise manifested natural law in the realm of political economy, and went hand in hand with republican institutions, comprising together the essential conditions of democracy, individual liberty, and increasing prosperity. To Wilson, much of whose economic thinking was based upon the assumption of the growing superiority of United

States industry, the arguments of Smith, Cobden, and Bright were compelling: they, in their day, spoke for an industrially supreme Great Britain, and recognizing Britain's position, argued that the optimum condition for the nation's economic growth and expansion rested upon the "natural" flow of trade, a "natural" international division of labor, uninhibited by "artificial" hindrances.

Taken together, Puritanism and Smithian-Manchestrian economics instilled Wilson with the compulsion to serve the strengthening and extending of the politico-economic system he knew in the United States as a positively moralistic commitment, since that would strengthen and extend the sphere of liberty, democracy, prosperity, and Providence, and accorded with natural law. As William Diamond observes, such assumptions were to become "basic" to Wilson's "thought on foreign policy."[2]

Third and finally, the organismic view of society that Wilson derived from Edmund Burke and Walter Bagehot provided him with the concept that whatever social phenomena or social system evolved "naturally" from the traditions and customs of the past, from the working of natural law through "irresistible" social forces, were not only inevitable as prescriptively ordained but morally indisputable. They represented both the evolution of the genius of human custom and institutions and the assertion

[2] William Diamond, *The Economic Thought of Woodrow Wilson* (Balt., 1943), p. 29. As revealed his his life, speeches, and writings, Wilson's concern was to protect the private enterprise system, as beneficient in itself and in its effects, from those dishonest, unscrupulous men who threatened to misuse and pervert it (and from socialists who threatened to abolish it). It was in keeping with his intense commitment to his moral principles that Wilson, early and late in his life, viewed an activist political career as his "heart's *first*—primary—ambition and purpose," as opposed to pure academic pursuits. Wilson to Ellen Axson, Feb. 1885, cited in Arthur S. Link, *Wilson: The Road to the White House* (Princeton, 1947), 19 (hereafter cited as Link, *Wilson*, 1). Emphasis in original, *Cf. ibid.*, 20, 23, 97, 123, 130; and Ray S. Baker, *Woodrow Wilson, Life and Letters* (8 vols., N.Y., various dates), I, 229, II, 98. It was therefore only natural that in the 1880's and 1890's and thereafter, far from being a head-in-the-clouds "idealist," Wilson made himself intimately conversant with the concrete political and economic issues of the day.

of God's will in human affairs. To Burke, whom Wilson revered and assiduously studied, the market economy manifested the working of natural law, which in turn manifested divine law. In Burke, Wilson could find a reverence for the market economy akin to religious awe: "the laws of commerce . . . are the laws of nature, and consequently the laws of God," Burke had said.[3] American Puritan doctrine, as developed by Jonathan Edwards, had itself become firmly anchored in the natural law of Newton and Locke; it required the intensive study of society's concrete development and condition, in order to comprehend God's work in the universe. In this respect, Puritanism and Burke stood on common ground. Here both religious and secular morality converged upon the affirmation of things as they were and as they appeared to be evolving. That which was "natural" was moral. The part of wisdom, morality, and statesmanship was to comprehend, affirm, and work for the necessary institutional adjustments to, "natural" evolution and "the well-known laws of value and exchange."[4] This evolutionary-positivist or conservative-historicist[5] approach to society served to modify whatever predilections Wilson may have had for atomized economic relations; it provided him with philosophical ground for rejecting the doctrine of unrestricted competition, as did the institutional economists he encountered at Johns Hopkins in the 1880's, and for affirming, as an inevitable result of the laws of commerce and natural social evolution, the demise of the freely competing entrepreneur at the hands of the large corporation.

[3] Burke, *Thoughts and Details on Scarcity* (World Classics edition), VI, 22, also 6, 9, 10.

[4] See, e.g., Wilson's "The Making of the Nation," *Atlantic Monthly*, LXXX (July 1897), in Ray S. Baker and William E. Dodd (ed.), *The Public Papers of Woodrow Wilson* (4 vols., N.Y., 1925, 1926), I, 328 (hereafter cited as *P P W W*); and "Democracy and Efficiency," *Atlantic Monthly*, LXXXVII (March 1901), *Ibid.*, 400.

[5] The term conservative-historicist is used in the technical sense defined by Mannheim, *op. cit.*, 120, 121, and is not meant here to denote "conservatism" as against "liberalism" as those terms are conventionally used.

As Wilson once remarked, explaining his approval of large-scale industrial corporations, ". . . No man indicts natural history. No man undertakes to say that the things that have happened by operation of irresistible forces are immoral things. . . ." [6]

To the extent that the characterization of Wilson's mentality as "moralistic" connotes Sunday school platitudes or Pollyanna ingenuousness, therefore, it is not only irrelevant, but fundamentally misleading. Since Wilson's writings, speeches, policy decisions, and actions simply do not correspond with such "moralism" the tendency of those who view his mentality in this manner is to judge both Wilson's utterances and actions, and the great events with which he was concerned, either in terms of a Faustian personality torn between the forces of high idealism and gross materialism, or less charitably, in terms of a sophisticated hypocrisy: ". . . Beneath the layer of Christian moralism is the shrewdness of the Puritan merchant. . . ." [7]

But Wilson's moralism was not simply a veneer "beneath" which lurked supposedly amoral "commercialism." It was a genuine and basic component of his ideological framework, though, it is submitted, no more so than in that of William Howard Taft, Philander C. Knox, Theodore Roosevelt, or Huntington Wilson. Woodrow Wilson's "wrung heart and wet hanky," we may be sure, were "real enough." [8] His thought in matters of political economy embraced a body of moralist concepts, just as his moralism presumed certain principles of political economy and corresponding social relations. Whether or not in human

[6] "Richmond Address," delivered before the General Assembly of Virginia and the City Council of Richmond, Feb. 1, 1912, *P P W W*, II, 377.

[7] Richard W. Van Alstyne, "American Nationalism and Its Mythology," *Queen's Quarterly*, LXV, 3 (Autumn 1958), 436.

[8] For this reference to Wilson by D. H. Lawrence, see his *Studies in Classic American Literature*, 1922 (Anchor edition: N.Y., 1951), 32-33, which contains a valuable insight into the morality showed by Wilson in the chapters on Benjamin Franklin and Hector St. John de Crevecoeur, 19-43.

thought and ideology the two have often failed to be inextricably interrelated, in Wilson they certainly were. A view of ideology that cast morality and ethics into one realm and political economy into another, that sees history as a struggle between the "ethical" men and the "materialistic" men, between the lofty and the commercialistic, suffers from an inverted economic determinism that overlooks the possibility that commitment to an economic way of life may go hand in hand with the most intense and highly systematized morality; with respect to Wilson, it forgets that just as classical political economy, "despite its worldly and wanton appearance—is a true moral science, the most moral of the sciences;" [9] so Puritanism, as the works of R. H. Tawney and Max Weber suggest, despite its heavenly concern, is a truly worldly doctrine.

For Wilson, like Burke, ideals and principles, to the extent that they validly applied to society, arose from and satisfied, not rationally deduced abstract precepts, but practical experience with the concrete conditions of society drawn in the light of "the inviolable understandings of precedent." [10] "Will you never learn this fact," he lectured Boston real estate men in January, 1912, "that you do not make governments by theories? You accommodate theories to the circumstances. Theories are generalizations from the facts. The facts do not spring out of theories . . . but the facts break in and ignore theories . . . and as our life is, as our thought is, so will our Government be." [11] Accordingly, Wilson insisted upon the necessity of adjusting legal institutions to the changed circumstances of economics and politics: ". . . if you do not adjust your laws to the facts, so much the worse for the laws, not for the facts, because law trails after the facts. . . . we must [adjust the laws to the facts]; there is no choice . . . because the

[9] Karl Marx, *Economic and Philosophic Manuscripts of 1844* (Foreign Languages Publishing House, Moscow, n.d.), 119.
[10] "The Ideals of America," *Atlantic Monthly*, XC (Dec. 1902), *P P W W*, I, 422; Baker, *Wilson, Life and Letters*, II, 104.
[11] "Efficiency" (Jan. 27, 1912), *P P W W*, II, 361.

law, unless I have studied amiss, is the expression of the facts in legal relationships. Laws have never altered the facts; laws have always necessarily expressed the facts; adjusted interests as they have arisen and have changed toward one another." [12] It was the necessity, the "facts," which Wilson recognized that determined his world view.

Time and again Wilson emphasized that the facts of modern life to which adjustment was most urgent were economic in character. Indeed, Wilson viewed economic relations as basic to all other social relations. He analyzed conditions in the United States, its troubles and opportunities, as essentially the result of rapid industrialization aggravated by the passing of the continental frontier. He conceived the major issues of his time as "questions of economic policy chiefly," and defined in this manner not only the tariff, coinage and currency, trust, and immigration questions, but also, significantly, "foreign policy" and "our duty to our neighbors." [13] The life of the nation, he declared in 1911, was not what it was twenty, even ten, years before: economic conditions had changed "from top to bottom," and with them "the organization of our life." [14] As New Jersey governor-elect Wilson noted, "the world of business [has changed], and therefore the world

[12] *The New Freedom* (N.Y., 1914), 33, 34, 35; "Richmond Address" (Feb. 1, 1912), *P P W W*, II, 376. For an interesting comparison worth noting here, see Karl Marx, *The Poverty of Philosophy* (1847): "Indeed, an utter ignorance of history is necessary in order not to know that at all times sovereign rulers have had to submit to economic conditions and have never been able to dictate laws to them. Both political and civil legislation do no more than recognize and protocol the will of economic conditions. . . . Law is nothing but the recognition of fact." Translation is that found in Franz Mehring, *Karl Marx, the Story of His Life* (London, 1951), 123. (*Cf. The Poverty of Philosophy* [For. Lang. Pub. House, Moscow, n.d.], 83). For a present-day view that regards law as subordinate to economic fact, specifically with respect to the rise of the corporation as the predominant form of business organization, *cf.* Edward S. Mason (ed.), *The Corporation in Modern Society* (Cambridge, Mass., 1959), 1, where Mason, in his Introduction, states: ". . . law in a major manifestation is simply a device for facilitating and registering the obvious and the inevitable. . . ."

[13] "Leaderless Government," address before Virginia State Bar Association, Aug. 4, 1897, *P P W* W, I, 354.

[14] "Issues of Freedom," address at banquet of Knife and Fork Club of Kansas City, Mo., May 5, 1911, *P P W W*, II, 285; *The New Freedom*, 3.

of society and the world of politics. . . . A new economic
society has sprung up, and we must effect a new set of
adjustments. . . ." And as candidate for the Democratic
presidential nomination in 1912, he declared, ". . . business underlies every part of our lives; the foundation of
our lives, of our spiritual lives included, is economic."
Business, he emphasized, "is the foundation of every other
relationship, particularly of the political relationship. . . ." [15]

Wilson's view of economic relations as basic to social,
political, and spiritual life, fit altogether consistently into
his conservative-historicist, natural law approach to society. Understood in these terms, Wilson's "idealism"
arose, therefore, from his conception of practical experience, of "natural" social evolution, of the genius of
evolved social institutions, custom, habit, and traditions,
of "irresistible" social forces, and the laws of commerce.
It was that mixture of classical nineteenth century liberalism with conservative-historicism that made Wilson the
Progressive he was: rational adjustments, determined by
enlightened men concerned with the general welfare, were
made to irrational processes, that is, to processes not determined by men but evolving irresistibly in accordance
with supra-human natural law or predetermination.

Wilson's position on the "trust" question cannot be
accurately understood apart from his firm conviction that
law must correspond with the facts of economic life, must
accommodate the people, their habits and institutions to,
and facilitate, natural economic development, and in the
process achieve the general welfare or national interest.

He defined the general welfare or national interest not
in terms of abstract reasoning or visionary dreams, or from

[15] Inaugural Address as gov.-elect of New Jersey, Jan. 17, 1911, *P P W W,*
II, 273; "Government in Relation to Business," address at Annual Banquet
of the Economic Club, New York, May 23, 1912, *ibid.,* 431, 432. In 1898,
Wilson had observed, "For whatever we say of other motives, we must
never forget that in the main the ordinary conduct of man is determined
by economic motives." Quoted in Diamond, *op. cit.,* 52 n.

"pure" moral principles, but historically in terms of the
"facts" of the existing economic structure and business
organization. To Wilson, the "facts" were that the large
corporation and large-scale industry had replaced the individual entrepreneur and small producing unit as the central and dominant feature of modern capitalism.
Accordingly, the adjustments to be made, in Wilson's
mind, involved not an attempt to restore the entrepreneurial competition of by-gone days nor the dissolution
of large corporations, but on the contrary, "the task of
translating law and morals into terms of modern business.
. . ." [16] More precisely, the problem to be defined was
that ". . . Our laws are still meant for business done by
individuals; they have not been satisfactorily adjusted to
business done by great *combinations,* and we have got to
adjust them. . . . there is no choice." [17] What was needed
were "open efforts to accommodate law to the material
development which has so strengthened the country in all
that it has undertaken by supplying its extraordinary life
with necessary physical foundations." [18]

Usually overlooked in discussions about the great
"anti-trust" debates of the pre-World War I period is that
the leading participants were concerned not so much with
the abstract idea of "competition versus monopoly" as
with the role of the corporation in the new industrial
order and its relation to the state. This was as true of
Wilson as it was of Roosevelt, Taft, George W. Perkins,
Elbert H. Gary, and Herbert Croly. In his writings and
speeches on the "trusts," Wilson placed particular emphasis upon "the extraordinary development of corporate
organization and administration," [19] as the dominant mode

[16] "Politics (1857-1907)," *Atlantic Monthly,* C (Nov. 1907), *P P W W,* II,
19.

[17] "Richmond Address" (Feb. 1, 1912), *Ibid.,* 376.

[18] *The New Freedom,* 117-118.

[19] "The Lawyer and the Community," annual address delivered before
the American Bar Association, Chattanooga, Aug. 31, 1910, *P P W W,* II,
253.

of modern capitalist enterprise, upon the corresponding decline of unrestricted competition and the growth of "cooperation," and furthermore, of particular importance, consistent with his over-all view, upon the legitimacy of the
process, the need to affirm and adjust to it. Large corporations were "indispensable to modern business enterprise";
"the combinations necessarily effected for the transaction
of modern business"; "society's present means of effective
life in the field of industry" and its "new way of massing its
resources and its power of enterprise"; "organizations of a
perfectly intelligible sort which the law has licensed for the
convenience of extensive business," neither "hobgoblins"
nor "unholy inventions of rascally rich men."[20]

As institutions that had developed "by operation of
irresistible forces," large corporations could not be considered "immoral"; ". . . to suggest that the things that
have happened to us must be reversed, and the scroll of
time rolled back on itself," Wilson declared in 1912,
". . . would be futile and ridiculous. . . ."[21] On more than
one occasion during the campaign of 1912, as he had in
the past, Wilson declared: "I am not one of those who
think that competition can be established by law against
the drift of a worldwide economic tendency; neither am
I one of those who believe that business done upon a great
scale by a single organization—call it corporation, or what
you will—is necessarily dangerous to the liberties, even
the economic liberties, of a great people like our own . . .
I am not afraid of anything that is normal. I dare say we
shall never return to the old order of individual competition, and that the organization of business upon a great
scale of co-operation is, up to a certain point, itself normal
and inevitable."[22] Or, as he put it on another occasion,

[20] *Ibid.*, 254-257, 262: "Bankers and Statesmanship," address before the
New Jersey Bankers' Association, Atlantic City, May 6, 1910, *ibid.*, 229:
The New Freedom, 5; Inaugural Address as gov.-elect of New Jersey (Jan.
17, 1911), *P P W W*, II, 271.

[21] "Richmond Address," *ibid.*, 376-377.

[22] Address accepting Democratic party presidential nomination, Aug. 7,
1912, *Official Report of the Proceedings of the Democratic National Convention*, 1912, 407. The "certain point" referred to by Wilson was the point

". . . nobody can fail to see that modern business is going to be done by corporations . . . We will do business henceforth when we do it on a great and successful scale, by means of corporations. . . ." [23]

With respect to remedies in the matter of "trusts," the task according to Wilson was "not to disintegrate what we have been at such pains to piece together in the organization of modern industrial enterprise"; a program of dissolution of the large corporations would only calamitously derange the economy; it would "throw great undertakings out of gear"; it would "disorganize some important business altogether." [24] Rather, the task was to prevent the misuse of corporations by individuals, make guilt and punishment individual rather than corporate, prescribe in law those practices corporations might and might not undertake, prohibit unfair and coercive methods of competition, require reasonable competition among the large corporations, and assure that corporations operate in the public interest.[25]

Historians have argued over when it was that Wilson first declared in favor of commission regulation of business, as if this were of fundamental importance to his

---

of diminishing returns. The enterprise that made money in the market without recourse to coercive or "artificial" practices was normal, its size justified by its pecuniary success.

[23] "The Tariff and the Trusts," address at Nashville, Tenn., Feb. 24, 1912, *P P W W*, II, 410-411. In this connection, more than a decade before Theodore Roosevelt denounced the "rural tories" as reactionaries whose passion for unrestricted competition and small business units would turn back the clock of progress, Wilson, in December, 1900, had applied the same criticism to Populists and Bryan-Democrats: ". . . Most of our reformers are retro-reformers. They want to hale us back to an old chrysalis which we have broken; they want us to resume a shape which we have outgrown. . . ." "The Puritan," speech before the New England Society of N.Y.C., Dec. 22, 1900, *ibid.*, I, 365.

[24] "The Lawyer and the Community" (Aug. 31, 1910), *ibid.*, II, 254.

[25] ". . . You cannot establish competition by law, but you can take away the obstacles by law that stand in the way of competition, and while we may despair of setting up competition among individual persons there is good ground for setting up competition between these great combinations, and after we have got them competing with one another they will come to their senses in so many respects that we can afterwards hold conference with them without losing our self-respect." Wilson, Jackson Day Dinner Address, Jan. 8, 1912, *ibid.*, 348.

over-all view of the trust question.[26] To Wilson, however, the question of commission regulation did not involve that of *laissez-faire* versus "positive" government, or regulation of monopoly versus enforcement of competition. It involved instead, the question of whether the ground rules of the new corporate system were to be left to arbitrary decisions of executive officers, subject to change with each administration, and possibly productive of both interference with personal and property rights and irrational attacks upon corporations, or whether, as he advocated, they were to become institutionalized in law. As had the corporate leaders themselves who testified before congressional committees, what Wilson wanted was "the certainty of law." Within that context, he favored "as much power as you choose." [27]

Whether one examines Wilson's thought before or during his "New Freedom" years, it is evident that what is thought of as *laissez-faire* Jeffersonianism is not one of its characteristics. In 1908, for example, pointing to "the necessity for a firm and comprehensive regulation of business operations in the interest of fair dealing," Wilson stated, ". . . No one now advocates the old *laissez-faire* . . ." [28] As if to emphasize his conviction that the popular notion of Jeffersonianism bore little direct relevance to

[26] See, *e. g.*, John W. Davidson (ed.), *A Crossroads of Freedom: The 1912 Campaign Speeches of Woodrow Wilson* (New Haven, 1956), 80.

[27] "The Vision of the Democratic Party" (New Haven Address, Sept. 25, 1912), *ibid.*, 264-265. Davidson points out (see in 26 above) that Wilson declared for commission regulation at his Buffalo speech of September 2, 1912, at least three weeks prior to the New Haven address, but the point Wilson made on these occasions was in no essential respect different from that which he made more than four years earlier, when insisting "everywhere upon definition, uniform, exact, enforceable," he stated (in criticism of the pending Hepburn amendments to the Sherman Act), ". . . If there must be commissions, let them be, not executive instrumentalities having indefinite powers capable of domineering as well as regulating, but tribunals of easy and uniform process acting under precise terms of power in the enforcement of precise terms of regulation." "Law or Personal Power," address delivered to the National Democratic Club, N.Y., April 13, 1908, *P P W W*, II, 28.

[28] *Ibid.*, 25.

the problems of modern times, Wilson took the occasion
of the Democratic party's Jefferson Day Banquet in 1912
to assert, ". . . We live in a new and strange age and reckon
with new affairs alike in economics and politics of which
Jefferson knew nothing." [29] With respect to the government's role in particular, as William Diamond summarizes the record, ". . . Throughout his political life . . .
[Wilson] was willing to use the government as a positive
instrument in the economic life of the nation. . . ." [30]

In two most basic areas of policy and thought, then,
that of the extent of government intervention in the economy and that of the "trust" question, Wilson was no more
a "Jeffersonian" than was Theodore Roosevelt, Edward
D. White, Oliver Wendell Holmes, George W. Perkins,
or Herbert Croly. If "Jeffersonian" is meant to connote a
return to an agrarian yeoman republic, or to the regime
of unrestricted competition among independent entrepreneurs or small business units, or a government policy of
laissez-faire, then much as it obscures more than clarifies
in applying the term of any leading twentieth century
figure in United States history, it certainly fails even alle-
gorically to characterize, or provide much insight into,
Wilson's thought or policy positions.

Accordingly, Wilson's "New Freedom" years, 1912-1914,
may be more accurately comprehended not as a break
with his past, just as his decision to make commission
regulation the core of his "trust" program may be better
understood not as a break with his "New Freedom" views.
Before, during, and after 1914, Wilson's views on the
"trust" question, like those of large corporate spokesmen
within the Chicago Association of Commerce, Nation
Civic Federation, and the United States Chamber of Commerce, and like those of Roosevelt and Bureau of Corporations chiefs James R. Garfield and Herbert K. Smith,
embodied the common law-Rule of Reason doctrine ulti-

[29] "What Jefferson Would Do," *ibid.,* 424.
[30] Diamond, *Econ. Thought of Wilson,* 130.

mately handed down by the Supreme Court in its American Tobacco and Standard Oil decisions of 1911. Like the others, Wilson had opposed the Court's earlier decisions prohibiting both "reasonable" and "unreasonable" restraints of trade; like them his approach affirmed large-scale corporate organization, sought the institutional legitimization of reasonable restraints of trade and the prohibition of unreasonable restraints or "unfair" competition, as determined at common law and by judicial precedent, with the public interest as the central consideration.

Wilson's position on the "trust" question as of 1912-1914 may be looked upon as a synthesis of the positions of Taft and Roosevelt: on the one hand, acknowledgment of the demise of *individualistic, entrepreneurial* competition, but the affirmation of and insistence upon reasonable *intercorporate* competition; on the other hand, the prevention of "unfair competition" and affirmation of "reasonable" combination and intercorporate arrangements consistent with the "public interest" or "general welfare," under a government regulatory policy rooted in the settled precedents and practices of common and civil law jurisprudence, whether enforced by the courts or by an administrative commission or by a combination of both.

To cite the fact that Louis D. Brandeis exerted decisive influence in Wilson's acceptance of the trade commission bill as evidence of a basic alteration in Wilson's views on the trust question, is either to overlook Brandeis' public utterances at the time and the program he advocated, or to disregard Wilson's previous writings and statements. Brandeis' position avowedly embodied the Supreme Court's Rule of Reason decisions of 1911; he advocated "reasonable" restraints of trade (including limitations upon competition by trade associations) and the prohibition of "unfair practices."[31] The issue involved in Wil-

---

[31] See, *e.g.*, Brandeis' testimony before House Comm. on the Jud., *Trust Legislation* (Ser. No. 2)—*Patent Legislation* (Ser. No. 1), *Hearings on H. R.*

son's abandoning the Clayton bill was primarily the impracticality of specifying every unfair practice to be proscribed, and the severity with which, in its original form, it threatened to interfere with corporate practices. The Rule of Reason decision, on the other hand, provided the general term, "unfair competition," with a recognized meaning at common law as evolved over the past decades in court decisions. And after its establishment, when the Federal Trade Commission sought to define "unfair methods of competition," it began by cataloguing all practices that had been found by the courts to be unreasonable or unfair at common law.[32] The trade commission act, while not providing full certainty of law, as Wilson had wished, satisfied the basic elements of his position in removing regulatory powers from the arbitrary decisions of commissioners and grounding them in judicial precedent.

It should also be noted, within the context of the community of agreement on the "trust" question between Wilson and large corporate spokesmen, that the circumstances surrounding the writing of the bill bear no anomaly. As Arthur S. Link shows, Brandeis and George L. Rublee worked closely together and in consultation with Wilson in drafting the legislation; Rublee actually wrote the bill.[33] Generally unknown, however, is that at the time Rublee worked in Washington writing the measure, he was serving as a member of a special committee on trade commission legislation of the United States Chamber

---

11380, H. R. 11381, H. R. 15926, and H. R. 19959, Jan. 26, 27, and Feb. 19, 1912, 62d Cong., 2d Sess. (Wash., 1912), 13-54 (Brandeis testified on Jan. 26, 1912); and Brandeis, "The Solution of the Trust Problem," *Harper's Weekly,* LVIII (No. 2968), Nov. 8, 1913, 18-19.

[32] *Memorandum on Unfair Competition at the Common Law* (printed for office use only by the Federal Trade Comm., 1915), cited and discussed in Thomas C. Blaisdell, Jr., *The Federal Trade Commission* (N.Y., 1932), 21-23.

[33] Link, *Wilson: The New Freedom* (Princeton, 1956), 436-438, 441 (hereafter cited as Link, *Wilson,* I). See also, George Rublee, "The Original Plan and Early History of the Federal Trade Commission," *Proceedings of the Academy of Political Science,* XI, 4 (Jan. 1926), 114-120.

of Commerce. (Brandeis had been an initial member of the Chamber's committee, but retired in favor of Rublee under the press of other affairs).[34]

But all this is not to imply that Wilson "sold out," that he was obliged reluctantly to submit to "implacable" forces, or that his views or policies had undergone any basic change. Rather, it is to suggest that, viewed within the context of Wilson's over-all thought and programmatic approach, the "New Freedom" years are not best understood as a distinctive period in his intellectual or political life, nor as "anti-Big Business" in nature or intent.

This view may be all the more forcefully substantiated if the interrelationship between the "New Freedom" legislation of 1913-1914 and promotion of United States economic expansion abroad is appreciated. Here again, it may be seen that, consistent with Wilson's previous and subsequent views, the "New Freedom" was not directed against large corporate developments at home or abroad.[35]

That prior to 1912-1914 Wilson had been a firm advocate of United States economic expansion abroad is a

[34] Senate Comm. on Interstate Commerce, "Promotion of Export Trade," *Hearings on H. R. 17350,* 64th Cong., 2d Sess., Jan. 1917 (Wash., 1917), 10-12.

[35] For a characteristic formulation of the conventional interpretation of the "New Freedom," particularly with respect to foreign relations, see Charles A. Beard, *The Idea of National Interest* (N.Y., 1934), 121, 122, 464. In this valuable theoretical work designed to demonstrate that United States foreign policy has historically been based not upon abstract ideals, but upon the pursuit of national interest as defined by the realities of political economy, Beard felt obliged to classify Wilson as an exception to the rule. According to Beard, Wilson "turned a cold shoulder" to the great economic interests that had "on the whole, supported and benefited by dollar diplomacy." "From the turn of the century," Beard explains, "the practice of giving aggressive support to the interests of American citizens abroad grew until it appeared to attain almost world-wide range and received the authority of a positive official creed in the conception of dollar diplomacy. . . . After a brief setback during the Wilson regime, the pattern was restored again with the return to power of a Republican administration in 1921. . . ." But, "in the main, the policies of President Wilson, both domestic and foreign, ran counter to corporate development and commercial expansion under the impulse of dollar diplomacy, with their accompanying interpretations of national interest. . . ."

matter of record upon which there is general agreement
by historians. His views in this respect have been sufficiently observed and analyzed elsewhere.[36] The main
elements of his thought may be briefly summarized here.
As an early adherent of Turner's frontier thesis Wilson
defined the nation's natural political-economic development and its prosperity as a function of westward expansion. With the end of the continental frontier, expansion
into world markets with the nation's surplus manufactured goods and capital was, in his view, indispensable to
the stability and prosperity of the economy. It was also no
more than a natural development in the life of any industrial nation, and, to him, in no way morally invidious
since in his view, the nation's economic expansion was a
civilizing force that carried with it principles of democracy and Christianity as well as bonds of international
understanding and peace. Given the United States' superior industrial efficiency she would assume supremacy
in the world's markets, provided artificial barriers to her
economic expansion were eliminated. Accordingly, Wilson
admired and championed Hay's open door policy and
advocated vigorous government diplomacy and appropriate government measures to attain the ends in view.

Within this broad framework of thought, the application of the expanding-frontier image to economic expansion abroad, assumed a significance more fundamental
than the invocation of a romantic metaphor: the West
had been developed by the extension of railroads, the
opening of mines, the development of agriculture—in
short by the extension of the sphere of enterprise and
investment that resulted in the widening of the internal
market and fed the growth of large-scale industry. Markets
for manufactured goods were in this way actively *devel-
open, created,* in the West, by the metropolitan industrial
and finance capitalists, and not without the significant aid
of the federal government. Similarly with such markets

---

[36] Diamond, *op. cit.,* 131-161.

abroad: foreign investments and industrial exports were seen by the corporate interests most heavily involved and by like-minded political leaders, such as Wilson, as going hand in hand, centered as their concern was on the needs of an industrial capitalist system in general and heavy industry in particular. Accordingly, the idea of "development" of agrarian areas in other parts of the world, and "release of energies," is prominent in Wilson's approach to economic expansion abroad.

Wilson's emphasis on exports of manufactures, his belief in their indispensability to the nation's prosperity, and his conception that the government should play a leading role in these matters, coincide in every essential respect with the views of the so-called Dollar Diplomatists, and of large corporate spokesmen within the U.S. Chamber of Commerce, the American Asiatic Association, the Pan-American Society, the American Manufacturers Export Association, and the National Foreign Trade Council. In like manner his advocacy of appropriate government measures to encourage an effective merchant marine and adequate international banking facilities flowed from this common concern for expanding the economic frontier; and his support of a low tariff was in large part informed by his belief that it was necessary to the nation's assumption of its proper role in world economic affairs.

But these were not merely the views of a supposedly "early" Wilson, later to be abandoned by the "New Freedom" Wilson; on the contrary, he carried them most emphatically, along with programmatic proposals, into his presidential campaign of 1912. Wilson's consistent theme, in this respect, during his bid for the presidency, is summarized in his address accepting the Democratic Party's presidential nomination: ". . . Our industries have expanded to such a point that they will burst their jackets if they cannot find a free outlet to the markets of the world . . . Our domestic markets no longer suffice. We need foreign markets. . . ." The alternative, as he had previously put it, was "a congestion that will operate calamitously upon the economic conditions of the country." The economic imperatives, therefore, required institutional adjustments on the governmental and private business levels to break an outmoded "chrysalis," in order to "relieve the plethora," and "use the energy of the [nation's] capital." They also pointed to "America's economic supremacy" (a phrase which Wilson shared with Brooks Adams): ". . . if we are not going to stifle economically, we have got to find our way out into the great international exchanges of the world"; the nation's "irresistible energy . . . has got to be released for the commercial conquest of the world," for "making ourselves supreme in the world from an economic point of view." He stressed three major reforms to meet the new necessities of the time—the downward revision of the tariff, the development of a strong merchant marine ("The nation that wants foreign commerce must have the arms of commerce"), and laws permitting foreign branch banking tied to a commercial-acceptance system (". . . this absolutely essential function of international trade . . .").[37]

Wilson's concern for the promotion of foreign trade and investment found expression in some of his key appointments upon assuming the presidency. To China, for example, he sent Paul S. Reinsch, long a prominent spokesman for economic expansion abroad. He appointed his intimate friend, Walter H. Page, as ambassador to Great Britain; as editor of *World's Work,* Page had published series of articles on such topics as "the industrial conquest of the world," to which Reinsch contributed.[38] Wilson's appointments of Edward N. Hurley and George L. Rublee to the newly formed Federal Trade Commission

[37] See in particular his speeches, "Efficiency" (Jan. 27, 1912), *P P W W,* II, 357-360, 372-375, 380; "The Tariff and the Trusts" (Feb. 24, 1912), *ibid.,* 407-409; and "Speech of Acceptance" (Aug. 7, 1912), *ibid.,* 471-472.

[38] See, *e. g.,* Walter H. Page to Paul S. Reinsch, Aug. 13, Nov. 15, Dec. 10, Dec. 28, 1900, in *Paul S. Reinsch Papers, Correspondence, 1892-1908.* Collection owned by State Historical Society of Wisconsin (Madison).

proved decisive, in its first few years, in making it a leading agency of foreign trade promotion, an aspect of its
activities that was not then widely anticipated nor since
been sufficiently appreciated.[39]

Wilson appointed William C. Redfield to head the Department of Commerce, which, with its Bureau of Foreign
and Domestic Commerce, shared with the State Department the central responsibility within the federal government for promoting foreign economic expansion. It is a
mistake to dismiss Redfield, as Link does with the remark
that "perhaps his chief claim to fame was the fact that he
was the last man in American public life to wear side
whiskers. . . ."[40] For Redfield was a prominent member of
the corporate community, enjoying the respect and confidence of corporate leaders. As a New York manufacturer
of iron and steel products he spent many years abroad
developing markets and as a "business statesman" much
of his time expounding the theme of expansion and downward revision of the tariff. Like Wilson he had been a
gold-Democrat, and the views of the two men were strik-
ingly similar in matters of trade expansion and the tariff.

[39] As a member of the Chamber of Commerce's special committee on
trade commission legislation, Rublee played a leading role in the Chamber's campaign to authorize the Commission to investigate world trade
conditions and make appropriate recommendations to Congress. Hurley
was a prominent Illinois industrialist who had introduced the pneumatic
tool industry to the United States, had been an active member and president of the Illinois Manufacturers Association, and, as an articulate advocate of economic expansion abroad, had played a leading role in the
organization of the National Foreign Trade Council. In 1913 he toured
Latin America as an official trade commissioner for Wilson's Department of
Commerce to investigate market and investment opportunities for United
States industry and finance.

[40] Link, *Wilson*, II, 139. It might also be noted that Link errs in stating
(*Woodrow Wilson and the Progressive Era, 1910-1917*, N.Y., 1954, 74) that
Rublee was prevented from serving on the Federal Trade Commission
due to the Senate's refusal to confirm his nomination in deference to
Senator Jacob H. Gallinger (Repub.—N.H.), who declared Rublee "per-
sonally obnoxious." Actually, Rublee served, under a recess appointment
by Wilson, for about eighteen months, from March 16, 1915, to Sept. 8,
1916, before he was obliged to retire. See *Federal Trade Commission
Decisions* (March 16, 1915, to June 30, 1919), Wash., 1920, I, p. 4; and
Rublee, *op. cit.*, 120.

Indeed, Wilson, in January, 1912, acknowledged that "I primed myself on Mr. Redfield's [tariff] speeches." [41] Of greater significance, indicating Redfield's prominence in the corporate community and the degree to which he represented corporate opinion, Redfield had been president of the American Manufacturers Export Association (organized in 1910), which, to use Robert A. Brady's terminology, was a peak association of large corporate interests. As Secretary of Commerce, with Wilson's support and approval, he immediately undertook to reorganize the Bureau of Foreign and Domestic Commerce for more efficient service in promoting foreign trade, and submitted a bill to Congress for the creation of a system of commercial attachés and agents, and trade commissioners, which Congress passed in 1914. Between the two of them, Redfield and Hurley, again with Wilson's approval, instituted many of the mechanisms of business-government cooperation in domestic and foreign trade, including the encouragement of trade associations, that are usually regarded as initially introduced by Herbert Hoover while Secretary of Commerce during the 1920's. Finally, it is important to note that while Wilson permitted Secretary of State William Jennings Bryan to make many ambassadorial appointments on the basis of patronage obligations, he refused to permit Bryan to disturb the consular service.

Against this background, the attitude of corporation leaders toward the three major pieces of "New Freedom" legislation of 1913-1914 (Underwood Tariff, Federal Reserve, and Federal Trade Commission acts), as well as the extent to which that legislation affected foreign trade expansion and to which, in turn, the nature of the legislation was determined by considerations relating to such expansion, may be more clearly understood.

Between 1910 and 1914, corporate leaders, particularly those connected with the large corporations and banking

[41] "The Tariff" (Jan. 3, 1912), *P P W W*, II, 330.

houses, were unusually active in organizing themselves for
the promotion of their interests and programmatic objectives in domestic and foreign affairs. In 1910 industrial
corporations organized the American Manufacturers Export Association (AMEA); in 1912, these corporations,
along with other business organizations, such as the American Asiatic Association (AAA), established the United
States Chamber of Commerce; and in 1914 the AMEA,
the AAA, and the Pan-American Society joined together
to form the National Foreign Trade Council (NFTC).
These were all what might be called "peak associations"
of large corporate interests; but the NFTC may be legitimately considered a peak association of peak associations.
The officers and memberships of these associations inter-
locked as intricately as did the directors of the huge industrial corporations and finance houses of the time.

Of the more significant manifestations of the Wilson
administration's concern for the promotion of foreign
trade and of the community of agreement between large
corporate interests and that administration, therefore, one
was its endorsement of the purposes of the first National
Foreign Trade Convention, convened in Washington,
D.C., May 27 and 28, 1914. The Convention, presided
over by Alba B. Johnson, and the National Foreign Trade
Council subsequently established, with James A. Farrell
as its president, were led and dominated by men representing the nation's greatest industrial, mercantile, and
financial corporations.[42] As Johnson related, "This Convention had its inception at a meeting in New York some
time ago" with Secretary of Commerce Redfield. He gave
the idea for such a convention "his most cordial approval,
and, therefore, it is fair to say" that he "is in a sense the
Father of this Convention. . . ."[43] Edward N. Hurley, the

---

[42] *Official Report of the National Foreign Trade Convention* (1914), 15,
16, 457-458 (hereafter cited as NFTC, Proceedings). Johnson was himself
president of the Baldwin Locomotive Works, and Farrell the president of
the United States Steel Corporation.

[43] *Ibid.*, 203-204.

first vice-chairman and later chairman of the Federal Trade Commission, also played a leading role in the organization of the Convention and in the Council's subsequent affairs.[44]

The Convention met in the afterglow of Secretary of State Bryan's appearance, in January, 1914, as guest of honor at the annual dinner of the American Asiatic Association, of which Willard Straight was then president.[45] At that time, the Underwood Tariff and Federal Reserve acts, measures most closely associated with the "New Freedom," had been passed by Congress. The Association's expressed purpose for inviting Bryan to the dinner, which was attended by leaders of the corporate community, was to exchange views with him on, and have him clarify, the administration's foreign policy. Emphasizing that the "era upon which we are entering is not only that of the Pacific Ocean, it must be one of Pacific development as well," Straight cited the new tariff as a stimulant for "carrying the war into the enemies' camp and competing abroad with those who will now invade our own market. . . ." And to the cheers of the diners, he observed that with the Panama Canal and the opportunity provided by the reserve act for the extension of foreign banking and investment, ". . . we are in a better position than at any time in our history aggressively to undertake the development of our export trade."[46] In response, Bryan pointed out that his duties as Secretary of State kept him "in touch with the expansion of American Commerce and the extension of American interests throughout the world," with

[44] *Ibid.*, 15, 17, 457.

[45] Straight had served as agent of the American Banking Group in China during the days of the Six-Power Consortium, was associated with the House of Morgan, and was a leading participant in the organization of the NFTC.

[46] The reserve act, as Straight noted, permitted "the establishment of branches of American banking institutions abroad," and with its provision for a commercial-acceptance system promised to "free vast sums for use in an international discount market and for the purchase of desirable foreign securities." *Journal of the American Asiatic Association*, XIV, 1 (Feb. 1914), 8 (hereafter cited as AAA *Jour*).

which both he and the President were in "deep sympathy," and he assured the business men that the administration "will see that no industrial highwayman robs
you. This government stands committed to the doctrine
that these United States are entitled to the greatest possible industrial and commercial development." In this
respect, like Straight, he singled out the tariff and reserve
acts as decisive instrumentalities for giving the doctrine
practical effect.[47]

The administration's endorsement of the National
Foreign Trade Convention the following May assumed
tangible forms. Secretary of Commerce Redfield delivered
the opening address of the Convention on the morning of
May 27 and he served as toastmaster at its banquet that
night; Secretary of State Bryan delivered the main after-
dinner speech at the banquet; and Wilson the next day
received the delegates at the White House for a short
interview.

As the Council later announced, the national importance of the Convention was "attested by the fact that its
purpose [to promote foreign trade and a coordinated national foreign trade policy based upon the cooperation of
government and business] was cordially indorsed by the
President of the United States, who received the delegates
at the White House; by the Secretary of State, who delivered, at the banquet, an outline of the administration's
policy toward American business abroad; and by the
Secretary of Commerce, who opened the convention. . . ."[48]

In his address to the delegates in the East Room of the
White House, after having been introduced to them by

[47] The reserve act, according to Bryan, as a law the nation "long
needed," would stimulate foreign trade "not only in the Orient but also
throughout South America"; the new tariff meant "a larger commerce
between our nation and the world, and in this increase the Orient will
have her share," to the advantage not only of the public in general, but
"especially" of "those merchants and manufacturers now turning their
eyes to the Far East." McKinley's advocacy of tariff reduction "as a means
of extending . . . our exports," was "a prophetic utterance": we "must
buy if we would sell." *Ibid.*, 12-13.
[48] NFTC, *Proceedings* (1914), 8.

Edward N. Hurley, Wilson declared his "wish to express
. . . the feeling of encouragement that is given by the
gathering of a body like this for such a purpose." For, he
said, "There is nothing in which I am more interested
than the fullest development of the trade of this country
and its righteous conquest of foreign markets." Referring
to Secretary Redfield's address of the previous day, Wilson
confided: "I think that you will realize . . . that it is one
of the things that we hold nearest to our heart that the
government and you should cooperate in the most intimate manner in accomplishing our common object." He
expressed the hope that this would be "only the first of a
series of conferences of this sort with you gentlemen." In
reply, Alba B. Johnson assured the President that as business men they realized "the deep interest which this
government takes in promoting legitimate foreign
trade. . . ." [49]

Bryan delivered two addresses at the banquet on the
night of May 27, 1914, the first a short, prepared statement
for release to the press, the second a lengthier extemporaneous speech. In the prepared speech Bryan declared
the administration "earnestly desirous of increasing American foreign commerce and of widening the field of
American enterprise. . . ." He reiterated its intention to
cooperate with the business community to this end, and
speaking for his own department he emphasized its
"earnest purpose" to "obtain for Americans equality of
opportunity in the development of the resources of foreign countries and in the markets of the world." Accordingly it was his "intention to employ every agency of the
Department of State to extend and safeguard American
commerce and legitimate American enterprises in foreign
lands," consistent with the "sovereign rights of other governments." [50]

[49] *Ibid.*, 392-393.
[50] *Ibid.*, 206, 207. That this represented administration policy, not
merely edifying rhetoric to win the favor of corporate interests, is cor-
roborated, *inter alia,* by the exchange of notes during the summer of 1913
between Bryan and E. T. Williams (U.S. Chargé d'Affaires at Peking).

In his extemporaneous remarks, Bryan explained to the men of capital that his department's policy was Wilson's policy—what it "does in foreign affairs is but what the President desires." This meant, he said, "policies which will promote our industry abroad as well as home"; already, in the short time of the administration's existence, it had taken measures that would "tend directly and neces-

---

Williams requested instructions "as to the attitude to be taken by this Legation towards financial transactions between American capitalists and the Chinese Government," in view of President Wilson's statement of March 18, 1913, repudiating the Six-Power Consortium and the Reorganization Loan. Referring to the passages in that statement that the American people "wish to participate . . . very generously, in the opening . . . [of] the almost untouched and perhaps unrivaled resources of China," and that the U.S. government "is earnestly desirous of promoting the most extended and intimate trade relationship between this country and the Chinese Republic," Williams suggested as his understanding of the administration's policy that the State Department would support "industrial" loans and investments for the development of railways and mineral resources, secured upon the assets and earnings of such enterprises, but not "financial loans" to the Chinese provincial and central governments secured upon government revenues. Bryan replied that ". . . the Legation is right in assuming that the Department is extremely interested in promoting, in every proper way, the legitimate enterprises of American citizens in China and in developing to the fullest extent the commercial relations between the two countries." He continued, "It may be stated, in general, that this Government expects that American enterprise should have opportunity everywhere abroad to compete for contractual favors on the same footing as any foreign competitors, and this implies also equal opportunity to an American competitor to make good his ability to execute the contract. . . . [This Government] stands ready, if wrong be done toward an American citizen in his business relations with a foreign government, to use all proper effort toward securing just treatment for its citizens. *This rule applies as well to financial contracts as to industrial engagements.*" (Emphasis added). Dept. of State, *Papers Relating to the Foreign Relations of the United States*, 1913, 183-187, 170-171. It is essential to note that the conditions outlined by Bryan in this note and in one cited by him from Secretary of State Richard Olney to Minister Charles Denby in 1896 (*ibid.*, 1897, 56), delimiting the extent of government support for U.S. enterprise abroad (*i. e.*, refusing special support for one U.S. firm to the exclusion of others, refusing to guarantee the execution of contracts or the success of an enterprise, and renouncing any commitment to intercede forcibly in the internal affairs of foreign nations on behalf of U.S. capitalists), were all well established principles affirmed alike by the Dollar Diplomatists (such as Taft, Knox, II, Wilson, Calhon, Straight) in their public statements and diplomatic notes, and by their predecessors. These delimiting principles were in no way peculiar to the Wilson administration, and cannot be considered as distinguishing its policy from that of Taft and Knox.

sarily to promote commerce," such as the tariff and reserve acts. But "more than that," Bryan continued, the administration's efforts to win friends for the United States, safeguard the peace, and conclude commercial treaties constituted a broad contribution to the stabilization and extension of foreign economic expansion. "One sentence from President Wilson's Mobile speech has done a great deal to encourage commerce." When he there renounced territorial conquest as an object of United States policy in Latin America, ". . . he opened the doors of all the weaker countries to an invasion of American capital and American enterprise. (Applause.)" [51] As Bryan had put it

[51] NFTC, *Proceedings* (1914), 208-210. Along with the Mobile speech, the statement repudiating the Six-Power Consortium is most often cited to substantiate the view that Wilson repudiated Dollar Diplomacy. If this is meant as a repudiation of government support of corporate interests in expanding investments and exports abroad, then as already indicated in the immediately preceding text and in footnote 50, above, neither the Mobile speech nor the consortium statement is amenable to such interpretation. Wilson's consortium statement not only emphasized the government's intention to promote United States participation in the development of China and the closest of commercial relations between the two countries, but also specifically declared, ". . . The present administration will urge and support the legislative measures necessary to give American merchants, manufacturers, contractors, and engineers the banking and other financial facilities which they now lack and without which they are at a serious disadvantage as compared with their industrial and commercial rivals. This is its duty. This is the main material interest of its citizens in the development of China. . . ." *Foreign Relations*, 1913, 171. Cf. the versions of and references to the statement in George H. Blakeslee (ed.), *Recent Developments in China* (N.Y., 1913), 159-160; John V. A. MacMurray (ed.), *Treaties and Agreements with and concerning China, 1894-1919* (N.Y., 1921), II, 1025; Charles Vevier, *The United States and China, 1906-1913* (Rutgers Univ. Press, N.J., 1955), 210. All these versions include the reference to banking and other financial facilities needed for effective competition in Chinese markets. (These facilities were regarded as essential by corporate interests to foreign economic expansion and were provided in 1913 by sections 13, 14, and 25 of the Federal Reserve Act, which permitted branch banking abroad and the establishment of a domestic discount market for foreign trade commercial acceptances). Unfortunately, in the widely used *Documents of American History*, edited by Henry S. Commager, the consortium statement, there entitled "The Repudiation of 'Dollar Diplomacy',", is entirely reproduced, except for the passage referring to the banking and other financial facilities (5th ed., 1949, Doc. #390). For further evidence regarding the Wilson administration's intentions in repudiating the consortium, see Secretary of State Bryan's address before the Asiatic Association in January, 1941, where he

at the Asiatic Association dinner, ". . . The doctrine of universal brotherhood is not sentimentalism—it is practical philosophy . . . The government could not create trade, but it was its "duty" to "create an environment in which it can develop."[52] He looked forward with "great expectations" to the extension of United States trade and investment abroad; the Convention itself provided "evidence that we are going forward," and the statistics showing the increase in exports of manufactured goods left "no doubt" that the United States could compete successfully with the European industrial nations "in the newer countries that are awaiting complete development," and that the United States would thus become "an increasing factor in the development" of such countries.[53]

Bryan's approach to economic expansion exemplifies a unified world view, embracing "moralism" and "commercialism" as interdependent and mutually consistent elements, that was so common to the expansionists of the time; the underlying assumptions of the "Good Neighbor" policy of later administrations were not basically different; and like the policy of Wilson or Straight it emphasized

---

explained, ". . . The new administration in withdrawing approval from the Chinese loan did not question the good faith or good intent of those who had seen in it a means of increasing our influence, prestige and commercial power in China. The President believed that a different policy was more consistent with the American position, and that it would in the long run be more advantageous to our commerce. . . ." See also Willard Straight's remark on the same occasion that though many business men ". . . have interpreted the announcement . . . to mean that the American Government would not extend to our bankers the support which those familiar with trade conditions in China consider necessary . . . I personally feel assured, that this impression . . . is not justified. . . ." AAA *Jour.*, XIV, 1 (Feb. 1914), 12, 8-9; *cf.* editorial in *ibid.*, 8. The present author examines this question in greater detail in his master's thesis.

[52] AAA *Jour*, XIV, 1 (Feb. 1914), 13. *Cf.* Straight's remark: "The true armies of world peace . . . are the merchants engaged in international trade. In this army, the Secretary of State is a Chief of Staff, and the Ambassador a Corps Commander. We of this [Asiatic] Association are the rank and file. . . ." *Ibid.*, 8. Also, that of M. A. Oudin, manager of the Foreign department of General Electric Co., that while the government could not create trade, it could "point the way to private enterprise." NFTC, *Proceedings* (1914), 366, 367, 379-380.

[53] *Ibid., Proceedings* (1914), 207, 208.

not merely trade but also "development" of agrarian countries, and the government's responsibility to foster those operations.

Promising the complete support of his Department for the extension of markets and investments abroad, and inviting the close co-operation between the business men and the State Department, Bryan told the corporate leaders, "I promise you that the State Department—every agency of it—will be back of every honest business man in pushing legitimate enterprise in all parts of the world. (Applause.)" To emphasize the community of purpose between the Department and the corporate interests, he continued by extending a colorful analogy: "In Spanish-speaking countries hospitality is expressed by a phrase, 'My house is your house.' . . . I can say, not merely in courtesy—but as a fact—my Department is your department; the ambassadors, the ministers and the consuls are all yours. It is their business to look after your interests and to guard your rights." If any of them failed to fulfill his responsibility, advised Bryan, "we shall be pleased to have you report them." For his part, the Department would "endeavor to open all doors to you. We shall endeavor to make all people friendly to you . . ."[54]

Given the general approach to expansion shared by men such as Wilson, Straight, Bryan, and corporate spokesmen, the question of "inner" motive is somewhat irrelevant. For example, what may be said of Straight's "inner" motive when he spoke of trade as the means to peace; or of the Steel Corporation's president, James A. Farrell, when he told the Convention: ". . . there is no factor which is so much involved in . . . [the nation's] material prosperity as the export trade," and then proceeded to say that "due to its great significance with respect to the economic conditions of our financial relations with the markets of the world, the export trade is likewise a vital factor in international affairs . . . The contest today is for supremacy in

[54] *Ibid.*, 210-211.

the trade of the world's markets, because that country which is a commercial power is also a power in other respects." [55] The important point is that they held in common the assumption that expansion of markets and investment abroad was indispensable to the stability and growth of the political economy. As Redfield had put it at the banquet while introducing Bryan as the next speaker, the mission of his fellow diners was "to make this land of ours one of continual increasing prosperity." For he continued:

. . . we have learned the lesson now, that our factories are so large that their output at full time is greater than America's market can continuously absorb. We know now that if we will run full time all the time, we must do it by reason of the orders we take from lands beyond the sea. To do less than that means homes in America in which the husbands are without work; to do that means factories that are shut down part of the time. And because the markets of the world are greater and steadier than the markets of any country can be, and because we are strong, we are going out, you and I, into the markets of the world to get our share. (Applause.) [56]

The record leaves no reason to doubt that the knowledgeable corporate leaders understood and accepted as genuine the administration's policy statements.[57] The difficulty in their view, lay not with the administration, but with the people. In this respect, upon closer examination, it is apparent that many of the pronouncements by business men in this period that have been interpreted as directed against the Wilson administration, were more often directed against an "unenlightened" public and/or hostile senators or congressmen. As one business man put it, the public must realize "that government assistance to American shipping and the American export trade is not

[55] *Ibid.*, 35, 36.

[56] *Ibid.*, 205. For similar expressions on the indispensability of exports to the nation's prosperity by business and political leaders, see *Ibid.*, 6, 7, 70, 74, 80, 86, 117, 140, 141, 214, 218, 230-231, 285.

[57] See, *e. g.*, the remark of M. A. Oudin of General Electric, *Ibid.*, 366, 367, 379-380.

only a business but a patriotic policy, pertaining to national defense as well as to our industrial welfare."[58] Or as Willard Straight phrased it, under current conditions of public opinion, "any administration may be attacked if it utilizes the power of the Government for the profit of private interests, no matter what indirect advantage might accrue to the country as a whole." The problem was to educate the people to accept government support of private foreign investments as action not on behalf of a special, but of the national, interest.[59]

In the context of Wilson's approach to both foreign trade and the "trust" question, and of the community of views between large corporate interests and his administration in these areas, the significance for foreign trade of the Federal Trade Commission Act, as the legislative embodiment of the Rule of Reason, may be better comprehended.

It was generally recognized in business circles that the large industrial corporations were most suited to successful export trade, and that the rapid rise in exports of manufacturers from the late 1890's to 1914 had been due largely to the operations of these corporations. The large corporations enjoyed low unit costs necessary for competition in world markets, particularly in the capital and durable goods industries. Their superior reserves and intimate connections with the great financial institutions enabled them to carry the expense of foreign sales promotion, offer attractive foreign credit facilities, and reap the benefits of foreign loans and concessions, all indispensable to an expanding and stable export trade. It was these corporations that were most intimately involved in the "development" of agrarian nations. Since the export of manufactured goods was considered primary in maintaining the nation's international exchanges, in liquidating foreign debts, and in guaranteeing domestic prosperity, the success of any

[58] P. H. W. Ross, president of the National Marine League, *Ibid.*, 143.
[59] *Ibid.*, 174-187.

business or governmental policy looking to the promotion of export trade and the achievement of these related objectives appeared to stand or fall with the large corporation. A domestic policy, therefore, designed to atomize large corporations could only prove self-defeating.

These were the points emphasized by such prominent spokesmen for large corporate interests as John D. Ryan, president of the Amalgamated Copper Company, M. A. Oudin of General Electric, and Alba B. Johnson of the Baldwin Locomotive Works.[60] As Johnson put it, "To attack our business interests because by reason of intelligent management they have grown strong is to cripple them in the struggle for the world's trade."[61] But their views, in so far as they related to the maintenance of large business units, were in no essential respect different from those of Wilson, whose attitude, as already indicated, may be summed up by the declaration in his Acceptance Speech: ". . . I am not afraid of anything that is normal."[62]

It is important to note, therefore, that the criticisms of "anti-trust" bills pending in Congress by speakers at the 1914 National Foreign Trade Convention were leveled not against Wilson and his administration, but against "radicals" in Congress and what was considered misguided and dangerous public opinion. They particularly applied to the policy of the previous Taft administration, which in its last year and a half had "mined the Sherman Act for all it was worth."[63] But Wilson's position on the "trust" question was clear to all who read or heard his speeches, at any rate by early 1914; indeed, in his special

[60] See their remarks in *Ibid.*, 167, 168, 375-378, 327-328.

[61] *Ibid.*, 327-328.

[62] *P P W W*, II, 464; *ibid.*

[63] Robert H. Wiebe, "The House of Morgan and the Executive, 1905-1913," *American Historical Review*, LXV, 1 (Oct. 1959), 58. *Cf. The Federal Antitrust Law with Amendments, List of Cases Instituted by the United States, and Citations of Cases Decided Thereunder or Relating Thereto,* Jan. 1, 1914, in Sen. Comm. on the Jud., *Hearings . . . together with Briefs and Memoranda . . . Compiled for Use in Consideration of H. R. 15657,* 63d Cong., 2d Sess. (Wash., 1914), 164-183.

address on the "trusts" to Congress in January, 1914, he
had specifically declared, ". . . no measures of sweeping or
novel change are necessary . . . our object is *not* to unsettle
business or anywhere seriously to break its established
courses athwart." [64] Programmatically his position centered upon the legislative proposals advanced since the
Hepburn amendments of 1908-1909, by large corporate
interests through such organizations as the Chicago Association of Commerce, the National Civic Federation, and
later the Chamber of Commerce. And by the end of 1914,
large corporate interests found that they could look with
satisfaction upon the status of the nation's "anti-trust"
laws.[65]

The "New Freedom" legislation on "trusts" bore upon
matters of foreign trade expansion in a more overt way.
In February, 1914, the Chamber of Commerce devoted
its principal session, in which Secretary Redfield participated, to a discussion of the administration's trust program.[66] It was here that the Chamber appointed its special
committee on trade commission legislation, of which
William L. Saunders and Rublee were members. Other
members included president of the Chamber R. G. Rhett,
Professor Henry R. Seager of Columbia University,
Charles R. Van Hise, president of the University of Wis-

---

[64] *P P W W*, III, 82, 83. Emphasis in original.

[65] See, *e.g.*, the report of William L. Saunders to the second National
Foreign Trade Convention in January, 1915. Chairman of the board of
the Ingersoll-Rand Company, Saunders was also a charter member of the
National Foreign Trade Council, and had served with Rublee on the
Chamber of Commerce's special committee that played a leading part in
drafting the trade commission act. Saunders observed that the Sherman
law prohibited only those restraints of trade that were "unreasonable or
contrary to the public welfare," and that there was "no likelihood" of its
becoming "any more drastic." The Clayton Act "defines a monopoly and
. . . announces certain moral principles to which we all agree;" while the
trade commission act "prevents unfair methods of competition," and as
such "is the most wholesome legislation . . . that has been passed recently"
in the matter of trusts. Saunders criticized *opponents* of the trade commission act for not seeing that "cooperation among business men—cooperation and concentration—is wholesome business and a good economic
condition." NFTC, *Proceedings* (1915), 54, 56.

[66] See *La Follette's Weekly*, VI, 8 (Feb. 21, 1914), 1-2.

consin, and Guy E. Tripp, chairman of the board of directors of the Westinghouse Electric Manufacturing Company. One of the committee's recommendations, issued in the spring of 1914, urged that Congress "direct the Commission [when established] to investigate and report to Congress at the earliest practicable date on the advisability of amending the Sherman Act to allow a greater degree of cooperation" in the export trade. By a vote of 538 to 67 the Chamber's membership approved this specific recommendation (as did the National Foreign Trade Convention in May, 1914), along with the broader one supporting a trade commission act.[67] Accordingly, in the drafting of the act, which Rublee wrote, it was this Chamber committee that inserted word for word section 6(h), which authorized the trade commission to investigate world trade conditions and submit appropriate recommendations to Congress.[68] With Rublee and Hurley appointed by Wilson as two of the agency's five commissioners, the FTC undertook and completed in its first year of operation four investigations, three of which dealt with foreign trade conditions.[69] One of these resulted in the two volume *Report on Cooperation in American Export Trade,* which recommended that Congress pass what was to become the Export Trade (Webb-Pomerene) Act of 1918 permitting cartels in the export trade, a bill which Wilson strongly supported.

The requirements of foreign trade promotion also influenced, in a negative way, the nature of the Clayton Act. As Oudin reported to the Foreign Trade Convention of May, 1914, ". . . the Committee on the Judiciary of the House . . . has reported a bill containing strict prohibitions against discriminations in prices for exclusive agencies, but providing that such prohibitions shall apply

---

[67] Sen. Comm. on Interstate Commerce, "Promotion of Export Trade," *Hearings,* 64th Cong., 2d Sess., 11.

[68] *Ibid.,* 10-12.

[69] *Annual Report of the Federal Trade Commission for the Year Ended June 30, 1916,* 18.

only in respect to commodities sold within the jurisdiction of the United States. This emphatic recognition of the distinction between domestic and export commerce reflects the growing disposition of the Government to render sympathetic assistance to American exporters. . . ." [70]

Just as the character of "New Freedom" legislation concerning the regulation of business related to the requirements of foreign trade promotion and reflected a community of views between the corporate community and the Wilson administration, the same was true, as already indicated, of the two most important "New Freedom" laws passed in 1913, the Underwood Tariff and the Federal Reserve Acts.

When Bryan, in his banquet address to the Foreign Trade Convention delegates, cited the tariff and reserve acts as measures taken by the administration for the promotion of foreign trade, he was not assuming the posture of protesting too much, nor was he merely waxing politically expedient to please his audience: the large corporate spokesmen among the delegates analyzed the two laws in precisely the same way. The two laws, it should be noted, were passed against the background of a trend among large industrial and financial interests, which had visibly emerged at least a decade before, toward tariff and banking structures oriented *(inter alia)* to their foreign trade and investment requirements. Bryan pointed to the elementary principle underlying the new tariff: "if we are to sell abroad, we must buy from people beyond our borders." The reserve act "will do more to promote trade in foreign lands than any other one thing that has been done in our history"; it had "set a nation free." [71] From no less a figure in large corporate circles than John E. Gardin, vice-president of the National City Bank of New York,

[70] NFTC, *Proceedings* (1914), 379; *cf.* House Comm. on Jud., *Hearings on Trust Legislation* (2 vols.), 63d Cong., 2d Sess., Serial 7, 1914, 11, 1960-1963.
[71] NFTC, *Proceedings* (1914), 208-209.

came a similar view. Complaining of the nation's imma-
turity in matters of international finance, Gardin found
encouragement in the tariff and reserve acts. ". . . The
administration . . . certainly has given us two things of
which we might be proud: one, the reduction of the tariff
. . . opening up the markets of the world,—if we want to
sell we have got to buy; and the other is the Federal Reserve Law, which relieves us from the bondage" of an outmoded banking law, providing "relief just as important
as the emancipation of the slaves. . . ." In view of these
laws, Gardin looked forward to the projected program of
the NFTC, as working "for the benefit of all those who
wish to partake . . . of the new freedom." [72]

Among those spokesmen of industrial and financial
interests who praised the Underwood Tariff, representatives of smaller interests were conspicuously absent. It is a
mistake to view the Underwood measure as part of a "New
Freedom" crusade against large corporations. It *was* part
of the "New Freedom" program; but the heathens were
not necessarily the large corporations. It was part of an
attack on "special privilege" conceived to be in conflict
with the national interest understood in terms of the conditions of modern times; but it was the special privilege
cherished by smaller and by non-industrial interests, no

---

[72] *Ibid.*, 249, 250-251. See also the remarks of Fred Brown Whitney,
chairman of the board of directors of the Lake Torpedo Boat Co., Alba B.
Johnson, Clarence J. Owens, managing director of the Southern Commercial Congress (at whose convention in 1913 Wilson had delivered his
Mobile address), Herbert S. P. Deans, manager of the foreign exchange
department of the Merchants Loan and Trust Company Bank of Chicago,
Edward N. Hurley, representing the Illinois Manufacturers Association.
Ibid., 251, 22-23, 90-91, 304, 291. Whitney: the reserve act represented the
people's "mandate—eternal and omnipotent—that the United States shall
become a World Power in international finance and trade. . . ." Johnson:
the new tariff was "part of the preparation . . . for this great forward
movement in the world's market;" the reserve act "is designed particularly
to facilitate exchange transactions with other nations. . . ." Owens: along
with the Panama Canal the reserve act "announced the beginning of a
period of direct financial relations" with Latin American markets, "giving
America the chance, for the first time, to compete in this regard with Great
Britain and Germany."

longer needed by the larger interests as export trade became increasingly more important to them.

Aside from its immediate intent to stimulate export
trade, the tariff, consistent with Wilson's views, sought to
enforce industrial efficiency by inviting world-wide competition, which would result in making United States industry and finance a more formidable competitor in world
markets. The larger industrial interests could withstand,
and expect to fatten on, such competition, but not the
smaller. Those items placed on the free list by the tariff
were, in the majority, articles of food, clothing, and raw
materials, industries occupied by the "little man." Large
corporations engaged in the capital and durable goods industries, and most heavily involved in the export trade so
far as manufacturers were concerned, could approve this
provision, because should the tariff have the intended
effect, it would operate to keep wage levels down, reduce
costs of materials, and in the process enable more effective
competition in world markets, aside from increasing the
profit rate. The issue was analogous to the great Corn
Law debates in England during the previous century,
where the industrialists sought to abolish import duties at
the expense of producers of food and raw stuffs. Wilson,
after all, had learned well from Cobden and Bright, the
apostles of what had been aptly termed the "imperialism
of free trade." [73]

At the same time, those items of heavy industry placed
upon the free list, such as steel rails and agricultural machinery and implements, were already produced by the
larger United States corporations with an efficiency and
at a cost of production sufficient to permit not only successful competition in world markets in general, but

---

[73] See John Gallagher and Ronald Robinson, "The Imperialism of
Free Trade," *The Economic History Review*, VI, 1, Second Series (Aug.
1953), 1-15. This is not meant to imply that the Underwood Tariff was a
free trade tariff; it was, in Taussig's terms, a "competitive tariff." F. W.
Taussig, *The Tariff History of the United States* (8th edition: N.Y., 1937),
418-422.

within the national markets of the European industrial nations as well, a point Wilson frequently made. Of further aid to such competition, moreover, the Underwood Tariff granted drawbacks on exported items comprised in part or in whole of imported materials subject to import duties.[74]

In effect, the Underwood Tariff strengthened the position of the larger corporations as against the smaller, and as against producers of agricultural materials. In this case, legal reform served the interest of those seeking to buttress the socio-economic *status quo,* while adherence to established law and institutions rallied those whose interest lay in forestalling the onward rush of that *status quo.* Accordingly, the greatest danger to the Underwood bill's downward revisions while pending in Congress "came from a horde of lobbyists," among whom the "owners and managers of industries that produced the great bulk of American industrial products were unconcerned and took no part. . . ." As Link concludes, the Underwood duties assumed their greatest significance "in so far as they reflected a lessening of the pressure from the large industrial interests for a McKinley type of protection."[75] It is understandable, therefore, that among the Congressional critics of the Underwood Tariff, as with the reserve law and the trade commission and Clayton acts, were "radical" and insurgent Democrats and Republicans claiming to represent the smaller and agrarian interests. In so far as the tariff, perhaps more dramatically than other issues, brought into unified focus the elements of efficiency, bigness in business, foreign trade, and an expanding sphere of enterprise—the last holding out the promise of more room for the "little man"—it may be accurately described as one of the high points of Wilsonian reform.

[74] Federal Trade Commission, *Report on Cooperation in American Export Trade* (2 vols.), June 30, 1916, I, 162; Taussig, *op. cit.,* 425-449.

[75] Link, *Wilson,* II, 186, 196. The lobbyists included representatives of such interests as wool, sugar, textile manufacturers, citrus fruits.

It is not meant to imply that the corporate community had no criticisms of the Underwood Tariff or Federal Reserve Act; but large corporate interests in particular viewed the new tariff either as a worthwhile experiment or more positively as sound policy, and business opinion overwhelmingly viewed the reserve law as basically sound, in need of perfecting amendments, rather than as a measure directed against their interests. The conflict over the reserve system bill during 1913 had not revolved so much around the provisions of the bill as around the question of how and by whom those provisions should be administered, except in so far as the "radical" and agrarian Republicans and Democrats insisted upon provisions that Wilson rejected. Otherwise, with respect to the manner of administering the system, the division lay not between Wilson and the "small" interests on the one side and "big business" on the other: the large corporate interests themselves were divided, particularly, the evidence indicates, along industrial and financial lines. As Link notes, the great mass of non-banking business opinion approved the bill, and in October, 1913, for example, both the Merchants Association of New York and the United States Chamber of Commerce (the latter by a vote of 306-17) endorsed it.[76]

The Federal Reserve Act may be interpreted, with respect to the issues raised here, in terms of a movement of large finance and industrial corporate interests, extending back to and before the National Monetary Commission, for branch banking, a commercial acceptance market for the facilitation of foreign trade and investment, and a reserve system that would protect the gold stock from foreign and domestic runs; a movement that, by expanding the credit structure, would reduce industrial corporations' dependence upon the money markets for investment capital, and insulate industrial operations from stock market fluctuations and speculators; a movement

[76] Link, *Wilson and the Progressive Era,* 51.

that Wilson approved and responded to favorably without himself being in any way responsible for its initiation, just as in the case of the movement for the Federal Trade Commission Act.

Indeed, upon his election, Wilson had no well-defined specific program; he had a general approach, and even his "specific" proposals were couched in general terms. He had identified himself with, and then given ideological and political leadership to, those movements with which his general approach corresponded, and which therefore corresponded with the concept of national interest embraced by that general approach. These movements—what are known as the Progressive reform movements (and they were reforms)—were movements led by and consisting of large corporate interests and political and intellectual leaders affirming the large corporate industrial capitalist system, and convinced of the necessity of institutionalized reforms, legal and otherwise, to accommodate the nation's law and habits, and the people's thinking, to the new corporate business structure and its requirements, domestic and foreign. As Wilson had put it, laws "meant for business done by individuals" had to be "satisfactorily adjusted to business done by great combinations," requiring "open efforts to accommodate law to the material development which has so strengthened the country."

Wilson's careful and emphatic distinction between the large corporation and the "trust" may be cited as one of the more forceful illustrations substantiating this formulation. A corollary of his evolutionary historicism, this distinction, in terms of Wilson's programmatic proposals, was decisive to his approach to the "trust" question, just as it was to that of the Bureau of Corporations under Garfield and Smith, and to that of Roosevelt, Taft, Perkins, Gary, and Croly. The large corporation, in this view, and the restriction of competition by corresponding forms of "cooperation," were the inevitable product of natural economic development. The "trust," however, was an artificial contrivance of predatory design, deliberately created by unscrupulous business men for undue ends. Accordingly, Wilson believed that while ". . . the elaboration of business upon a great co-operative scale is characteristic of our time and has come about by the natural operation of western civilization," this was different from saying that the "trusts" were inevitable. ". . . Big business is no doubt to a large extent necessary and natural. The development of business upon a great scale, upon a great scale of cooperation, is inevitable, and . . . is probably desirable. But that is a very different matter from the development of trusts, because the trusts have not grown. They have been artificially created; they have been put together not by natural processes, but by the will, the deliberate planning will, of men who . . . wished to make their power secure against competition." On the other hand, ". . . any large corporation built up by the legitimate processes of business, by economy, by efficiency, is natural; and I am not afraid of it, no matter how big it grows. . . ."[77]

Conservative-historicism, with Edmund Burke as one of its more prominent spokesmen, regards the politico-economic sphere of society "as a completely irrational one which cannot be fabricated by mechanical methods but which grows of its own accord. This outlook relates everything to the decisive dichotomy between 'construction according to calculated plan' and 'allowing things to grow.' . . ." ". . . A mode of thought is thus created which conceives of history as the reign of pre- and super-rational forces."[78] This mode of thought, transmitted to Wilson in particular from Burke, may be traced as a central thread winding not only through the early twentieth century liberalism (Progressivism) of Theodore Roosevelt, Croly, et al., as well as Wilson, but also through the liberalism of such presently prominent bourgeois ideological

[77] The New Freedom, 163-165, 166.
[78] Mannheim, Ideology and Utopia, 120, 121.

leaders as Adolf A. Berle, Jr., who states: ". . . Unlike the socialist commissariat, the American corporation is not a product of doctrine and dogma; it is an organic growth. . . ."[79] With respect to the basic structure of society, modern liberalism regards as legitimate only those institutions that it conceives as emerging independently of and beyond the deliberate, conscious determination of men; the underlying principle is submission to natural law, as distinguished, for example, from Marxism, which demands the understanding of objective laws of social development operating independently of man's will precisely in order to subject social development to man's conscious will; and as distinguished also from French Enlightenment social thought, which assumed that man could determine his society in accordance with Reason.[80] Conscious determination by men assumes its legitimate and proper function, from the modern liberal standpoint, only in facilitating natural evolution (as manifested in the basic structure of society as it is), and devising appropriate adjustments to it through parliamentary means (reforms).

The sharp and protracted ideological and social conflicts of the late nineteenth and early twentieth century, revolving around the corporate reorganization of the economy and erupting in the great "anti-trust" debates of that period, suggest that the growth of the corporation was not so "organic" as modern United States liberals

[79] In his Foreword to Mason (ed.), *The Corporation in Modern Society*, p. ix. In the same way, and characteristically, Wilson anticipated the downward revision of the tariff not "because men in this country have changed their theories," but because "the condus of America are going to bust through [the high tariff]. . . ." "Efficiency" (Jan. 27, 1912), *P P W W*, V, 360.

[80] In this connection, Wilson's conservative-historicism was reinforced by his adaptation of Darwin's theory of biological organic evolution to social evolution, though not in the form of survival-of-the-fittest "Social Darwinism" associated with Spencer, Sumner, and Fiske. See *Constitutional Government in the United States* (N.Y., 1908), 56-57, 199-200, and *The New Freedom*, 46, 47-48, where Wilson describes his view of government and social life as organic, Darwinian, as distinguished from the mechanistic, Newtonian conception of Montesquieu, the Enlightenment thinkers, and Jefferson. *Cf.* also, Diamond, *Econ. Thought of Wilson*, 39, 47, and Link, *Wilson*, I, 21-22.

insist; that capitalists and like-minded political and intellectual leaders fought hard and consciously, with "doctrine
and dogma" and with economic, political, and legal
strategem, to establish the large corporation, in an historically short period of time, as the dominant mode of
business enterprise, and to attain popular acceptance of
that development. Nevertheless, the "allowing-things-to-
grow" doctrine achieves a triumphant renaissance, as the
unifying conception, in twentieth century United States
liberalism, which may be accurately referred to as cor-
porate-liberalism (though now Burke is left neglected
backstage and Croly given the curtain calls). It is the
fundamental element that makes modern United States
liberalism the bourgeois Yankee cousin of modern European and English social-democracy.[81]

Within this essentially natural-law framework, while
consistently holding that the large industrial corporations
were natural and beneficent products of social evolution,
Wilson attributed much of the evils with which they were
popularly associated to financiers, *dei ex machina,* manip-
ulating corporate securities and practices for speculative
profit and creating artificial corporate structures for
monopolistic advantage.[82] At the same time, by tying
credit and currency mechanisms to the "natural laws" of
commerce, that is, by basing the banking system upon
commercial paper rather than upon government bonds,
and building up a reserve system, measures long sought
by large financial and industrial corporate interests, the
federal reserve law corresponded with Wilson's view that
trade and investment should be set "free" to pursue their
"natural" course, unhindered by the arbitrary will of a

[81] Herbert Marcuse, *Reason and Revolution* (2nd edition: N.Y., 1954),
398-401. Since completing this essay the author's attention has been drawn
to Arnold A. Rogow's "Edmund Burke and the American Liberal Tradition," *The Antioch Review* (Summer, 1957), 255-265, which analyzes the
decisive relevance of Burke to Wilsonian liberalism in particular and
modern U.S. liberalism in general.

[82] See, *e. g.,* "Law or Personal Power" (Apr. 13, 1908), *P P W W,* II, 29.

few financiers; in theory, it would encourage greater competition (through greater opportunities for investment
borrowing), and permit "little men" to obtain credit with
which to start or maintain a business enterprise of their
own, though no longer in the central areas of production,
transportation, or communication. *Mutatis mutandis,* Wilson's position on the tariff flowed from similar considerations: the government's role was to provide business with
the "environment" best suited to the assertion of its "natural" course.

Wilson held no dogmatic views on the question of the
extent of government intervention in economic affairs—
he had long believed that the state should intervene so
far as "experience permits or the times demand"—and
with respect to the reserve law, he had by June, 1913,
firmly decided upon government control of the central
board, in the face of stiff banker opposition. The compromise that resulted constituted a concession to the large
banking interests. After the bill's passage, and the announcement of Wilson's appointments to the central reserve board, the large banks' spokesmen, as well as
spokesmen for large industrial corporations, expressed
widespread satisfaction,[83] just as they had in the case of
the Underwood Tariff and Federal Trade Commission
acts.

[83] See annual address of American Bankers' Association president Arthur Reynolds at the 1914 convention, and his later remarks at the same
convention. *Proceedings of the Fortieth Annual Convention of the American Bankers' Association,* Richmond, Va., Oct. 12-16, 1914, pp. 57-68, 312-
315. See also letters expressing approval of the Federal Reserve Act from
George M. Reynolds, president of Continental and Commercial National
Bank of Chicago, A. Barton Hepburn, chairman of the board, Chase National Bank, and A. J. Hemphill, president of Guaranty Trust Company
of N.Y., to F. H. Goff (president of Cleveland Trust Co.), president of
Bankers' Association's Trust Company Section, dated Sept. 23, Oct. 9,
Oct. 5, 1914, respectively, in *ibid.,* 305-308. *Cf. La Follette's Weekly,* Vl, 4
(Jan. 24, 1914), 3, where Jacob H. Schiff of Kuhn, Loeb & Co., is quoted
praising the reserve law as "legislation highly pleasing to me." La Follette,
who opposed the measure, remarked, ". . . The published reports that Wall
Street banking interests were fighting the Administration's currency bill
tooth and nail now appear somewhat pale in the light of the enthusiastic
approval Wall Street is bestowing upon this law." See also, Link, *Wilson,*
II, 451-452, 454-455.

In this way, Wilson emerged as a foremost ideological and political leader of a social movement affirming industrial corporate capitalism, and as the pre-eminent personality in the nation's public life acting as a bridge of communication between that movement and the public (or, the electorate to which the movement appealed), popularizing the movement's ideology and program, and making them understandable and acceptable to the people in terms of the nation's traditions, evolutionary development, and "destiny." The ideology embraced a neo-Comtean positivism that (in European terms) Wilson, the conservative-historicist and modified Manchestrian liberal, was eminently qualified to serve. Wilson's position was not that of a representative of the "little man," or the "middle class," *against* "big business"; but that of one who, affirming the large corporate industrial capitalist system, was concerned with establishing the legal and institutional environment most conducive to the system's stability and growth, while at the same time preserving some place within the system for the "little man." His formula was fair competition and impartial access to credit at home, and expansion of the economic frontier abroad, upon the assumption that the wider the market and the more impersonal its conditions, the more room and opportunity for the "little man" to coexist side by side with the big. The very conditions of industrial production and of foreign economic expansion, however, made the "little man," as an independent entrepreneur, increasingly irrelevant to the national economy, except in peripheral spheres of services and distribution. Theodore Roosevelt sought to meet this disturbing reality by acknowledging it and insisting upon equal opportunity for every young man to rise within the established corporate structures. While similarly insisting upon such equality, Wilson refused to concede the irrelevance of the "little man"; but his refusal was not a matter of sentimentality: it stemmed from his fear that given a growing irrelevance of "little men" in the nation's economy, fewer and fewer people would retain a stake in the capitalist system, and more and more would lose hope for betterment under capitalism and turn toward socialism or other forms of radicalism.[84] As such, the Wilsonian and Rooseveltian variants of Progressivism signified, if not the birth, then the coming of age, of twentieth century United States liberalism, whose present-day fundamentals, converging upon large-scale corporate capitalism at home and economic expansion abroad, remain genetically true to the components of Wilson's world view, their immediate parental source.

According to the generally accepted interpretation offered by Arthur S. Link, Wilsonian Progressivism, as applied and developed during Wilson's two terms as

[84] As Wilson advised leading business men in his address at the Annual Banquet of the Economic Club in New York, May 23, 1912 (*P P W W*, II, 446, 449-451): ". . . How would it suit the prosperity of the United States, how would it suit the success of business, to have a people that went every day sadly or sullenly to their work? How would the future look to you if you felt that the aspiration has gone out of most men, the confidence of success, the hope that they might change their condition, if there was everywhere the feeling that there was somewhere covert dictation, private arrangement as to who should be in the inner circle of privilege and who should not, a more or less systematic and conscious attempt to dictate and dominate the economic life of the country? Do you not see that just as soon as the old self-confidence of America, . . . as her old boasted advantages of individual liberty and opportunity are taken away, all the energy of her people begins to subside, to slacken, to grow loose and pulpy, without fibre, and men simply cast around to see that the day does not end disastrously with them."

"What is the alternative, gentlemen? You have heard the rising tide of socialism . . . Socialism is not growing in influence in this country as a programme. It is merely that the ranks of protestants are being recruited . . . If it becomes a programme, then we shall have to be very careful how we propose a competing programme . . . the programme of socialism would not work; but there is no use saying what will not work unless you can say what will work.

". . . If you want to oust socialism you have got to propose something better. It is a case, if you will allow me to fall into the language of the vulgar, of 'put up or shut up.' . . . It is by constructive purpose that you are going to govern and save the United States. . . .

"Very well, then, let us get together and form a constructive programme, [that posterity will say that after America had passed through a simple age] . . . when the forces of society had come into hot contact, . . . there were men of serene enough intelligence, . . . of will and purpose to stand up once again . . . [and who found out] how to translate power into freedom, how to make men glad that they were rich, how to take the envy out of men's hearts that others were rich and they for a little while poor, by opening the gates of opportunity to every man. . . ."

president from 1913 to 1921, can be divided into two periods: the first, the period of the "New Freedom," characterized by government attempts to regulate and stand in hostile posture apart from "big business," and directed at restoring some semblance of a *laissez-faire*, free-competition social order; the second, characterized by a government policy of cooperation with "big business" and active regulatory intervention in the economy. The divide, according to this view, lay somewhere around November, 1914 (though at points the divide is rolled back to early 1914, as a response to the continuing depression, leaving scarcely a year to the "New Freedom" phase). Thus, it is argued, the "New Freedom" was capable of serving the cause of Progressivism for only a short time; Progressivism gained new life after November, 1914, through the abandonment of the "New Freedom" and the move toward Herbert Croly's and Theodore Roosevelt's "New Nationalism."

If Wilson is properly understood in terms of the widely current evolutionary-positivistic world view that he shared alike with leading industrial and finance capitalists and with prominent politicians and intellectuals within the bi-partisan Progressive movement, and if the approaches taken by his administration to both foreign and domestic affairs are viewed as basically interrelated, rather than compartmentalized, as affecting each other, rather than operating in isolated spheres, then it is of greater analytical value to view the attitude assumed by Wilson and his administration toward "business" before and after November, 1914, as undergoing consistent development, rather than fundamental change. That attitude corresponded with a world view that affirmed large-scale corporate industrial capitalism as the natural and inevitable product of social evolution, and that regarded foreign investments and exports, defined in terms of the needs of industrial and finance capital, as indispensable to the nation's prosperity and social well-being. Beneficence at home and abroad, in this view, was a function of necessity.

Large corporate production appeared as the vehicle of domestic material progress; foreign economic expansion, considered a decisive condition of such production, promised to carry "civilization," bourgeois-liberal ideas and institutions, and a better way of life, to the agrarian areas of the world, particularly as "development" of natural resources in those areas was considered essential to such expansion.

It no more occurred to such liberals as Wilson than it did to the so-called Dollar Diplomatists before him, or than it does today to the "internationalist" liberals, that investment in, and ownership of, other nations' resources, railroads, and industry, by United States capitalists, constituted imperialism or exploitation. Imperialism to them meant British- and European-style colonialism or exclusive spheres of interest; exploitation meant unscrupulous gouging, exorbitantly profitable concessions gained by undue influence with corrupt government officials, and the like, in short, "unfair practices" analogous to those characteristics that distinguished the "trust" from the large corporation in domestic affairs. Open door expansion, on the other hand, appeared to them as simply the implementation of the natural international division of labor between the industrialized and agrarian nations; it meant mutually beneficial (and beneficent) business relationships and trade; it meant the assumption by the United States of its natural place in the world economy *vis-à-vis* the other industrial nations, by the elimination of "artificial" impediments to the operation of the laws of competitive commerce; it meant "free trade." [85]

[85] See, *e. g.*, Wilson's "Be Worthy of the Men of 1776," July 4, 1914, *P P W W*, III, 142-143: "The Department of State . . . is constantly called upon to back up the commercial . . . and the industrial enterprises of the United States in foreign countries, and it at one time went so far in that direction that all its diplomacy came to be designated as 'dollar diplomacy.' . . . But there ought to be a limit to that. There is no man who is more interested than I am in carrying the enterprise of American business men to every quarter of the globe. I was interested in it long before I was suspected of being a politician. I have been preaching it year after year

In the Wilsonian manner, former president Truman recently remarked, "The Open Door policy is not imperialism; it is free trade." Unfortunately, the bourgeois-liberal mind seems unable to understand how any transaction that involves the exchange of equivalent for equivalent can carry with it any quality of injustice or exploitation. In the economic realm, morality and justive are defined as exchange at value, so long as it is devoid of any element of extra-pecuniary coercion; in more sophisticated ideological terms, morality and justice correspond with natural law. But it is precisely in the relationship defined by natural law, precisely in the exchange of equivalent for equivalent (assuming the free and competitive exchange of equivalents in the first place, though this is often not the case), that the exploitation, the injustice, the immorality, from the point of view of the agrarian peoples, resides. For, while the relationship is reified by the liberal mind as purely an exchange of goods, a confrontation of things, of private properties, what is really involved is a relationship between human beings. Concern for the nicely balanced exchange of things according to their market value —"a fair field and no favor"—blinds the liberal mind to the real relationship between people, of which the exchange of goods is but a consequence, and to the resulting conditions of life (the "human relations" and "individual dignity" with which the liberal is so articulately preoccupied.)[86] Hence, the innocent shock consistently evinced

---

as the great thing that lay in the future for the United States, to show her wit and skill and enterprise and influence in every country in the world. . . . [But if] American enterprise in foreign countries, particularly in those . . . which are not strong enough to resist us, takes the shape of imposing upon and exploiting the mass of the people . . . it ought to be checked and not encouraged. I am willing to get anything for an American that money and enterprise can obtain except the suppression of the rights of other men. I will not help any man buy a power which he ought not to exercise over his fellow-beings."

[86] ". . . we are told that free trade would create an international division of labor, and threby give to each country the production which is most in harmony with its natural advantages. You believe perhaps, gentlemen, that the production of coffee and sugar is the natural destiny of the

by liberals at anti-Americanism and resentment in the agrarian areas of the world regardless of whether United States foreign policy is of the "Dollar Diplomacy" or the "Good Neighbor" variety.

For, the essence of open door expansion involved an international system of economy identical to that established by England and the European industrial nations with their colonies and other agrarian areas. The latter were to become increasingly familiar with modern relations of capital and labor, but with capital appearing in the form of the foreigner and labor in the form of the indigenous population; they were assigned the role of suppliers of raw materials and markets for industrial goods and capital investment; and, of particular importance, control over, and investment decisions affecting, decisive sectors of their economies were to be transferred from their determination to that of capitalists in the United States. Those sectors of their economies were to become "complementary" to, and integrated with, the United States corporate economy, each an *imperium in imperio* within its respective nation, with all the implications of economic dislocation, political instability, and restriction of national economic and political independence. To Wilson, such implications were no necessary part of open door expansion, but rather of imperialism and exploitation as he narrowly conceived them; as for the rest, it all appeared as only natural in relations between "capital surplus" and

---

West Indies. Two centuries ago, nature, which does not trouble herself about commerce, had planted neither sugar-cane nor coffee trees there." "If the free-traders cannot understand how one nation can grow rich at the expense of another, we need not wonder, since these same gentlemen also refuse to understand how within one country one class can enrich itself at the expense of another." ". . . the protectionist system is nothing but a means of establishing large-scale industry in any given country, . . . of making it dependent upon the world market, and from . . . [that] moment . . ., there is already more or less dependence upon free trade. . . ." Marx, "On the Question of Free Trade," public speech delivered before the Democratic Association of Brussels, Jan. 9, 1848, in *The Poverty of Philosophy*, 22-223, 224.

"capital deficient" nations, and as the mode of progress
in international affairs.[87]

It was the part of statesmanship to make law the expression of the necessities and facts of the time: to institution-

[87] See, *e. g.*, the report of Edward E. Pratt, chief of the Bureau of Foreign and Domestic Commerce under Wilson, for the fiscal year July 1, 1914, to June 30, 1915: ". . . we can nver hope to realize the really big prizes in foreign trade until we are prepared to loan capital to foreign nations and to foreign enterprise. The big prizes . . . are the public and private developments of large proportions, . . . the building of railroads, the construction of public-service plants, the improvement of harbors and docks, . . . and many others which demand capital in large amounts. New countries are generally poor. They look to older and richer countries to supply them with the capital to make their improvements and to develop their resources. The country which furnishes the capital usually sells the materials and does the work . . . there is no doubt that the loans of one nation to another form the strongest kind of economic bond between the two. It is commonly said that trade follows the flag. It is much more truly said that trade follows the investment or the loan." ". . . A foreign commercial policy . . . is gradually taking shape under a wise and careful administration. American investments abroad are being encouraged. The fact that investment must precede trade and that investments abroad must be safeguarded is fully recognized." *Reports of the Department of Commerce*, Oct. 30, 1915 (Wash., 1916), 247, 249. *Cf.* the more recent statement of the prominent liberal spokesman, Dean Acheson: ". . . in the nineteenth century an international system of sorts not only kept the peace for a century but also provided highly successful economic working agreements. It brought about the industrialization of Europe and of many other parts of the world—our own country, for one. It stimulated production of raw materials and led to a great, though unevenly distributed, rise in the standard of living. This was accomplished by the export of capital, primarily by Great Britain, but also by all of Western Europe." ". . . a system for the export of capital, much greater than our present . . . efforts, is necessary. The system has been destroyed which expanded the power of Western Europe. . . . One to replace it will be devised, managed, and largely (but not wholly) financed by the United States; otherwise, it is likely to be provided by the Soviet Union, under circumstances destructive of our own power. . . ." "Foreign investment can provide wider opportunity for use of national energies. This can well enhance pride in national achievement and relieve frustrations among members of the populace now denied opportunity to use their full capabilities and training. This should tend to lessen xenophobia, strengthen social fabric and political stability, and bring new meaning to national independence. . . ." Acheson, *Power and Diplomacy* (Cambridge, Mass., 1958), 18, 19-20, 22. The first chapter of the book includes a subsection entitled, "The Collapse of a World Order," referring to the disintegration of the imperial system of the 19th century, and argues the necessity of replacing it with one similar to it, in its economic aspects, led by the United States. Acheson prefaces the chapter with lines of verse from Alfred Noyes: "When his hundred years expire / Then he'll set hisself a-fire / And another from his ashes rise most beautiful to see!"

alize the ground rules of the corporate economy at home and the mechanisms of economic expansion abroad, so that day to day business, the laws of commerce, and the government's role with respect to them, might flow smoothly along settled paths, rather than by the fits and starts of fire-brigade policy or executive fiat. As Wilson had put it in 1907, " . . . an institution is merely an established practice, an habitual method of dealing with the circumstances of life or the business of government. . . . " [88] In Wilson's view, it was this, with respect to modern circumstances of the modern industrial order, that the legislation of 1913-1914 promised to do.

Historians who have studied Wilson appear to harbor guilt-feelings about capitalism: a policy based upon considerations of the economic imperatives of capitalism is sordid, immoral, or amoral; a policy based upon non-economic principle is moralistic. The corporate and political policymakers of the United States, Wilson included, have had no such guilt-feelings or compulsion to make such a division in their thinking. To them there was (and is) nothing immoral about capitalism; it embraces the highest morality. The strength and spread of morality appear as the function of the strength and spread of capitalism. Historians, however, disregarding the imperatives of modern capitalism, while assuming its existence all the same, seem to have created an ideal construct of what liberalism ought to be, arbitrarily imputing to it certain characteristics of a transcendent nature and withholding from it others, particularly those relating to the affairs of political economy. It is an academic, idealized liberalism, not the responsible political liberalism as it operates as a functional ideology outside the university walls; it is a liberalism from which historians have written history in the manner of advice, consent, and dissent, rather than history that analyzes the nature of liberal ideology as it operates and appears in the hurly-burly of political econ-

[88] Wilson, *Constitutional Government*, 14.

omy. Accordingly, historians have tended to appraise the nature of the Wilsonian liberal (or Progressive) movement by deduction from, and in comparison with, the supposed nature of its ideology, instead of basing their analyses on an empirical study of the movement and comprehending the ideology of its leaders as emerging from and interacting with that movement and its adversaries. Particularly is the latter approach essential to an analysis of Wilson, to whom the great issues of his day turned upon concrete economic interests and questions.

Finding that Wilson's thought and policies often deviated from the ideal model, many historians have concluded superficially that Wilson was a "hypocrite" or a conservative in liberal's clothing. The point raised here, however, is not a quarrel as to whether Wilson was in fact a liberal or Progressive; on the contrary, it is submitted that a successful, comprehensive effort at analyzing precisely what Wilsonian liberalism or Progressivism was (and modern United States liberalism in general) has yet to be made.

It would be conducive to a move impartial and comprehensive understanding of Wilson and Wilsonianism to discard as a tool of analysis both the "New Freedom" —"New Nationalism" formula and the "Moralism"-*vs.*-"commercialism" presumption. This approach sees behind the "New Freedom" the shadow of a misconstrued Brandeis, who is taken inaccurately to symbolize an anti-"big business" program for the restoration of some sort of *laissez-faire*, free-competition society; more accurately, it sees behind the "New Nationalism" the shadow of Croly as represented in his book, *The Promise of American Life*. At the outset, and only at the outset, it may be more pertinent and analytically suggestive to a re-evaluation of Wilson and Wilsonianism, to see instead the shadow of Croly-the-adolescent behind the earlier years of Wilson's presidency, Croly-the-strapping-young-man behind the later (and lingering into the 1920's), with Croly-the-nearly-mature biding his time until the advent of the New Deal. In view of the present "national purpose" campaign of corporate spokesmen, liberal political and intellectual leaders, the Luce publications and *The New York Times,* short of a basic reordering of United States society, Croly-the-mature may yet arrive, and then the nation will surely be in need of a new freedom.

Gompers and the New Liberalism, 1900–1909

BY *James Weinstein*

Volume V, No. 4
Fall 1965

James Weinstein here reviews a book by one of the best of the old left historians. His essay is an attempt to criticize from a New Left point of view some of the limitations of old style Marxist thinking in the United States.

With *The Policies and Practices of the American Federation of Labor, 1900-1909,* Philip S. Foner* has completed three volumes in his projected comprehensive history of the labor movement in the United States. His accomplishment to date, and his announced plans for volumes on the Industrial Workers of the World and labor and the Socialists from 1910 to 1917, indicate that Foner is well on his way toward the most important single history of the American labor movement. In part, this is the result of the scope of Foner's research, particularly impressive in this volume, in the vast incoming correspondence files of the American Federation of Labor, almost all of which were subsequently destroyed when the Federation moved to new headquarters in Washington about fifteen years ago. Foner uses this material to get behind the formal debates and convention proceedings which usually fill labor histories. His volume supplies a

---

* New York. International Publishers. 1964.

much needed look at the relations between the trade
union leadership and the employers, at the labor leaders'
attitudes toward the workers who made up their constituencies, at their politics and social values. His greatest contribution is a picture of the way in which the "business"
values of the labor leaders, and their acceptance of a
subordinate role in a capitalist system dominated by the
large corporations, led them into a position as mediators
between business and the workers, rather than as representatives of their class interests. In this respect Foner's
book is sharply distinguished from the tradition of
apologia for the AFL represented in the works of Selig
Perlman and Philip Taft, and other John R. Commons
school historians.

Foner's class conscious view of the labor movement in
the early 1900's and his concern with the extent to which
the AFL met its responsibilities to its worker-constituents
in these years leads him to ask important questions of his
material. His book is best, and that is very good, in its
discussion of the process by which the trade union bureaucracy developed its conservative practice. He makes
clear not only the failures of the AFL leadership to organize unskilled, immigrant, Negro and women workers,
but the way in which this was related to their acceptance
of business principles and prevailing social values. The
corruption of the AFL bureaucracy took two forms: direct
graft-taking (for failure to organize, for settling strikes on
terms advantageous to corporations, for selling union
labels) and a more subtle, but more pervasive desire to
emulate the business leaders they confronted—to gain
personal influence and prestige by close association with
the leaders of the large corporations. Foner describes this
process well and correctly emphasizes the importance of
the National Civic Federation and its role in developing
the second form of corruption. His picture of the process
through which the AFL leadership became increasingly

committed opponents of independent politics, organization of the unskilled and united strike action is convincing
and important for those who would understand our present labor movement. His discussion of the role of the
Catholic Church is equally important. As Foner shows,
the Catholics made up almost half the membership of the
AFL, and were the dominant religious group among the
officers of the international unions and on the Executive
Council of the Federation. In the AFL, the Church,
through several labor societies and later the Militia of
Christ, was the most consistent and most powerful opponent of Socialism. There was no outside force more active
in pressuring the Federation to avoid independent class
conscious political action, or working for cooperation between labor and capital. Foner does not explicitly say so,
but his chapter on the Church and Labor makes it clear
that as long as Catholics made up half the AFL membership, Socialists could not hope to win control of the Federation. At times, Socialists had two-thirds of the non-
Catholic voting strength in conventions, but the active
participation of the Militia of Christ and other Catholic
organizations in the AFL restricted the areas of activity
open to them.

Unfortunately, on the questions most relevant to contemporary politics and to radicals of today, Foner is at
his worst. These involve the nature of American radicalism in the years from 1900 to 1909 (actually until the
First World War), and, more important, the relationship
of the large corporations to the development of American
liberalism, the welfare state and the New Deal. In these
two areas Foner never transcends the level of sophistication of the dominant school of liberal historians who see
the Socialists as irrelevant in the face of Theodore Roosevelt's progressivism and Woodrow Wilson's liberalism,
and who view liberalism itself simply as a popular movement in opposition to big business. Foner does devote two

chapters to the National Civic Federation, the organization through which many executives of America's biggest trusts and financial institutions worked with the conservative trade unionists (and later with representatives of the Grange and other farmers' organizations and with professional groups). But Foner fails to explain the role these men played in developing the concepts of liberal consensus, or the politics that led them to these concepts. He does relate that "rather than smash unionism," the business leaders in the Civic Federation "sought to emasculate it, to ensnare the labor leaders into a conscious program of collaborating with the employers, robbing the workers of their vigor, militancy, and the spirit of their class." (p. 61.) What he does not see is that these men were the ideological parents of Franklin D. Roosevelt (who was a member of the National Civic Federation) and of the many sophisticated big businessmen who supported Roosevelt's slightly more advanced programs during the New Deal. The leaders of the Civic Federation understood and constantly acted on the need to distinguish between those social reforms that did not threaten the underlying relationships of the system, and socialism. They supported the former as long as Socialists or middle class progressives such as Robert M. LaFollette threatened the political hegemony of the large corporations. In short, they provided the ideological foundation on which Lyndon Johnson's "Great Society" rests. One would never know this from reading Foner's book.

The National Civic Federations general approach to social reform and to the trade unions was expressed by many business and liberal political leaders in the years from 1900, when the Federation was formed, to 1917, when many of its functions merged into those of the wartime Administration. Samuel Insull, Chicago utilities magnate, expressed one motivation for reform in 1909. Seeing that it was only a matter of time before public clamor would lead to regulation of utilities, Insull told

Ralph Easley of the Civic Federation that he preferred
to "help shape the right kind of regulation," rather than
have "the wrong kind forced upon him." [1]

In a more general expression of this approach, George
W. Perkins, partner of J. P. Morgan and company and a
director of both the United States Steel Corporation and
the International Harvester Company, told the Civic
Federation that "if this new order of things is better for
capital and better for the consumer, then in order to
succeed permanently it must demonstrate that it is better
for the laborer." [2]

In its first few years the National Civic Federation was
not primarily concerned with social reform as such, but
rather with mediating industrial disputes and strengthening the conservative currents among the craft unionists.
Foner makes this point effectively, but fails to see that
the big businessmen in the Federation were genuine progressives in the sense that they were prepared to make
those adjustments in the system made necessary by the
emergence of giant corporations in almost every area of
economic activity. Unions were clearly here to stay, but
class antagonism and conflict were to be reduced wherever
possible. This put reform on the agenda; it also dictated
big business opposition to the reactionary anti-union
drives of the National Association of Manufacturers,
launched in 1903. Ralph Easley of the Civic Federation
observed in 1904 that the Federation and its big business
sponsors simultaneously faced "the hatred of socialism
and the opposition of the recently formed employers'
associations." Easley enjoyed pointing out that the latter
were not in themselves a threat, although they did cause
political problems, because they included "none of the
great employers of labor representing the basic industries,

---

[1] Ralph M. Easley to George W. Perkins, New York, June 9, 1909, Box
38, National Civic Federation papers, New York Public Library.
[2] Address to the *Tenth Annual Meeting of the National Civic Federation, New York, November 22 and 23, 1909* (New York, 1910), 144.

such as coal, iron, steel, building trades and railroads.[3] Louis D. Brandeis, an active member of the Massachusetts Civic Federation, supported Easley's position, arguing that collective bargaining was essential to the survival of capitalism against the rising tide of socialism. "The trade unions also stand as a bulwark against the great wave of socialism," Brandeis insisted. Conservative businessmen outside the Civic Federation were warned by Brandeis that "among a free people every excess of capital must in time be repaid by the excessive demands of those who have not the capital." What this meant was that "if the capitalists are wise, they will aid us in the effort to prevent injustice." [4]

Seeing that their long range class interests lay in taking Brandeis' advice, the Civic Federation moved steadily in the direction of social reform after 1905. By 1909, as *The Survey* pointed out, business leaders in the Federation had "clearly recognized the public necessity for the choice between unionism and state socialism." Espousing the cause of trade unionism "as consonant with American institutions," and as an "antidote for the socialistic propaganda," the Federation placed itself squarely against the NAM and its new president, John Kirby, Jr. This, commented *The Survey,* was "most significant," because the National Civic Federation numbered among its officers Seth Low, the banker Isaac N. Seligman, President William H. Taft, Secretary of the Treasury Franklin Mac-Veagh, Elihu Root, Andrew Carnegie, August Belmont and "a score more of equally representative men." [5]

One area in which the Federation took the lead was that of workmen's compensation legislation. By 1909 it had embarked on a full scale campaign for compensation laws. President Seth Low appointed August Belmont to

[3] *National Civic Federation Monthly Review,* 1,4 (June 1904), 12.
[4] Quoted in Alpheus T. Mason, *Brandeis* (New York, 1946), pp. 141, 149, 130.
[5] Graham Taylor, "Industrial Survey of the Month," *The Survey,* XXII (August 7, 1909), 668-9.

head the Federation's Workmen's Compensation Committee and the annual meeting was devoted almost entirely to discussion of the new reform. That year not one state had a general compensation law on its books, but by 1917, after an intensive campaign by the Civic Federation, with the strong support of its leading business members, forty-two states had adopted such legislation. The significance of this reform, and, more important, the manner in which it was made, was pointed to by the assistant general solicitor of the United States Steel Corporation. He suggested that the "progress of workmen's compensation should be a rebuke and a rebuttal" to those who "assert that workingmen get nothing from employers except by contest and struggle." It was the hope of the steel company's lawyer that the role of employers in promoting this legislation would "strengthen those leaders among workmen" who "believe that capital can be fair to labor and labor can be fair to capital [6] Theodore Roosevelt understood all this very well. He was delighted to cooperate with such enlightened and responsible representatives of great wealth and power. As he told the assembled magnates at the annual meeting of the Civic Federation in 1911, their activities and organization approached the ideal in that progress was being "made in such a manner that the progressive people will not part company with the bulk of the moderates." In other words, Roosevelt enthused, this movement was taking "the form of evolution rather than revolution." [7] Many of the big businessmen supported Roosevelt's candidacy as a Progressive in 1912 precisely because they understood the vital importance of distinguishing between socialism and social reform. Almost all the corporate executives in the Federation, whether Progressive, Republican or Democratic in

[6] Raynall C. Bolling, "Results of Voluntary Relief Plan of United States Steel Corporation," *Annals*, 38, 1 (July 1911), 43.

[7] *National Civic Federation Annual Meetings, 1911-1912* (New York, 1912), 188-89.

1912, understood "that a distinction should be made between proposals and direct undertakings that are socialistic . . . in principle," and those that would be favored by Socialists, but which were "not necessarily in conflict with the underlying principles of the existing industrial order."[8] This understanding was clearly not restricted to one party. In 1913 Elihu Root told a big business-dominated meeting of New York Republicans that workmen's compensation was a necessity. A resolution in its favor carried unanimously, and the conference further resolved that "changed and changing social and industrial conditions impose new duties on government." It sympathized "with the humanitarian spirit now abroad in the world," and recognized "that there are other social measures besides workmen's compensation which have been adopted in other countries and states, which must be seriously considered." The Republican party, the resolution concluded, must "meet industrial and social demands of modern civilization, so far as they are reasonably consistent with our institutions."[9]

Foner misses entirely this dimension of the National Civic Federation and of the big businessmen who supported it. One result is that he tends to overestimate the effect of the open shop drive, led by employers' associations and the National Association of Manufacturers (at that time organizations mainly of smaller manufacturers). Indeed, on this point Foner presents three apparently conflicting pieces of evidence in different parts of the book, each supporting a different argument. In the section on the open shop drive he tells us that union membership, after growing steadily in the decade up to 1904, declined some 220,000 between 1904 and 1906 and did not

[8] Memorandum Concerning the Policy to be pursued by the Department of Industrial Economics of the National Civic Federation (1914) Box 84, NCF papers.

[9] Minutes of the Conference of Republicans of the State of New York, Waldorf Astoria Hotel, New York City, December 5, 1913, 34. Low papers, Columbia University.

surpass the 1904 figure until 1911. (p. 32.) This, he implies, was a result of the open shop drive. Later, in a section on business unionism, he quotes Joseph R. Buchanan to the effect that two-thirds of the decline in union membership in these years was the product of graft and dishonesty in the internationals. (p. 163). Still later, in a section on the immigrant worker, Foner quotes Isaac Hourwich to the effect that immigrants swelled the ranks of organized labor (rather than hindering its development), and that in the years from 1901 to 1910 membership *increased* "from about 1,300,000 to about 2,625,000." (p. 264). It would seem that only one of these can be correct; I think Buchanan comes nearest the truth.

A more important corollary of Foner's view of the National Civic Federation is his mistaken insistence that behind the leaders of the open shop drive "stood the finance capitalists, the monopolists who dominated American economic and political life," (p. 41.) and that "at the helm of the NAM were the finance capitalists," who were active in the NCF (pp. 42, 89.) Foner himself points out that forty-three of the top industrial capitalists and leading executives of sixteen of the sixty-seven largest railroads were members of the National Civic Federation. But few of these men were in the NAM, which Ralph Easley and other NCF leaders viewed as an organization of irresponsible small businessmen. As Easley wrote to Senator Joseph L. Bristow in 1909, Frank Vanderlip of the National City Bank and George W. Perkins had come around to the view that unions were desirable; other big businessmen were moving in the same direction, "but it is almost an individual question." There were, Easley explained, "no corporations but what are themselves divided in opinion. Take the United States Steel Corporation: Judge Gary, George Perkins and Henry Phipps are friendly to our work, whereas Henry C. Frick and W. E. Corey hate the Federation and believe it is doing great harm by recognizing the labor leaders. They would smash every union in the country if they could. In fact, our enemies are the Socialists among the labor people and the anarchists among the capitalists." [10]

Foner's view of Big Business as monolithic and as re-actionary leads him into a number of factual errors, too. He concludes that by 1908 the Civic Federation had ac-complished most of what it set out to achieve and thus declined. In fact, the opposite was so. Between 1908 and 1916 the Federation was more active than at any other period. It took the lead not only in agitation for work-men's compensation, but in the movement that led to the Federal Trade Commission Act in 1914, and in the investi-gation of many other reforms. It conducted an active campaign against the Socialists in and out of the labor movement, and it came to win the support of an increasing number of business and top political leaders. Foner cites Charles W. Eliot's anti-union statements when he was a member of the Civic Federation as evidence of its anti-unionism, but he does not tell his reader that Eliot quit the Federation in 1907 because he did not share its views on labor. He asserts that unions were driven out of all trustified industries, but in coal mining union membership increased from one hundred thousand in 1900 to over four hundred thousand by 1914.

I do not mean to imply that Foner is entirely wrong about the attitudes of the big businessmen in the Civic Federation. Much of what he says is accurate. Many busi-ness leaders took positions in the abstract debates of the Federation that they did not take in their factories. When they did support the unions and social reforms it was often in direct response to the threat of more radical de-mands in the labor movement or from the Socialists. But this is exactly the motivation that led business to support the liberal reforms in the New Deal and that impels the Johnson Administration to war on poverty and sponsor a

[10] Easley to Senator Joseph L. Bristow, New York, July 17, 1909, Box 46, NCF papers.

voting rights bill. It is precisely this flexibility and sophistication on the part of American businessmen that has
given the system its strength and durability. A consciousness of the role of the corporation leaders in developing
this ideology is extremely important for radicals today,
both the new ones and those who lived through the New
Deal and never understood it. Foner's book in no way
contributes to such an understanding.

Foner's second major area of weakness is related to his
general ideological position even more directly. His view
of the old Socialist Party is crabbed and one-sided. His
method of analysis is to pick through the available documents in search of damaging quotations and to construe
his findings in their worst light, rather than in their historical context. Foner's presentation of Victor Berger's
views is at best a bad caricature. He attributes to Berger
a set of attitudes toward the AFL leaders and toward
working class politics that were not his. Indeed, in a footnote, in a chapter on the political policies and practices
of the AFL, Foner quotes Berger to the effect that
Gompers deserved a prison sentence for his trade union
policies; yet in the chapter on the Socialist he implies (by
equating Berger with Max Hayes, a leading socialist trade
unionist) that Berger hoped to win the AFL leaders to
the Socialist position. All in all, Foner repeats all the old
slanders and ends up by attacking the party for recruiting
middle class members, for lacking militancy and for failing to recruit and involve Negroes and women in the
party work or to fight for their rights. At the end of his
chapter on the Socialists, Foner first criticizes the party for
failing to introduce a resolution in favor of Socialism at
the AFL convention in 1904, and on the very next page
comments that Socialist militants (the Good Guys) "were
not impressed by the mere passage of resolutions introduced by Socialist delegates at union conventions." (p.
391.)

It is difficult to criticize Foner's treatment of the Socialists in detail since his chapter on the party is a series of true but inadequate statements and snide asides. Suffice it to say that Foner misses entirely the immense strength that the party gained from including under its loose organizational hegemony a diversity of ideological tendencies. These included not only the right, center and left (inadequately described by Foner), but also the ex-populists (who were close to the left in Texas and Oklahoma, and to the right in Washington) and the Christian Socialists (who were closer to the center and left than to Berger). In his discussion of Socialist attitudes toward Negroes, Asian immigrants and women, for example, Foner has no trouble finding statements that reflect a very low level of political sophistication. The party itself recognized this on occasion, but Foner uses such recognition as evidence of its backwardness rather than of its consciousness of the need to change. To show that the Socialist party "did little to involve women in the work of building this new social order," Foner quotes *The Worker* (1904) to the effect that too many men, "good socialists in most respects" looked with "irritating contempt on any participation by women in the affairs of the movement. (p. 382.) Foner concludes from this simply that "such attitudes dominat[ed] the Socialist Party," and thus fails entirely to take into account the period in which these men lived, the wide diversity of their social backgrounds and earlier political experience, and, most important, the direction in which the party was moving. Reading this, one would never guess that from 1910 onward there was always a woman on the National Executive Committee; that the Socialist Party was instrumental in securing the passage of suffrage amendments in Kansas (1912), Nevada (1914) and New York (1917); that Anna A. Maley was the Socialist candidate for governor in Washington in 1912, the year of the party's greatest strength in that state; or that Ella Reeve Bloor and Jesse Wallace Hughan were the Socialist candidates for lieutenant governor and state treasurer in New York in 1918, the first election after the suffrage victory. The period from which Foner draws almost all of his quotes runs only from 1901, the year the Party was organized, to 1904. Foner himself acknowledges, *in a footnote,* that as a Congressman (in 1911) Berger "did try to rectify his earlier stand" on the Negro. (p. 381.) But he does not indicate that party attitudes changed and became more consistent with Socialist principles as the years went on.

Foner's treatment, or lack of treatment, of the Socialists and the National Civic Federation is a good example of his general approach. He devotes two chapters to the Civic Federation and one to the Socialists. He attacks the Socialists for introducing resolutions at AFL conventions and not following through in the internationals. He asserts that Socialists were "quiescent" from 1904 to 1912. But he does not tell us that Socialist agitation in the United Mine Workers forced John Mitchell to resign his post as chairman of the Mediation Department of the National Civic Federation in 1911, and that similar activity in the Carpenters union forced the withdrawal of their president from the Federation in 1912. As Ralph Easley complained to Walter Weyl, the Federation "had this spirit to contend with through the labor movement in the crafts where the Socialists are strong. We have expected the Carpenters to take [president] Huber out for the last two years, as they practically control that organization." [11]

Foner's treatment of the Socialist Party is similar in style to that of Ira Kipnis.[12] Like Kipnis, Foner apparently has an ideological need to downgrade the impact of the old Socialist Party on American politics, and especially its

[11] Easley to Walter Weyl, New York, September 28, 1912, Box 49, NCF papers.
[12] See my review of Kipnis' *The American Socialist Movement, 1898-1912* (New York, 1952) in *Studies on the Left,* III. 4 (Fall 1963). 88 *et. seq.*

success in developing among millions of workers and farmers a consciousness of socialism as an alternative to the prevailing economic and social system. Foner is particularly critical of the Socialists' argument "that while the trade unions were of great value in the struggle against the exploitation of labor, this could only be achieved by a political revolution which would give ownership of the instruments of production to the entire people." (p. 387.) He misses entirely the historical context of this argument, which was aimed at the syndicalist idea (also operative in the Communist Party for the last thirty years) that struggle in behalf of economic or immediate social demands was enough to transform people's consciousness and to contribute to the building of a radical movement. The great virtue of the Socialists in the early 1900's was that they knew better, that they understood that their first responsibility as Socialists was to bring the theories and vision of a Socialist transformation into the arena of public debate. This, of course, did not preclude working in the trade unions or in social reform movements, and indeed, most Socialists were active trade unionists, but it did mean that they viewed education for Socialism and the building of an explicitly Socialist movement as their central task.

I have made much of what I consider to be Foner's shortcomings in this volume of his *History of the Labor Movement in the United States* not out of a desire to minimize the magnitude of his accomplishment. Quite the contrary, Foner's three volumes published so far are the best available labor history written in the United States, and the series appears destined to remain the key work in the field for many years to come. The criticisms made here are important and should, I think, be kept in mind in reading this volume; but no student of American history, and no radical who wants to know how the trade union movement in the United States got to where it is today, can afford not to read it.

Reply:
Historical Materialism
and Labor History

BY *Philip S. Foner*

Volume VI, No. 2
March–April 1966

I am grateful to James Weinstein for the kind comments
in his review. However, I received the impression that
Weinstein was often commenting on volumes of my labor
history yet to be written rather than the one under discussion. Thus in many of the points he raises he cites
evidence for the years after 1909, with which period I
shall deal in later volumes, and he blames me for not
having written a book which I never intended to write
on this particular occasion, namely, a historical analysis of
the New Deal and the Great Society.

Weinstein is particularly critical of two portions of my
book, those dealing with the National Civic Federation
and with the Socialist Party. Readers of my book will note
for themselves that I did not say, as Weinstein asserts, that
the NCF's work was done by 1909. What I did say was
that so far as its work in converting the leadership of the
AFL to accept its class-collaboration outlook, the NCF's
work was accomplished by 1909. Any student of the American labor movement knows that the greatest period of the
NCF's activity occurred after 1910, but its ideas and relations with the leaders of the AFL had been fully worked
out before 1910, and what remained thereafter was merely
a refinement of these policies.

Weinstein disputes my statement that leaders of the Na-

tional Association of Manufacturers who spearheaded the
open-shop drive were finance capitalists who were also
active in the NCF, but he ignores the statement of Ralph
M. Easley, NCF Secretary, that the Civic Federation included more leaders of the NAM "than the whole Parry
outfit," the "Parry outfit" representing the ruling clique
of the NAM. In his study of the National Civic Federation
(unpublished Ph.D thesis, Princeton University, 1956)
Gorden Maurice Jensen demonstrates that many of the
top financial and industrial capitalists who dominated the
NCF were also active in the NAM. Certainly the top
leaders of the most important employers' associations in
the country belonged to both organizations.

After disputing much of what I say about the NCF as
being onesided, Weinstein makes the following concession: "I do not mean to imply that Foner is entirely wrong
about the attitudes of the big businessmen in the Civic
Federation. Much of what he says is accurate. Many business leaders took positions in the abstract debates of the
Federation that they did not take in their factories." But
Weinstein bases his judgment on the NCF, not on what
the business leaders did in their day-to-day relations with
their workers in the factories, but on what they said at
NCF meetings and dinners. This may be a pleasant way
to write history, but it is clearly not historical materialism.
Moreover, Weinstein does not do justice to the point I
was making. I did not confine myself merely to demonstrating that there was a contradiction between what the
business leaders in the NCF said and did, but I proved
that the key figures in the open-shop drive were leaders of
the Civic Federation, and cited specifically the officers of
the employers' associations who were breaking agreements
with unions in their industries and instituting the open
shop precisely at the time that they were voicing at NCF
meetings the need to achieve capital-labor harmony. The
United States Steel Corporation had a president and three
directors—Charles M. Schwab, Henry Phipps, Marvin S.
Hughitt and George W. Perkins—active in the National

Civic Federation. Yet U.S. Steel was the model for the open-shop drive, and by 1909 had all but destroyed trade unionism in the iron and steel industry. The leaders of U.S. Steel spouted "welfare capitalism" at meetings of the NCF, but to the unorganized steel workers engaged in back-breaking labor twelve hours a day, seven days a week for pitiful wages, the conditions they faced were closer to industrial feudalism.

Did the NCF ever criticize the officials of U.S. Steel for failing to apply the principles espoused at Civic Federation meetings? On the contrary, they protested when-even this was exposed. In its report on the Steel Strike of 1919, the Interchurch World Movement condemned the hypocrisy of the heads of U.S. Steel for upholding "welfare capitalism" at NCF meetings while practicing the worse tyranny against workers in the industry. "The bulk of unskilled labor," the report stated, "worked a twelve-hour day, seven days a week, and earned less than enough for the average family's minimum comfort. The steel industry was under the domination of a policy whose aim was to keep out labor unions. In pursuit of this policy, blacklists were used, workmen were discharged for union affiliation, 'under-cover men' and the 'labor detectives' were employed and efforts were made to influence the local press, pulpit and police authorities." These conditions were true in the industry ever since the steel strike of 1901 was crushed (with the assistance, as I point out, of the NCF). Yet throughout this entire period the leaders of the industry were among the most active of the business leaders in the NCF.

Instead of criticizing the leaders of the steel industry, the NCF worked hard to suppress the Interchurch report. Easley forwarded a copy of the report to an official of U.S. Steel, suggesting that efforts be made to oust the men who drew up the report. "There ought certainly to be no trouble in getting the loyal American members of the Protestant churches to have these men kicked out of their positions, at any rate put in places where they can not poison anyone but themselves." (New York *World,* August 5, 1920; *Weekly People,* August 15, 1920.)

It is not difficult to understand Easley's concern. As I have demonstrated, the House of Morgan which dominated U.S. Steel was the leading financial supporter of the National Civic Federation.

Having devoted fifty pages in my book to the NCF, it is hardly necessary to prolong the discussion further here. I am willing to stand by Weinstein's acknowledgment that "Many business leaders took positions in the abstract debates of the Federation that they did not take in their factories . . ." for this is precisely what the workers in these factories pointed out to Gompers, Mitchell and other AFL leaders who defended the NCF business leaders as "enlightened" capitalists. As the Philadelphia Central Labor Union, an AFL affiliate not noted for its radicalism, put it: "The National Civic Federation is financed by capitalists who are bitterly opposed to their own employees becoming organized." (Philadelphia *North American,* March 14, 1911; New York *Call,* March 14, 1911.)

Since Weinstein neglected to tell in his review what my view of the Socialist Party was, even though he describes it as "crabbed and one-sided," I would like to acquaint your readers with some of the points I made. The chapter in my book referred to is entitled "The Socialists, 1900-1905: 'Boring From Within.'" As the title implies, it is primarily an analysis during the years indicated of the theory and practice of the Socialists who advocated boring from within the American Federation of Labor and its affiliated unions instead of organizing dual labor organizations. These Socialists contended with considerable logic that it would weaken the labor movement to establish dual unions, and that more could be accomplished by agitating within the organizations already in existence. But the true test of the validity of this theory, in the eyes of many workers, was what the Socialists agitated for in the existing unions. Did they agitate for industrial unionism in place of the already outmoded craft unionism; did they agitate for organization of the unorganized, especially the foreign-born, Negro, women and young workers; did they agitate against those features of the AFL which, as I demonstrated in several chapters, were retarding the organization of American labor? The record, unfortunately, proves that the Socialists, with some notable exceptions, did not conduct such a campaign, and this record is set forth in my discussion. As a result of the failure of the Socialists to conduct a campaign for these principles within the existing labor organizations, radical forces were encouraged in the belief that "boring from within" was pointless, and that only by working outside of the framework of the AFL could the mass of the unorganized workers be organized. This conclusion resulted, as I note, in the formation of the Western and American Labor Unions, sponsored by the Western Federation of Miners, and ultimately in the organization of the Industrial Workers of the World with which I deal at length in Volume IV of my labor history just published. Socialists were bitter in denouncing these organizations, but their arguments were weakened by their own failure to conduct a real program of boring from within.

Weinstein discusses various activities of the Socialist Party, most of them related to events after 1909, but he fails to disprove the major thesis of my treatment. Nor can he, for the evidence proves that the Socialists in the period covered by the volume under discussion did not agitate within the exicting labor movement for the key principles I have outlined above. I have great admiration for Weinstein's contribution to the understanding of the role played by the Socialist Party in American life in his unpublished and published work, but these relate to the Socialist movement after 1910 when partly as a result of criticism within the Party over the deficiency of its work in the labor movement before 1910, and partly as a result of the impact of the rise and militant struggles of the IWW, the Socialists began to pursue a different policy within the AFL. It is significant, in this connection, to

note that the first extended, serious discussion in the Socialist press, apart from the writings of Eugene V. Debs,
whose views were frowned upon by the rest of the Socialist
leadership, of the significance of industrial unionism occurred late in 1910 after William D. Haywood criticized
the Party for its failure to champion this form of organization.

I appreciate Weinstein's view that "Foner's three volumes published so far are the best available labor history
written in the United States." I have written this communication simply to take issue with what I feel are erroneous bases for some of the criticisms he raises.

Reply

BY *James Weinstein*

Volume VI, No. 2
March–April 1966

Philip S. Foner's communication usefully sharpens the
questions at issue between us. I hope this brief reply will
clarify the intention and nature of the criticisms in my
review. I did not blame Foner for not having written a
book on the New Deal, as he asserts, nor did I imply that
he should have done that. But, presumably, the writing
of history should help us better to understand the present.
Foner's book so misrepresents the essential nature of the
National Civic Federation that it makes difficult an understanding of later developments in the New Deal and
the Great Society. From 1900 to 1916 business leaders in
the NCF worked out their attitudes toward the trade
union movement, social reform as a means of stopping
the growth of Socialism, and the role of government in
rationalizing and stabilizing the political economy. Most

of the social reform and regulation programs later developed or institutionalized in the New Deal and the Great Society were discussed and examined in the NCF in these years. Neither in his book nor in his communication does Foner recognize or understand this. Instead he insists on exposing the Bad Guys. It was not my purpose to picture big businessmen as truly concerned with making life easier for the workers. I looked at the process by which the leaders of large corporations became fully class conscious, as opposed to narrowly interest conscious, and at what this meant in terms of their attitudes toward unions and the working class.

In his communication Foner says that the NCF's work of converting the leadership of the AFL to accept its class collaborationist outlook was completed by 1909. I agree. But his book says that "by 1908 the Civic Federation had already accomplished most of what it had set out to achieve." (p. 110.) In the context of the book, the implication is clear that this refers to the NCF in general. But the NCF had not set out simply to convert the *leadership* of the AFL, although that was one side of its activities. As Mark Hanna said, the aim of the NCF was nothing less than to "lay the foundation stone of a structure that will endure for all time." To Hanna the cornerstone of this foundation was "a relation of mutual trust between the laborer and the employer." Notice that Hanna speaks of the laborer, not the leadership of the AFL. Up until 1904 or 1905 the main thrust of NCF activity was to encourage the conservative tendencies in the AFL, in part by trying to win businessmen to a more sympathetic view of such unions. This emphasis changed after 1905 because 1) the leadership of the AFL had been won over but the rank and file were unimpressed with the very limited gains from such cooperation and were moving toward independent politics, (The Socialist vote increased fourfold from 1900 to 1904, for example.) and 2) many employers, including several NCF members, would not abandon their anti-union views and practices. Starting in 1905-1908 the NCF turned to the state (both state and federal governments) to solve the problems of rationalizing and stabilizing the large corporation system, and, at the same time, to paternalistic "welfare work" in order to win over anti-union businessmen. From this period on, the NCF examined in great detail a series of social reform and regulation programs. Municipal ownership, workmen's compensation, unemployment insurance, trust and utilities regulation, social security, minimum wages and many other questions were examined and discussed by commissions of experts and concerned parties and at many conferences under NCF auspices.

These were attended by thousands of leading businessmen, trade unionists, professionals and academics. Sometimes (as with the case of workmen's compensation and trust regulation) agreement was reached and legislation proposed and pushed by the NCF. Sometimes there was no immediate result. From the point of view of the business leaders involved (and of the NCF leadership), these conferences were an essential part of developing a consciousness and a political economy that would provide "that habitual normal sense of social solidarity which is the foundation stone of democracy." The activities of the NCF after 1908 were not merely refinements of their earlier programs, they were a working out of a new approach to the role of the state as regulator and mediator that has since triumphed.

Some specifics. 1) I did not ignore Ralph Easley's statement that the Civic Federation contained more leaders of the NAM "than the whole Parry outfit," I merely understood what Easley meant. The NAM was organized in 1895. For its first seven years it was not anti-union, but was concerned almost entirely with the promotion of foreign trade. Its first president, Theodore Search, was also a founding member of the NCF. He viewed "questions involving the relations between manufacturers and employer" as outside the province of the NAM. In 1902

David M. Parry, John Kirby, Jr. and James W. Van
Cleave, all relatively small manufacturers, organized
secretly to win control of the NAM by electing Parry to
the presidency. Parry's main opponent, Charles Schieren
(hand picked by Search) and the other three candidates
were all foreign trade advocates. Only Parry stood for
militant anti-unionism. He was elected with 46 votes in
a total of 124 cast. Thus Easley's statement that there were
more NAM leaders in the NCF "than [in] the whole
Parry outfit."

2) To Foner "historical materialism" seems to include
only a knock on the head or working a twelve hour shift.
Class consciousness and discussions of program or attitudes
are, I suppose, subject matter only for philosophical ideal-
ists. If Foner does not mean that, then he must mean that
what the businessmen said at NCF conferences was cyn-
ically designed to fool the public in order to allow business to operate as before. But that position does not make
sense unless one thinks that all the reforms of liberalism
are the result of victories of "the people" or "the workers"
over business leaders. Arthur M. Schlesinger, Jr. believes
that "liberalism in America has been ordinarily the
movement on the part of the other sections of society to
restrain the power of the business community." Apparently Foner does too. But if this were the case, then after
all the liberal victories we have suffered in the Progressive
Era, the New Deal, the New Frontier and the Great Society, the large corporations would be on the ropes and
the people would hold power. In fact, each liberal reform
has seemed to strengthen the system, make revolutionary
politics more difficult, reduce conscious class antagonisms,
even though only partially. Can business leaders be only
the accidental beneficiaries of these attacks upon them?
Or is it perhaps possible that they were doing more than
spouting "welfare capitalism" at meetings of the NCF, as
Foner suggests?

But much of what Foner says *is* accurate. I recognize
that; I was not making a concession to him in saying it,

merely confirming that his view is one-sided, rather than no-sided. Furthermore, it is true that the original impetus for reform and welfare usually comes from those on or near the bottom of society. The business leaders in the NCF knew this too, and further understood the need to make concessions and to anticipate some movements in order to shape reforms so that they were consistent with and bolstered the interests of the corporations. Some concessions they made only when the pressure was great, when impending losses to their system (in the form of a growing radical movement) outweighed their immediate or particular interests (such as keeping a non-union work force). These men and their corporations often appeared self-contradictory because their new understanding of the value of liberalism was only partly formed, but also because their long range class interest often contradicted their short range particular interest. Nevertheless, Foner to the contrary notwithstanding, their class interest was as material as their immediate interest and many of them understood this.

I agree with the substance of Foner's comments on the Socialists in his communication. I did not mean to disprove his major thesis in regard to Socialist activity in the AFL from 1900 to 1905. My objection to his treatment is that it fails to look at the party as a newly formed organization of diverse groups and to examine the direction of its development. The Socialist Party was not formally organized until the middle of 1901. By 1912 it had 135,000 members and controlled one-third of the AFL. Yet Foner does not treat the party in its historical development, but passes judgment upon various aspects of its work. Thus he uses a statement that indicates awareness of the shortcomings of some members on the woman question as evidence of party backwardness, rather than as the beginning of change in what he and I agree is the right direction. In that sense I believe his treatment is one-sided.

The Corporate Ideology of American Labor Leaders from Gompers to Hillman

BY *Ronald Radosh*

Volume VI, No. 6
November–December 1966

In this article Ronald Radosh attempts to develop a new view of the political role of American trade union leadership and the ideology of the labor movement. His concern is with the problem of the subjugation of long-range class consciousness in the labor movement to the immediate interests of workers and trade union leaders. He does not deal with the process by which unions were able to organize. As Philip S. Foner observes in his comments, Radosh's discussion is an abstraction that does not come to grips with the immediate forces that compel the corporations to recognize unions at a particular point in history. Foner criticizes Radosh for this, but does not himself deal with what is central, although only implicit, in the Radosh essay: the failure of the old left to work out a strategy to create and sustain an independent class consciousness in the union movement. The Radosh article and Foner's commentary were originally presented at the Second Annual Socialist Scholars Conference in New York, September 1966.

Historians of American labor usually describe two strains in trade unionism: the "pure and simple" business unionism of Samuel Gompers, and the social unionism of Sidney Hillman or Walter Reuther. But beneath these avowed differences there is a fundamental concensus shared by both kinds of labor leaders—that a corporate society offers the best means of achieving industrial stability, order and social harmony.

Corporate thinkers view society as composed of various functional economic groups caused by the division of labor. Workers are defined as producers rather than as a social class. Therefore they hold an equal stake with management in developing efficient industrial production. The goal of such thinkers is peaceful industrial relations in which each sector of the economy has political representation and is coordinated by an impartial administration. Ideally, an economic congress should be created in which each functional group would be represented. Such a congress of economic groups would work more equitably than the system in which the different groups blindly scramble for power.

C. Wright Mills was perhaps the first social scientist to emphasize that labor leaders framed unions as instruments for integration into the existing political economy, not levers for changing it. It was the labor leader's desire to "join with owners and managers in running the corporate enterprise system and influencing decisively the political economy as a whole." The result, in Mills' words, was a "kind of 'procapitalist syndicalism from the top.'"[1]

In this paper I hope to present some tentative but provocative suggestions as to the way in which Samuel Gompers in the 1920's, and Sidney Hillman in the 1930's, sought to find a place for labor within a corporate capitalist economic structure.

After defeats suffered by labor in the Homestead, Pullman and Coeur d'Alene strikes of the 1890's, Samuel Gompers concluded that unions could not beat the growing "trusts" in head-on collisions.[2] Accepting the growth

[1] Mills, C. Wright, "The Labor Leaders and the Power Elite," in A. Kornhauser, R. Dubin, A. Ross, *Roots of Industrial Conflict*, N.Y., 1954, pp. 144-152; Mills, *Power, Politics and People*, ed., Irving L. Horowitz, N.Y., 1963, pp. 108-109.

[2] Mandel, Bernard, "Samuel Gompers and the Establishment of American Federation of Labor Policies," *Social Science*, vol. 31, no. 3, June 1956, pp. 165-176.

of the large corporations as natural and inevitable, Gompers sought to organize the worker within the system as an alternative to socialism. The problem was to find means whereby the employer and worker could function together harmoniously.

This problem was met by espousing labor participation in the National Civic Federation. Organized in 1900 by Ralph Easley, Mark Hanna and Samuel Gompers, the Federation sought to resolve class conflict and institute cooperative relations between capital and labor. The employer who led the Civic Federation hoped to establish a community of interest between previously warring groups and create one unified corporate body. Gompers' association with men like Hanna led him to believe that industrial peace would reign, since the "men who control wealth in this country are at bottom human and adaptable to the changed order of relations." Hanna signed a collective bargaining agreement with the AFL union in his steel plant, and worked to convince capitalists to concede "the rightful demands of labor." [3]

From the birth of the Civic Federation to 1914, Gompers' ideas about labor were molded by his association with those sophisticated employers who saw the AFL as a conservative and disciplined junior partner in a stable corporate order. It was Gompers' wartime experience, however, that led to maturation of his thought. The wartime need for an uninterrupted flow of goods and services, the participation of union leaders in the Administration and the growth of union membership impressed upon labor leaders the desirability of taking a new position. Before the war the AFL was indifferent to production and efficiency, scorned productivity theories and was hostile to the scientific management movement. The war years taught the AFL leaders the value of preaching cooperation and efficiency to increase production. It was then that

[3] Gompers, Samuel, "Union Labor and the Enlightened Employer," March 5, 1921, Samuel Gompers MSS (State Historical Society, Madison, Wisconsin).

Gompers began a close association with scientific engineers from the Taylor school.[4]

During the war the Wilson Administration tried to institutionalize cooperative relations between labor, industry and government. The War Industries Board, Bernard Baruch reported, established price fixing, allocation and priorities policies under which the "manufacturing facilities of the Nation were almost as effectively transformed into governmental agencies as though the Government had absorbed them."[5] Baruch's board worked with Gompers and sought to adjust disputes over wages, hours of labor and working conditions. Gompers was never "a class champion obstructionist," Board secretary Grosvenor B. Clarkson reported, and he proved a "strong believer in the scheme of close cooperation with industry and was one of the first to endorse the program of industrial group committees to facilitate government dealings with private business."[6]

As the government developed a large cartelizing program that kept up prices and stabilized industry under administration tutelage, Gompers came into contact with leading corporate figures involved in this reorganization. Daniel Willard, President of the Baltimore and Ohio Railroad and the first head of the War Industries Board, was close to Gompers. As members of the Advisory Commission to the Council of National Defense in 1916, Willard noted that he and Gompers found themselves "in very full accord concerning most questions of fundamental importance."[7]

[4] McKelvey, Jean Trepp, *AFL Attitudes Towards Production, 1900-1932*, Cornell Studies in Industrial and Labor Relations, Ithaca, New York, vol. II, p. 27, p. 116.

[5] United States, Senate, 74th Congress, 1st Session, *Special Committee on Investigating the Munitions Industry*, Final Report of the Chairman of the United States War Industries Board to the President of the United States, February 1919 (Washington, 1935) no. 3, p. 51.

[6] Clarkson, Grosvenor B., quoted in *The American Federationist*, vol. xxx, no. 8 (Aug. 1923) pp. 672-673.

[7] Willard, Daniel, to John P. Frey, Dec. 21, 1926, John P. Frey MSS (Library of Congress) Washington, D.C.

After the war Gompers' contact with such sophisticated industrialists continued. The 1920's saw a revival of the National Civic Federation. Industrialists such as Edward A. Filene, of Filene and Sons, and former Secretary of Commerce William C. Redfield were among the luminaries active in trying to forge a new community of interest. Charles A. Coffin, chairman of the Board of General Electric, expressed the Civic Federation's position when he observed that the task of industry was to find methods by which the "best among labor and the best among the employers" could cooperate. Coffin branded employers who supported the open-shop movement as "oppressive." "Sympathetic, broad-minded employers," he said, should be ready to "discipline and denounce the radicals among the employers, and to meet on that ground men like Mr. Gompers and his associates who are combatting the radical movement in labor."[8] The NCF position was also supported by former Assistant Secretary of the Navy Franklin D. Roosevelt, who sat on the Civic Federation Executive Committee. During the seven and one half years that he supervised a ship building industry of one hundred thousand, Roosevelt did not have "a single strike in a single trade in a single Navy yard." FDR attributed this stability to the agreement that if a dispute occurred, management and labor would "sit around the table and talk it over," a plan which always worked. Roosevelt criticized both the old-fashioned employer who refused to accept modern conditions and the radical worker who dreamt of far-off ideals. He urged labor-capital cooperation to meet domestic problems, and called for elimination of misleading socialist schemes such as those emanating from the Rand School in New York.[9]

The man whose thought most affected Gompers was the

---

[8] National Civic Federation Executive Committee Meeting, Bankers Club, New York, April 15, 1921; National Civic Federation MSS (New York Public Library).

[9] *Ibid.*

prolabor Secretary of Commerce Herbert Clark Hoover. Hoover analyzed the American industrial system as composed of three basic units—capital, labor and government. His objective was to have these groups function together harmoniously. He therefore demanded a voice in labor policy in President Harding's Cabinet. Defining labor and management as producers, not as social classes, Hoover saw large areas of mutual interest that had to be cultivated. Once in office Hoover began the pattern of prolabor intervention by government that culminated in the New Deal. As coordinator of Woodrow Wilson's Second Industrial Conference, Hoover had favored collective bargaining, had criticized company unions and urged an end to child labor. E. D. Howard, the labor negotiator for the firm of Hart, Schaffner and Marx, was among those who in 1920 urged that "it would be a great step forward if Mr. Hoover were appointed Secretary of Labor." While there was evidence that many "reactionary employers" wanted to eliminate unions, there were "also a great number of more thoughtful and more liberal-minded employers who would like to carry on the work started by the President's conference," and "block the efforts of the reactionaries and also of the radical people on the other side" and "do something constructive." [10]

In May of 1924 Hoover gave a speech before the United States Chamber of Commerce in which he presented his concept of self-determination in industry. Hoover pleaded that new regulations favoring human rights had to be developed out of the voluntary forces in the nation. Legislation entered the business world only when abuses existed, and remedies had to come "out of the conscience and organization of business itself; these restraints which will cure abuse . . . eliminate waste . . . that will march with larger social understanding." The United States, Hoover stated, was "in the midst of a great revolution,"

[10] Howard to Sidney Hillman, Nov. 18, 1920, Sidney Hillman MSS (Amalgamated Clothing Workers Headquarters) New York City.

a transformation from a period of "extremely individualistic action into a period of associational activities."
Through autonomous associational bodies, America was
moving "towards some sort of industrial democracy." [11]

After reading his speech Samuel Gompers wrote Hoover
that he found "genuine inspiration" in the address; it was
"the most valuable contribution to the understanding of
industrial organizations" and would "without doubt further constructive progress for which I share your concern." [12] Gompers proceeded to use the speech as a vehicle
for a major statement. Writing that Hoover's views met
and "match perfectly the policy and philosophy of the
American Federation of Labor," Gompers agreed that
those who sought "retention of our basic institutions" had
to cure "the abuses which naturally" develop. Gompers
endorsed the concept of self-government in industry,
claiming that the legislative world lacked the informed
intelligence necessary to deal with industrial problems.
American labor "goes all the way with Mr. Hoover,"
Gompers wrote, "or Mr. Hoover goes all the way with
Labor." Hoover had a "keen understanding of our industrial order, including Labor's part in the operation
thereof—and that is all Labor asks of any man." Gompers
departed from Hoover in only one respect; he emphasized
the need to grant unions "greater participation in the
impending changes." [13]

Gompers' evolving corporatist outlook became clear in
his evaluation of the wartime experience. 1924 saw
Bernard Baruch argue for a new scheme to institute price
fixing of all commodities and to reinstitute wartime type
controls, when "wages had to be the same as were then
prevailing in the industry." While labor was satisfied with
that, Baruch wrote Gompers, he was concerned that Gom-

[11] Address of Herbert Hoover at the Annual Meeting of the U.S. Chamber of Commerce, Cleveland, Ohio, May 7, 1924, Gompers MSS.

[12] Gompers to Hoover, May 24, 1924, Gompers MSS.

[13] Gompers, Samuel, "The Road to Industrial Democracy," *American
Federationist,* vol. 31, no. 6, June 1924, pp. 481-485.

pers was "opposed to . . . my plan for mobilizing industry." Baruch could not understand this because he knew
that "neither you nor any of the men associated with me
. . . during the war, could be opposed . . . because it is
only what we were endeavoring to put into execution at
that time." [14]

Gompers assured Baruch that he was aware that many
did not have "your sympathetic attitude towards labor."
Moreover, labor had given its wholehearted support during the war because the War Industries Board recognized
unions, and had arranged that "representation be provided for all elements concerned in producing including
labor." Industrial policy of the future would have to be
the result of decisions reached by "a thoroughly representative group" which would have the "confidence of
industry."

Gompers believed that society moved not through the
exercise of political power, but through the recognition
that decision making power was concentrated directly in
autonomous functional economic units. He emphasized
that the WIB worked through "the organized agencies of
industry and enforced decisions by economic means." The
methods, machinery of operation and decisions were far
different than any which could be secured through political means. In fact, Gompers recalled, "the complete
collapse of political machinery during the war emergency
has remained in my mind as a most significant feature.
During the months of our intense activity we were scarcely
aware of the existence of Congress." [15]

Baruch was pleased to find that Gompers shared his
conception. "It gave me great pleasure to receive your
letter," he wrote, and to find that "your thoughts are
exactly in accord with me on this whole subject." Baruch
expressed his debt to Samuel Gompers. "My recommendations," he informed him, "were based on our mutual ex-

[14] Baruch to Gompers, April 5, 1924, Gompers MSS.
[15] Gompers to Baruch, April 18, 1924, Gompers MSS.

perience. None of my contacts in Washington were of more benefit or of greater pleasure to me than the one I had with you." [16]

The attempt to organize, balance and coordinate functional economic groups took final shape in the demand that a new economic parliament be created. As AFL Vice-President Matthew Woll expressed it, the Federation hoped that there would "come into existence an economic and industrial chamber, in which all factors in industry will be fairly represented, and which will determine the rules and regulations that industries will impose upon themselves." [17] The most explicit statement was to be made at the 1923 Convention in the Executive Board's statement "Industry's Manifest Duty." Here the AFL leadership revealed that it sought the "conscious organization of one of the most vital functional elements for enlightened participation in a democracy of industry." State regulation was undesirable because decisions that affected people's daily lives were made by men in autonomous economic groups. Functional elements in our national life had to work out their own problems without regulation. The mission of industrial groups was "to legislate in peace," and to develop an "industrial franchise comparable to our political franchise." [18] It was Gompers' corporate conception that led him to respond positively to Benito Mussolini's attempt to build a corporate state in Italy. Despite differences in method, Gompers saw a set of common assumptions shared by Italian fascists and liberal American trade unionists.[19]

[16] Baruch to Gompers, April 19, 1924, Gompers MSS.

[17] Woll, Matthew, editorial, *The American Photo-Engraver,* vol. 16, no. 1, December, 1923, pp. 661-662.

[18] *American Federationist,* report of the Executive Council to the 1923 Convention at Portland, vol. 30, no. 11, 1923, pp. 890-895.

[19] Gompers, Samuel, "Significant Movements in Europe," *American Federationist,* vol. xxxi, no. 7, July 1924, pp. 565-570; "An Analysis of Fascism," *American Federationist,* vol. 30, no. 11, November, 1923, pp. 927-933; *cf.,* Ronald Radosh, "Corporatism, Liberal and Fascist as Seen by Samuel Gompers," *Studies on the Left,* III, no. 3, 1963, pp. 66-77.

Gompers' corporate overview, with its stress on functional democracy, efficiency and production, is often viewed as a pragmatic response to paternalism of open-shop employers. When confronted with benevolent employers, some argue, labor sought to prove that "it was industry's most able helpmeet." [20] Others view the AFL's emphasis on efficiency as an admission that they were in a period of decline. By striving to improve output, the declining AFL hoped to gain the employer's acceptance. As one labor historian has written, the emphasis on production was "a kind of 'if you can't lick 'em, join 'em philosophy,'" to which most employers "did not want to be 'joined.'" [21]

Writers taking this view contrast the AFL approach with that developed by CIO leaders in the 30's. The latter are praised for organizing unskilled workers, for their use of militant tactics and for purportedly developing a new labor ideology. But the corporate ideology of American labor leaders actually matured in the New Deal era. CIO leaders stressed efficiency and productivity, and favored a formal corporate state. The difference was that in the 30's they hoped that the CIO industrial unions would be the labor bodies given representation in the new industrial parliament.

In the 1930's labor leaders became involved with a new group of far-sighted industrialists who wanted to establish a place for unionism in the corporate capitalist economy. Gerard P. Swope, architect of his own plan for a corporate state—the Swope Plan—was one industrialist who wanted to integrate labor into the system. As early as 1926 Swope had sought to convince William Green to form a nationwide union of electrical workers organized on an industrial basis. Swope felt that having an industrial union

[20] Rayback, Joseph G., *A History of American Labor,* New York, 1959, p. 293, pp. 306-307.

[21] Bernstein, Irving, *The Lean Years, A History of the American Worker, 1920-1933,* New York, 1960, pp. 99-102; James O. Morris, *Conflict Within the AFL,* Ithaca, New York, 1958, p. 56.

might mean "the difference between an organization with which we could work on a business like basis and one that would be a source of endless difficulties." [22]

William Green, maintaining his commitment to the craft union bloc in the AFL, rejected Swope's pleas. Swope preferred industrial organization for one simple reason; he saw his industry "intolerably handicapped if the bulk of our employees were organized into different and often competing craft unions." They could deal easily with one bargaining agent, but not with more than one dozen. When the CIO was organized and the left-led United Electrical Workers began to organize G.E., Swope rejoiced. He informed one of his vice-presidents that "if you can't get along with these fellows and settle matters, there's something wrong with you." The UE was praised by Swope as "well led, the discipline good." [23] Julius Emspak, a top official of the union, recalled that Swope was an "enlightened" employer who told him that the time had come when "industry would have to recognize that" a union representative should sit on the company's board of directors.[24]

Not only did Swope favor industrial organization, but he supported the Black Bill for a thirty-hour week and the minimum wage amendment introduced by Frances Perkins. While William Green opposed the amendment urging that it would reduce the hourly earning of skilled labor, Swope supported it because he claimed that the AFL did not cover all unskilled labor. It was a necessity since out of the "millions of men employed in industry, a very small proportion is in the American Federation of Labor." The legislation was on behalf of the unskilled worker "who needs protection . . . those who have no organization working for them." Congress, Swope said,

[22] Loth, David, *Swope of G. E.*, N.Y., 1958, p. 168; Gerard Swope, Columbia University Oral History Memoirs.

[23] Loth, *op. cit.*, p. 172, p. 259.

[24] Emspak, Julius, Columbia University Oral History Memoirs.

had to act on behalf of the "millions of men who are not members" of the AFL and "for whom no one is talking." [25]

The early New Deal was to be characterized by the introduction of planning techniques that had antecedents in the trade associations of the 1920's. The War Industries Board cartelization reached fruition in the National Recovery Administration. One of NRA's key architects was Donald Richberg, who had been chosen for his position because of his labor background. As a young Chicago lawyer, Richberg had written both the Railway Labor Act of 1926 and the Norris-La Guardia Act of 1932. In 1933 Richberg argued that industrial unions would have to be the prerequisite for an American corporatism. "If industrial workers were adequately organized," he wrote, "it would be entirely practical to create industrial councils composed of representatives of managers, investors and workers and then to create a national council composed of similar representatives of all essential industries." In the council "all producing and consuming interests would be so represented that one group could hardly obtain sanction for a policy clearly contrary to the general welfare." Richberg was critical of craft union leaders. He wished that they had "seized" labor's "great opportunity to organize the unemployed," and had ignored "the hampering tradition of craft unionism," simply organizing men and women "denied their inherent right to work." Labor should have demanded that "their government should no longer be controlled by rulers of commerce and finance who" had failed to "meet their obligations." If such a movement had been built, if labor had created one "mighty arm and voice" of the "unemployed millions," Congress would have listened to the dispossessed.

Richberg also forecast the conservative role which in-

[25] United States, House, Committe on Labor, *Thirty-Hour Week Bill,* 73rd Congress, 1st Session, April 25-28, May 1-5, 1933, pp. 91-111.

dustrial unions would play. "Let me warn those who desire to preserve the existing order," he cautioned, "but intend to do nothing to reform it, that if this depression continues much longer the unemployed will be organized and action of a revolutionary character will be demanded." To avoid this people had to be put back to work. The answer was to mobilize the nation "through the immediate creation of a national planning council, composed of representatives of major economic interests who recognize the necessity of a planned economy," or, in other words, the American corporate state—or the NRA.[26]

NRA, as Eugene Golub has observed, revealed that "the basic idea of corporatism had been accepted as part of the American scene."[27] Businessmen in each industry were given exemption from antitrust prosecution, and were granted permission to draw up codes of fair competition which the government would enforce as law. The codes also established minimum wages in each industry, and price and production quotas. Labor was to receive the protection offered in Section 7-a, which guaranteed its right to organize. Despite the obvious corporate origins and function of NRA, liberals and radicals ignored its conservative heritage because of what Arthur K. Ekirch called their "widespread confidence in the broad nature and humanitarian goals of the New Deal's planning." FDR's use of big business methods and wartime regimentation was forgotten because the goal was more jobs and better working conditions.[28] The commitment to support reform if liberals would bypass criticism of the conservative nature of NRA was understood by Richberg himself. NRA would win the allegiance of liberals by

[26] Richberg, Donald, "Depression Causes and Remedies," testimony submitted Feb. 23, 1933 to the Senate Committee on Finance, Donald Richberg MSS (Library of Congress).

[27] Golub, Eugene, The Isms: A History and Evaluation, N.Y., 1954, pp. 97-123, quoted in Bernard Sternsher, The New Deal, Boston, 1966, pp. 157-159.

[28] Ekirch Jr., Arthur A., The Decline of American Liberalism, N.Y., London, Toronto, 1955, pp. 274-278.

providing Title II which offered a program of public
works. In a draft prepared for the NRA planning committee Richberg suggested that "it would be at least a
tactical error not to begin the bill with a public works
program," with the provision for trade agreements following as further stimulation to stabilization of industry.
"If this is not done," he explained, "the reaction of the
host of people expecting, advocating and convinced of
the value of public works will be antagonistic to the general program." If "industrial control leads off, with public
works as a secondary, incidental part of the program, it
will be difficult to avoid violent opposition from those
now clamoring for public works who might swallow a
somewhat 'fascist' proposal to get their 'democratic' measure of relief." [29] In facetiously using the terms he expected
critics to cite in the future, Richberg showed awareness
that reformers would acquiesce in the corporate state if
reform was part of its program.

The most significant success that the Roosevelt Administration had was the integration of organized labor into
the corporate system. The old line craft unions were in-
sufficiently structured to aid unskilled labor. Therefore
unions that had a sudden revival under NRA were industrial outfits such as the United Mine Workers and the
Amalgamated Clothing Workers. NRA turned unionism
into a semi-public institution whose organization was part
of the new government program. NRA officials understood
that the AFL unions were not capable of fulfilling the
NRA program for a rise in labor's condition. As Benjamin
Stolberg wrote in 1933, "in short, the socialist unions,
whose militancy has been kept alive these last few years
by an inner left wing opposition, fitted very easily into
the drift towards state capitalism, which characterizes the
New Deal." [30]

It is not surprising to find that Sidney Hillman, the

---

[29] Richberg memorandum, n.d., (1933) Richberg MSS.
[30] Stolberg, Benjamin, "A Government in Search of a Labor Movement," *Scribner's*, vol. xciv, no. 6, Dec. 1933, pp. 345-350.

Jewish immigrant who built the Amalgamated Clothing Workers, would emerge as a major exponent of a corporate state in which labor would be guaranteed a formal position. Hillman's contribution to corporate ideology is usually ignored. Hillman was originally a socialist and led a union whose rank and file was Marxist inclined. Moreover, he favored industrial unionism and his own Amalgamated was created in an internal rebellion against the AFL garment union in Chicago.

The truth about Hillman's attitude was carefully explained by William H. Johnston, the President of the AFL Machinists. Trying to reassure Baltimore and Ohio President Daniel Willard about the effect of radical workers on the B and O, Johnston urged that Willard disregard rhetoric and look at reality. "I believe it is a mistake to be too much disturbed by every unfortunate phrase or differing angle" some labor groups use, he wrote. What Willard had to realize is that "in labor circles discussion is free and often acrimonious, that labor people have their own traditions" and use their own terminology. It was essential "not to confuse phrases with the reality." Johnston's example was relations between the hat firm of Hart, Schaffner and Marx and Hillman's Amalgamated Clothing Workers, "no strikes having taken place in the plant and cooperative experiments having been developed to a high degree." Yet, Johnston commented, "the union itself is full of 'revolutionary' propaganda, and even its officers are far more outspoken in their radical political and industrial doctrines than the officers of any railroad unions." If the "well disposed employers had taken this sort of thing too seriously or had allowed themselves to be upset by everything that was said in the union, then friendly relations with their employees might have been broken off a hundred times." But these employers "were realistic and concentrated on the job in hand. They did not confuse realities with phrases."[31]

[31] Johnston, William H., to Daniel Willard, April 1924, box 38, Otto S. Beyer MSS (Library of Congress).

The record indicates that the employers acted wisely in disregarding the Amalgamated's radical rhetoric. Hillman's role was that of champion of cooperative schemes in the garment industry. Like Gompers, Hillman received the aid of government during the First World War. In August of 1917 Secretary of War Newton D. Baker had composed a directive assuring that sound industrial conditions would be in force in firms manufacturing army uniforms. A control board was established to see that standard wages, the eight hour day and union conditions were met. With this agreement the Amalgamated grew rapidly and organized most of the clothing industry. By 1919 Hillman was advocating stabilization of the industry by creation of one national organization of clothing manufacturers, a move opposed at the time by other union officers. As Hillman's biographer observed, his "intellectual approach . . . was sympathetic to 'statism,' an attitude formed during World War I, when a constructive policy toward organized labor had been adopted by the Federal Government."[32]

When rank and file unionists opposed administration policy, such as American participation in the World War, the union moved to curb antiwar agitation. Amalgamated officer Frank Rosenblum wrote that the union's newspaper had "overdone itself in its criticism of the government." While Rosenblum agreed that the war was unjust, he felt that attacks on it should not be given "the space and prominence it has until now," and that the union should "not do anything which will antagonize any one." To Rosenblum it was "a question of expediency." To criticize the war meant an opening for those who wanted to harm the union, since there were "enough forces in and out of the labor movement seeking to destroy the Amalgamated without getting the U.S. Government on the job to assist them." If it kept up an antiwar stance,

[32] Josephson, Matthew, *Sidney Hillman, Statesman of American Labor*, N.Y., 1952, p. 346.

the union would "lose friends which it might need in the future." [33]

The union did not lose its friends. By the 1920's Hillman was the leading advocate of "the new unionism," whose supporters put their stress on efficiency. They argued that an industry which was not productive could not be prosperous, and that industry would yield benefits to all groups if it was efficiently administered. Hillman introduced what were called standards of production into the clothing trade, in which a specified shop production was agreed to by representatives of both sides, and was guaranteed by the union.

For this attitude Hillman won praise from important figures. Ray Stannard Baker saw the Amalgamated representing "in the labor question what the League of Nations represents in international relations," substituting in place of militancy "a system for the prevention of war and conflicts between employers and employees." The result of Hillman's program would be that workers would not be "compelled in despair to turn to radical movements in the hope of securing what they consider their right—a joint voice with the employer in the determination of conditions of labor." [34] Since the Amalgamated was supposedly a radical union, this was a substantial achievement.

Most satisfied with the work of the Amalgamated were employers. Joseph Schaffner had signed the first binding agreement with the union. The result, he stated in 1915, was that "in our own business, employing thousands of persons . . . many of them in opposition to the wage system and hostile to employers as a class, we have observed astonishing changes in their attitude during the four years under the influence of our labor arrangement." Workers knew that "justice will be done them" once the company

[33] Rosenblum, Frank, to Jacob Potofsky, June 2, 1917, Hillman MSS.

[34] Baker, Ray Stannard, "Collective Bargaining: A Strong Asset," *Maryland Women's News*, vol. x, no. 4, April 23, 1921, p. 29. (All clippings pertaining to Hillman and the Amalgamated are catalogued in the Hillman scrapbooks, Hillman MSS.)

gave the union a voice.[35] Another employer explained
that before the union entered his New York firm the
workers often simply refused to produce. After he signed
with the union the Amalgamated gave its permission to
dismiss hostile workers, "and with their sanction we discharged every man in the shop, and are now building up
a new force." Years ago, the employer explained, such
discharges would have meant a "general strike," but now
his firm "had the disciplinary power of the union behind
us."[36] The union's worth was also demonstrated by E.
Strouse, a leading Baltimore clothing manufacturer.
Writing to Hillman in October of 1919, Strouse complained that the local leader in Baltimore was so loaded
down with work that he was unable to be reached "when
we need him most." Asking that the union representative
meet with him once a day, Strouse noted that "I have
been trying to get more production for weeks and have
been unable to do so." Could you "not do something that
we might have him oftener," Strouse asked, "because I
feel that with his finesse he is able to get for us what we
want, better than we can ourselves and it is urgent from
many angles that we get our production."[37]

By 1919 Hillman had called for "the organization of
every industry, beginning from the raw materials, completing with the agencies for distribution, and providing
representation from all the factors in industry, and placing
upon all of them the responsibility of running the industry."[38] The result, Robert W. Bruere wrote, was that
continuity of production was guaranteed, and strikes and
lockouts did not occur. Hillman had proved the "ability
of rightminded employers and trade union leaders to
sublimate class conflict into integral class concert." Labor's concern shifted from the haggles of getting more to

[35] Creel, George, "A Way to Industrial Peace," *The Century,* July 1915.
[36] Baker, Ray Stannard, *New York Evening Post,* Feb. 18, 1920.
[37] Strouse to Hillman, Oct. 3, 1919, Hillman MSS.
[38] "A New Experiment in Industrial Relations," *The City Club Bulletin,*
Dec. 1, 1919, vol. xii, no. 43, speech of Nov. 21, 1919.

the joint concern for achieving "efficient production." [39] Like Samuel Gompers, Hillman's approach led him into the camp of Herbert Hoover. After Hoover was elected to the Presidency Hillman termed his efforts the "first definite national move to carry out the plans favored by the Amalgamated for the last fifteen years." [40]

By 1931 Hillman actively called for creation of a formal corporate state structure. Speaking at a conference held in March with leading progressive Senators, Hillman demanded that government step in to alleviate bread lines and the plight of the poor, which he attributed to the lack of "planning in industry." Hillman called for creation of an "economic council for industry" similar to the one Bernard Baruch operated during the First World War. The council should have "representatives of all the parts that make up industry management, capital, labor and government representing the public," and should be empowered to make recommendations to both industrial leaders and Congress. [41]

From 1931 on Hillman became the main labor advocate of a corporate society. Gerard Swope and other industrialists favored mobilization of industries into trade associations that would regulate and stabilize prices and production. Hillman's model differed only in that it demanded labor representation as an equal factor in industry. "Planless production for uncoordinated distribution" was attacked by Hillman as the "core of our individualistic social system." Instead of *laissez-faire* one had to substitute "purposive intervention in social processes," and begin to think "in terms of economic planning" by creating a national economic council. Hillman made it clear that he did not favor socialist planning in which capitalists would

[39] Bruere, Robert W., "A Strike Against Strikes," *Industry*, Dec. 15, 1925.

[40] "Clothing Workers for Hoover Industrial Program, Says Hillman," *Rochester Democrat*, Dec. 21, 1929.

[41] Proceedings of a Conference of Progressives, Wash. D.C., March 11-12, 1931, Hillman MSS.

play no role. Rather, he envisoned a corporate state in which authority would rest in a "national house of industrial representatives" on which both management and labor leaders sat.[42]

Hillman had come to sound like Hoover in the 1920's, since he emphasized a joint employer-worker attack on instability by "increasing individual productivity, reducing cost, eliminating waste . . . and taking advantage of the new technical advances in industry." Unions would assume greatly increased responsibility for the quantity and quality of output, which meant "a revolutionary change in the attitude of the worker toward his job." But for this to work nationally, a government "instrumentality" was needed to "guide a national economic plan."[43] The national program that would gain Hillman's favor was the NRA, and Hillman became its most ardent champion. NRA, he wrote, provided "for a measure of national economic planning, in business enterprise and productive activity." It could be used by labor to throw open union doors, and hence "unorganized industries and areas must be invaded by union organizers. Existing and functioning organizations," Hillman warned, "must abandon the narrow craft outlook. Labor must think of itself in terms of the whole working class."[44]

Speaking to the 1934 Amalgamated convention, Hillman told delegates that NRA was "a new constitution for both labor and industry." By eliminating the sweatshop employer it provided "a basis of equality for labor." Hillman predicted that NRA would "remain a permanent part of our industrial life," because it recognized the "need for planning" and because the codes of fair competition made "further development possible." NRA gave

[42] Hillman, Sidney, "Unemployment Reserves," *Atlantic Monthly*, November, 1931.

[43] Hillman, Sidney, "Labor Leads Toward Planning," *Survey Graphic*, March, 1932.

[44] Hillman, Sidney, "National Economic Planning—The Industrial Recovery Act and Labor's Chances," March 22, 1932, Hillman MSS.

labor "representation in the governing of industry and it assigns to the government the place of an umpire." Roosevelt had seen the need to create an organization representing "all elements in industry." [45] NRA, Hillman asserted, proved that a social organization could be changed within its own shell. It aimed at a coordinated balance of production, and saw the "fundamental necessity for government regulation and supervision of industrial processes and of economic forces." It was "the beginning of national economic planning," and those who wanted "to ride into the land of promise" had to first "lay the road." Moreover, employers through NRA were "becoming accustomed to consider the demands of labor an integral part of the industrial situation." [46]

In March of 1935 Hillman cited NRA as proof that "we have come to maturity as a nation in our understanding and in our handling of the problems arising out of a complex economic system." Workers knew that they had "an economic interest with employers in the successful operation of the establishment." That is why they favored increased productivity, and denied the autocratic employer who held that business was their own exclusive affair. It was to NRA's credit that it recognized the social "nature of industry." It truly forecast "a new birth in industrial relations," and the "responsible labor leaders" had learned "the lessons of cooperative relations under the New Deal." They knew that "the source of our prosperity is increased production," and Hillman guaranteed that labor thought in these terms whenever it strived to gain a just share of the product.[47] As he put it, "organized labor, with the full feeling that it 'belongs' and that

[45] Amalgamated Clothing Workers 10th Biennial Convention, 1934, pp. 42-55.

[46] Hillman, Sidney, "The Quest for Economic Security," *The Listener*, Nov. 28, 1934, pp. 894-895.

[47] Hillman, Sidney, "Management, Labor and Governmental Relationships," March 8, 1935 speech, Univ. of Cincinnati, NRA Press Release 10399.

everyone recognizes it is an essential part in industry, will cooperate to make it more efficient, more productive, more humane." [48]

Hillman's support of NRA was unique in that he backed its extension long after the majority of organized labor had concluded that NRA was resulting in the spread of company unions. Attacking those Congressional liberals who blamed NRA for monopolistic price-fixing, Hillman compared them with those who favored ending unions because they were not perfect. Asking radicals "not to hurry things beyond their natural course," Hillman asked that labor support NRA and demand increased authority to "impose a code on every industry." [49]

Hillman then worked in Washington to affect a rapproachement between dissident labor leaders and the administration. The labor leaders agreed to stop attacking NRA, Philip Murray was appointed to the National Industrial Recovery Board and the administration began to show a sympathetic attitude to the pending Wagner labor disputes bill. More important, Hillman's close associate Robert Soule revealed that Hillman began "discussions which may lead to the evolution of a labor organization which can cooperate with the government in place of the American Federation of Labor." Labor, adopting this path, would "have ready access to the White House." [50]

Hillman had begun to take steps that would lead to representation for industrial unions in the corporate state. The industrial unions, he assured all, would function responsibly. In a 1937 interview Hillman stressed that the CIO emphasized "that industry is based on three factors of equal importance," and that the "labor factor" was entitled to a fair share. The CIO was "not a movement to change the competitive system," but was, rather, trying

[48] Hillman, Sidney, speech at the joint meeting of the Wisconsin State Bar and Milwaukee City Bar Association, Dec. 7, 1934, NRA release 9129.
[49] *The Advance*, April, 1935.
[50] Soule, Robert G., "Sidney Hillman Turns Architect," *The Nation*, April 3, 1935, pp. 383-384.

"to make the system workable." It asked only a "proportionate share of the progress of industry" in which labor was one of the three "vital and participating elements." Commenting accurately that Hillman subscribed to the "principle enunciated by the late Samuel Gompers," the interviewer quoted Hillman as advising that after a contract was signed, "every employee should lend himself to complete cooperation with the employer in the interest of efficient management of industry." Responsible labor shared a set of common economic goals with the employer. Hillman stressed that the CIO objected in principle to sit-down strikes. He "chuckled" as he told the press that "Wall Street is beginning to recognize the CIO." [51]

Hillman always stressed that if studied, industry would see that the CIO recognized the need for a prosperous industry. In fact, the CIO had contributed to this end "in choosing the form of industrial organization." It had rejected craft unionism precisely because "it permits of no responsibility in the relationship between labor and management." Sounding like Gerard Swope, Hillman pointed out that no employer could enter into seventeen agreements with seventeen unions, and be sure of avoiding jurisdictional strikes "which make it impossible to have responsible leadership." [52] By 1933 Hillman was explaining that "efficiency in the men's clothing industry" had reached its highest point. The union had "helped many manufacturers to introduce efficiency methods because" at the same time they helped their members by enabling the employers to stay in business. Hillman added, *"Industry-wide union organization is, of course, essential if cooperation and efficiency are to be brought to this degree."* [53]

[51] "Hillman on Political Possibilities of CIO," *St. Louis Post-Dispatch*, April 26, 1937.

[52] Hillman, Sidney, "Outstanding Problems of Labor and Industry," *The Concensus*, vol. xxii, no. 1, May 1937, pp. 17-20, speech of April 29, 1937.

[53] Finney, Ruth, "Strikes Nipped in Bud Under Plan Followed by Clothing Firm," *Washington Daily News*, Oct. 19, 1938.

While Sidney Hillman was leading the industrial work-ers into absorption in the corporate capitalist system and towards political commitment to the Roosevelt Admin-istration, some criticism was beginning to emerge from labor's ranks. It came, however, from the remaining de-scendants of the Gompers machine in the AFL. Men trained by Gompers, such as Matthew Woll, president of the Photo-Engravers and an AFL vice-President, and the old pro-war socialist William English Walling, were two who quickly became disenchanted with NRA and became outspoken critics of the New Deal. Originally both had hoped that NRA would lead to a new partnership be-tween equal factors in industry. As it turned out, workers were not given equal protection, and no guarantee existed that labor was to be organized as efficiently as the em-ployers were in trade associations. Woll and Walling dis-sented from Hugh Johnson's belief that strikes were eco-nomic sabotage against the government. They defended the right to strike as the sole assurance workers had as a preventative to compulsory labor. As for the plea of John-son that labor be subject to government control, Woll and Walling viewed that demand as one pointing "in the direction of Fascism" and as the "opposite of self-govern-ment in industry." [54]

In 1935 Woll emerged as a full-scale critic of the New Deal. While he favored an economic congress that would represent functional groups, Woll wanted it to be volun-tary and labor to be afforded equal representation. NRA gave only a "semblance of recognition" to all factors. It worked not to create unity, but to accentuate differences and to "undermine every vestige of concord in the func-tional groups in industry." Industry was functioning under a form of "capitalistic syndicalism" in which labor had no direct voice.[55] Under NRA codes monopoly had

[54] Woll, Matthew, and William English Walling, *Our Next Step—A National Economic Policy*, N.Y., 1934, pp. 117-125.

[55] Woll, Matthew, *Labor, Industry and Government*, N.Y., 1935, pp. 198-199, 207, 226-228, 233.

grown, cartelization of the economy had been encouraged and "corporate control had been permitted to strengthen its grip upon the economic life of the nation." Woll felt that while NRA held out the promise of a corporate society, the goal had been subverted by its actual practice. Labor "might well assert," he wrote, "that the seed of Fascism had been transplanted" and that political government reigned supreme. The NRA's system of "compulsory trade association, of code membership, and of code observance borders closely upon the corporate or syndicalist form of organization characterized by Fascism in Italy." Labor might "well be concerned regarding its future hope and policy to deal effectually with such a strongly entrenched and cartelized system of industry."[56]

Rather than urge compliance with code authorities, Woll suggested that labor should remove its support from the concept of NRA itself. "Not anywhere this side of Fascism, or complete control by the Government," Woll wrote, "could code provisions be adequately enforced." Woll worried that the unions might become the equivalent of Fascist labor groups, in which industries were organized "along lines somewhat akin to what has taken place in each of our major industries operating under a code." In Italy labor was subordinate to the state in the guise of governmentally controlled unions. Woll explained that "the cartelization of American industry which has gone on under codes is a familiar story in the early history of Fascist Italy." "Are we," Woll queried, "heading toward a business Fascism?"[57]

Another aspect of New Deal policy questioned by Woll was American foreign policy. Woll argued that an economic surplus was being invested abroad instead of being put to use at home. While the internationalist view was "put before the world as a form of idealism," it was sustained "mainly by private international banking and

[56] *Ibid.*, pp. 59-63.
[57] *Ibid.*, pp. 71-72, 171-172, 124-225.

trading interests." Implying that internationalism actually meant interventionism, Woll saw no relation between "the internationalist idea of free trade and peace." On the contrary, "economic activities of private interests outside of national boundaries were likely to "carry us toward war than toward peace." Many plans for economic ties were meant to "cover growing economic conflicts" due to foreign investments.[58]

Commenting that many saw the "chief cure for the present depression and for unemployment . . . in the development of the export market," Woll dissented from Cordell Hull's path of gaining security through increase of reciprocal trade treaties. "The arguments of those who made possible" that legislation, Woll wrote, "are precisely the same as have been used by all those who see the solution of our present economic problem not in the increase of American purchasing power, but in plunging our nation into the mad and illusory race for foreign markets." [59] While Woll's vision of creating a viable home market for existing surpluses was marred by the faulty argument that the export trade was unimportant for the economy, he did not hesitate to demand creation of an order that did not have to seek its prosperity through foreign expansion. "To attempt any radical extension of our foreign trade through 'reciprocal tariffs,' " he stressed, "is not only likely to get us into economic conflict with the nations excluded . . . but involves us in difficulties due to 'most favored nation' provisions." The only solution was at home. Woll hoped that capitalism would prove itself by developing full employment through a highly developed home market. Rising surpluses had to be absorbed by the home market "through increasing the income of wage-earners."[60]

The 1930's revealed the apparently strange picture of conservative craft union leaders developing a fairly rigor-

---

[58] Woll, Matthew, and William E. Walling, *op. cit.*, p. 186.
[59] Woll, Matthew, *op. cit.*, pp. 299-300.
[60] *Ibid.*, pp. 300, 304.

ous critique of the direction taken by the leaders of corporate capitalism. They urged that problems be solved
at home, and opposed the expansionist course of the New
Deal abroad and its corporatism at home. During these
years industrial unions were flourishing under a New
Deal aegis. Their leaders renounced a critical approach,
and urged the absorption of labor into the very mechanism of the corporate state. Although the AFL leaders
began to criticize, their reliance on craft organization
made their critique irrelevant and allowed it to go virtually unnoticed. Most misread their views as the desperate pleading of old-line conservatives. Liberals and radicals
forgot that the militant tactics of the CIO soon ended,
and as William A. Williams has explained, the "labor
movement rather rapidly settled down into the syndicalist
pattern that was by then clearly emerging from the ex-
citement and flux of the New Deal." [61]

The labor movement and its leadership chose to align
itself with American business and its path of foreign expansion. In exchange labor received government protection as it entered a stage of rapid growth. The labor
leaders developed an ideological view of reality in which
they asserted that the old capitalist system with its manifold problems had basically changed. In failing to point
out the fallacies of this view, and by failing to explain
that labor's victories were byproducts of continued expansion abroad, American radicals quietly forfeited their
responsibility of providing a radical alternative.

While radicals worked hard to organize workers into
industrial unions and at times won the leadership of CIO
branches, they unwittingly became the allies of those
whose concern was to fit labor into the corporate structure.
John L. Lewis explained in December of 1935 that the
"dangerous state of affairs" might very well have led to
" 'class consciousness' " and "revolution as well." Lewis

[61] Williams, William A., *The Contours of American History*, Cleveland
and New York, 1961, p. 445.

hoped that it could "be avoided," and he pledged that his own industrial union was "doing everything in their power to make the system work and thereby avoid it." [62] The CIO leaders gained the aid of the left in the attempt to make the system work. Once it was on its feet the services of the left were no longer appreciated, and radicals were purged from the labor movement with only a ripple of protest emanating from the rank and file. Labor's postwar position of acquiescence in the policies of different conservative administrations had been assured, and the corporate ideology of American labor leaders remained dominant and unchallenged.

Comment

BY *Philip S. Foner*

Volume VI, No. 6
November–December 1966

For some time now there have been signs of disenchantment with the nature of the American labor movement. Paul Jacobs' *The State of the Unions*, B. J. Widick's *Labor Today: The Triumphs and Failures of Unionism in the United States* and Paul E. Saltan's *The Disenchanted Unionist* are several of the recent books which have bemoaned the stagnation in the unions, the absence of militancy and the lack of consciousness of mission, and the steadily increasing role of the labor movement as an ally of the government in carrying out a reactionary foreign policy. There has been no lack of articles pointing

[62] "John L. Lewis Tells of Plans in First Interview Since A.F. of L. Resignation," interview with Selden Rodman, Dec. 20, 1935, William Green MSS (State Historical Society of Wisconsin, Madison, Wisconsin).

out the failure of the CIO to realize its bright promise of becoming the labor movement with a mission and the vanguard of progress in American society. Nevertheless, no one has provided an over-all conceptual framework by which to explain why the labor movement became allied with business and government, and acquiesced in conservative domestic and foreign policies. Indeed, most labor historians have tended to evade dealing with this central problem. Mr. Radosh, however, does attempt to explain why the labor movement developed as it did in recent years, and how it became aligned with American business and government. He has described how this alliance began, developed and matured.

While I agree that Radosh has clarified much of what was until now obscure, I feel that he has overemphasized the significance of the relationship between labor leaders and sophisticated employers. One comes away from reading his paper with the impression that from the turn of the century to the era of the New Deal the most important American labor leaders and the employers who controlled the major industries of the country achieved an arrangement whereby employer and worker functioned together harmoniously. Peaceful industrial relations resulted because of the understanding by both labor leaders and sophisticated employers that labor deserved a place within a corporate capitalist economic structure. There were, to be sure, "radical" employers who insisted on trying to destroy unionism rather than accepting it as an ally in operating the corporate enterprise system. But these men were old-fashioned in their thinking, and, in any case, did not exercise the dominant influence in American industrial society.

One might never suspect that in the majority of cases recognition of unionism came after militant struggles by the workers involved. Actually, many employers who later acknowledged the value of giving the union a voice in administering industry had to be convinced to accept this position not so much by the ideology of the union leaders as by the power of the workers. Radosh, however, implies that the radicalness and militancy of the rank-and-file was not to be taken seriously, since in the end it was the labor leadership that fixed the character of the relationship with the employers, a relationship predicated primarily on the community of interests between labor and capital in the corporate society.

I do not deny that there were sophisticated industrialists who saw the value of cooperating with labor leaders in combatting the growth of radical influences in the labor movement, and, at the same time, assuring themselves of increased production and efficiency. The question is to what extent did this element represent a truly significant section of American industry? Then again, to what extent did those who preached the doctrine that employer and worker could function together harmoniously actually practice this policy in their day-by-day relations with workers in their plants and factories? Mr. Radosh writes, "From the birth of the (National) Civic Federation to 1914, Gompers' ideas about labor would be molded by his association with that group of sophisticated employers who welcomed the AFL as a conservative and disciplined junior partner in a stable corporate order." He then cites the fact that Mark Hanna, president of the Civic Federation, signed a collective bargaining agreement with the AFL union in his steel plant. But Hanna died in 1904, and August Belmont, who succeeded him as President of the Civic Federation, destroyed the AFL union on his Interborough Rapid Transit Co. The United States Steel Corporation had a president and three directors—Charles M. Schwab, Henry Phipps, Marvin S. Hughes and George W. Perkins—active in the National Civic Federation. Yet U.S. Steel was the model for the open-shop drive, and by 1909 had all but destroyed trade unionism in the iron and steel industry. Gompers could say that his experience in the Civic Federation had led him to believe that the "men who control wealth in this country are at bottom human and adaptable to the changed order of relations." But a study of the U.S. Commission of Labor showed in 1910 that of the one hundred fifty-three thousand employees in the blast furnaces, steel works and rolling mills owned by U.S. Steel, fifty thousand customarily worked seven days a week, and twenty per cent of them worked eighty-four hours or more a week, which meant a twelve-hour day, including Sunday. Labor conditions in the company's plants were far below "the American standard of living as to sanitary and moral conditions." The wages paid, assuming constant employment and the ordinary family as the basis, "are barely enough to provide subsistence."[1] The men who headed the company where such conditions existed appeared very human indeed to Gompers and other AFL officials at Civic Federation dinners. But it is not surprising that the steel workers did not share the enthusiasm of labor leaders for such employers. I might also mention other leading members of the Civic Federation like J. Ogden Armour, Louis F. Swift, Elbert H. Gary, Cyrus H. McCormick, who operated open shops in their plants and resisted attempts at unionization. It is well known that many of the important employers' associations which were leaders of the drive to destroy the unions were represented in the Civic Federation in the person of their officers.

The point I wish to emphasize is that a historian should pay attention not only to what people said but to what they did, that it is insufficient to draw conclusions about the labor policy of the leading corporations by basing them on positions their spokesmen took at meetings or conferences. What is more essential is to judge these policies on what these same men did in their own factories. Gompers was always impressed by the pro-labor utterances of employers, but the incoming correspondence in the

[1] Foner, Philip S., *History of the Labor Movement in the United States*, vol. III, New York, 1964, p. 86.

archives of the AFL contains many letters from workers complaining that these same employers were discharging and blacklisting them if they dared to unionize.

Along with his failure to deal with the problem of representativeness, Radosh is vague on the way the material forces of history are shaped. He affirms that "the 1930's saw labor leaders becoming involved with a new group of far-sighted industrialists who desired to establish a place for unionism in the corporate capitalist economy." But when it comes to demonstrating the validity of this thesis, he is content to tell us what a few men thought and then to jump to the conclusion that this determined the course of events in the 1930's. We are left with the notion that the organization of the unorganized in the mass production industries was in some way a product of the ideas of a Gerard P. Swope and a Donald Richberg. Then, too, we are given the impression that the success of industrial unionism was the result of a definite policy initiated by the NRA. But there is a wide gap between the statement of abstract ideas and their implementation. The implementation came not from the government but from the pressure of the millions of unorganized workers. Radosh asserts that Section 7-a of the NRA "guaranteed labor's right to organize." But Hugh Johnson, administrator of the NRA, was closer to the truth when he told the National Association of Manufacturers on December 8, 1933, "We have a mandate under this act—positive and direct—to foster the organization of industry for cooperative action among the trade groups. . . . But we have no such mandate as to labor. The only thing that labor gets here is a right to organize (if it so desires) and to bargain (as it may elect) either individually or collectively—without employer interference. . . . As a matter of fact, I cannot see how industry being given not only the right (long denied it) but full governmental assistance for organization to the ultimate can greatly object to the

naked right of labor—without assistance at all—to organize also." [2]

What transformed "the naked right of labor" into
meaningful collective bargaining through an organization
chosen by the workers? The story of organization in the
mass production industries illustrates that it was not
transformed by discussions between labor leaders and
sophisticated employers, not even fundamentally by the
role played by the government. To achieve their goal of
union recognition, the workers had to overcome company
unionism, espionage, the use of armed guards, the denial
of constitutional and civic rights by local authorities. In
the end the powerful companies capitulated before the
mass strength of the workers exhibited so well in the wave
of sit-down strikes which swept industry, especially the
automobile industry, in late 1936 and early 1937. Radosh
reports Sidney Hillman as stressing in April 1937 that the
CIO objected in principle to sit-down strikes, but Hillman goes on to remark with a chuckle that "Wall Street
is beginning to recognize the CIO." Would this recognition have occurred if the sit-down strikes had not taken
place? The great victory in the General Motors sitdown
of January 1937 gave rise to a union impulse unequalled
in labor history, bringing new millions of workers into
the organized effort against open-shop employers. Before
this power employers reluctantly yielded. Labor was guaranteed a position in the industrial life of the nation because of its strength and solidarity, and not because
Hillman was able to convince the employers that workers
knew they had "an economic interest with employers in
the successful operation of the establishment."

It seems to me that what Hillman succeeded in doing
was to convince the once arrogant antiunion employers,
the ones who dominated the most important basic industries of the country, that they should abandon any attempt

[2] *NRA Notes,* January, 1934, p. 2.

to destroy the unions they had been forced to recognize and learn to live with them, and that, indeed, they would be served better by cooperative relations with labor than by continuing to plot head-on collisions. Naturally they could only be convinced of the value of this policy if they were simultaneously guaranteed that the new industrial unions would not seek to change the existing system, but make it work even better to provide higher profits. As for labor, it would be content with "a fair share." A minority of the employers—the sophisticated element—saw the value to industry of this approach at the very outset of the New Deal. But the decisive element of American industry accepted it because it really had little choice. In most cases the industrial unions were too well entrenched to be destroyed by the usual methods of antiunionism.. Unquestionably, the fact that the new industrial unions eliminated the radicals and assured the employers that they stood to gain profitwise by dealing with them accelerated the process. Even then it would be a mistake to conclude that concessions to the unions came automatically. Many were gained by strikes and are still being won in this manner.

Radosh concludes his paper with the observation that the radicals were purged from the labor movement "with only a ripple of protest emanating from the rank and file." He then states, "Labor's postwar position of acquiescence in the policies of different conservative administrations had been assured, and the corporate ideology of American labor leaders remained dominant and unchallenged." Yet, except for the little depression of 1937, this ideology has been tested only in a period of rising prosperity, more or less full employment and vast government activity in the military program. But suppose that the economic picture should change and the boom be replaced by a serious business decline? Herbert Clark Hoover is cited by Radosh as pleading in 1924 for "new regulations favoring human

rights," and urging that "capital, labor and government
. . . function together harmoniously." Yet this was the
President who in the great depression hardly lifted a finger
to assist the thirteen million unemployed, and closed his
doors to the bonus marchers. What happened then to
Hoover's concept of "new regulations favoring human
rights"?

Although he did not label it corporate ideology, Harold
J. Laski threw interesting light on this problem in his
book *Trade Unions and the New Society*, published in
1949, which made up the Sidney Hillman lectures he delivered that same year. Laski discussed the theory that
"there is harmony of interest between employers and employed." He observed, "It then follows that with goodwill
all differences can be settled on the basis of that harmony;
that disputes, and especially violent disputes, are the result of a failure to recognize the reality of that harmony."
He then noted, "This doctrine has never proved convincing to organized labor except in times of overwhelming boom; and it is one of the first concepts to be thrown
overboard as boom conditions decline and the signs of a
depression begin to make themselves felt." Laski predicted
that with wages falling, the hours of labor increased, the
number of unemployed growing quickly, the rank and
file would see the fallacy of the ideology of class harmony.
"They see in the losses they suffer when a pay envelope
is reduced, or an injunction is used against the union, or
grounds are found to call out the militia or federal troops,
the very doctrine he [the labor leader] has urged them to
reject." Then, Laski predicted further, the radicals would
exercise an influence in the labor movement quite out of
proportion to their strength in numbers.[3]

I am not looking forward hopefully to the time when
Laski's theory can be tested. But I do suggest that it is

[3] Laski, Harold J., *Trade Unions and the New Society*, New York, 1949,
pp. 33-37.

premature to conclude that the corporate ideology of American labor leaders will remain "dominant and unchallenged."

On the surface the labor movement should seem to be satisfied with the results of class collaboration. Organized workers have gained many concessions and have achieved, in many cases, a standard of living which seemed out of reach only a few decades ago. But beneath the surface there is much that should give the labor movement cause for concern. Organized labor still represents only a minority of the working class; the AFL-CIO has 13.5 million of seventy-three million employed workers. Large sections of the unorganized workers, particularly those on the poverty level, are alienated from the labor movement. The skilled craft unions affiliated to the AFL-CIO still continue to maintain the traditional practice of excluding nonwhites from skilled occupations. The majority of Negro wage-earners are forced into unskilled and menial job classifications in the industrial economy. As a consequence, Negro workers are more vulnerable to be displaced due to technological change than any other group in the labor force.

The labor movement cannot afford to ignore this problem. The day will surely come when the organized workers will need allies, and it would be a serious error to think that when that time comes it will be simple to overcome the years of indifference, indeed, of hostility to those who should be organized labor's allies.

What can American radicals do under these conditions? They can dismiss the labor movement as an essential part of the establishment, an ally of American imperialism, an obstacle to further progress in American society, and too completely dominated by a class-collaborationist labor bureaucracy to offer any hope for change. But this is what was said by liberals about the labor movement in the 1920's, when it seemed that the prospect of changing the craft character of the AFL and its indifference to the organization of the unskilled and semiskilled seemed remote. But many radicals of that period decided to make the effort to achieve a change, and devoted themselves to working within the existing unions for a progressive trade union policy. This effort, in part, produced the great organizational achievements of the 1930's. To be sure, once the organization was achieved, many of the radicals were dispensed with. But the organization of millions of workers was a fact, and exists today as a base from which to move forward.

No change in the labor movement is possible unless we first thoroughly understand its structure and character. Radosh has made an important contribution to that understanding. But we cannot stop here. We cannot merely conclude that the corporate ideology is dominant and unchallenged. We must begin to think about how to organize the challenge that will end the domination.

The Hoover Myth

BY *Murray N. Rothbard*

Volume VI, No. 4
Summer 1966

Murray N. Rothbard is the author of several books, including America's Great Depression *(1961), and the editor of* The Libertarian Forum. *He is a free-market conservative and individualist whose anti-imperialism and proscriptions of bureaucracy and the corporatist state coincide with those of the New Left. Rothbard's evaluation of Herbert Hoover is similar to the revisions of New Left historians: both emphasize the continuity in Herbert Hoover's thought and actions with those of Woodrow Wilson and the New Deal. Rothbard is Associate Professor of Economics at the Polytechnic Institute of Brooklyn.*

Herbert Clark Hoover* has gone into history as one of the great myths of modern Liberalism: a bumbling reactionary advocate of pristine nineteenth-century capitalism whose *laissez-faire* methods of coping with the Great Depression left America a shambles. In Liberal eyes the *laissez-faire* shambles supposedly bequeathed by Hoover makes the accomplishments and grandeur of Franklin Delano Roosevelt all the more lustrous. There are, however, two grave problems with this Liberal mythos: (1) that the New Deal did *not* cure or even alleviate the depression, which yielded only to America's entry into World War II, and (2) that Herbert Hoover, far from being an exemplar of *laissez-faire,* created all the lineaments of the New Deal program. The latter point is ex-

---

* Romasco, Albert U. *The Poverty of Abundance: Hoover, the Nation, the Depression.* Oxford University Press. New York. 1965.

tremely difficult for Liberals to concede: for if the hated
reactionary Hoover really differed but little from the be-
loved progressive FDR, what does that make FDR? What,
indeed, does that imply about the realities of our contemporary Liberal New Deal-Fair Deal-New Frontier-Great
Society?

Historians were at first content to portray Hoover as
the quintessence of *laissez-faire;* but, as reappraisals of
Hoover's program have accumulated in recent years, this
simplistic view has become increasingly untenable. And
so Liberal historians have begun to mount a second line
of defense, elaborated most recently by Professor Albert
Romasco. Romasco knows full well that Hoover can
hardly be described as precisely an advocate of *laissez-
faire;* his salvaging operation for the Liberal line consists
in describing Hoover's position as *close* to *laissez-faire* and
as firmly voluntarist. Romasco accomplishes this by consistently downgrading Hoover's extensive use of government action, and by playing up his windy voluntarist
rhetoric. Unprecedented acts of federal intervention are
transmuted by Romasco into "the new individualism,"
"cooperative individualism," and—especially loaded term!
—"enlightened conservatism." Romasco's vision, then, is
merely a sophisticated version of the old Liberal morality
play: at one pole are the Bad Guys, the unregenerate
champions of *laissez-faire;* slightly better than, but close
to them is the Hoover Administration, whose actions
were all dedicated to the voluntary approach of "cooperative individualism"; and at the opposite pole, waiting in
the wings, are the happily coercive Liberals of the Roosevelt New Deal. To Romasco it was only the *failure* of
the Hoover "voluntarist" approach that by horrid example
ushered in the coercive New Deal, not a more direct
filiation. But Hoover *was* slightly better than the *laissez-
fairists* insofar as he was willing to use the power of government. Apparently to the liberal Romasco, one's
political soundness is apparently in direct proportion to

one's willingness to exercise the powers of the federal government.

Trapped in his orientation Romasco completely misconceives the cast of Herbert Hoover's mind as he ascended the Presidency. According to Romasco Hoover was a "cooperative individualist," an individualist who merely tacked on to *laissez-faire* a wish to have the government, in the Pollyanna phrase of Romasco, "assist the flowering of the cooperative spirit." Rather than a man caught short by the Depression who simply tried to extend cooperative individualism, as Romasco implies, Herbert Hoover came to it armed with a "new economics" which he was eager to apply should a depression strike: and the Hooverian new economics was remarkably similar to the Roosevelt New Deal.

The first thing to be understood about Hoover is that his career down to 1928, was the very model of a modern Liberal; his "voluntarism" was a ragged cloak of traditional rhetoric covering his willingness greatly to accelerate the powers of the federal government. Down through the years the Hooverian style was the mailed fist in the velvet glove: offering a program for "voluntary" cooperation, but with the threat of federal coercion always evident and held ready in case anyone had the temerity to exercise his voluntary choice and opt out of the program.

Typical of Hoover's social philosophy was the Reconstruction Program which he had developed after serving in his high post as Food Czar in the Wilsonian "war collectivism" of World War I. The program envisioned a system of governmental planning in which the federal government's "central direction" would preside over the "voluntary" cooperative action of the nation's economic groups. The government was supposed also to eliminate industrial "waste" (i.e. vigorous competition), build dams, encourage unionization, develop health and education,

"conserve resources" (i.e. restrict production), stabilize
employment, increase inheritance taxes and regulate the
stock market so as to eliminate "vicious speculation." So
"forward-looking" was Hoover's program, indeed, that
such progressive Democrats as Louis Brandeis, Herbert
Croly of the *New Republic,* Colonel Edward M. House
and Franklin Delano Roosevelt eagerly boomed Hoover
for the Presidential nomination on the Democratic ticket
in 1920.

One of the great deficiencies of Romasco's book is his
complete failure to treat Hoover's view of unionism, or
the union leaders' attitude toward Hoover's program for
fighting the depression. That attitude, being wildly favorable, hardly fits Romasco's portrayal of Hoover as the
last, if not the most doctrinaire, of conservative indi-
vidualists. On the contrary, Hoover not only favored
unionism, he believed in using the power of government
to encourage workers to join large-scale, "responsible"
unions that could avoid strikes and be readily integrated
into the new non-individualist economic order. Hoover
enunciated these principles as early as 1909, and continued
promoting them assiduously throughout the 1920's: in
federal labor-management conferences, in the drive to end
the twelve-hour day in steel, in the railway strike of 1922,
in the creation of the Railway Labor Act of 1926. Indeed,
Hoover was very close to such labor leaders as William
Green and Sidney Hillman; in 1928 Hillman and many
other leading Liberals backed Hoover for the Presidency.

Early in his career Hoover also developed a proto-New
Deal approach toward curing depressions by vast programs of federal public works. As early as the 1921 depression he pushed for such a program in collaboration
with Otto Tod Mallery, the nation's foremost advocate of
public works in depressions, the AFL, the United States
Chamber of Commerce and the American Association of
Labor Legislation, an organization of eminent economists,

industrialists and Liberals, dedicated to government intervention in the fields of labor, unemployment and welfare.[1]

The most striking example of Hoover's collaboration with Liberal intellectuals was his adoption of the highly inflationist public works scheme of the economist Dr. William Trufant Foster and the banker and industrialist Waddill Catchings. Foster and Catchings were an unsophisticated 1920's version of later Keynesianism, promoting underconsumptionist theories of the causes of depression as well as continued inflation and public works as the preferred solution. Hoover enthusiastically adopted the Foster-Catchings public works plan for curing all future depressions, leaking it to the public through Governor Ralph Owen Brewster of Maine in the Governor's Conference of late 1928. A large part of the press hailed the plan as "prosperity insurance" and as a "pact to outlaw depression"; William Green of the AFL hailed it as the most important pronouncement on wages and employment in a decade; John P. Frey of the AFL announced that Hoover had now accepted the AFL theory that depressions are caused by low wages and underconsumption. The press reported that "labor is jubilant, because leaders believe that the next President has found . . . a remedy for unemployment which, at least in its philosophy and groundwork, is identical with that of labor."

If Hoover was armed with labor union support to face any economic vicissitudes, he was armed also with the latest conclusions of "scientific" economics. As Foster and Catchings exulted: "The Plan . . . is business guided by

[1] The roster of American Association of Labor Legislation officials in this era is an instructive lesson in itself on the development of the ideology and practice of corporate liberalism in America. It included Liberals Ray Stannard Baker, Mrs. Mary Beard, Joseph P. Chamberlain, Morris Llewellyn Cooke, Paul H. Douglas, Morris L. Ernst, Herbert Feis, Walton H. Hamilton, Broadus Mitchell, Wesley C. Mitchell, William F. Ogburn, Roscoe Pound, Father John A. Ryan, Ida Tarbell, Mary Van Kleeck and Leo Wolman; and industrialists: Bernard Baruch, Henry S. Dennison, S. Fels, Thomas I. Parkinson, Mrs. George D. Pratt, Julius Rosenwald, Gerard Swope, Mrs. Frank A. Vanderlip and John G. Winant.

measurements instead of hunches. It is economics for an
age of science—economics worthy of the new President."

Thus, Herbert Hoover, by the advent of the Great
Depression stood as a "Great Humanitarian" bolstered by
the enthusiastic support of labor unionism. As a "Great
Engineer" he had discarded the old credo of *laissez-faire*
that had prevailed in previous depressions. Armed with
the latest findings of "scientific" economics, allied to liberal intellectuals, he stood ready to use boldly the powers
of the federal government to eliminate the business cycle
and to encourage unionism. Above all, as Romasco blithely
puts it, "to assist the flowering of the cooperative spirit."
What this "flowering" actually amounted to, however, was
a cartelization of the American economy: a cartelization
aided, encouraged and regulated by the federal government. Here was the new economic order of which Herbert
Hoover was one of the first heralds and to the formation
of which he bent his energies. It was to be a harmonious
reign of cooperating monopolies, each raising prices and
restricting production under the aegis of the central government. During the 1920's Hoover was extraordinarily
active as Secretary of Commerce in promoting this goal:
notably by aiding the establishment of trade associations
throughout industry, hopefully to flower eventually into
self-regulation by industry in collaboration with suitably
responsible unionism.

One of Hoover's favorite candidates for cartelization—
and one of the main reasons for his continual emphasis
on public works—was the construction industry, with
which he was intimately connected from the first as a
prominent engineer. During the depression of 1920-21
federal and state authorities charged the New York construction industry with price-fixing; in reaction to these
charges Hoover and Franklin Delano Roosevelt jointly
formed the American Construction Council in 1922. The
Council was not only to serve as a trade association; it was

to cartelize the industry, to plan for it as a whole, and to impose various codes of "fair practice" upon its members. Originated by Hoover, the codes were a device to restrict production and raise prices; as President of the Council Franklin Roosevelt repeatedly denounced rugged individualism and unbridled profit-seeking by the individual. In short, the maverick competitor, the "unfair" "chiseler" who is ever the bane of monopolists, must be brought to book. Hoover also collaborated with Roosevelt and the American Construction Council in pushing the idea of public works programs, which of course would constitute a huge subsidy to the construction industry.

One of the major programs of government-sponsored cartelization put through by Herbert Hoover came in the field of agriculture. Here, where Hoover was the person mainly responsible for the shift from a free market to governmental cartels, Professor Romasco so misconceives the Hoover farm policy as to call it the "new individualism." Romasco depicts Hoover as reluctant to accept the farm bloc proposals for cartelization and corollary support of farm prices. But on the contrary, Hoover had pushed for cartelization throughout his term as Secretary of Commerce. One of the earliest proponents of a Federal Farm Board to create a system of agricultural cooperatives, Hoover campaigned in 1928 for such a board to sponsor and subsidize co-ops and to support farm prices. Thus his alacrity in setting up the Federal Farm Board in mid-1929. This pre-depression program was not designed to meet any cyclical emergency, but radically to transform much of agriculture from a free-market to a centrally cartelized industry. Romasco dismisses the Hoover farm program as being voluntarist and therefore a failure; he gives no indication that the vast loan and price-support program of the Federal Farm Board and its subsidiary crop corporations was the direct prescursor of the New Deal-to-Great Society farm program. Virtually the only element missing from the later New Deal was compulsory

crop restrictions—a policy that would complete the New
Deal's creation of a true "poverty of abundance," taxing
the mass of impoverished citizens to induce and force
farmers to restrict form output at the very time when
poverty and starvation pervaded America. Even for this
final step such influential and "conservative" Republicans
as Senator Arthur H. Vandenberg were urging the government to compel farmers to restrict their production.
Hoover simply would not go all the way.

Romasco also follows the lead of all too many historians
in ignoring the realities of the composition of the Federal
Farm Board; like all Liberal historians he is so content
with government intervention *per se* as a progressive step
that he fails to explore the underlying reasons for and
the nature of that intervention. He fails, in short, to realize that political action is not the imposition of an abstract
good upon the community but an act by which some
people gain at the expense of others, and where we therefore must inquire: *who* does what to *whom?* In the case of
Hoover's Federal Farm Board, its composition demonstrates its cartelizing, monopolistic intent. Chairman of
the FFB was long-time Hoover associate Alexander Legge,
protegé of the powerful Bernard M. Baruch and president of the International Harvester Company, a leading
manufacturer of farm machinery with a direct economic
stake in farm subsidization. Others appointed to the FFB
were prominent tobacco, cotton, fruit, grain, dairy and
livestock producers.

Complete neglect of Hoover's pre-depression record of
support of government intervention is one of the crucial
ways by which Romasco can present Hoover as basically
a voluntarist and individualist. The other major device
is to exaggerate greatly the voluntary aspects of the Hoover
depression program and to deprecate or ignore the ways
in which the program approximated the extensive intervention of the Roosevelt New Deal. Thus, Romasco dep-
recates the influence of the White House conferences of

leading industrialists which Hoover organized immediately after the stock-market crash in October 1929 to get
business to pledge to keep wage rates up and let profits
fall rather than cut wage rates—a revolutionary new program in American depressions, supervised by Julius
Barnes, head of the United States Chamber of Commerce.
Romasco intimates that the wage-maintenance agreements
were not carried out, and dismisses the conferences simply
as ineffectual exercises in voluntarism. Actually the White
House agreements succeeded phenomenally, and all too
well. For the first time in a severe depression, monetary
wage rates in manufacturing remained almost constant
for two whole years, with the result that *real* wage rates
(wage rates corrected for price changes) rose by over ten
per cent. Even when wage rates finally began to fall under
the enormous pressure of the depression, real wage rates
in manufacturing barely fell at all, and remained over
eight per cent higher than 1929 at the depth of the depression in March 1933.[2]

The extent of Hoover's interventionism is also obscured
by Romasco's failure to mention the union hosannahs for
the wage-maintenance program. Thus, the journal of the
AFL hailed the fact on January 1, 1930 that: "The
President's conference has given industrial leaders a new
sense of their responsibilities. . . . Never before have they
been called upon to act together . . . in earlier recessions
they have acted individually to protect their own interests
and . . . have intensified depressions." By the following
March the AFL was lauding the large corporations for
not lowering wage rates, and hailing the fact that big
business was now adopting the purchasing power gospel
of W. T. Foster; the United States, it exulted, will "go
down in history as the creator of (an) . . . epoch in the
march of civilization—high wages." In late 1930 William
Green hailed Hoover's virtual suspension of immigration

---

[2] See the study by Sol Shaviro, "Wages and Payroll in the Depression,
1929-1933" (Unpublished M.A. essay, Columbia University, 1947).

as a method of keeping up wage rates and reducing the
labor-market pressure upon those rates, and also supported Hoover's similarly motivated program for the
massive deportation of "undesirable" aliens. Throughout
1930 and 1931 Hoover and Commerce Secretary Robert
P. Lamont were active in trying to induce the nation's
industrialists to meet in formal conference with the leaders of organized labor.

It is typical of Romasco that he devotes almost more
attention to the "voluntary" bank-financed loan program
of the short-lived National Credit Corp. than to the direct
governmental lending of its successor Reconstruction
Finance Corporation, established by Hoover in 1932 and
continued as a linchpin of the Roosevelt program. This
despite the fact that the NCC was conceived as a strictly
temporary program; furthermore, Romasco characteristically omits the fact that the NCC was only imposed
upon by the nation's bankers by Hoover's threat of governmental coercion should they reject the program. Pro-
ceeding on his course of praising the *idea* but minimizing
the *extent* of any of Hoover's ventures in direct governmental intervention, Romasco slides over the important
activities of the RFC in 1932, and omits its function as a
method for the American citizenry to subsidize the bailing
out of shaky banks, especially those that held the bonds
of bankrupt railroads. One of the main enthusiasts for the
latter policy was the originator and chairman of the RFC,
Eugene Meyer, Jr., a protegé of Bernard Baruch. Meyer
also just happened to be the brother-in-law of a partner
of J. P. Morgan and Co., one of the main beneficiaries
of RFC *largesse*.

Romasco also misconceives the role of Colonel Arthur
Woods, chairman of Hoover's President's Emergency
Committee for Employment and a trustee of the Rocke-
feller Foundation and Rockefeller's General Education
Board. Romasco thinks of Woods as having completely
voluntarist views on relief identical with those of the

President. But, on the contrary, Woods repeatedly urged upon Hoover a more thoroughgoing interventionist program, as well as even greater public works than Hoover himself was launching. Nor does Romasco give any attention whatever to Hoover's extensive public works program or his joining with Mallery to put through Senator Wagner's Employment Stabilization Act of February 1931. Hoover's Home Loan Bank Act of 1932, again a typical New Deal measure, is also brushed aside quickly. Neither does Romasco show any grasp of the crucial monetary situation, including: the revolutionary, proto-New Deal nature of Hoover's program of inflation and bank credit expansion, the role of this program in causing bank failures and an outflow of gold, the willingness of Hoover by the end of his term to put into effect the FDR programs of bank holidays and bank deposit insurance, as well as the willingness by that time of Hoover's Secretary and Undersecretary of the Treasury to go off the gold standard. Instead, Romasco's only contribution to analysis of the monetary picture is to chide the bankers for being personally responsible for their own liquidation by not being inflationist enough; this from a writer who chides conservatives for thinking in purely personal terms about the large economic forces!

Romasco may accord with the liberal image when he writes of Hoover as not wishing to tamper with the operations of the stock market, but he is again dead wrong. All his life, in fact, Hoover had been extremely hostile to the stock market—perhaps from a corporate manager's native antagonism toward the outsider financier, perhaps because the free-wheeling stock market is the most difficult institution in capitalism to monopolize or bring under central control. Thus, R. E. Treacy has shown that, as early as his *Principles of Mining Valuation* in 1909, Hoover had lashed out bitterly at the speculators, and had asserted that it is "the duty of every engineer to diminish the opportunity of the vulture as far as possible"; some day, Hoover declared, "people will not ask, who paid for a thing, but who built it." By 1912 Hoover was praising industrial "insiders" and denouncing "outsiders," and asserting that: "from an economic point of view . . . capital in the hands of the Insiders is often to more reproductive purposes than if it had remained in the hands of the idiots who parted with it."[3] And Hoover was highly critical throughout the inflationary credit expansion of the Coolidge Administration, especially insofar as the credit went into the booming stock market.

As soon as President Hoover took office he moved against the stock market. During the first half of 1929 he tried to deny bank credit to the stock market while keeping it abundant to "legitimate" commerce and industry— a feat bound to fail in an interrelated economy. In the fall of 1930 Hoover launched the first of a series of attacks on his old *bête noire* the New York Stock Exchange. He threatened federal regulation of the Exchange, and, under this threat, forced its head, Richard Whitney, to agree "voluntarily" to withhold loans of stock for short-selling, which Hoover naively held to be responsible for the fall of stock prices. Despite this compliance, as well as further restrictions on short selling by the Exchange in late 1931, Hoover called in the Exchange authorities in early 1932 and threatened them with government coercion unless short-selling were purged to his satisfaction. Indeed, Hoover absurdly denounced as "vicious" and "sinister" the fall in stock prices that reflected the enormous fall in earnings; somehow he felt that this "pounding of prices to a basis of earnings" was "rotten" and subversive. It was Hoover's constant stream of hysterical denunciations that led to a Senate investigation of the Stock Exchange, and to further restriction of short-selling. Hoover, furthermore, went on to propose additional controls of the stock market which virtually became the New Deal SEC pro-

[3] Herbert Hoover, "Economics of a Boom," *The Mining Magazine* (May, 1912), pp. 370-73.

gram: including compulsory stock prospectuses and Congressional rules for security exchanges. It is no wonder that Hoover was later to have a highly benign attitude toward the New Deal's SEC.

Hoover also proceeded during the depression on a direct cartelizing program for the vital oil industry. In the face of an increasing abundance of oil finds, the oil companies turned to the power of state and federal government to compel a drastic restriction of oil production, and the assigning of restrictive quotas of crude oil output to each producer in order to effect a drastic rise in the price of oil. Hoover came to favor oil restrictions even before the depression, and when the depression struck he and his Secretary of Interior persuaded Texas, Oklahoma and other oil-producing states to enact proration laws to compel a vast cutback in production to raise the price of oil. The President cooperated further by cancelling permits to drill for oil in large parts of the public domain, by pressuring private oil operators near the public domain to restrict their production, and by establishing a "Voluntary Committee" of the Federal Oil Conservation Board to assist the state efforts. And even though the monopoly program was put through under the specious guise of "conserving" oil, Hoover bolstered the cartel further in 1932 by establishing a tariff on imports of petroleum. If conservation instead of monopoly had *really* been the goal of the government action, imports of oil would of course have been welcomed rather than penalized. Not one word, however, of the Hoover oil policy appears in the Romasco volume.

All this leads to the conclusion that Herbert Hoover played a vital role in moving America toward a new economic order. Throughout his career culminating in the Presidency, Herbert Hoover sought to transform the American economy into one of collaborating, self-regulating monopoly groups, all under the benevolent aegis and central direction of the federal government. Banded together under this direction would not only be American industry but also three important co-opted groups: a cartelized agriculture, a strong, federally-imposed and cooperative labor unionism, and an articulate Liberal *intelligentsia* to provide the theoretical apologia for the new system and to provide also the efficient technical help of running its central plans. Helping to fuel the system and inducing its various parts to cooperate would be a structure of permanent if carefully controlled inflation, provided by a continual expansion of money and credit under the direction of the central government. Thus, there is more to Hoover's thoroughgoing anticipation of the Roosevelt New Deal than the various particular measures, striking though they may be. Even more important is Hoover's approach to the system as a whole, the overall political economy that would be cemented by Roosevelt. That new system, which replaced the quasi-free-market capitalism of the nineteenth century America, can be and has been called by various names, each more or less appropriate to understanding its nature: interventionism, neo-mercantilism, the Welfare State, political capitalism, state monopoly capitalism, the corporate state, neo-fascism. It is one of the great failings of Romasco's book that not once is there mention of fascism, that new economic system of the 1920's that provided such a large degree of attraction for American businessmen—and for Liberal intellectuals. The whole program of corporate and group monopolies directed by the State, fought for all his life by Hoover and brought to a culmination by FDR, was essentially the corporate economy of fascism.[4]

[4] That neither Hoover nor FDR envisioned a one-party dictatorship on the fascist model is not really very important. For, after all, does not a democracy in which the two major parties both subscribe to the new order add up to a more subtle and less vulnerable version of a one-party state?

On the attraction of the Italian fascist model for American Liberal intellectuals, see John P. Diggins, "Flirtation with Fascism: American Pragmatic Liberals and Mussolini's Italy," *American Historical Review* (January, 1966), pp. 487-506. There is, moreover, a remarkable similarity in the linkage between fascism, Social-Democratic collectivism and the New Deal in the analyses of such diverse thinkers as F. A. Hayek and R. Palme Dutt (in the pre-Popular Front phase of the international Com-

The major difference, indeed, between Hoover and
FDR is that during the course of the Hoover regime, big
businessmen began to turn swiftly toward a rapid acceler-
ation of the existing trends toward an outright corporatist
economy, a turn that increasingly left the more moderate
and cautious Hoover behind. The signal for this new turn
came in September 1931 when the "enlightened" industrialist Gerard Swope, head of General Electric, presented
the Swope Plan to a convention of the National Electrical
Manufacturers Association. The Plan, which garnered a
great deal of publicity, amounted to a scheme for compulsory cartelization of all American business—an obvious
imitation of fascism and a direct anticipation of Roosevelt's NRA. Every industry was to be forcibly mobilized
into trade associations, which would regulate (raise) prices
and (restrict) production, and enforce codes of "fair practices." All this would function under the control of the
federal government through a national economic council,
a joint administration of representatives of industrialists
and workers, to plan the overall result and "coordinate
production and consumption."[5]

The Swope Plan swiftly gained the approval of the
corporate world. In December, led by its new president,
Henry I. Harriman of the New England Power Company,
the United States Chamber of Commerce endorsed the
plan by a large majority. In the report he wrote for the
Chamber Harriman exulted that "We have left the period
of extreme individualism. . . . Business prosperity and
employment will be best maintained by an intelligently
planned business structure." With business forcibly organized through trade associations and a national economic

---

munist movement). Thus, see Friedrich A. Hayek, *The Road to Serfdom*
(Chicago: University of Chicago Press, 1944), and R. Palme Dutt, *Fascism
and Social Revolution* (New York: International Publishers, 1934).

[5] B. A. Hughes points out that as early as December 1926 Swope had
unsuccessfully appealed to William Green to organize the unskilled (such
as at General Electric) into industrial unions: "It might make the difference between an organization with which we could work on a businesslike basis and one that would be a source of endless difficulties."

council, any dissenting business competitor would be
"treated like any maverick. . . . They'll be roped, and
branded, and made to run with the herd." The eager
president of the National Association of Manufacturers
wanted to go beyond the Swope Plan to compel the inclusion into the scheme even of firms employing less than
fifty workers. Also endorsing the Swope Plan were:
Swope's friend Owen D. Young, Chairman of the Board
of General Electric, Benjamin A. Javits, who had already
developed a similar plan, Paul M. Mazur of Lehman
Brothers, who deplored the "tragic lack of planning" in
the capitalist system, Henry S. Dennison of the Dennison
Manufacturing Co., Rudolph Spreckles, president of the
Sugar Institute, H. S. Person of the Taylor Society, former
Secretary of the Treasury William Gibbs McAdoo, and
Ralph F. Flanders of the Jones and Lamson Machine
Company. Charles F. Abbott of the American Institute
of Steel Construction hailed the Swope Plan as "a measure
of public safety," as providing "an industrial traffic officer"
who would discipline "the blustering individual who
claims the right to do as he pleases." In short, thundered
Abbott, "we cannot have in this country much longer
irresponsible, ill-informed, stubborn and non-cooperating
individualism."

An unconsciously amusing note in boosting the Swope
Plan was provided by highly conservative academicians
Nicholas Murray Butler, president of Columbia University, and Wallace B. Donham, dean of the Harvard School
of Business, both of whom admiringly cited the central
planning of the Soviet Union as a guide for the new
American collectivism. To Butler, the Soviets had the
"vast advantage" of a plan, and Donham cited the Soviet
Union as demonstrating the value and necessity of a
"general plan for American business."

Perhaps the earliest direct inspiration for the Swope
proposal had been provided by Swope's friend Bernard
Baruch who as early as 1925 had conceived of an economy
of giant trusts, regulated and run by a federal commission.

All in all, Dr. Virgil Jordan, economist for the National Industrial Conference Board, was entirely accurate when he approvingly declared that American business was ready for an "economic Mussolini."

Liberal intellectuals also hastened to co-opt themselves into the projected new dispensation. Stuart Chase, Royal W. France, Will Durant and Louis Brandeis endorsed the Swope or equivalent plans, and in the National Progressive Conference of 1931 John M. Clark, George Soule and Edwin S. Smith endorsed a slightly less pro-business version of the same scheme. Rexford Tugwell has acknowledged the close similarity between the Swope-Harriman planners and the views of the "collectivists in Franklin's Brain Trust." Among union leaders the most enthusiastic supporters of the Swope-led drive for government planning were John L. Lewis and Sidney Hillman, both of whom called for a national economic council for central planning consisting of representatives of labor and industry. Even the liberal Arthur Schlesinger, Jr. correctly concludes that "Lewis and Hillman, in the end, differed little from Gerard Swope and Henry I. Harriman." [6]

The onrushing development of New Deal collectivist thought in America had passed Herbert Clark Hoover by. While his speeches were increasingly peppered with calls for "cooperation" and the "elimination of waste," Hoover drew back decisively from the abyss and stoutly and accurately denounced the Swope Plan or anything like it as "fascism." In a vital though neglected confrontation during the 1932 campaign Henry Harriman warned Hoover that FDR had agreed to enact the Swope Plan, and that if Hoover persisted in his opposition the big business world would shift to Roosevelt. The threat was carried out as Hoover refused to yield, and the rest is history. The Swope Plan soon took shape as the NRA,

---

[6] Rexford Guy Tugwell, *The Democratic Roosevelt* (New York: Doubleday and Co., 1957), p. 283; Arthur M. Schlesinger, Jr., *The Crisis of the Old Order, 1919-1933* (Boston: Houghton Mifflin Co., 1957), p. 186.

with Swope and Harriman helping to draft the bill. Swope stayed on to help run the NRA, the chairman of which was General Hugh S. Johnson, a friend of Swope's and a disciple of Baruch's. Head of NRA's sister AAA turned out to be George Peek, who with Johnson had first proposed cartelization of agriculture in the early 1920's, and Henry Harriman found a congenial berth as a leader of FDR's agricultural Brain Trust. Meanwhile, former President Hoover, without in the least bit repudiating any of his own quasi-fascist actions, remained outside of the new dispensation to attack the developed corporatism of the New Deal, thereby gaining an unwanted reputation from one and all as a proponent of *laissez-faire* individualism.

There is much wrong with Professor Romasco's book, not in the least a skimpiness reflected in a bibliography that shows no acquaintance whatever with the important work of Benjamin M. Anderson, Murray Benedict, Irving Bernstein, Joseph Brandes, Lawrence Clark, Daniel Fusfeld, Charles O. Hardy, Seymour Harris, William E. Leuchtenberg, Harold M. Levinson, David Loth, Lionel Robbins, Sol Shapiro, H. Parker Willis, William Appleman Williams, or Thomas Wilson. Romasco also indulges in a habit of all too many historians: after first disclaiming any discussion of the causes of the depression for lack of economic training, he proceeds to slip in casually his own *ad hoc,* unsupported and inevitably fallacious causal theories. Neither can he furnish us with an analysis of the economic consequences of Hoover's actions during the depression. But the most important defect of the book is a failure of overall vision: a failure to grasp the fundamental meaning of the Hoover record, or for that matter, of the subsequent New Deal. It is, in fine, a failure to realize that the difference between Hoover and FDR is that Hoover refused to go all the way to a highly centralized state capitalism.

McCarthy and the Liberals

BY *John Steinke* AND *James Weinstein*

Volume II, No. 3
Summer 1962

John Steinke, in a revised portion of his Master's Thesis (written at the University of Wisconsin) here has undertaken one of the first efforts to point out the ways in which the Cold War Socialists contributed to the development of the ultra-right in the United States. Steinke is Assistant Professor of History and Government at the Michigan Technological University. He is the author of Wisconsin Farm Politics, 1948-1964 *(1969)*.

The late Senator Joseph Raymond McCarthy enjoyed the distinction, shared by few other men, of having had his name become the root of a common noun while he was still alive. This honor was a tribute to the excellence of the Senator in his chosen profession of witch-hunting and red-baiting. And yet, though he deserves some recognition for his outstanding success, the particular tribute is somewhat misleading: for McCarthy did not invent the art, he merely became its leading practitioner. Nor, as many liberals complain, did he abuse or misuse an otherwise useful tool: he simply carried it to its logical conclusion.

But this was precisely his offense. It is the reason "mccarthyism" bears his name. He rode the monster too hard, turning it against its creators, and they, realizing finally that their creation was out of control, attempted in flaccid defense to turn it back upon him. By naming the beast after the Senator the liberals have tried to conceal its origin, and, indeed, have even sought to prove that Mc-

Carthy himself was the creation of the Communists, just as he sought to do with them. "Mccarthyism," however, was from the beginning a Frankenstein begging to run wild. Created by the Cold War, the new ism was an inevitable product of a policy of which the liberals were the chief architects. Their unchivalrous attempt to give their child another's name is unworthy of the defenders of the finest traditions of Western Civilization.

In 1946, circuit judge Joseph R. McCarthy defeated Senator Robert M. LaFollette, Jr. in the Republican primary, and went on to win the general election for United States Senator over Democrat Howard J. McMurray. In the course of these two campaigns, McCarthy evolved as a militant anti-Communist crusader; however, these four months (from mid-July to election day, 1946) were not one of innovation for the future Senator, but of learning.

Within the Republican Party, it was a widespread practice at this time to discredit President Truman's various recommendations as Communistic. Representative B. Carrol Reece, for example, then Chairman of the Republican National Committee, observed that the coming elections represented a "choice between Communism and Republicanism," since "a radical group" committed to the Soviet Union constituted "the policymaking force of the Democratic Party."[1] Similarly, Senator William Stanfill, of Kentucky, charged that the Washington bureaucracy was infested with "Communist Party workers and Communist sympathizers," who were purloining America's "top secrets." Claiming that the Communists had selected the State Department as their principal target, Stanfill proposed that the President authorize the F.B.I. to investigate it and to foil this Soviet attempt to infiltrate the Government.[2]

Finally, Representative Joseph Martin of Massachusetts

[1] *The Milwaukee Journal,* June 18, 1946.
[2] *Ibid.,* August 19, 1946.

predicted the election of a Republican Congress in 1946, and promised that first "we will direct our efforts toward cleaning out the Communists, their fellow travelers and parlor pinks from high positions in our government." [3]

In Wisconsin, too, there was no paucity of strident anti-Communism. The Reverend Dr. Walter A. Maier, a Lutheran radio evangelist, for example, warned that "we have banished Nazism, only to find ourselves confronted with the ascendency of a far greater, more sinister force which is uncompromisingly opposed to God." The Communist crusade, Dr. Maier warned, threatened the "abolition of private property and public worship." [4] And the Appleton *Post-Crescent* attacked the Democratic Party for having "made love to these Commies," for having "sloppily kissed them in public," and for having given them "the combination of the front door as it told them how it trusted them." Commenting on Secretary of State James F. Byrnes' removal of one hundred five State Department employees as "untrustworthy," the editors concluded that "the Democratic national leadership sold the nation for its individual gain and put Benedict Arnolds as sentinels on the wall for a few thousand lousy votes in [the] slum districts." [5]

The Republican Party in the State was busily trying to make the most of the issue that the Truman Administration had created for it. The Democrats were particularly vulnerable. They had been in power during the war, when the Soviet Union and the United States cooperated to defeat Germany, and then they had repudiated their own wartime alliance to initiate the Cold War. To defend their wartime policy was to undermine their postwar policy. The Republicans, of course, faced no such problem. They were in the enviable position of being able to

[3] *Ibid.*, September 21, 1946.

[4] *Ibid.*, March 11, 1946, II, 1. See, also speech of the assistant director of the F.B.I. to the convention of the Wisconsin American Legion, *Ibid.*, August 5, 1946, II, 1.

[5] Appleton *Post-Crescent*, October 9, 1946.

support Truman's Cold War, and at the same time to use
it against his Party. Thus, the Wisconsin Republican
Party censured the Truman Administration for appease-
ment of Soviet Russia: Governor Walter S. Goodland
attacked the New Deal's flirtation "with Communism,
fellow travelers, Socialism and other untried and wholly
theoretical idealism," while Senator Alexander H. Wiley
pronounced that the "people want their government to
stand for American principles—instead of Communism." [6]

In the meantime, McCarthy lagged behind. Although
he endorsed the Truman Administration's opposition to
the Soviet Union, he also registered minor protests against
the Cold War. At least twice, McCarthy echoed Henry
Wallace's recommendations to negotiate a *modus vivendi*
with the Soviet Union, arguing that the United States
could not sustain her domestic prosperity and political
democracy following a third world war. On June 20,
1946, McCarthy visited Wisconsin Rapids and endorsed
negotiations and accommodation with the Soviet Union.
A great many people, he declared, "apparently are all out
for world co-operation generally but they back off when it
gets down to specific cases." There were, he continued,
"things I don't like about Russia, but nothing is gained by
damning them." If enough of our leaders "keep on cursing
Russia we're going to have a war," he declared, concluding
that "one can pick up votes by attacking Russia," but
that it would serve only "to destroy our nation for even
if victorious, we could not survive the tremendous economic and social upheaval which would accompany another war." [7]

Following his election in November, McCarthy stated
again that he did not believe a war was in the offing. Ob-
serving that "Russia does not want war" and was not

[6] *Capital Times* (Madison), October 22, 1946; Beloit *Daily News*, October 29, 1946.

[7] Wisconsin Rapids *Tribune*, June 20, 1946.

ready to fight one, the Senator-elect praised "Stalin's proposal for world disarmament" as "a great thing," about which Stalin "must be given credit for being sincere."[8] Nor were these comments merely campaign devices, for one statement was made after the election, and the other was not repeated in the industrial sections of the state, where the Communists still had considerable strength in the United Automobile Workers and in the machinery of the state C.I.O.

On the whole, however, McCarthy clearly remained a disciple of the Truman-Vandenberg program, which pictured the United States as the citadel of human freedom and characterized the Soviet Union as an instrument of tyranny. He endorsed the application of America's political leadership and economic power to the problem of integrating the non-Communist nations into an American-led system, in opposition to the Communist world. Thus, four days before the primary, McCarthy had pledged his "vigorous opposition" to world communism.[9] Later, he re-endorsed "the Vandenberg-Byrnes policy," proposing that we "retain a grip both in Western Europe and in Eastern Asia" to prevent these people from falling "easy victims" to Russia. The candidate concluded that "we should use our economic might as a weapon in Western Europe and Eastern Asia."[10]

Like his fellow Republicans, McCarthy occasionally resorted to red-baiting during the 1946 campaign, stating, for example, that his candidacy offered the Wisconsin electorate an opportunity to thwart Communist infiltration in the Democratic Party at home and to foil Soviet expansion abroad. Thus during the primary campaign he observed that LaFollette's opposition to the Connally Resolution "paved the way" for Communism in Poland and "the rest of Eastern Europe."[11]

[8] *The Milwaukee Journal*, November 10, 1946.
[9] *Wisconsin State Journal*, August 9, 1946.
[10] Beloit *Daily News*, October 30, 1946.
[11] *The Milwaukee Journal*, August 8, 1946.

He did not concentrate on the Russian issue, however, until he discovered the liberal vulnerability to anti-Communism.

The issue matured after Fred B. Blair, Wisconsin chairman of the Communist Party, dispatched a telegram to the *Daily Worker* explaining LaFollette's loss to McCarthy in the primary. Blair was highly critical of McCarthy and endorsed McMurray in the election. "The correct emphasis of McMurray's campaign," Blair affirmed, was his attack on LaFollette's "red-baiting and anti-Sovietism." McCarthy, on the other hand, was characterized by Blair as "an open imperialist red-baiter." Warning that McCarthy was "a good campaigner" and would be "heavily financed," Blair recommended "McMurray's candidacy on the Democratic ticket" as affording an opportunity "for the broadest possible coalition of labor and liberal forces to win victories in November." [12]

Ten days after Blair's dispatch appeared, Norman Thomas addressed the forty-sixth annual picnic of the Wisconsin Socialist Party. Assailing Blair's message, Thomas wondered aloud whether McMurray intended to "accept the 'fellow travelers' label" that the *Daily Worker* had pinned on him, or if he was "just hard up for an issue" when he attacked LaFollette's foreign policy.[13] These statements were picked up by two Republican newspapers, the Appleton *Post-Crescent* and the Green Bay *Press-Gazette,* and paraphrased in identical editorials entitled "The Challenge to McMurray." [14] A few weeks later, McCarthy followed suit.

Indicting his Democratic opponent during their joint debate before the Milwaukee League of Women Voters, McCarthy stated that McMurray's campaign was part of a Communist conspiracy to capture the government. Following Thomas' lead, he went on to inquire if McMurray

[12] Quoted in *The Milwaukee Journal,* August 8, 1946, II, 12.
[13] *Ibid.,* August 26, 1946.
[14] *Post-Crescent,* September 5, *Press-Gazette,* September 6, 1946.

welcomed the *Daily Worker's* endorsement. McMurray maintained that he was oblivious to Blair's recommendation, but replied that "if I have the support of the *Daily Worker,* I certainly repudiate that paper and their whole tribe." [15] The following week the two candidates met again in Appleton, and McCarthy reiterated his charge that the *Daily Worker* recommended McMurray's election and considered him a " 'fellow traveler,' meaning a Communist." In addition, McCarthy twitted McMurray for disregarding Norman Thomas' suggestion that he repudiate the *Daily Worker's* endorsement. Again McMurray pleaded ignorance, and attempted to purge himself by repeating his repudiation of Communist support.[16]

Having found Achilles' heel, McCarthy set his teeth firmly into it. It had no doubt occurred to him by now that since the Democrats had been in power during the war, they were much more vulnerable on the question of pro-Communism than were the Republicans. Only three weeks before the November election, he promised to expand his anti-Communist endeavors, and to "make every effort toward removing the vast number of Communists from the public payrolls." [17] Finally, in his last campaign address, McCarthy unveiled his original contribution to the new popular art. Charging that the American people had "been victimized by a seditious serpent which has wrapped us in its conniving constriction until we stand in a perilous position," McCarthy revealed that that "snake is Communism." He then went on to contend that the Communists had penetrated into governmental, industrial and labor circles, and that Russian agents threatened the very existence of the Democratic Party. Of course, he conceded, "all Democrats are not Communists," but there were enough Democrats voting the "Communist way to make their presence in Congress a serious threat

[15] *The Milwaukee Journal,* October 17, 1946.
[16] *Ibid.,* October 23, 1946.
[17] Eau Claire *Leader,* October 16, 1946.

to the very foundations of our nation." McCarthy had found the most "vital issue in America," and considered it his duty to expose the Democratic Party in general, and his opponent in particular, as Soviet agents who disregarded Communist infiltration into federal agencies.[18]

McCarthy's tactics left his liberal opponents in an awkward position. If they accepted his basic assumptions regarding Communism, and merely denied being contaminated by it, they left the initiative with him. This, as McMurray found out, proved ineffective. On the other hand, if they denied his assumptions and attacked him as a myth-maker they would have pulled a major prop from under their Cold War edifice. It was, after all, their myth. Finally, they could refine McCarthy's crudities and turn them back against him. This they attempted to do.

Senator LaFollette had the honor of being the first to accuse McCarthy of being a Communist dupe. Only six days after his primary defeat, in early August, LaFollette rationalized his loss by claiming that his anti-Russian statements had led the "extreme left in the labor movement" into a coalition with the "extreme right in the Republican Party" to assure his defeat.[19] Supporting LaFollette in this piece of premature "mccarthyism," Morris Rubin of *The Progressive* complained that the Communists, "who own the Milwaukee County CIO lock, stock and barrel," had repudiated LaFollette because he rejected their "Russia can do no wrong philosophy." [20]

This counter-attack, conceived, one might charitably say, out of unprincipled desperation, received its first major incarnation in a book by Jack Anderson and Ronald W. May, published in 1952. The authors contend that "Wisconsin Red-complexioned CIO leaders" supported McCarthy against LaFollette because of LaFollette's con-

[18] Janesville *Gazette,* October 30, 1946.
[19] Appleton *Post-Crescent,* August 19, 1946.
[20] *The Progressive,* August 26, 1946, 1. Rubin listed other possible causes for La Follette's defeat, but this was listed first.

sistently anti-Communist record, and that in the primary
the Communists "cranked out reams of hate-LaFollette
literature and rallied the workers behind McCarthy." [21]
This attempt was followed by another book, *McCarthy
and the Communists,* that accused McCarthy of seeking
Communist support in the 1946 primary, and alleged that
the Communists were only too happy to help McCarthy
"to defeat LaFollette, arch-enemy of Communism." [22]
These efforts have been followed by widespread acceptance
of the thesis on the part of liberal journalists. Thus, both
the *Milwaukee Journal* and the Madison *Capital Times*
now view McCarthy's election as the product of an anti-
LaFollette Communist conspiracy,[23] although, as we shall
see, they both know better.

True, the Communists had opposed LaFollette in 1946
after the Senator criticized the Soviet Union's international behavior. LaFollette had accused the Soviets of vio-
lating Polish sovereignty, of disregarding the Atlantic
Charter, and of ignoring their Yalta commitment, concluding that the Soviet Union exhibited the same expansionist tendencies previously practiced by Czarist Russia.[24]
The pro-Communist leadership of the state CIO reacted
sharply to this foreign policy pronouncement, and the left-
wing *Wisconsin C.I.O. News* berated the Senator, suggesting that its readers "take proper action at the next
election" against LaFollette.[25] After LaFollette's defeat in
the primary, the *Daily Worker* commented that "The
People Won't Mourn LaFollette." [26]

[21] Jack Anderson and Ronald W. May, *McCarthy: The Man, The Senator, and the "Ism"* (Boston: Beacon Press, 1952), 104.

[22] James Rorty and Moshe Dector, *McCarthy and the Communists*
(Boston: Beacon Press, 1954), 150.

[23] See, for example, William T. Evjue's comments in the *Capital Times,*
March 3, 1960, where he writes of "McCarthy's courtship of the Commu-
nist support in the 1946 primary," and of McCarthy "campaigning against
La Follette with Communist support."

[24] *The Congressional Record,* Seventy-Ninth Congress, First Session,
May 21, 1945, 5315-30.

[25] *Wisconsin C.I.O. News,* June 18, 1945.

[26] Rob F. Hall, "The People Won't Mourn LaFollette," *Daily Worker,*
August 19, 1946.

However, at the time, the liberal *Milwaukee Journal* also viewed the Senator's anti-Soviet oration as endangering co-operation with the Soviet Union, sabotaging the San Francisco Conference and benefiting "isolationism."[27] Similarly, the conservative *Wisconsin State Journal* opined that LaFollette did not possess sufficient information to indict Soviet policies toward Poland and the Atlantic Charter. Admitting that they were "suspicious of Russia," the *State Journal* conceded that "certainly we have not always played fair with Russia," and concluded that LaFollette's proclamations were "a major factor" contributing to Soviet hostility towards the United States.[28]

Although LaFollette's anti-Sovietism certainly alienated the Communists, the decisive factor in losing left wing labor support was the Senator's decision to dissolve the Progressive Party and return to the Republican fold. As Howard J. McMurray stated during the primary in 1946, LaFollette had abandoned "liberalism" when he repudiated the Roosevelt Administration. McMurray further revealed that Roosevelt had despised LaFollette, commenting to him: "Howard, I've made many mistakes and one of the worst ones was in Wisconsin."[29] Other New Deal elements also criticized LaFollette's invasion of the Republican primary and the Senator's failure to repudiate Robert A. Taft's endorsement of his candidacy.[30] Recommending that labor disregard the senatorial primary, Peter Schoemann, president of the Milwaukee Labor Committee, stated that "an endorsement of Bob LaFollette at this time is an endorsement of the entire Republican ticket."[31] The Milwaukee County Labor Committee, representing the AFL, CIO and railroad brotherhoods, concurred and refused to endorse any senatorial aspirant.[32]

[27] *Milwaukee Journal*, June 3, 1945.
[28] June 4, 1945.
[29] *Milwaukee Journal*, August 7, 1946.
[30] *Capital Times*, May 5, 1946; "Teamsters Ask Bob to Speak Up," Racine *Labor*, June 7, 1946.
[31] *Milwaukee Journal*, June 5, 1946.
[32] *Ibid.*, August 15, 1946.

It was, therefore, not Communist hostility, but the fact, in David Lawrence's words, that "many labor organizations went over into the Democratic Party" that defeated LaFollette.[33]

The Communists, meanwhile, disregarded the Republican senatorial contest and concentrated instead on the Democratic Fourth Congressional District primary in which they supported Edmund Bobrowicz against incumbent Thad F. Wasielewski. Bobrowicz, a supporter of Senator Claude Pepper's and Henry A. Wallace's program of negotiation and accommodation with the Soviet Union, advocated international control of nuclear power and denied that the atomic bomb should be the private possession of the United States. He endorsed the United Nations, supported postwar cooperation "with our wartime Allies," championed Roosevelt's "economic bill of rights," and criticized the alliance of poll-tax Democrats and Northern Republicans.[34] Six years later, Harold Christoffel, former president of Local 248 of the Allis-Chalmers Union, conceded that "the CIO and progressive forces" invaded the Democratic primary to nominate "an entire slate of candidates." Bobrowicz's campaign against "the renegade New Dealer, Congressman Thad F. Wasielewski," furnished the principle incentive behind their intervention in the Democratic primary.[35] Thus, although Communist participation in the Democratic primary undoubtedly diminished LaFollette's strength, there was no conspiracy between their organization and

[33] Appleton *Post-Crescent*, August 15, 1946. At the time William T. Evjue also admitted that labor had abandoned La Follette to return to the Democratic fold. See *Capital Times*, August 14, 1946. McMurray also made this claim. *New Republic*, August 26, 1946, 217. As did Lawrence S. Eklund in *Milwaukee Journal*, August 15, 1946.

[34] *Milwaukee Journal*, August 5, September 20, 1946. Many Communist leaders, including Sigmund Eisencher, Communist candidate for Governor, and his brother Edmund, a photographer for the *Wisconsin C.I.O. News*, circulated Bobrowicz's nominating petitions, and other Communists were active in his campaign. See *ibid.*, September 13, 1946.

[35] Harold Christoffel to William T. Evjue, March 1, 1952, in Evjue's possession.

the Republican machine to prevent LaFollette's nomination.

Bobrowicz's fate after winning the Democratic primary adds an interesting sidelight on the origins of "mccarthyism." One month after the primary, the liberal *Milwaukee Journal* attacked Bobrowicz as a pro-Communist candidate, charging him with having joined pro-Soviet organizations during World War II, with praising the Communist system, and with authorizing Communists to circulate his nominating petitions. Asserting that the candidate had never repudiated his friendship with Communist officials, the *Journal* observed: "Whether Bobrowicz is a card-carrying member of the Communist Party is not vital. In thought and action he has shown himself a communist spelled with a small 'c'." [36]

In reply, the accused candidate described himself as "a New Deal Roosevelt Democrat," denied any affiliation with the Communist Party, and went on to attack the Milwaukee press for practicing the Republican strategy of identifying the Democratic Party with Communism.[37] Nevertheless, the Wisconsin Democratic leadership scurried to a conference with Democratic National Chairman Robert Hannegan, and then repudiated Bobrowicz' candidacy to prove their ideological purity. Among others, Howard J. McMurray, Democratic candidate for the Senate, Daniel Hoan, former Socialist mayor of Milwaukee and Democratic gubernatorial candidate, and Representative Andrew J. Biemiller, censured Bobrowicz for his alleged affiliations. Repudiating Bobrowicz, they endorsed the incumbent Wasielewski.[38]

Despite the Democrats' disavowal of Bobrowicz, and the Party's disavowal of Communism in general, the Communists continued to support the Democratic ticket, even going so far as to withdraw their own senatorial candidate

[36] September 13, 1946.
[37] *Milwaukee Journal,* October 3, 1946.
[38] *Ibid.,* October 2, 9, 1946.

in order to support McMurray against McCarthy.[39] Fred
Blair, the withdrawn candidate, and Sigmund Eisencher,
the Communist gubernatorial candidate, recommended
that "progressive Democrats, former Socialists, Progressives and liberal Republicans" combine with the Communist Party to defeat "reactionary Democrats of the
stripe of Wasielewski or reactionary Republicans like
McCarthy, O'Konski, Kerstan, etc."[40] In addition, Blair
wrote to Evjue of the *Capital Times* to reaffirm the Communists' support of McMurray. Blair conceded that "we
have little use for . . . McMurray, yet," he went on, "we
are not going to be responsible even in a small degree
for [his] defeat." Eight years later, Blair reiterated his
defense of Communist strategy "towards unity around the
candidacy of . . . Howard J. McMurray in the hope of
defeating Joe McCarthy."[41] Clearly, the Communists did
not support McCarthy, but attempted to do whatever they
could to prevent his election.

Furthermore, we have seen that McCarthy did not
originate "mccarthyism." Indeed, before the late Senator
adopted the technique as his own he had observed regular
Democrats using it successfully against a left wing Democrat, and then had watched Norman Thomas use it with
effect against a regular Democrat. Since, at the time, Mc-
Carthy believed himself invulnerable from such attack,
and since all Democrats could, with more or less justification, be smeared in this way, it is not surprising that he
abandoned himself to his new pleasure. The liberal response to this tactic—red-baiting McCarthy in return—is
symptomatic of the moral degeneration engendered by
the Cold War. In its original form, however, it was too
crude to gain wide acceptance. It could not withstand

[39] Fred Blair, "A Political Myth Debunked," Waukesha *Daily Freeman,*
August 9, 1954.

[40] *Milwaukee Journal,* September 14, 1946.

[41] Fred Blair to William T. Evjue, October 28, 1946, in Evjue's possession; Blair, "A Political Myth . . .", *loc. cit.*

comparison to external reality. In its place, the liberals concocted the principle that mccarthyism must be fought, not because it is based on a myth, but because *objectively* it strengthens Communism. McCarthy was branded a tool of the Russians, even though his sincerity as an anti-Communist was no longer questioned. He was attacked for making the United States *appear* less democratic in other people's eyes, for handing the Soviets another weapon in their ceaseless struggle to undermine the posture of American democracy in the uncommitted nations of the world. This sophisticated bit of pragmatic principle has replaced the original, more innocent, lie. It seems destined to remain the last liberal word on the subject.

PART II

AN
AMERICAN
SOCIALISM

The Decline of American Radicalism in the Twentieth Century

BY *Gabriel Kolko*

Volume VI, No. 5
September–October 1966

Gabriel Kolko is the author of several books including The Triumph of Conservatism *(1963), a key book in the development of a new view of the Progressive Era and modern American liberalism. This article argues that the essential failure of the old Socialist movement was its inability to come to terms with the emerging corporate liberal order after World War I. Kolko's thesis complements the general view developed in* Studies on the Left *that the primary failure of the left in the United States has been its own theoretical poverty.*

I

Existing theories on the failure of American socialism in the twentieth century provide ample opportunity for American society to indulge in self-congratulation, and this perhaps explains why no one has defined a truly satisfactory view of the problem. The absorption of third party platforms by major parties, the economic prosperity of a society that met the economic grievances that led to the formation of socialist parties in other nations, the consensual, Lockean basis of an American liberalism which was broad enough to accept the demands of the left, the religious and racial conservatism of the American workers, social mobility, or limited trade union job consciousness—all these generally accepted interpretations have permitted a narrower view than is justified of the nature of the historical context in which American radicalism failed. If each has some merit, their collective thesis by-passes a somewhat less attractive possibility that American socialism failed partly because of its own internal life and ideology, but primarily because in crucial respects American society and politics in the twentieth century have also failed in a world wracked by war and repression. Indeed, given the cataclysmic nature of a great part of the century, tepid views of the demise of socialism avoid the tenor of the period by ignoring the relationship of the failure of organized American socialism to the failure not just of American politics and diplomacy, but also to the intellectual and political collapse of the left everywhere in the Western world. It is worth considering some of the internal and external causes of the decline of American radicalism.

The intellectual and political heritage of Marxism did not prepare the left in America and Europe for the complexities of the twentieth century, if only because, exegetical citations notwithstanding, Marxism and all its later varieties and schools prior to World War I accepted a paralyzing and debilitating optimism which was inherited from the intellectual tradition of the idea of Progress. Defeat as a possibility of long-term, even permanent duration was never entertained, and a social theory that cannot consider this option is not merely intellectually unsatisfactory but misleading as a basis of political analysis and action. Ignoring the intellectual issue of possessing an accurate account of past events, mechanistic optimism led socialists to slight the negative consequences of action or inaction in relation to desired goals, and to try to fit every major event of political and economic development into a pattern of inevitable progression that justified optimism. Such determinism led to quietism, even celebration and opportunism, as socialists everywhere welcomed the events

that led to their undoing. Never was it considered that
societies have options to succeed and to fail in the attainment of desired goals, and that the precarious relationship
of means to ends warranted continuous concern. Social
democracy and bolshevism alike, sharing the premises of
historical liberalism, avoided considering the possibility
of tragic history, a viewpoint that might be based on secular premises but which placed, as the price of success, a
greater burden on superior thought and appropriate social
action at critical junctures in history. The need for decisive action in unpredictable situations had no meaningful place in either socialist, or, after 1918, bolshevik
political strategy, since the normal evolution of things did
not warrant it, and for this reason the paralysis of the left
in the face of reaction before World War I or between
the two World Wars is quite explicable.

The relevance of Marxism to the twentieth century depends less on its function as an inspiration of radical
faith and commitment than its value as an intellectual
system capable of being applied in an elucidating manner
to social reality. After the demise of Austrian socialism
and Rosa Luxemburg it may be argued that, on the level
of social and economic analysis, Marxists produced remarkably little of value, and hence Marxism's function
as an ideology and exaltation of social change was hopelessly limited for the tasks at hand. And since the Western
left in general was theoretically impoverished, it should
come as no surprise that the American left was not much
below the intellectual par of the international movement.
There is nothing "exceptionalist" about the fact that not
one important or original theoretician emerged in the
entire history of American socialism—at best it produced
charismatic figures or men of rare degrees of integrity
admired for their constancy and dedication. Although
American socialism on an organizational level was infinitely weaker than European socialism, what is important
is that Western European social democracy and bolshevism

could never translate mass political movements into political success—in the form of a substantially new social
order—and for many of the same reasons that prevented
the emergence of a serious American left.

What were the intellectual causes of the impotence of
socialism and its failure to develop a dynamic social theory
appropriate to the complicated economic and political
realities of this century?

Marx undoubtedly wished his intellectual system to
serve as the beginning of a theoretical reservoir that his
successors were to continuously apply and amplify, but
the fact is that it was not. What may have been a stimulus
for social change eventually constricted it as the left failed
to keep abreast of the evolution of modern capitalism
and society. This widening gap between theory and reality
often led to the application of nineteenth century premises
to twentieth century conditions, and Marxism became the
deadening burden on the left—the opium of optimism
and certitude Marx assimilated in the prior century disarmed the revolutionists of the twentieth century save,
as in the case of Lenin, where the will to power led to
the abandonment of ideology. The socialists certainly did
not fail because of Marxism, but because their reliance
on a stultified view of it was used to justify action for
which no better rationale was found. Marxism was primarily effect rather than cause, but it failed to correct
opportunism and optimism.

Marx and Engels early took their stand against the
assumption of the utopian socialists that industrial tech-
nology was malleable and capable of decentralized controls and direction by men for their own social purposes.
To Marx and the Marxists the inevitable centralization
and monopolization of industry under capitalism was not
only a prerequisite to a new social order but its best guarantee. Marxists, from the American Socialist Party to the
Mensheviks, dismissed tampering with this inexorable
trend as a hopeless undertaking. After the economic im-

peratives of the system had spun itself into a giant tangled superstructure, capitalism would presumably choke under its own weight and contradictions.

Such an interpretation of the evolution of capitalism logically led to a consideration of the fragility of the economy in the larger social context rather than an inquiry into the extent to which big business might have weaknesses not necessarily involving constant and variable capital, surplus value, or rates of profitability, but rather weaknesses reflecting innovation, decentralization of the market, or the international economy. American socialists, with the possible exception of William E. Walling, hardly discussed the prospects for the economy in a way that hinted that the character and function of the political order might be deeply influenced by the needs of the economy, changing the features of both politics and economics in some decisive fashion requiring a political theory of change superior to Engels' last expression of Marxism. This shortcoming was just as true in Europe among the dominant schools of socialism as it was in America.

It is not unfair to suggest that the parliamentarian and legalist theory of social change which the American and European socialists accepted in theory and practice before the First World War, and that the bolsheviks of Western Europe accepted in practice from the mid-1920's onward, was also a logical outcome of Marxist theory. It would be very easy indeed to catalog Marx and Engels' comments concerning the need for revolutionary action, but both in their response to anarchism and the spectacular electoral triumph of German Social Democracy Marx and Engels eventually opted for left *politics* as the crucial means of social change in the West, and hence implicitly for a liberal political theory that assumed that the political structure, in the last analysis and despite corruption, was a classless tool available to the workers.

The belief in the efficacy of the ballot box and the ultimate neutrality of the state laid the basis for the subsequent parliamentary mechanism, naïveté and failure of Western European socialism. A logical conclusion of this premise was a serious misconception of the functions of the state in the economy and society. American socialists could therefore see state intervention in the economy as a kind of surrogate socialism, perhaps reflecting the interests of small business against big industry, as Walling interpreted it, but an important step toward true socialism. And with their faith in parliamentarianism European socialism was led down the less uncomfortable path of the "politics of responsibility," and an accommodation to a fragile and reluctantly liberal order that failed after 1914 to stem the demise of that system before the challenges of war and reaction. Responsibility to an irresponsible society did in fact lead to the attainment of certain minimal goals in Western Europe—to a kind of welfare state—but the socialist movement failed to reverse the deeply regressive aspects of Western capitalism that periodically expressed itself in crises that threatened to wipe out, and frequently did so, welfarism and much else besides, including the socialists. The view of socialists in America and Europe alike by 1914 was that for all their limitations the existing political forms could be utilized for a clean fight for a clean victory, a victory that would not be borne in terror, struggle and counter-terror. For the new world the socialists wished to create before 1914, the outlines of which Marx, Engels and their successors only vaguely specified, the inherited structural forms were still viable. Both the American and European socialists accepted this assumption.

The vehicle for exploiting this structure was the working class, which in its dynamism, strikes and organizations created in the face of repression and conflict, seemed to be engaged in a continuous process which was, certainly in its American context, best characterized by the term "struggle." The socialists interpreted this struggle as having a revolutionary meaning involving decisive social change rather than limited ends, a confusion that historical experience has yet to prove justified. It seemed inconceivable that this epic of heroism and sacrifice might be directed toward something less than heroic and ennobling goals. The American socialist movement, and certain revisionist schools in Europe as well, also saw the need for winning over men of good will from the middle-classes, classes that had economic problems also driving them to socialism, but in the last analysis the concept of the working class was the core of the theory of change.

Looking at the emergence of new efforts to regulate the economy prior to the First World War, socialists everywhere failed to understand the political-economic process they were living through, a process that was pragmatic, haphazard and hardly comprehended by even its most sophisticated advocates. Nothing in socialist theory, much less *laissez faire* and marginal economic theory, prepared socialists for the possibility that a class-oriented integration of the state and the economy in many key areas would rationalize and strengthen capitalism. This process could only reinforce modern capitalism in a way that not only made Marxian economics obsolescent, but which made democratic social change, and the political instrumentalities supposedly available for that purpose, more remote. In this process of development, socialists, almost without exception in the United States and generally in Europe, misinterpreted capitalism's desire to strengthen itself with seemingly neutral techniques of sophisticated economic planning, techniques which nothing in the socialist intellectual heritage helped them to understand and which by their endorsing helped lead to the almost willing demise of the left. Like orthodox advocates of *laissez faire,* many socialists believed that state intervention in the economy was a step toward socialism.

II

Yet the distinctive American causes for the failure of socialism and radicalism in the twentieth century also deserve reconsideration. These causes were both external to the organized socialist groups, rooted in the unique character of the larger social order, and internal, reflecting the special qualities of parties and their followers.

The political and intellectual history of the Socialist Party, much less the Communist Party, is far better described and understood by historians than that of perhaps either major party over a similar period, and this fascination with causes that have failed rather than those that have succeeded affords me the luxury of generalizing on the thorough research of others. The genesis of American socialism until 1900 was colorful, like an intellectual hothouse, but not more so than that of the British Labor Party, which was at least as exotic. Socialism as a cause touched every interesting intellectual current—Christians who saw in polite socialism a way to bring a piece of heaven to earth, funny-money advocates seeking deeper solutions than free silver, cooperative colonization groups, led by Eugene Victor Debs, that could appeal to John D. Rockefeller as a "Christian gentleman" to bring the frontier opportunities back to America, discontented intellectuals seeking to end the alienation of industrial society, followers of Edward Bellamy's Nationalist movement, and, of course, the Marxist-oriented elements that were to effectively dominate the party after 1901 when the Socialist Party was formed out of an amalgam of various groups.

The internal world of the Socialist Party until 1912 was not unlike that of German Social Democracy, from which it absorbed many of the doctrinal positions of both Eduard Bernstein's revisionist school and his seemingly left critics. The Party was not merely partially German on ideological issues—borrowing from the Bernstein-Kautsky debate was a convenience, not a cause—but also in the classic bureaucratic sense described by Robert Michels in *Political Parties*. From this viewpoint the Socialist Party was a party of functionaries, officials and an elite quite impatient with rank-and-file democracy and dissent. The Party, like most pre-World War I European Social Democratic parties, was bolshevik in structure though fairly democratic in organizational theory. Later in 1919 the men who controlled the Party before the war were to expel the vast bulk of the members for their support of bolshevik theory as well, just as they had expelled the embarrassingly non-parliamentarian Industrial Workers of the World faction at the 1912 convention. The Party had never actively sought to enlist the vast slum and industrial working class, and in purging the IWW it broke with its already minimal pre-war mass working class contacts. It was, to cite Trotsky's unkind but apt remark, a party of dentists, and always remained so at the leadership levels.

The middle-class character of the majority of Socialist leaders reflected their belief that the middle-class and skilled workers were the most promising for membership, and this unconsciously required a crucial conformity to dominant prejudices, assumptions that guaranteed that the political strength of the Socialists could never exceed the nine hundred thousand votes of the 1912 election unless the Party radically altered its tactics—which it never did. In the area of trade unionism the Party always maintained its primary contacts with the AFL, which at this time was the most conservative major union in the world.

The position of the Socialist Party on civil rights and racism was hardly designed to win support from the Negro community either. Before the war the Socialist Party tolerated within its ranks social segregation, the exclusion of Negroes from Southern white locals and theories of racial superiority. The Party passed only one resolution on Negro rights—a weak one—between 1901-12. Anti-Oriental prejudice was common as well, and on this question, as well as the larger issue of immigration restriction, the Party followed the conservative, even reactionary leadership of the AFL.. It made little effort before the war to enroll immigrants or to publish sufficient non-English materials, and what little was produced in this field was generally from local and individual initiative.

The expulsion of the IWW in 1912 soon cost the Party an important minority of its 125,000 members, but new circumstances were nevertheless to result in a victory for its left wing. The Party lost most of its intellectuals to the pro-war cause, but its intransigent position against the war—until 1917 there was nothing unique about its neutralism—attracted vast electoral support. In the 1917 municipal elections it increased its percentage of total votes received from three to eight times by campaigning on an anti-war platform, its vote being considerably greater in areas with large Yankee populations. Indeed, by 1919 the Party's membership was almost restored to its 1912 peak, but the complexion of that membership had radically altered. Thirteen per cent of the Party belonged to foreign language sections in 1912, fifty-three per cent in 1919. The Socialist Party had moved to the left for the first time, had become a party of immigrants, and was making significant electoral gains.

Although internecine disputes have wracked the Socialist Party since 1919 and would have destroyed it in any case, it is worth noting that at the very moment American Socialism appeared on the verge of significant organizational and political success, it was attacked by the combined resources of the Federal and various state governments. Elected candidates were denied their seats in Congress and various state assemblies, immigrant leaders were deported under the Espionage and Sedition Acts, numerous leaders of the Party were jailed, newspapers were denied mailing privileges and otherwise harassed, and in many localities the club, lock and prison ended Party activity. If the Government used war and patriotism as justification, it should be recalled that leading progressives, with rare exceptions, also supported the Red Scare and repressive laws for reasons always implicit in pre-war progressive ideologies. Progressives wished to integrate the labor and immigrant community into an ordered, homogeneous society, and they feared socialism might be the consequence of their failure to do so. Roosevelt had never equivocated on the use of force against dissident labor, and consistently endorsed major infractions of the civil liberties unions and their leaders. Progressivism to men such as Roosevelt was designed, among other things, to head off the threat of socialism by reforming capitalism. The United States Steel Corporation, accepted by Roosevelt as a model of enlightened business, could introduce both welfare measures and Pinkertons when needed. In brief, if labor could not be voluntarily integrated into the social order by good works, it was to be tailored to size by chopping off its unmanageable left by any means appropriate to the task, including suppression. Only when one takes this equation into account can we comprehend the near unanimity of pre-war reformers in favor of Wilson's Red Scare and the Espionage and Sedition Acts.

In a sense the failure of American radicalism was due, at least between 1917 and 1920, to the failure of American politics to operate according to the conventionally accepted but rarely practiced ideal theories of democratic political processes. American Socialism was unable to appreciate the limitations this breakdown might have for their own concept of change, a view that remained static until it was too late. To the extent the true character and the efficacy of a political structure is revealed only under the test of pressure and crisis, it can be suggested that Socialists shared a generally-held sublime innocence concerning the resilience of American democracy during crises. For Socialists this naïveté was decisive, since their stake in the validity of existing mechanisms of change was vital—for others, the fixity of the political machine merely reinforced their interests in the status quo.

Looking at American society and politics before the First World War the Socialists could see a class structure as an objective fact, and sufficient tumult and noise within it to impute to it a seemingly dynamic aspect. Such dynamics could be measured, and if amplified held out hope of vindicating the socialist theory of change. Classes, strata and competing interests were recognized by Marx, though he neither created them nor was he the first to discover their existence. Since politics was based ultimately on conflict, the class context of such conflict might lead to decisive social change. Yet one other possibility existed which socialists refused to consider, but which Thorstein Veblen had proposed before the war. American society could also be understood as a class structure without *decisive* class conflict, a society that had conflict limited to smaller issues that were not crucial to the existing order, and on which the price of satisfying opposition was relatively modest from the viewpoint of the continuation of the social system. In brief, a static class structure serving class ends might be frozen into American society even if the interests and values served were those of a ruling class. A sufficiently monolithic consensus might voluntarily exist on the fundamental questions indispensable to the continuation of the existing political and economic elites, and their primary interest would be respected in the last analysis. The functionally dominant conception of interests, the prime values of the society, did not have to be essentially classless, as Louis Hartz and recent theorists of consensus have argued, but merely accepted by those segments of society without an objective stake in the constituted order. This, I believe, was the point that Veblen was making, not in order to rationalize the dominance of business in American life but to explain the extent of its obvious spiritual and material pervasiveness.

The best argument for such an interpretation is the fact that at no time in American history in this century has the labor movement or the dispossessed translated their struggles for specific demands into a larger demand for fundamental change. The mythology of American society as one that welcomes opportunity and equality for all—as if a vaguely defined rhetoric is more realistic than a frank appreciation of the functionally inegalitarian and class nature of America—extends not only to labor, but even to civil rights activists who seek entry of the Negro into a society that is inherently stratified and class-oriented in decisive ways having nothing to do with race. And if everyone does not share this consensus consciously, and indeed even if the majority neither agrees nor disagrees but is apathetic on such matters, the least that can be said is that no one has been able to redirect such apathy toward a meaningful alternative. Indeed, even the apathetic usually permit the consensual ideology of American life to be defined for them during times of crisis and pressure, and they accept erstwhile national goals which are in fact class goals and interests. The apathy itself proves less than the fact that conscious deviations from manipulated consensual values have been roughly disparaged in this century as "Hunism," "pacifism," "bolshevism," or what have you, suggesting that although voluntary most of the time, the power of legal authority has also reinforced and defined consensus to save society from dangers the possibility of functional democracy posed to the existing order.

The failure of the Socialist Party, therefore, also reflected the consensual and voluntarily accepted total domination of American political ideology, an ideology that was conveniently described as classless, and in recent years as the end rather than the total triumph of ideology, in order to reaffirm the ideal view of the neutral, free and untrammelled nature of the political mechanism. American radicals accepted this mythology and tried to play the game according to rules that were quite irrelevant to social and political reality, a reality that was obscured until the exercise of nominal political rights threatened to become unmanageable and Red Scares, the manipulation of electoral laws and the like were required to reinforce a consensus that was equivalent to class domination. And since the force of challenges to this control was rarely very great, and the American left was usually incapacitated by its own internal weakness, the true character of politics as a means for confirming and legitimizing the existing order was rarely revealed. For the American left to regard this historical experience frankly would also have required a willingness to reorient their descriptive social theory and their concept of change. To consider the union movement as wedded to reform capitalism would have called for a less reverent, flexible view of labor. To regard the electoral structure as free only when it was not exercised would have demanded new tactics, tactics which also might have been inappropriate in light of the seemingly pervasive support for the social order by those with the smallest stake in it. That the society might have been, quite voluntarily and even happily, functionally totalitarian in its monolithic character would have required the rejection of the political optimism of the nineteenth century, an optimism that not merely rationalized unimportant gestures that constituted a make-believe world of democratic rhetoric concealing controlled politics, but also offered the left some hope of eventual success. That success was perhaps unobtainable in a game so completely loaded required a realism that bordered on a willingness to accept a tragic view that possibly involved writing off America as an arena for social progress in the twentieth century.

And rather than consider these unpleasant alternatives the American left after 1919 continued in its ritual acts of self-destruction.

One of the more common interpretations of the failure of the American left—defined to include both the Socialist and Communist Parties after 1919—ascribes its demise to the success of American capitalism. This view might make sense applied to a period of full employment, but for a decade after 1929 both the left and the larger social structure in which it operated had failed, and well before the New Deal reforms allegedly stole its thunder and presumably impinged on its basic demands, the Socialist Party was quite dead. It existed, of course, but never as a serious factor in shaping American politics or labor unionism toward some socially meaningful new departure. What it called "life" was a factional precociousness that sharpened the polemical talents of its brighter young followers, talents many were later to employ to their own advantage as key spokesmen for anti-communism after the Second World War.

The leaders of the Socialist Party during the 1920's fell into quieter, bureaucratic ways, managing their existing institutions, building their private careers and maintaining a doctrinal purity which was by this time well to the left of that prevalent in the pre-war party. The Communists, despite their anti-parliamentarian rhetoric, ran their first Presidential candidate in 1924, and differed only slightly from the Socialist Party in their functional political premises. The Communist Party too was primarily a party of recent immigrants, and during the 1920's its amoebic internal life kept it preoccupied with Trotskyists and Lovestonites. Though it created its own organizational forms for the purpose, it duplicated the union and other activities of the Socialists. In brief, just as Social Democracy was bolshevized into bureaucratic channels before the war, Bolshevism was being social democratized toward parliamentarian and unionist directions after 1924 in a way hardly designed to create a new order where others had failed.

The divisions in the Socialist Party after 1933 do not

warrant much consideration. Factors having to do with
age, politics or psychology kept the Party in factional
turbulence to the extent that from twenty-two thousand
members in 1934 it dropped to seven thousand in 1938
and two thousand in 1941, and has not exceeded the last
figure since that time. During the 1930's the majority of
the Socialist Party's members were foreign-born or first
generation, and this pattern of immigrant domination was
even more widespread in the Communist Party. In this
context both parties became a kind of fraternal center—
the majority of the literature of the Socialist Party was not
in English—for lonely migrants who might raise funds at
banquets for the Scottsboro boys but were essentially adjusting as best they could to a strange, new life. What was
ultimately more important to such leftists was the con-
viviality of the banquet hall and comrades who spoke the
mother tongue. These activists might also finance the
work of the more earnest younger men who were wholly
committed to politics as they defined it and, especially in
the case of the Communists after 1935, might be caught
in the euphoria and passion of organizing the CIO, going
to Spain or participating in student movements. Even
when the Communists lost their capacity to attract the
young and the earnest they could still, even in the worst
days of McCarthyism, retain their banquet hall followers
whose social roots were grounded in the activities of the
IWO or other organizations—aging and bewildered people who were transformed in the social imagery into con-
spirators posing a serious danger to society.

The intellectual problems of the Socialists and Communists in America were very much like those of their
associates in Europe. Throughout the 1930's the European
left was fighting a losing, rear-guard battle and drifting
along with the capitalists toward a world conflagration.
The left was characterized by futile efforts to respond to
the initiatives of reaction. The Western European left,
the Communist Parties included, was incapable of break-

ing out of the mold of a parliamentarianism no longer resilient enough to provide the decisive leadership necessary for social change capable of stopping the tide of the Right. "Socialism" from this time onward became merely another, more technically sophisticated way of managing an effete European capitalism, and after the Popular Front period, and especially during 1944-47, the Communists frequently shared in this game by courting respectability via cabinet posts in France, Belgium and Italy, an effort that frequently made the practical domestic function of the Communist Party in Western Europe indistinguishable from that of the Social Democrats and liberal centrist parties.

It may perhaps be suggested that in fact the institutional and economic heritage of Western capitalism limited the European left, and hence doomed it to failure. If so, the left in both Europe and America never seriously acknowledged the dilemma, but persisted in giving obeisance to socialist doctrines that molded their political action to a concept of change. The dominant political leaders of these movements rarely contemplated that the left was participating in the strengthening of capitalism. This lack of reflection characterized the American left even more than the European, for here there was no intellectual core capable of grasping these dilemmas.

III

The sins of the Bolshevik left after the Second World War are well documented, so much so that the history of the American Communist Party in all its dimensions has become a major, well financed and thoroughly debilitating concern which has been both a cause and reflection of the demise of the American left. In its worst aspect it suggested that the Communist Party was an important experience in post-World War I American history, just as paranoid McCarthyites had suggested. At best it was a dialogue with McCarthyism on terms and issues defined by that movement, critical only insofar as it applied higher canons of evidence. This concern engaged an articulate sector of the non-Communist Party left that implicitly regarded a discourse on an unimportant and impotent party as a more serious undertaking than a confrontation of basic social and political questions. Indeed, the issue of the Communist Party gave the left an excuse to postpone and ultimately avoid dealing with the much more significant and difficult issues facing it in an age of nuclear terror.

It was not unexpected that the non-Communist left might focus so closely on the Communist Party, since anti-Communist had become a categorical imperative of American life, and a way for the left to integrate itself with the larger assumptions of their society and perhaps make itself more plausible. Succumbing to the mood of the times, even while proclaiming a higher if not clearly defined morality, the American left gradually took over even more of the crucial assumptions of conventional politics, aligning itself with the more liberal wings of the Cold War in the hope, quite as chimerical, that it would succeed with the liberals in a way it had not been able to do with the workers. Turning an astringent eye on the faults of the bolsheviks, the post-war left could not recognize its own, much less see that their moral defects were very much in the same category as those it attributed to the bolsheviks. Both had lost critical perspective toward their favorite side, neither had anything new to say in regard to the American scene and its mechanics of change. The Eastern European situation was described by the socialists in the blackest detail, but little was said, for example, about the actions of French socialist ministers who in Indo-China, Madagascar and Algeria committed horrors on behalf of an old order that paled those of bolsheviks groping their way against resistance toward

new societies. The moral distinctions that were evoked
on behalf of anti-Communism were obscured when it was
necessary to give critical support to the West.

Such policies were a logical concomitant of social democratic biases, but not entirely conscious. With the exception of those who gave up socialism for sociology and a
technical precociousness which produced formal structural
theories with less historical relevance than even hobbled
socialist theses, American socialism of the non-Communist
variety was characterized by a pervasive dilettantism.
Crucial political judgments were made on the basis of the
most casual information, and a precise focus on the institutional operation of society, politics and foreign relations
was just as lacking as before the war. Socialism as an intellectual system became, for the most part, impressionist
and literary, which added a sensitivity to subtle problems
in only a few areas. Alienation and mass culture—the
former had been a familiar complaint of radicals for decades—were deemed worthy of closer inquiry than economics or diplomacy. The post-war left preferred taking
its insights from political novelists who, for all their perception, saw the world through a looking glass that obscured important distinctions that could be defined only
by viewing society directly. A mediocre novelist such as
George Orwell was far more influential than considerably
more intelligent social scientists, and his success was based
on the political favor with which his views were held.

Once socialists regarded totalitarianism, much less bolshevism, as a cause of the world crisis, rather than as the
effect of the collapse of liberalism and Western politics,
it was possible for socialists to enlist, with reservations that
did not change their basic commitment, in the cause of
the "Free World." The results were catastrophic. American radicals soon found themselves cutting the edge of
their criticism and explicitly acknowledging the community of interests and assumptions with American
politics and society that had always been implicit. In this

position they were at a premium, their talents and books overpraised as they titillated a jaded and casual upper middle-class professional audience. A few might sincerely maintain a semblance of critical integrity by dissecting marginal aspects of American life and politics, aspects that if altered would leave the larger society intact, but by 1952 no important neutralist or third-camp foreign policy position could be found among articulate radicals. And what was never willingly tolerated, above all, was a hard, dispassionate, uncommitted look at the competing worlds, their attainments as well as their shortcomings, much less a searching view of the foundations of American society and its purposes and historic role in the post-1945 crisis. Stronger claimants to intellectual and literary importance who failed to accept these premises were isolated or ignored by upper bohemia and the intellectual set connected with universities and the "cultural media." Only the subterranean world of the beats and isolated renegades claimed Kenneth Patchen; Europeans published Karl Korsch, who built a major reputation in France without ever being acknowledged in the country he resided in the last twenty-five years of his life; the anti-Communist left read but also reviled C. Wright Mills. The post-war generation recognized the need for new ideas, and the call for the application of intelligence became a static posture, but little more. Intelligence was rarely applied to specific American issues in a way that increased knowledge, and studies of Communism failed to alter this deficiency.

In the name of humanism, socialists in the United States gradually but firmly aligned themselves with the American cause in the deepest political and cultural sense—Castro, the Vietminh and the victims of the post-war world crisis became first as guilty as their potential executioners, as culpable morally, and then deserted in a manner that increasingly absolved the executioners. The impact of the Western resistance against revolutionary movements, especially in Eastern Europe and China, was rarely considered in evaluating the social systems that emerged. Again victims were condemned for their responses to the crimes of their executioners, as if the Cubans, Vietnamese and Chinese had chosen with deliberate malice to violate a humanist tradition they too evoked and claimed to act upon. The power of the old orders to shape the form of the new systems, and what was transitional or permanent, defensive or deliberate in the synthesis was never considered. Economic development as a justification of their action was dismissed as narrow economism, as if economic development were worth nothing. The losses involved in such a process were carefully examined, but never weighed and balanced against the gains, particularly in those areas that had precious little intellectual freedom or political democracy to lose. Growth rates and their distribution struck many as meaningless, and for *litterateurs* as uninteresting. That the difference between bolshevik totalitarianism with bread, and capitalist totalitarianism without bread, is the elimination of hunger, filth and death was gainsaid. That a dynamic society that ends starvation is freer in a crucial sense, and saves far more life than it may willingly or unwillingly destroy, is a point that was never confronted, even when politically meaningful options to the *status quo* or controlled planned economies did not exist.

To have considered these questions would have meant a rupture between the non-Communist American left and the social order to which it had accommodated itself. To re-examine the political context of socialism closely might have meant a new and sympathetic alignment with forces throughout the world that have rejected the hegemony of American leadership, and it would have meant a return to isolation and discomfort. By the end of the 1950's the left which emerged from the Socialist Party tradition of the 1930's was incapable of making this adjustment. For fifty years the American left, because of ideological roots and optimistic belief in the efficacy of transforming the

existing order, had been grounded in the acceptable
myths and premises of the existing order. In the context
of the world conflict, to refuse to align itself with the
United States would have been equivalent to breaking the
illusion of being political men with a political future. To
assume otherwise would have been to take the unenviable
and pessimistic position that radicalism, given the social
and political realities of America, had moved beyond
politics not because it had no political ideas but because
it finally acknowledged it had no political means. The
left would have been beyond politics not because politics
is unimportant, but because the control and exercise of
power is nominally democratic but in reality voluntarily
totalitarian. To refuse to support the American cause
would have shattered the last illusions concerning the
nation's ability to tolerate dissent which does not choose
to mark out areas of agreement on fundamental assumptions.

Instead radicals sought to remain politically "relevant"
at the expense of their ability to protest against injustice
emphatically and negatively. They found it necessary to
argue for the existence of a viable political structure in
the hope description would eventually assume the nature
of self-fulfilling prophecy, even if their description of the
political process sounded strangely similar to those of the
academic schoolmen who confused liberal rhetoric with
reality. At no time did they attempt to articulate a sense
of history which generalized on the consistency in United
States' policies at home and abroad, for this could only
lead to seeing the politics of liberal rhetoric as a trap, and
the pessimistic consequences of such a realization were not
considered to be worth the loss of the assumption, if not
illusion, that radicals were still free agents of potential
power in a situation that was plastic and retained cause
for hope.

The failure of the left by the end of the 1950's did not
eliminate the need for a left, nor did their forced opti-

mism alter the graver realities which underlay American
domestic affairs and foreign policy. That a "New Left"
should have emerged was both predictable and logical,
and that it should have all-too-many of the characteristics
of the older left should not be surprising. Its factionalism
is debilitating, and its view of the Negro and poor is not
unlike that of the old leftists or Wobblies who cultivated
illusions concerning mass industry or migrant workers.
There is no serious awareness that modest gains for the
Negro and poor may make far-reaching success, the prerequisite of permanent social change, impossible. A society
that is poisoned produces poisoned responses and men,
and those who do not succumb to these pressures may find
themselves a very small minority of the white and black
community—a rare minority of principled radicals with a
commitment that is not likely to gain followers in the
milieu of aborted movements of progress.

The New Left has had the political courage to challenge the politics of the status quo, though it too frequently hopes that the existing political mechanism may
somehow be applied to serve its own radical ends. But it
has not asked sharp or relevant questions concerning the
intellectual premises of the old left, and has merely rejected its chronic anti-Communism and myopia concerning the liberals in the Democratic Party. To succeed
intellectually where the old left failed, the New Left will
have to find fundamentally new and far-reaching premises,
premises that are not obsequious in the presence of the
ghosts of the eighteenth and nineteenth centuries. And to
succeed politically it must find dynamic possibilities and
forces of movement in a social order in crisis, forces it
must frankly acknowledge may not exist as permanent or
decisive factors for social change. Having rejected the
conservative, futile politics of the old left, the New Left
has yet to define a solid alternative, much less begin to
create it.

Given the consensual basis of American politics and

society in the twentieth century, and the will of the beneficiaries of consensus to apply sufficient force and power
at home and abroad when resistance to consensus and its
hegemony arises, the New Left must confront the prospect
of failure as an option for radical, democratic politics
in America. Rational hopes for the twentieth century now
rest outside America and in spite of it, and the least the
American political and intellectual resistance may do is to
encourage the efforts of those elsewhere who have more
options than we to build a new democracy and society.
At best a New Left may only be able to define a new
intellectual creed at home which permits honest men to
save their consciences and integrity even when they cannot
save or transform politics. This little cannot be gainsaid,
for we have yet to win even this, and once this much is
obtained perhaps there will be a realistic basis for a new
politics that may yet eventually emerge.

Socialism's Hidden Heritage: Scholarship Reinforces Political Mythology

BY *James Weinstein*

Volume III, No. 4
Fall 1963

This review-essay was written before the publication of James Weinstein's The Decline of Socialism in America, 1912-1925 *(1967) and represented his view of the limitations and weaknesses of previous work done on the history of American socialism.*

Since 1952, when Princeton's two volume study of *Socialism in American Life* appeared, a small stream of histories of American Socialism and Communism has fitfully trickled forth.* Ira Kipnis and H. Wayne Morgan have examined parts of the Socialist Party experience; Irving Howe and Lewis Coser, Theodore Draper and James P.

---

* Daniel Bell, "The Background and Development of Marxian Socialism in the United States," in Donald D. Egbert and Stow Persons (eds.), *Socialism and American Life*. Princeton. Princeton University Press. 1952.

James P. Cannon, *The First Ten Years of American Communism*. New York. Lyle Stuart. 1962.

Theodore Draper, *The Roots of American Communism*. New York. The Viking Press. 1957. And *American Communism and Soviet Russia*. New York. The Viking Press. 1960.

Irving Howe and Lewis Coser, *The American Communist Party: A Critical History (1919-1957)*. Boston. Beacon Press. 1957.

Ira Kipnis, *The American Socialist Movement: 1897-1912*. New York. Columbia University Press. 1952.

H. Wayne Morgan, *Eugene V. Debs: Socialist for President*. Syracuse. Syracuse University Press. 1962.

David A. Shannon, *The Socialist Party of America*. New York. The Macmillin Company. 1955.

Cannon have done the same for the Communists; and David A. Shannon and Daniel Bell have dealt with both movements. In all, these books have made available a great deal of information. Three or four of them are invaluable for the interested student. Yet they reveal only this: there was a thriving socialist movement in the United States before the First World War; by the mid-1920's, at the latest, it had become an exotic collection of sects; in the 1930's it failed to utilize the unprecedented opportunities presented to it to build a meaningful movement for socialism in the United States.

What these books fail to do is explain what went wrong. In large part this is the result of glossing over the central problem of the change in the nature of the movement for socialism in the United States that took place in the years from 1918 to 1924. There are two reasons for this. (1) All the books, except Daniel Bell's essay, are party histories. (2) The historians of the early Socialist Party have been incapable of transcending their own memories of, and relationships to, the faction-ridden movement of the decades following 1920.

The initial conception of these histories as party histories obscures the central problem in American socialist history—why, during the years of the crisis of American capitalism (1929-1940), the socialist movement failed to surpass its pre-1919 vigor and mass following. It would seem that historians would be interested in this central question if they are interested at all in American socialism. Instead we are treated to histories which end in the middle, or begin there. In fact, there is even one (David A. Shannon's *The Decline of American Communism*) that begins at the end, in 1945.[1]

Despite the unfortunate consequences, it is easy to see how such histories were conceived. The Socialist Party grew to its maturity and exerted its maximum influence

---

[1] In fairness to Shannon it should be noted that it was not he but Clinton P. Rossiter, editor of the Ford Foundation series on American Communism, who is responsible for this chronological atrocity.

before the communist parties were organized. By 1925 it had all but ceased to exist as a propagator of radical consciousness. The communist parties, on the other hand, were not organized until 1919. They did not cause so much as a ripple on the political surface until most of them were reorganized into the Workers' Party in December 1921. They did not make a significant impact on American politics until well into the 1930's. By the time the Communist Party began to influence American society the Socialists had long been isolated from their earlier sources of support and had developed anti-Soviet attitudes out of keeping with the popular mood of the time. Since the periods of ascent of the two movements were discontiguous, and since communist inspiration and ideology were more closely connected to the Russian Revolution than to American radical traditions, it was not unnatural for historians to view the two movements as subjects for separate treatment.

But even if the Communist movement is viewed as something that sprang *de novo* out of the revolutionary euphoria of the New International in 1919, its real significance, especially during the first five years of its existence, lies in the impact it exerted on the overall movement for socialism in the United States. And a *party* history cannot deal adequately with this subject, as the Draper and the Howe and Coser books attest. Draper correctly notes (in the introduction to his second volume) that the key period in Communist history is the first decade of the Party's life. It was then that American Communism assumed the characteristics it was to retain throughout its existence as a party. And yet, although the interaction with the Socialist Party and with the various labor and farmer-labor parties of 1919-1924 is a vitally important part of the history of the early communist parties, it is examined from only one side both by Draper and by Howe and Coser.

In both studies, of necessity, the farmer-labor movements are underestimated, their politics and ideology misunderstood; and in both the Socialist movement of the 1920's is hardly mentioned at all. From the other side, Shannon's history of the Socialist Party does no better with respect to the farmer-laborites, and, of course, Shannon virtually ignores the communists.

Perhaps the most unfortunate result of these approaches is that the Labor Party movement of 1919, and the farmer-labor party movements—in Chicago, Minnesota, Washington, New York, and elsewhere—of 1920-1924 are nowhere treated adequately.

While the form of these party histories leads to fragmentation of the radical past, the myths and traditions of post-1920 radicalism (in which our historians are hopelessly entangled) blur the distinction of the periods before and after that year. Thus we have a series of projections into the pre-1920 period of the characteristics of the movement in the years that followed. Two ubiquitous errors ensue: an obsession with the factional disputes of the pre-split movement, which is pictured as narrow, isolated, and divided into irreconcilably hostile factions; and a concept of left and right wings analogous to those in Europe during the First World War.

Thus our historians under review tend to treat left *versus* right as a conflict between worker and petit bourgeois, of industrial unionist *versus* craft unionist, fighter for equality *versus* racist, anti-war *versus* pro-war; in short, they view the left as true to traditional socialist principles and the right as opportunist. But few such polarities existed. The differences between left and right in the old Socialist movement were frequently rhetorical, more of mood than of substance; and where they were of substance they were as often the opposite of what one would expect as not. On a question such as land tenure, for example, the left wing Texas and Oklahoma Socialists[2] favored

___

[2] The Texas and Oklahoma Socialists considered themselves left wingers and have been treated as such by Bell, Kipnis and Shannon. They were

private ownership of small farms, whereas Victor Berger
espoused the traditional Marxist position of collective
ownership of the land. Again, on the question of centralization of party organization the left stood for local
autonomy, and Berger, Hillquit, and their followers for
increased authority for the National Executive Committee. This line-up was not unrelated to the fact that before
1917 the right had control of the national organization;
nevertheless it is directly contrary to the post-1919 positions on this question. On other issues, such as the war,
there was no more militant spokesman for what has come
to be known as the left position of opposition than Berger,
whereas many leading leftists, as we shall see, supported
American participation.

This is not to say that there were no meaningful
divisions in the pre-war years. But even where these
existed, communication and genuine debate characterized
relations among the various groups within the Party, and
the groups themselves remained amorphous and fluid. In
the pre-World War I period of the party's ascendency,
irreconcilable differences crystallized only around the
related issues of syndicalism and the use of sabotage. This
occurred in 1912 and 1913, when the Party placed a constitutional ban on the advocacy of crime, sabotage, or
other methods of violence, and later recalled William D.
Haywood from his position as a member of the National
Executive Committee of the Party after he advocated
sabotage at a public meeting.
These events, along with Debs' strong showing in the
1912 presidential elections, have led to another misconception: that 1912 was the watershed of American Socialist
history. Ira Kipnis, for example, projects the futilitarian

---

allied with other leftists in the party, with the Christian Socialists and
with Debs. At the time of William D. Haywood's recall from the National
Executive Committee in 1913 Texas Socialists voted more heavily in Haywood's favor than those of any other state.

nature of the post-1919 socialist movement back into the
pre-war period in an apparent attempt to obviate the
necessity of explaining what happened in 1919 and after.
Kipnis has gone so far as to end his book, called *The
American Socialist Movement,* at the year 1912. At that
time, he asserts, overcome by opportunism, racism, and
lack of inner-party democracy, the Socialist movement
started on an irreversible decline.

It is true, of course, that if any one year can be considered the high point of American Socialism it is 1912. But
that does not mean that 1912 was a great divide; for
neither in its internal development nor in its impact on
American society did the movement change significantly
then, whereas it did in 1919. Contrary to Kipnis' thesis,
left activity and strength increased after 1912, despite the
departure of several thousand IWW sympathizers following Haywood's recall. By 1917 the various left tendencies
were clearly in the ascendancy.

In trying to force the facts into his thesis, Kipnis makes
several serious errors, both theoretical and factual. For
example, he equates Haywood's pseudo-syndicalism with
industrial unionism. The majority in the Party opposed
Haywood's advocacy of dual unionism and sabotage; Kipnis uses this as evidence to imply that it opposed industrial organization. In doing so he tends to lump Debs and
Haywood together, whereas in fact Debs strongly opposed
the IWW and its dual union activities after 1910.[3] As the
Party's Information Department commented in 1915, all
Socialists believed in the industrial form of labor organization, although they disagreed with the IWW as to the
best method of bringing it about.[4] Indeed, not only was

[3] See, for example, "Debs Denounces Critics," *International Socialist
Review,* XIV, 2 (August 1913), 105.
[4] The IWW and the Socialist Party (Socialist Party Information Department, January 13, 1915); See also *The Christian Socialist,* May 16,
1911, for the Christian Socialist Fellowship endorsement of industrialism;
and *The Rebel,* May 16, 1914, for the endorsement of the Texas party of
industrialism.

Debs an industrial unionist, but in New York Hillquit's main strength after 1914 came from the newly organized Amalgamated Clothing Workers, while in Milwaukee Berger's basic support came from the Brewers. Both unions were industrially organized and Socialist-led.

Debs did disagree with Berger and Hillquit, as well as with Max Hayes, Duncan MacDonald and others, over whether socialists should work within the AFL; but the issue here was one of tactics, and on this question Debs had little to offer after 1908 when he dropped his membership in the IWW. In 1914 Debs made a last attempt to act as a catalyst in the formation of a new federation of industrial unions—after Charles Moyer of the Western Federation of Miners proposed a merger to the United Mine Workers. However, when the UMW turned a deaf ear to the ailing metal miners union, Debs' pleas became mere rhetoric. In the end, Berger was vindicated in his program of working within the AFL in order there to agitate for socialism, even though this approach came to naught after the war for other reasons.

In the period from 1912 to 1917 (which, according to Kipnis, is one of swift disintegration), Socialists in the AFL succeeded in winning the leadership of the state federation of labor in Pennsylvania and Illinois, and maintained their leading positions in Wisconsin and Missouri. Furthermore, they retained their strength in such international unions as the International Association of Machinists, United Mine Workers, Western Federation of Miners, Brewery Workers, Quarry Workers, Typographers, in addition to gaining control of the Ladies Garment Workers and organizing the Amalgamated Clothing Workers Union in 1914.

In attempting to prove his thesis Kipnis falls into more narrowly factual error, too. Thus as evidence that the National Office of the party lost concern over unionism and the working class Kipnis asserts that it stopped giving aid to strikers after 1912. His figures are $21,000 donated in 1912, $400 in 1913, nothing in 1914. In fact, the figure for 1914 was $39,428.41, donated to the coal miners of Ludlow, Colorado, and the striking metal miners of Calumet, Michigan.[5]

More serious because it involves the omission of a great deal of accessible evidence is the treatment Kipnis gives the attitude of Socialists toward Negroes (racism), and toward women. He attacks the "center" and "right" for racism, and for opportunism in relation to women,[6] and states or implies that the Party became worse on these questions as time went on, causing the decline after 1912. (pp. 305, 278.) As his own evidence shows, however, the attitudes of Socialists toward Negroes and women cannot be correlated with their adherence to right or left wings. Moreover, and of greater significance, Kipnis presents no evidence that his speculations are valid after 1910. In fact, directly contrary to his thesis, women played an increasingly important role in the Party after 1910, and the Party as a whole became more active in behalf of suffrage.[7] In 1910 Lena Morrow Lewis was elected as one of the seven members of the National Executive Committee of the Party. In 1912 Kate Richards O'Hare was elected, and in 1916 Anna Maley followed her. Further, the Socialists were instrumental in helping win the adoption of suffrage in Nevada in 1914 and in New York in 1917.

Similarly, Kipnis stops his inquiry at the point the Party begins to develop interest in the Negro question. Again, his last evidence to prove that the Party was the victim of opportunism after 1912 is something that hap-

---

[5] Condrad F. Nystrom, "Socialist Corner," *Galesburg* (Illinois) *Labor News,* June 25, 1915. See, also, *The Appeal Almanac and Arsenal of Facts for 1915* (Girard, Kansas, 1915), p. 62, which gives a total of $33,075.46 for 1914.

[6] It is true that some right wingers were unabashed racists, as was Victor Berger; but Kipnis presents his evidence in such a way as to indicate increasingly racist attitudes, whereas the process was the opposite.

[7] Kipnis does attempt to cover himself on this by admitting that women were more active in the fight for equal rights after 1910, although "with little aid from the male members of the party." (p. 265)

pened in 1910. And again, the Socialists displayed increasing interest in the organization of Negroes after 1912. This is not to argue that the Party's understanding of the Negro question was adequate to conditions, but only that one cannot explain the decline of a movement in terms directly contrary to the direction of its development.

Another error Kipnis falls into is his involvement in the cult of proletarianism and his acceptance of the popular myth (which grew up in the 1930's) that the right wing and center Socialists—that is, those concerned with electoral victories—were middle class, and that the left Socialists were working class. (pp. 307-11, 361-64.) In this Kipnis is not alone, but is in the tradition supported by Debs' biographer, Ray Ginger, who wrote that Socialists elected to public office "were mainly ministers, lawyers and editors,"[8] and by such a recent historian as H. Wayne Morgan, who, writing in 1962, could agree that Socialist officeholders were no more than reformers and were dominated by "writers, professionals, lawyers or newspapermen." (pp. 120-121.)

In reality, trade unionists or ordinary workers filled a majority of the public offices held by Socialists in the years from 1912 to 1920. A survey of the occupations of Socialist state legislators, for example, shows that of the sixty-three individuals for whom there are available biographies, sixty-two per cent were workers at the time of their election or had been for most of their lives.[9] In regard to municipalities the evidence is spotty, but information from some twenty cities (of a total of about two hundred where Socialists elected officials between 1911

[8] *The Bending Cross* (New Brunswick: Rutgers University Press, 1949), p. 207.

[9] Socialists filled 131 state legislative posts from 1912 to 1920, but because many served more than one term only 80-85 individuals were elected. The sixty-three whose biographies are available do not include seventeen legislators elected in Idaho, Kansas, Montana, Nevada, New Mexico, Oklahoma, and Utah. If these were included it is likely that the percentage of workers and farmers would be higher.

and 1920) indicates that in the smaller towns and cities
most Socialist officeholders were workers, while in the
larger cities there was a tendency to elect ministers or
professional men to the highest offices. Thus, for example,
in Star City, West Virginia, the Socialists elected an administration comprising a carpenter, a laborer, and five
glassblowers for four successive terms (1911-1915), while
in Schenectady, New York, the mayor (George Lunn) was
a minister and the president of the council (Charles P.
Steinmetz) a well-known physicist (1911, 1915). Socialist
administrations were most often elected in small or me-
dium-sized railroad, mining or industrial centers, and
when the mayor was not a worker or trade unionist himself others in the administration often were. Thus in
Butte, Montana, where the Socialist mayor was a minister,
the police judge elected with him in 1913 was a miner.
And in Lackawanna, New York, where the mayor's occu-
pation is unknown, the councilmen elected with him
(1919) were trade unionists. Similarly, in Davenport,
Iowa, a doctor was elected mayor (1920), but his city clerk
was a machinist. Of course, in Milwaukee a majority of
the councilmen and administrative officials were workers
and active trade unionists. And in Minneapolis Thomas
Van Lear, the Socialist mayor (1916), was a business agent
of the International Association of Machinists.[10]

More important than the social class from which the
Socialist elected officials came, however, were their attitudes toward workers, and particularly toward the use of
the police power during strikes. Here, even the middle-
class mayors violated the stereotyped expectation. Actively
pro-labor, these Socialist administrations aided the unions

---

[10] The Socialist mayor in Beatrice, Nebraska (1911) was a teamster, in
Flint, Michigan (1911), he was a cigar maker, in Conneaut, Ohio, (1913)
a railroad conductor, whose director of public services was a day laborer;
in Frontenac, Kansas, (1917) a railroad trainman; in Massilon, Ohio, (1919)
a tinner. In Berkeley, California, on the other hand, the mayor, (1911,
1913) was a minister, J. Stitt Wilson; and in Los Angeles the candidate
for mayor in 1911 and 1913 was an ex-minister and lawyer, Job Harriman.

in many ways. One of the first acts of the Socialist mayor of Eureka, Utah, for example, had been to arrest and fine a Pinkerton man for carrying a concealed weapon.[11] More substantial was the approach of Marshall E. Kirkpatrick, Socialist mayor of Granite City, Illinois (1911, 1913, 1917), a railroad and metal processing suburb of St. Louis. Kirkpatrick wrote that during strikes, neutrality on the part of the city administration was impossible, and that he had chosen to be true of his socialist principles and support the workers. This could almost always be done, he asserted, by using the police power simply to allow a "fair fight." During a strike of three hundred metal workers, Kirkpatrick refused a company request for police protection in running scabs through the picket line.[12] Similarly, during the Paterson textile strike of 1913, when the IWW strikers were refused permission to speak in Paterson, the Socialist mayor of nearby Haledon invited the workers to hold their meetings on his territory.[13] And during the IWW strike in Little Falls, New York, Mayor Lunn of Schenectady helped organize a Relief Committee, which supplied the nearby strikers with money, food and clothing. This was gratefully acknowledged by William D. Haywood who praised the Socialist office-holders for their active support.[14]

In short, none of Kipnis' reasons for the rapid decline of the Socialist Party after 1912 stand up. This, however, should not be too surprising since the thesis of rapid decline is itself invalid, as we shall see.

Kipnis, of course, does not deny the viability of socialism as a political movement in the United States, but

[11] J. W. Morton, "How the Socialists Governed Eureka," St. Louis Labor, November 8, 1913.

[12] St. Louis Labor, October 25, 1913. For a similar incident during a garment workers strike in Milwaukee, see Kipnis, op. cit., 361.

[13] Alexander Scott, "What the Reds are Doing in Paterson," International Socialist Review, XIII, 12 (June 1913), 854.

[14] William D. Haywood, "On the Picket Line," International Socialist Review, XIII, 7 (January 1913), 522-523.

simply argues that because of opportunism, that is dis-
loyalty to socialist principles, the movement steadily de-
teriorated after 1912. Daniel Bell agrees that after 1912
the road for American Socialism was steadily downhill,
but he implies that this happened because of the irrelevance of socialism within the context of a society dominated by Wilsonian liberalism.

In his essay on Marxian Socialism in the United States
Bell raises important questions, although he fails to come
to grips with them. It is true, as he points out (p. 216),
that although the depression of the 1930's represented
American Socialism's great opportunity, no socialist movement emerged. And he is correct in seeking the reason in
the nature of the movement, rather than in general conditions. The problem, however, is not a narrowly ideological one, as Bell makes it; or, rather, if it is essentially
ideological, the question of how the particular ideologies
developed must still be answered. Bells' thesis is that the
Socialist movement, because it rejected capitalism, "could
not relate itself to the specific problems of social action
in the here-and-now, give-and-take political world." (p.
217.) This means, if it means anything, that American
Socialism never was a viable political movement, and that
whatever fleeting popularity it had was the result of
fortuitous circumstance. But the existence of a viable political movement with deep roots among workers and
farmers in the pre-World War I days (when conditions
were much less favorable for a socialist movement than
in the depression years) threatens Bell's thesis. Thus the
rapid decline of the movement after 1912 becomes a
necessary condition for the logical validation of the entire
thesis. Ideologically, Bell solves this predicament by at-
tributing the success of the pre-World War I movement
to Debs' romanticism and messianism, which worked until
the war "finally broke through the facade." [15] Historically,
he goes to great pains to show that "the eclipse of Amer-

[15] *The End of Ideology* (Glencoe: The Free Press, 1960), p. 276.

ican Socialism took place in 1912"; that "the rest of the
years were a trailing penumbra." (p. 291.)

While Bell's logic may not be bad, his history is. One
of his most striking illustrations in support of the 1912
thesis is the assertion that of the two hundred sixty-two
periodicals (Bell's figure) published in 1912, only forty-
two remained in 1916. (p. 313.) The figures are wrong at
both ends. First of all, there were three hundred twenty-
three socialist periodicals publishing in 1912, of which
two hundred sixty-two were English language weeklies.[16]
Of these, however, over one hundred fifty should be discounted at the outset, for this number, according to National Secretary John Work, were cooperatively published
papers, a highly transitory experiment in socialist journalism that lasted no more than three or four years.[17]

For example, one socialist cooperative publishing company in Iola, Kansas, printed fifty-nine such papers at its
plant in 1912.[18] By early 1915 so many had dropped off
that the company ceased publishing socialist papers.[19] By
late 1916 only three of the original fifty-nine weeklies survived.

Assuming the experience of the Iola company to have
been typical of cooperative publishers, about ninety-five
per cent of the one hundred fifty-odd cooperative papers
should be discounted from Work's figure of three hundred

[16] "Report of National Secretary John Work to the 1912 Socialist Convention," Socialist Party, Proceedings of the National Convention, 1912,
p. 221.

[17] Designed to allow even the smallest Socialist local to publish its own
paper while returning a profit to the cooperative publishing house, the
undertaking quickly failed. In Arkansas, for example, the Party Secretary
complained in 1913 that owning their own papers had "left the locals
busted financially," had "drained the movement without returns," and
had left the comrades "sore." (Ida Callery to Carl D. Thompson, Bonanza,
Arkansas, June 5, 1913, Socialist Party Papers, Duke University.)

[18] List included in a letter from M. F. Wiltse to Carl D. Thompson,
Marshalltown, Iowa, June 4, 1913, S. P. Papers, Duke.

[19] J. H. Bard to Carl D. Thompson, Iola, Kansas, March 2, 1915. Not
all the papers had failed, but enough to make it unprofitable to continue,
Bard wrote.

twenty-three for 1912. If this is done, about one hundred eighty non-cooperative papers remain. I have found one hundred eighty for 1912, and of these I have verified that one hundred sixty remained in business in 1916 or had been replaced by others. The rate of decline of the non-cooperative papers of which traces remain, in other words, was about eighteen per cent, compared to ninety-five per cent for cooperative periodicals. But the general rate of decline of American weekly newspapers in the years from 1914 to 1920 was about twelve per cent.[20] The performance of non-cooperative socialist papers was only slightly worse than that of commercial papers in these years.

This distortion of fact is not an isolated instance. Bell also tells us, for example, that during the war "the final blow, perhaps," was the party's "loss of the *Appeal to Reason*" (p. 313), which switched to support of the Administration in December 1917, following Wilson's enunciation of the principles to be contained in his Fourteen Points. What Bell does not tell us is that even during the remainder of the war the paper did not attack the Party, and that by early 1919 it had repudiated its pro-war stand and was able to distribute a special issue of 900,000 copies in support of amnesty for Debs. After rejoining Socialist ranks and initiating a campaign for the nomination of Debs and Kate O'Hare for President and Vice President in 1920 the *Appeal* boasted of its return to the "old revolutionary spirit." [21]

In general, in the years from 1912 to 1917 Socialist strength and organization seem to have remained stable. Gains were made in some areas, losses suffered in others, but no substantial downward trend is observable. In municipal elections, for example, Socialists elected fewer officials in the years after 1911.[22] This, however, was often

[20] Edwin Emery and Henry Ladd Smith, *The Press in America* (New York: Prentice-Hall, Inc., 1954), pp. 514, 517.

[21] *Appeal to Reason*, March 1, 8, May 24, 1919.

[22] 73 mayors in 1911, 8 in 1912, 32 in 1913, 5 in 1914, 21 in 1915, 5 in 1916, 18 in 1917.

the result of fusion against Socialist administrations—so that a majority was required where a plurality had previously sufficed. Or it was the result of the adoption of a commission or manager charter, which had the same effect as fusion.[23] In Milwaukee, for example, the Socialists elected a mayor with a little over a third of the vote in 1910, but lost to fusion despite an increase in the party's poll in 1912 and 1914. Not until 1916 did the party gain an absolute majority in that city. Similarly, in Granite City, Illinois, the party elected mayors in 1911 and 1913 in three-way contests, lost to fusion in 1915, and won a majority in 1917. In many other cities, especially in Ohio, the party increased its vote in the years after 1911 despite losses of office.[24]

In elections to state legislatures, on the other hand, the Socialists improved their showing after 1912—from twenty legislators in nine states in 1911-1912 to thirty-three in fourteen states in 1913-1914, twenty-nine in nine states in 1916-1917, and thirty-two in four states in 1918-1919. After 1912, also, the Party extended its influence to new areas. In 1915, for example, Socialists won several offices in the South, including the election of one of three commissioners in Birmingham, Alabama. In 1916 the Socialist trade unionist, Thomas Van Lear, was elected mayor of Minneapolis, and in that year in Nevada the Socialist candidate for United States Senator polled thirty per cent of the vote, losing to Key Pitman by only three thousand votes. Space does not permit a more detailed recitation of the evidence, but it must be said that the facts simply do not coincide with Bell's description.

If there was no precipitous decline in Socialist strength or influence between 1912 and 1916, the war years emerge

[23] See James Weinstein, "Organized Business and the City Commission and Manager Movements," *Journal of Southern History*, Vol. XXVIII, No. 2 (May 1962), 77.

[24] In Dayton, Ohio, for example, the party won 25% of the vote in 1911 and elected two councilmen and three assessors. In 1913, after the adoption of the manager charter, the Party increased its vote to 35% and elected nobody. Again in 1917 the Party polled 44% and elected no one.

as the crucial period in which Bell's thesis must stand or fall. Indeed, to protect himself Bell appends to his "trailing penumbra" the dicta that by opposing the war the Party embraced a "policy bordering on adventurism," and thereby "isolated itself completely from the mainstreams of American political life." (p. 328.)

It is, of course, impossible to refute Bell's assertion in a few sentences, but some observations are mandatory. First of all, Bell is not alone in this thesis. Indeed, it is shared by all historians who have commented upon the Socialists in this period. Even Shannon, for example, accepts this general proposition, although he takes note of the great increase in the Socialist vote in Northeastern cities in November 1917. (pp. 104-105.)

On the surface there is much to support the idea of Party decline during the war. By opposing the war the Party lost some of its best known members, it was cut off from access to the leadership of most trade union internationals, its newspapers were banned from the mails, its leaders were jailed and hounded by local, state and federal agents, and its members were assaulted, and even lynched by various private groups—organized and encouraged by loyalty leagues, chambers of commerce and other patriotic bodies. Yet, the Party remained intact, lost few members (from 83,000 in 1916 to 74,000 in 1918), greatly increased its vote everywhere in 1917, and in those places where its organization was intact in 1918, and it was able to keep its newspapers going and even to increase circulation where it was physically possible to publish. This should indicate that its position in opposition to the war was not unpopular.[25] What happened immediately after the war should be even more persuasive. In the first four months of 1919 Party membership rose to 107,000, the *Appeal to Reason* came back, and scores of trade

[25] For a description of the 1917 and 1918 election campaigns see James Weinstein, "Anti-War Sentiment and the Socialist Party, 1917-1918, *Political Science Quarterly*, Volume LXXIV, No. 2 (June, 1959), 215-239.

unionists attacked the administration for its actions and explicitly or implicitly endorsed the Socialist wartime positions. In Illinois, for example, John H. Walker, a pro-war Socialist who had resigned his membership and attacked the Party as traitorous during the war, was replaced as president of the State Federation of Labor by Duncan MacDonald, a loyal Party member.

In his first presidential address, MacDonald bitterly attacked the Wilson administration for its hypocrisy in presenting the war as having been one for democracy. Nor was his address an isolated example. Rather it was indicative of widespread disillusionment with the war, and of a climate of opinion entirely consistent with Socialist analyses of the war. When the war ended, in other words, the Socialists found that a great reservoir of goodwill waited only to be tapped. It never was tapped, but that was not because Socialist wartime policy had bordered on "adventurism."

The latest treatment of pre-1919 American Socialism, H. Wayne Morgan's *Eugene V. Debs: Socialist for President,* is essentially derivative and narrative. It is, of course, welcome that the Debsian tradition should be kept alive and that students should be reminded of the once vital movement. But Morgan's book serves primarily to set the attitudes and myths embedded in Bell's, Kipnis', and (to a lesser degree) Shannon's histories into an even more rigid pattern. The book is organized around Debs' five presidential campaigns from 1900 to 1920, and deals also with the one campaign in these years in which Debs was not his party's candidate—1916, when Allan Benson led the Party ticket. Covering the entire span of the Socialist Party's vitality, Morgan touches upon all the major developments and issues of these years, and might have provided a useful introductory guide to American Socialism. As it is, he has uncritically accepted Kipnis' description of increasing factionalism within the party, as well as his picture of growing middle-class domination, and has also adopted Bell's view of the increasing irrelevance of Socialism in the face of Wilsonian reform.

Morgan is at his worst in dealing with the war and its aftermath, here going beyond the errors of his predecessors. He observes that the "stresses and strains introduced by the Russian revolution . . . were the final straws that broke" the Party and led to its decline. (p. 142.) But he goes on to show that he understands neither the issues involved nor the process by which they developed. For example, Morgan takes Shannon's speculation (p. 91) that "perhaps" Benson's emphasis on anti-preparedness in 1916 "played right into the hands of the advocates of preparedness" (which opinion Shannon supports with an equally speculative quote from the pro-war leader of the National Civic Federation, Ralph M. Easley), and makes the flat assertion that "Benson played into the hands of the preparedness supporters, who now used him as a scapegoat." (p. 151.) But within the Party Benson's position on anti-preparedness was so popular that his series of articles in opposition to it in *The Appeal to Reason* won him the nomination, despite the fact that he was previously virtually unknown. And outside the Party, opposition to involvement in the war was so great that in order to defeat Hughes Wilson found it necessary to campaign as the man "who kept us out of war," despite his distaste for that appellation.

Again, after noting Socialist gains in November 1917, Morgan asserts that the large anti-war vote was "more a protest vote than a socialist vote," by which he means a protest against the violations of civil rights by the Wilson Administration. But the increase in the Socialist vote began too early to attribute it to protest against the suppression of socialist newspapers and the prosecutions under the Espionage Act. In April 1917, for example, Socialists scored heavy gains in such places as Chicago, Rockford, Granite City, and Sylvis, Illinois, Duluth and

Two Harbors, Minnesota, Sheboygan, Wisconsin, and Frontenac, Kansas, in all of which mayors or new councilmen were elected. Of course, these gains were minor compared to those of the fall primaries and the November elections, but they were all clearly based on Socialist opposition to the war. And all these elections took place before the first oppressive acts of Postmaster-General Albert Burleson.

Morgan's errors concerning the popularity of the Socialist position on the war reveals an amazing ability to misuse evidence. Thus, to show that the Party's position was unpopular, he recounts the membership figures for 1916 through 1921. These show an increase from 83,284 in 1916 to 104,822 at the end of 1918, and a decline to 26,766 in 1920. Morgan asserts that the rise in 1918 was "due to the specially-created foreign language federations," implying that these were organized in that year, when in fact they had all affiliated in the years from 1911 to 1915. (It is true that most of the increase in membership came from foreign born, and particularly Russian immigrants, who flocked into the Party after the revolution in Russia, but no one has yet demonstrated that English-speaking membership declined in 1918.) And, of course, the great drop in membership after 1918 was the result of the split of 1919, and had nothing to do with the Party's wartime popularity. Finally, Morgan places the Palmer Raids of January 1920 before the split of September 1919, and implies these were directed against the Socialists when in fact they were aimed at Communists and IWW's in the main.

Furthermore, Morgan does not fully understand the attitude toward the Soviets of Debs or his party. The basic issue between Socialist and Communist in 1919 and 1920 was not "the status of the new communist state in Russia," as Morgan asserts, but the assessment of revolutionary prospects in the United States. The split took place on this issue, with the Communists accepting the dicta of the New International that the revolution in the West was imminent (as well as necessary to the survival of the Soviets), while the Socialists insisted that American capitalism had emerged strengthened from the war, and that there were no immediate prospects for revolution in the United States. The question of anti-Sovietism did not arise in these years except insofar as the International defined anyone who opposed immediate insurrectionary programs as objectively anti-Soviet. Debs understood this difference, although he was not always clear in his expression of it. He was essentially anti-Communist, even though pro-Soviet. His refusal to become a Communist had nothing to do with what Morgan calls his inability to "go all the way in his radicalism." (p. 167.) Rather it was the result of his understanding that the way in which American radicals could best fulfill their international responsibilities was to maintain the integrity and health of the American movement for socialism. In making these errors Morgan is in good professional company. But this is precisely the danger of relying on the existing secondary works.

The histories of the Communist Party suffer from many of the same weaknesses as the Socialist, as well as from some of their own. Of the three works under consideration here, Draper's is the most substantial, and the only one which is destined to remain indispensable for any serious student of American Communism. Draper covers the first ten years of the Communist Party's history in two volumes, *The Roots of American Communism,* and *American Communism and Soviet Russia,* and he plans to carry the story to 1945 in future volumes. In dealing with the Communist Party (or parties) itself, that is with the years after 1919, Draper's work is almost entirely original, his research meticulous and painstaking, and his thoroughness likely to overwhelm the casual reader. Draper's books are most useful in tracing out the factional developments within the Party, as well as its relationship to the International and to developments within the Russian Communist Party in the 1920's during Stalin's rise to power.

The weakest part of Draper's study is his attempt to trace the pre-communist roots in the American Socialist movement during the World War. Here he falls into many of the worst errors of his predecessors, and commits a few of his own.

His treatment of the war follows the popular myth of left intransigence and right acquiescence. He misunderstands the meaning of the joint authorship by Hillquit and Ruthenberg of the St. Louis Declaration against the war, seeing it as a maneuver on Hillquit's part, rather than as representing a genuine consensus of party opinion. He calls Victor Berger pro-war, and misunderstands the meaning of the vote of the New York Socialist aldermen for the war loan in 1918. He writes that the "Left Wing" might have stood out more clearly as "the only one to live up to the letter and spirit of the St. Louis resolution" had it not been for government attacks. (p. 95.) And he gives as an example what he describes as the one left-led mass demonstration against the war—that in Boston in early July 1917 where some eight thousand demonstrators were attacked by a mob and hundreds of the demonstrators arrested.

In this section Draper's facts and interpretation are all incorrect. Berger and the Wisconsin movement were most consistent in their anti-war activity. Indeed, Ludwig Lore himself, an editor of what Draper calls the "theoretical magazine" of the new "Left Wing," (p. 87) wrote after the November 1918 elections that "the aggressive attitude of the Socialist movement of Wisconsin under this [Berger's] leadership" had "very much to do with" the "splendid" showing of the Wisconsin Socialists in the 1918 election. Lore believed that despite Berger's "many sins of omission and commission," he should have been in Congress during the war, where "he would not have been afraid to speak out against the government whenever the interests of the Socialist and labor movement demanded it."[26] Again, the vote of the Socialist aldermen in the spring of 1918 resulted from a general state of confusion in Socialist ranks after the Russian Revolution and the continued German advances into Russia. Not only the "right wing" aldermen, but such leftists as Max Eastman and Eugene Debs expressed confusion and advocated crushing the Germans. True, Debs quickly reversed his ground, but so did most of the others. And, in any case, the motivation of the right was precisely that of the left— to defend the revolution in Russia.

Finally, Draper's implications that the left was the only wing to lead mass demonstrations against the war, and that the Boston demonstration was the last of these, are both incorrect. Meetings of protest against the war of five thousand to ten thousand people were common throughout the summer and fall of 1917 in Minnesota, Ohio, Wisconsin, and other states, and they were led both by left wingers and right—in Minnesota, for example, by the left wing farmer, J. O. Bentall, and the right wing Machinist, mayor Thomas Van Lear of Minneapolis. Draper asserts that despite the breakaway of the open pro-war group, "closer examination" reveals the same cleavage in the American Party as existed in the ranks of European Socialism. But closer examination reveals something entirely different: that there is no meaningful correlation between left-right positions and pro- or anti-war attitudes or actions. Right wingers such as Berger, Hillquit, James H. Maurer, and many lesser figures were in the forefront of anti-war activity, while left wingers such as Rose Pastor Stokes, Frank Bohn of the *International Socialist Review*, William English Walling, Jack London, and others supported the war. Indeed, when Ruthenberg campaigned against the war the *Cleveland Plain Dealer*

---

[26] Ludwig Lore, "The Elections," *The Class Struggle*, Vol. II, No. 5 (December 1918), 621.

attempted to indicate how militant he was by describing him as "The Hillquit of Cleveland."[27] And in New York, where Hillquit ran for mayor on an anti-war platform, he was bitterly opposed by Henry L. Slobodin, a former left wing stalwart whose articles in the *International Socialist Review* had often complained of the lack of principle of the right wingers.

If Draper fails in his attempts to recreate in the United States the wartime pattern of European Socialism, his efforts to find organized secessionist movements within the Party are no more successful. He asserts that after 1912 the Left Wing (which he incorrectly capitalizes) "became a stranger in the Socialist house," (p. 48) and attempts to trace the development of an organized Left Wing within the Party, especially from 1915 to 1918. To do this Draper relies heavily on the Socialist Propaganda League, organized in Boston in 1915, on *The Class Struggle,* which began publishing in May, 1917, and on *Revolutionary Age,* an organ of the Boston Left in 1918-1919.

But, as we have seen, the left was not a stranger in the house at all after 1912. Instead it occupied more and more of its rooms. This was admitted by the old left winger, L. E. Katterfeld in July 1915 in connection with the seating of the "radical" party delegates from Texas and Michigan at a National Committee Meeting. This action, Katterfeld wrote, symbolized the reversal of the "trend toward centralization" of 1912-1914, and reflected the fact that although many leftists had resigned their membership following Haywood's recall, the Party contained "more clear-cut revolutionists than ever before," and was "sound to the core."[28] There were, of course, individuals and some small groups whose connection to the Socialist Party was tenuous or non-existent, and it is these that

[27] November 3, 1917.
[28] "The 1915 National Committee Meeting, *ISR*, July 1915, 56-7.

Draper inflates to the position of a meaningful seccessionist or pre-secessionist movement within the Party. His treatment of the Socialist Propaganda League, organized in Boston in 1915, is a case in point, for (as Draper shows) the League was the creature of the Lettish Federation in Boston, and the Lettish Federation, although affiliated with the American Party, still functioned as a branch of the Latvian Socialist Party. Its ties, in other words, were with Europe and with the Left Wing there. Its contacts and influences either in the American party or in American politics were few and slight. Similarly, Draper's heavy reliance on Louis Fraina (later known as Lewis Corey) as a central figure in the formation of the American Communist Party reveals the marginal nature of the self-conscious left. As Draper tells us, Fraina was a member of the Socialist Party for six months when he was fifteen (in 1909), and although he rejoined in 1917 after war had been declared, his ties were not strong, nor his influence widespread.

Draper's difficulties here are tied up with his treatment of what he calls "the literary left." (p. 48.) First, he made the point that the "Left Wing expressed itself in publications outside official Party control," as if this situation were peculiar to the left. In fact, all major Socialist publications were privately published. Indeed, before 1914 there was no official Party organ, and after that, until May 1917 when it was suppressed by the United States Postmaster-General, there was only one such journal, *The American Socialist*. In his treatment of *The Class Struggle* as the "theoretical magazine" of the "Left Wing" Draper compounds the error. To speak of a "theoretical organ" of a capitalized Left Wing is strongly to imply that a communist-style organization—that is, a sectarian faction as we know such groups today—had been created within the Socialist Party in 1917. But *The Class Struggle* was no such organ. It published articles by the right wing "reformists" James O'Neil, Florence Kelly, Adolph

Germer, National Secretary of the Socialist Party, and Joseph Whitehorn, Socialist state assemblyman in New York. Further, for a short period Debs himself was an editor, at least nominally, of *The Class Struggle*. Of the original editors, Louis Boudin, Louis Fraina, and Ludwig Lore, one (Boudin) did not become a Communist, another (Lore) remained not unfriendly to old right wingers such as Berger almost until the split occurred, and the third, who really was an ideological predecessor of the Communist Party, had few roots and little, if any, influence in the ranks of the Socialist Party. At the end of his chapter on "The Left at War," Draper writes of the need of the left to be led "from the Wilderness of Left Wingism to the promised land of communism"; but this was a need no one felt at the time. The "promised land" of the left was control of the Socialist Party, which meant simply deposing Hillquit and Berger from the leadership. As late as June 1919, only two and a half months before the split, the new Left Wing voted two to one against secession and for "capturing the Socialist Party for revolutionary socialism." (p. 167.) And this was several months after the new Third International had called upon the Left to follow the lead of the Bolsheviks and form their own (Leninist) party.

The search for ideological and political predecessors of the Communist Party is a valid enterprise, and in a book examining the roots of American Communism the inflation of such antecedents is perhaps preordained; but the distortions inherent in the undertaking are unfortunate. The point is not that American Communism had no ideological or political forerunners among radicals in the United States. It *is* that there were no issues dividing the Socialist Party that arose from the American experience. The only question over which the left and "right" were irretrievably opposed was that of immediate insurrection, and on that issue the left received its ideas from the new

International. That is why the split was almost entirely
along lines of national origin. The overwhelming bulk of
Socialists who quit the Party to form the communist
parties were not only foreign born but recent immigrants
from Eastern Europe—Russians, Latvians, Ukrainians,
Lithuanians, Hungarians, South Slavs, and Poles—all of
whom were much more cognizant of conditions in their
homelands than of those in the United States. That is also
why the outstanding leaders of the left in the Socialist
Party, Eugene Debs and Kate Richards O'Hare, remained
in the Socialist Party.[29] It is true that several lesser American left wing leaders joined the language federations in
splitting the Party, but this was partly because of the
manner in which the old guard defended its position of
leadership, and partly because of the enhanced prestige
these leaders gained by being elevated into the top leadership of the new movement. Draper's weakness in dealing
with this latter group of leftists is not in what he has to
say of them as individuals. By and large he does this very
well. But in trying to uncover a substantial historical
secessionist movement in the Socialist Party he distorts the
nature of the Party prior to late 1918.

One thing more. Draper's treatment of the pre-Communist movement within the old Socialist Party leads him
to consider the new parties "a new expression of American
radicalism," which by later seeking Russian help in the
solution of American problems was perverted into an
"American appendage of Russian revolutionary power."
(p. 395.) But if these parties were in fact an appendage of
the Russian revolution they were that from the beginning.
Draper demonstrates that the Communists became more

[29] The best known left winger to join the Communists was C. E. Ruthenberg, and he was a leader of the Cleveland local, not a national figure
in the sense that Debs or O'Hare were. Other local leaders, such as Emil
Herman, an old-time left winger, state secretary of the party in Washington, as well as a former member of Herman F. Titus' group (which included William Z. Foster and Alfred Wagenknecht), remained in the
Socialist Party following the split.

and more dependent on the Russians for the month to month functioning of the Party in the years from 1919 to 1929, but this is not the point. Given the manner in which the party originated, at Russian urging over an issue on which the old-line Socialists were right and they were wrong, it was inevitable that the Communists become increasingly dependent upon the new Socialist state. After all, the only political capital the Communists had during most of the 1920's (it was also a liability at times) was their position as the "recognized party." Thus, at the time of the split when Alexander Stoklitski attacked the so-called right wing it was for failure to adhere to the new International's call for insurrection, rather than because of a demonstrated possibility of successful insurrection in the United States. And in 1924, when Harry Wicks called on all dissidents to rally to the Worker's Party it was not in terms of the demonstrated ability of the Worker's Party that he argued. He relied, rather, on the threat that failure to do so would lead to isolation from the world Socialist movement. For the Party to oppose the will of the International, in other words, would have been to deny itself its reason for existence.

The balance of Draper's two volumes, that part dealing with the communist parties after 1919, is extremely useful. Draper has reconstructed the events of these years with care and with substantial accuracy. The major weaknesses are a result of the limitations of the scope of the books—of their being Party histories. Here Draper occasionally misinterprets the meaning of particular policies. Most noteworthy is his treatment of Communist participation in the Farmer-Labor movement in Minnesota in 1924. Draper writes of the role of the Communists in pushing for a convention in St. Paul to form a national farmer-labor party as one which caused great confusion, since the Conference for Progressive Political Action had already called a convention for July 4, 1924, at which

LaFollette was expected to be nominated. But the Communists were far from alone in their support of the Minnesota convention and of a new farmer-labor party. The CPPA, under the leadership of the railroad brotherhoods, had made it clear that it would not start a third party, but would only consider running a third candidate. Further, until William Gibbs MacAdoo was smeared with the oil of Teapot Dome in February 1924, Edward Keating, editor of *Labor,* and many other railroad leaders favored him over LaFollette, who was the choice of the Minnesota movement from the beginning. There was considerable support for a class party among non-Communist farmer-laborites not only in Minnesoto, but in the Dakotas, Montana, Nebraska, Wisconsin, Washington, and elsewhere. The Communist policy of supporting a separate convention to nominate LaFollette and form a party of workers and farmers was not a sectarian maneuver, as Draper says, but was highly successful until reversed, despite strong opposition from the leadership of the Nonpartisan League, the railroad brotherhoods, and Samuel Gompers and the AFL apparatus.

There are a few other instances where Draper's work suffers from an overdeveloped concern with proving the dependence of the American party on the International and the determination of the International to run the American party. For those interested in the history of American radicalism, as opposed to Communist antiquarianism, more attention to the effects of Communist policies on the general left in the United States—as well as the extent to which events in the United States helped mold Communist policies—would have been more valuable. As it is, Draper's history will be most useful to historians as a source book, to ex-Communists wanting to know how the Party developed into what it was in the 1930's, or to Socialists in search of sticks with which to beat upon the dead horse. For the general reader it will probably prove to be a little too much of an inside job.

In contrast to Draper, Irving Howe and Lewis Coser have written a one-volume history of the Communist Party that covers the whole span of its vitality—1919 to 1957. This, too, is essentially an inside history of the Party, one that, as the last chapter indicates, is largely concerned with developing "a theory of Stalinism," rather than with the examination of American radicalism. As a result it is not surprising that the best parts of the book are the earlier chapters. Howe and Coser repeat many of the errors common to other Socialist histories in their brief description of the early Socialist Party, but they are very good in the section dealing with the split of 1919, and in the early chapters on the Communist Party. After 1924, when Stalin began his consolidation of power, Howe and Coser became increasingly obsessed and self-righteous. Although their account is informative up through 1945, it becomes more and more polemical and enmeshed in Cold War presentism. This is particularly apparent in their treatment of the Wallace movement of 1948, where non-Communist opponents of the Cold War are described as men whose mental habitat is in perpetual fog. (p. 472.) The last chapter of Howe and Coser's work, "Toward a Theory of Stalinism," reveals the bias of the authors as well as their fundamental inability to comprehend the world revolution and the relation of the Soviet Union to it. A detailed critique of this "theory" cannot be attempted here, but anyone undertaking to read those chapters of the history dealing with the period after 1925 should first read the concluding chapter.

The final book to be considered is James P. Cannon's reminiscences of *The First Ten Years of American Communism*. This is really not a history but a series of letters in answer to questions put to Cannon by Theodore Draper as part of the latter's research for his history. This part of the book, which takes up two hundred twenty-seven of three hundred thirty-three pages, is of little interest to a general reader, especially if he has read Draper. Cannon's memories seem to be unusually accurate, and he has the ability to look back upon past events with a good deal of personal detachment, but of course what he remembers is only a small part of what was happening even within the Communist Party in these years.

The rest of the book is devoted to three essays and reviews of Draper's two books. Of these, the most interesting is Cannon's discussion of Debs and Lenin, in the course of which he attempts to defend the concept of the "Leninist" party against that of an open, multi-tendency party. Cannon appears to say that the Leninist party is a universal absolute because the revolution succeeded in Russia. The Socialist Party of Debs, Cannon tells us, is to be condemned not for its failure to lead a revolution, "but for its failure to work with that end in view and to select its membership accordingly." (p. 274.) The inclusion of "petty-bourgeois reformists and proletarian revolutionists in one political organization" inevitably led to the breakup of that party and movement.

To Cannon the form of a socialist party is more a matter of revealed truth than a function of political and social reality. Thus he ignores both the differences in the conditions under which the American and Russian Socialist movements had to work, and the differences in the history and stability of the two societies themselves. But surely the fact that Socialist agitation was illegal in Russia, that Party work had to go on underground, that many leaders were forced to live in exile has some relevance to the form of organization of Lenin's party. And surely the disintegration of the Russian political structure, accompanied by mass disillusionment and privation, both among the general population and in the army, helped determine the success of a tightly disciplined party capable of unified action in the midst of chaos. While the Russians developed their party in the most backward, semi-feudal country of

Europe, American Socialists did so in the most advanced and democratic industrial nation. Cannon admits that the main achievement of the early Socialist Party was that it "gave many thousands of people their first introduction to the general perspective of socialism," and that it "provided the arena where the main cadres of the revolutionary movement of the future were assembled." (p. 274.) But what more could one expect in the United States in the years from 1900 to 1920? Indeed, compare this accomplishment to that of the several Leninist parties during the years of the Great Depression. If there was ever a time when an American socialist party should have been able to live up to Cannon's standard and act "as the conscious agency in preparing the workers for the necessary revolution," it was from 1929 to 1940. Yet not one of the Leninist parties on the scene was capable of building a conscious movement for socialism even remotely comparable to that stirred up by the party of Debs, Berger, and Hillquit.

Relying on the breakup of the old Socialist Party as an argument against its viability, Cannon points to the alleged "unceasing internal conflict" as proof of the inadequacy of a multi-tendency party. But he fails to note that it was the successful revolution in Russia, or rather the policies of the International, that inspired the sundering of the Party. And surely the multiplicity of communist and Leninist parties that have hatched like maggots in the body politic since 1919 hardly argues for the stability of the Leninist party—especially in the light of a history of no such splits in the Socialist Party from 1900 to 1919. Cannon has rejected Stalinism and has in some ways remained truer to the original ideas of Lenin than his Communist comrades; but, since he split with the Communists in 1929, he has as much at stake as they in the defense of the earlier history of the Communist parties, or at least of their non-Stalinist aspects. Cannon praises the formation of the Communist Party in 1919 as a break with the conception of a common party of "revolutionists and opportunists." The closer one studies the old Socialist Party and its Communist heirs, however, the clearer it becomes that this particular change is purely illusory. The Socialist Party was no more a party of revolutionists and opportunists, whatever these loaded words may mean to Cannon, than the later parties have been. On the other hand, it was a party in which the freest debates took place unceasingly, and in which the differences rarely became so great as to interfere with Party work. Neither can be said of Cannon's allegedly superior Leninist parties.

The most striking thing about these books as a body of historical literature is the extent to which they reinforce, rather than dispel, the ideological fog in which the American Socialist past has been enshrouded. In large part this is the result of a predilection, common to our historians, to downgrade the early Socialist movement and to deny the existence of a meaningful tradition of indigenous anti-capitalist radicalism. This hidden heritage points clearly away both from acquiescence in a society dominated by the giant corporations and from the assumptions underlying the Cold War; but since it can provide no comfort for those who are unwilling or unable to do the hard work of developing their own radical analyses and sets of alternatives, it is useful neither to liberals nor communists. Every generation of historians rewrites its history to fit its needs and the books under review here demonstrate that their authors are no exceptions. Incapable of escaping the framework of political ideologies that permeated the period since 1919, these men have provided little that is usable to the newly emerging American left. But not all generations have an equal stake in obscuring the past. Hopefully, the new historians of American radicalism will be more disposed to learn from it, and less inclined to bend it, however unconsciously, to their more narrow and immediate purposes.

Proletariat and Middle Class in Marx: Hegelian Choreography and the Capitalist Dialectic

BY *Martin Nicolaus*

Volume VII, No. 1
January–February 1967

This essay is part of a new discussion of Marx based on his Grundrisse der Kritik der Politischen Oekonomie, *sections of which Martin Nicolaus is translating into English for the first time. The article helps dissolve the old notion that Marxist theory was relevant only to the competitive period of rapid capital accumulation. Nicolaus discusses what he calls (and Marx called) a new middle class of unproductive workers. This concept has also been explored by William A. Williams in* The Great Evasion *(1964) and by others in* Studies *and in* SDS. *But where Nicolaus writes of a new middle class, the* Studies *and* SDS *people view the same development as an increasing proletarianization and speak of a new variegated working class. The key element common in both analyses is a similar view of the process of capital accumulation.*

I. HEGELIAN CHOREOGRAPHY

To bring more clarity into the delicate subject of Marx's Hegelianism, it is necessary to make a distinction among three aspects of the dialectic. There is, first, the *context* of the dialectical movement, which in Hegel is either the timeless realm of pure logic or a sphere which is called History but is only the ephemeral context in which an abstract Idea unfolds its purpose. Second, there is the *content* of the dialectical categories, which in Hegel is typically abstract, void of concrete reference. Finally, there is the dialectical *movement* itself, the inevitable process by which contradictions unfold, affirm, negate and gracefully vanish from the scene with a dazzling *Aufhebung*— annulment, preservation and supercession in one motion. With polemical intent I have called this *movement* of the categories in Hegel his "choreography," for, it seems to me, Marx remained under the spell of this dance long after he had succeeded in bringing the *context* and the *content* of the dialectic down to earth and under a plain light. It was Marx's captivation with this choreography, I shall argue, which led him to the prediction that capitalist society must inevitably become polarized into two directly antagonistic classes, and that, in this polarization, the industrial proletariat must play the role of successful negation.

That this prediction has proved to be mistaken, and that its fulfillment seems least probable precisely where it was most to be expected, namely in the *advanced* industrial nations, has been apparent for some time. In the second section of this paper, I argue that Marx himself developed the theoretical principles on which this prediction can be shown to be invalid, and that on occasion these principles led Marx himself to make predictions which explicitly contradict those of the *Communist Manifesto.* My thesis is that Marx's major contributions to the understanding of capitalism—the labor theory of value, the theory of the surplus, the law of the tendential decline of the profit rate—constitute a body of theory from which the failure of capitalist society to polarize, the rise of a new middle class, and the declining militancy of the industrial proletariat—in other words, the essential features of advanced industrial society—can be accurately predicted and explained, and indeed that Marx himself did so. In discussing Marx's theory of classes I shall be concerned chiefly with his theory of classes arising out of industrial capitalism and not with his general theory. By the latter I understand the series of propositions centered on the ideas that class struggles are the moving force of history, that classes and their conflicts arise out of contradictions in the means and modes of production, etc. Nothing in this general theory, unfortunately, permits instant and spontaneous deductions to the specific conditions which prevail in a given society. In the *German Ideology* Marx was quite unambiguous about the necessity for empirical investigation. The general theory is that "given individuals who are active in production in a given way, enter into certain social and political relationships." However, "The connection between production and the social and political structure must in every case be uncovered by empirical observation, without mystification or speculation."[1] But Marx himself did not carry out a program of thorough empirical investigation of capitalist production until several years after the *Manifesto,* and it was the resulting weakness in his understanding of the capitalist social structure which permitted the Hegelian choreography to exercise so strong a hold over him.

Although biographical information about the genesis of an idea can provide no more than circumstantial evidence, that sort of evidence has its usefulness when it arouses skepticism; and when skepticism leads to a fresh examination of certain ritual formulations, then the introduction of biographical evidence may prove to be instrumental in bringing back to life an idea long after the period out of which it first arose. In the present case, the key item of circumstantial information which should arouse our skepticism and lead us to look at Marx afresh is the biographical fact that Marx proclaimed the historic liberating mission of the proletariat *before* he had more than the vaguest notions of the political economy of cap-

[1] Die Deutsche Ideologie," in Karl Marx, Friedrich Engels, *Werke* (Dietz, Berlin) Vol. 3, p. 25.

italism, before he had read the bourgeois economists of his day, and long before he had grappled with the economic problems to which his mature theory is the solution.

The proclamation that the proletariat would make the revolution came in the third of a series of philosophical papers in which the young Marx worked out a critical stance toward Hegel and his followers. In the first of these papers, the *Kritik des Hegelschen Staatsrechts* (written summer 1843, when Marx was twenty-five years old), he still held, with the Hegelians, that the French Revolution had created a political state in which the distinctions that existed in the private lives of its citizens, in "civic society," had no material relevance, or, in other words, that rich and poor were equal in the political sphere.[2] In the second paper *Zur Judenfrage* (autumn 1843), he amends this position drastically by stating that differences of civil standing might not be of importance in the political sphere, but that the political sphere itself was of little importance,' and that civil distinctions nevertheless remained civil distinctions, which must not be ignored.[3] A short time later in the *Kritik der Hegelschen Rechtsphilosophie, Einleitung* (winter 1843-1844), the "distinctions" of civil standing become "contradictions within civil society," a most important change; the relevance of the political sphere and of the philosophy that deals with it as if the state were the celestial realm here on earth is completely denied; philosophy itself is given a properly philosophical funeral with the proclamation that deeds, not words, will change society; and finally, the men who will wield the historical broom to sweep German thought and German politics clear of their interlocking cobwebs are ushered onstage:

Where, then, is the *positive* possibility of German emancipation? *Answer:* In the formation of a class with *radical chains,* a class within civil society which is not a class of civil society,

[2] Cf. *Werke,* Vol. 1, esp. pp. 283-4.
[3] Cf. *Werke,* Vol. 1, esp. pp. 354-5, 368-9.

an estate which is the dissolution of all estates, a sphere which possesses a universal character because of its universal suffering. . . . This dissolution of society as a special estate is the *proletariat*.[4]

Here the Hegelian context has been liquidated, and the Hegelian categories have received a historical content, but the choreography has, for all that, emerged more strongly. Marx has discovered no more about the proletariat than that it develops and grows larger as industry does,[5] and already he has it dancing the leading negative role in the dialectic of History. Only after this proclamation did Marx begin to read the political economists to find, as he wrote later, the anatomy of civil society.[6]

The record of the collision between Hegelian philosophy and the political economy of Adam Smith, Ricardo, and others, appears in Marx's *Economic-Philosophic Manuscripts of 1844*. None of his works reveals more clearly the difficulties Marx experienced, and probably those which anyone must experience, in attempting to grasp the dismally pragmatic confusion of data and theory that prevails in so unpoetic a discipline as economics with the intellectual equipment of a sphere so clear, uncluttered and even elegant as the Hegelian philosophy. The struggle is uncompromising and complex. On the one hand, Marx writes that ". . . my conclusions are the fruit of an entirely empirical analysis, based upon a careful critical study of political economy."[7] And then: "Political economy has merely formulated the laws of alienated labor."[8] However: "Hegel's standpoint is that of modern political economy. He conceives *labor* as the *essence,* the self-confirming essence of man."[9] Nevertheless: Hegel is wrong

[4] *Werke,* Vol. 1, p. 390.

[5] *Ibid.*

[6] "Zur Kritik der Politischen Oekonomie. Vorwort," *Werke* 13, p. 8.

[7] For reasons unclear to me, the *Werke* edition does not contain the 1844 MSS. Because of its reliability and wide availability, I have quoted from the Bottomore translation, in Erich Fromm, *Marx's Concept of Man* (Ungar, New York, 1961). The present quotation is on p. 91.

[8] *Ibid.,* p. 106.

[9] *Ibid.,* p. 177.

"because his conception is *formal* and *abstract,* [and therefore] the annulment of alienation becomes a confirmation of alienation."[10] This is a battle of methods, of ways of seeing and explaining the world, a struggle between disparate epistemologies. Here the dialectic power of German idealism struggles like Hercules against the giant, Antaeus, the son of Earth; and, it must be said, the outcome is the same as in that mythical trial: philosophy lifts its antagonist off the ground, away from the source of his strength, and crushes him in midair. Thus Marx seizes upon the capitalist production process, its relations of property, together with its system of exchange and circulation, and lifts this entire edifice of empirical fact and empirical fancy into the Hegelian air, where he compresses the pragmatic giant into the single concept of "alienated labor." And Marx aims higher than Hercules; he not only crushes his antagonist, but he also believes that he can then reconstitute him on a higher level by unfolding the content of the fundamental core to which he has been reduced. Thus he writes, as only a philosophical idealist could write:

As we have discovered the concept of *private property* by an *analysis* of the concept of *alienated labor,* so with the aid of these two factors we can evolve all the categories of political economy, and in every category, e.g. trade, competition, capital, money, we shall discover only a particular and developed expression of these fundamental elements.[11]

Here metaphysics has won over empiricism, not only in method but also in substance. Marx's theory of classes, as it was forged in this crucible, represents a two-fold defeat for economics. First, Marx sees both the division of society into classes and the division of labor as equivalent aspects of the touchstone concept "alienated labor."[12] Only from

[10] *Ibid.,* p. 189.

[11] *Ibid.,* p. 107.

[12] "The consideration of *division of labor* and *exchange* is of the great-interest, since they are the *perceptible, alienated* expression of human *activity* and *capacities* as the activity and capacities *proper to a species.*" *Ibid.,* p. 161.

a perspective beyond economics can one afford to ignore the difference between them. A political economist, on the other hand, must grasp and explicate the fact that the division of labor is not the same thing as class division, or else his entire craft runs into confusion. As late as the *German Ideology* (1846) Marx still stands outside political economy in that respect, as is shown by his famous remark that communism will abolish the division of labor, so that man may be a hunter, a fisherman, or a critic as he pleases.[13] This is a brilliant philosophical vision, but a less poetic spirit would not have ventured it without first asking where the hunter is to get his rifle, the fisherman his rod and reel, and the critic his books—and the answer to those questions is again within the realm of the economist, not of the philosopher. There is a measure of irony in the fact that Marx puts the division of labor and the division of classes into proper economic perspective only when he notes that Proudhon has committed a similar philosophic confusion—for Marx himself, he later wrote, was responsible for "infecting" Proudhon with Hegelianism.[14]

The second and more disastrous effect of the victory of philosophy over economics on Marx's theory of classes was his discovery that the antagonism of labor *vs.* capital could be made to "fit" neatly into the dialectical pattern. The earlier proclamation of the proletariat as universal negation was strengthened and amplified here to the point where the development of capitalist industrialization appeared to Marx as a fateful unfolding of a contradiction whose path *must* conform to the choreography *because* it was dialectical. "The relations of private property," he writes—and here he still speaks of "private property"

---

[13] *Werke* 3, p. 33. A page earlier, Marx writes that "private property and division of labor are identical expressions" for the same thing, i.e. that the division of classes is only another aspect of the division of labor, and vice versa.

[14] "Ueber P.-J. Proudhon" in *Werke* 16, p. 27. For Marx's clarification of the difference between division of labor and division of classes see *Misère de la Philosophie* (1847) in *Werke* 4, pp. 122, 144-156.

instead of capitalism, of *"buergerliche Gesellschaft"* (civil
society) instead of bourgeois society—"are capital, labor,
and their interconnections." And then the pattern that is
fundamental to his thought: "The movements through
which these elements have to go are: First—*unmediated
and mediated unity of the two* . . . [then:] *opposition between the two* . . . *opposition* of each *to* itself . . . [and]
clash of reciprocal contradictions." [15] Although it became
filled out with a great deal of historical material, this
dialectical schema remained the basis of Marx's view of
social classes and their conflict up to and including the
Manifesto, and to a great extent for the rest of his life.
The notion that "capital" and "labor" may not be the
only determining components of a fully developed capitalist society, and the idea that "the movements through
which these elements have to go" may not be the movements through which any self-respecting dialectical contradiction must go, but that these movements may be
determined by the specifically capitalist contradiction,
which may be quite different—these notions do not occur
until later in his work and will be discussed in the second
part of this paper. Meanwhile, however, the movement
of history seemed to confirm the dialectical prognosis,
making a detailed analysis of the capitalist economic
process unnecessary; for it was a fact, as Engels reported
in his *Condition of the Working Class in England,* that
the onrush of industrial capitalism was destroying the
previous small middle classes of tradesmen, manufacturers
and craftsmen, and that the social and economic distance
between a small number of big capitalists and the swelling propertyless proletarians was growing wider and
wider.[16] Was it so wrong to project the impact of primary
capitalist accumulation into the future, as in this crucial
passage from the *Manifesto?*

[15] "Economic-Philosophical Manuscripts of 1844" in Fromm, *op. cit.,*
pp. 117-118.
[16] "Lage der arbeitenden Klasse in England," in *Werke* 2, pp. 250-251.

Our epoch, the epoch of the bourgeoisie, possesses, however, the distinctive feature that it has simplified class contradictions. The whole society more and more splits into two great antagonistic camps, two great classes directly opposed to one another: Bourgeoisie and Proletariat.[17]

Only a small leap of faith was required to envision a society in which this initial polarization had continued to sharpen, finally reaching the outer limits of human endurance; that is, a society in which an absolutely wealthy capitalist class confronts an absolutely impoverished proletariat—and one does not need to be a Hegelian to predict that a revolution will occur under such circumstances. Yet is was a peculiarly Hegelian exaggeration, a Hegelian leap of faith, to assume that the contradiction between capital and labor would continue to develop and unfold in this manner until the two classes confronted each other with all the unmediated antagonism of a pure negation confronting an absolute affirmation. To assume without further analysis of the capitalist economic process that the dialectic of capitalism must conform to the dialectic of ideas was a most Hegelian error of procedure; and the error of procedure resulted in an error of substance. The advance of capitalist society has not meant increasingly sharp conflict between capital and labor. The most industrially advanced capitalist nations typically have the most quiescent, noninsurrectionary proletariats—witness the United States; and in every capitalist country there has arisen a broad, vocal and specifically new middle class to thwart Marxist theory and to stifle and crush Marxist action. Marx's captivation with the Hegelian choreography has cost his followers in advanced industrial society a heavy price. The prophets of class conflict have too often stood powerless to explain or to deal with the

[17] "Manifest der Kommunistischen Partei," in *Werke* 4, p. 463. I have relied in general on the English translation appearing in *The Communist Manifesto* (Monthly Review Press, New York, 1964) for my renderings of the original. However, some of the technical economic terms in that translation are not quite accurately put; see footnotes 20 and 23 below.

class structure of the society that their reading of Marx leads them to think should never have been.

II. THE CAPITALIST DIALECTIC

A. THE MODEL OF CAPITALIST ECONOMICS IN THE MANIFESTO

Marx's contributions to political economy—the labor theory of value, the theory of the surplus, the law of the tendential fall of the profit rate—all date from about 1857-1858, the years during which Marx wrote the *Grundrisse*.[18] None of these discoveries is foreshadowed in the *Manifesto* (1848), and indeed this early work shows no clear evidence that Marx had yet become aware of the *problems* to which his later contributions were the *solutions.*

Although Marx writes repeatedly in the *Manifesto* that capital employs labor in order to increase or augment itself *(vermehren),*[19] one looks in vain here for a theory of precisely how this process of capital accumulation takes place. The closest approach to an understanding of capitalist accumulation, and thereby to a theory of the surplus, comes when Marx mentions that communism wants to do away with the capitalist's appropriation of the net yield *(Reinertrag)* of production.[20] But this insight remains unconscious of itself, and the various references to capital accumulation are so rudimentary and cursory that no systematic theory of accumulation can be extracted

[18] Karl Marx, *Grundrisse der Kritik der Politischen Oekonomie (Rohentwurf),* Marx-Engels-Lenin Institut, Moscow (Dietz, Berlin, 1953). The actual *Grundrisse* of 1857-58 occupy 760 pages in this huge volume. A complete translation, or at the very least a translation of selected excerpts, would be highly desirable.

[19] *Werke* 4, pp. 468, 473, 475.

[20] *Ibid.,* p. 476. "Reinertrag" is misleadingly rendered as "surplus" in the English translation cited above, footnote 17.

from them or projected into them. The *Manifesto's* economic theorizing in general suffers from a great amount of vagueness. Here, for instance, is one example of a powerful prediction based on a chain of diffuse economic reasoning:

The essential condition for the existence, and for the sway of the bourgeois class, is the formation and augmentation of capital; the condition for capital is wage-labor. *Wage-labor rests exclusively on competition between the laborers.* The advance of industry, whose involuntary promoter is the bourgeoisie, replaces the isolation of the laborers, due to competition, by their involuntary combination, due to association. The development of Modern Industry therefore cuts from under its feet the very foundation on which the bourgeoisie produces and appropriates products. What the bourgeoisie therefore produces, above all, are its own gravediggers. Its fall and the victory of the proletariat are equally inevitable.[21]

I have italicized the phrase "wage-labor rests exclusively on competition between the laborers" in order to emphasize what strikes me as the weakest link in this argument. The statement is at best a half-truth; it is not even a full truth if one says that the *level of wages* rests exclusively on competition. But even if the statement were correct, then the conclusion that workers' associations will bury the bourgeoisie does not follow; the only thing that follows is that wage labor will get more expensive, from the capitalist's standpoint. And that, of course, is precisely what has occurred wherever workers' associations (unions) have succeeded in defeating competition from non-unionized labor; the reduction of competition has by no means done away with wage labor or with capitalism. Only if the bourgeoisie were absolutely economically incapable of granting wage demands put forth by associated workers would there be any necessary revolutionary consequences in the elimination of competition between the laborers. Had Marx at this time worked out an economic

[21] *Ibid.,* p. 474.

theory to account for the fact that the bourgeoisie is *not* incapable of raising wages, this particular prediction would have had to be argued differently. What the excerpt above shows chiefly is that Marx's analysis of bourgeois production had at this point penetrated little further than the insight that the bourgeoisie turns all human values into market values, all human beings into commodities. Thus, here and elsewhere in the *Manifesto,* Marx sees the *market* as the center of gravity of bourgeois society; in this case he goes so far as to believe that a change in the market (the labor market, here) will produce a drastic change in the whole social structure. While this emphasis on the importance of the market cannot be discounted, Marx himself in his mature economic works came to see the market as a dependent variable, and he then identified *capital accumulation* and *production* as the real fulcrum around which all the other phenomena of bourgeois society gravitate.[22]

Insofar as the *Manifesto* contains any theory of capitalist accumulation and production at all, which is debatable, that theory centers on the concept of exploitation. "Wage labor," Marx writes, "creates capital, i.e. that kind of property which exploits wage labor, and which cannot increase except upon condition of creating a new supply of wage labor for fresh exploitation."[23] But here all clarity stops, for what exactly does exploitation mean? It should be noted that in *Capital,* after Marx had developed the theory of the surplus, he gives this term a very precise, quantifiable meaning; here, however, it is more a physical and moral term, denoting suffering, degradation, destruc-

---

[22] For example, see Marx's polemic against the tendency to "explain" capitalist economics with reference to the so-called laws of supply and demand, i.e., the laws of the market, in *Kapital* III, *Werke* 25, p. 191 and elsewhere.

[23] *Werke* 4, p. 475. The English translation renders "erzeugen" as "getting" instead of "creating" a new supply of wage labor; the point, however, is not vital.

tion, dehumanization, etc. The closest economic term for this usage of "exploitation" would be destructive consumption; that is, capital is accumulated by using up, destroying the labor commodity in the act of production. The more the capitalist deprives the laborer of his commodity, labor, the richer the capitalist gets; the fatter the capitalist, the leaner the worker. Eventually the workers will become absolutely impoverished, and at the same time, the capitalists will have all the wealth of any kind in the nation. The capitalists will have everything but no one to sell it to, and the workers will have nothing but a world to win. Then, in the terms of the *Manifesto,* a classic overproduction crisis sets in ("too much civilization, too much means of subsistence, too much industry, too much commerce,")[24] or rather, there is a series of such crises, which culminates in the grand, final crisis which will bring the revolution. That approximately is the *Manifesto's* model of capitalist accumulation, and this also appears to be the model many Marxists still cling to.

The affinities between this model and the Hegelian choreography should strike the eye. For if this is indeed how capitalism operates, then it follows that capitalism must throw all possible parts of the population into the industrial labor supply, which means that all intermediate classes must and will be destroyed (which is exactly what the *Manifesto* says), thus creating a society perfectly polarized between an absolutely rich capitalist class and an absolutely poor industrial proletariat, the two facing each other with the undiluted antagonism of a logical contradiction. And then indeed the *Aufhebung* is nigh.

But, to return a last time to this economic model, what if for one reason or another the total wealth of the nation were not a fixed constant; what if there were an increment, say x, which arose to augment the total without diminishing the wealth of either labor or capital pro-

[24] *Ibid.,* p. 468.

portionately? The existence of this extra increment, this surplus, removes the weight of the iron law of destructive consumption. Absolute wealth on one side would not necessarily mean absolute impoverishment on the other side; which means that capitalist accumulation would not necessarily mean absolute social polarization. And this would be especially true if it were discovered that this x were not an arbitrary *deus ex machina* conjured into the system from outside, but a regular and essential feature of capitalist production itself.

B. THE DISCOVERY OF SURPLUS VALUE

If I am correct in saying that the validity of the Hegelian social choreography depends on the validity of the simple, surplus-less model of destructive consumption outlined above, then the liquidation by Marx of the Hegelian choreography can be fixed in time and space with considerable precision. The spell of that dance is broken in principle in the *Grundrisse der Kritik der Politischen Oekonomie (Rohentwurf)* of 1857-1858, a voluminous work which has not been translated into English. After a lengthy critique of economic theory which treats capitalist production as if it were production in general, as if its special characteristics were not worth investigating, Marx brings up the central problem of the theory of capitalism and proceeds to solve it. How is it, he asks, that at the end of the production process the capitalist has a commodity which is worth more than the elements that went into it? He pays the price of machinery, raw materials and the price of labor, yet the product is worth more than all three together. What, in other words, is the source of the surplus value *(Mehrwert)* which the capitalist appropriates? The problem is insoluble, Marx writes, so long as "labor" is considered a commodity like any other commodity (as it was, specifically, in the *Manifesto*).[25] If labor were such a commodity, then capitalist production would be: price of machinery + price of raw materials + price of labor = price of product. Where, then, is the capitalist's profit? If we evade the question by saying that the capitalist fixes an arbitrary profit percentage and simply adds it to the price of the product, as high as the market will bear, then it appears that the buyer of the commodity is the source of the capitalist's profit. Yet what the capitalist gains in this way, the buyer loses, and it is impossible to see how an aggregate surplus could arise out of such transactions. Marx rejected this mercantilist theory, according to which one nation could get richer only by cheating another in commerce. This theory is overcome, and the problem of surplus value is solved, when one realizes that the worker sells the capitalist not "labor," but labor *power (Arbeitskraft)*. Although its price varies with supply and demand, this specific commodity has the exceptional quality of being able to produce more value than is necessary to reproduce it.[26] For example, all the commodities necessary to keep a worker alive and able to work, i.e. groceries, clothes, shelter, etc., have a value represented by the letter n. Working in a favtory, the worker produces for the capitalist a quantity of commodities whose value is equal to the value of the commodities he needs to consume, in n hours. This n is what Marx calls necessary labor time, that is, the time necessary to produce enough value to allow the worker to live and work on. But once he is fed

---

[25] "Der Preis einer Ware, also auch der Arbeit, ist aber gleich ihren Produktionskosten." *Ibid.*, p. 469. The editors of the *Werke* duly note that Marx would have said "Arbeitskraft" instead of "Arbeit" in his later writings, a crucial difference on which may be said to hinge the entire distinction between Marxist and non-Marxist economics—as well as the distinction, perhaps, between the "young Marx" and the "mature Marx." See *Ibid.*, footnote 298, p. 649, and footnote 198, p. 636.

[26] This definition is restated frequently, notably in "Lohn, Preis und Profit," *Werke* 16, pp. 121-132, in *Capital*, and elsewhere.

and clothed, the worker is able to continue to work more than n hours, and that is exactly what the capitalist forces him to do. If at a given stage of social productivity it takes on the average six hours to produce enough for the worker to live, i.e. if n is 6, then any hours worked in addition to 6 are what Marx calls surplus labor, and the product of this surplus labor is the surplus product, which, when sold, yields surplus value, a part of which the capitalist pockets as profit.

The specific nature of capitalist production, then, is the creation and appropriation of surplus value by the capitalist class. To increase surplus value, the capitalist must increase the amount of the workers' surplus labor. Marx distinguishes between two methods of increasing surplus labor. In the early stages of industrialization the first method was the prolongation of the working day over and above the necessary labor time, thus stretching the day to twelve, fourteen, sixteen and more hours, up to and beyond the limits of human endurance. This form of surplus accumulation Marx calls the production of "absolute surplus."[27] However, eventually the labor force becomes exhausted in this way; the worker dies too young, the laboring population diminishes through disease and wages must rise. Then, Marx writes, the capitalist class finds it in its own interests to limit the working day by law to a humanly endurable "normal" length.[28] Once that stage has been reached, a point which according to Marx occurs when capitalism has taken over all branches of production and becomes altogether the dominant form of production,[29] then the capitalist class turns to the creation of what Marx calls "relative surplus," that is, the extraction of more surplus labor within a fixed number of hours.[30] While the production of absolute surplus is

[27] *Kapital I, Werke* 23, p. 532.
[28] *Ibid.,* p. 281.
[29] *Ibid.,* p. 533.
[30] *Ibid.,* p. 534.

possible with the instruments and machinery of earlier
periods, the relative surplus can only be increased by
revolutionizing the whole basis of production, which
means principally the rapid introduction of modern machinery. Machinery raises the productivity of each worker,
so that he produces the equivalent value necessary to sustain him in less time; that is, *n,* necessary labor time,
is reduced relative to surplus labor time. In this way, the
capitalist can appropriate greater and greater amounts of
surplus without necessarily working the worker to death
in the process, although he can also do both. For Marx,
the production of relative surplus by the use of ever more
efficient machinery resulting in ever greater productivity
was one of capitalism's fundamental historical tendencies.

Here we must briefly discuss what Marx called the
solution to the mystery which had plagued all of political
economy since Adam Smith, namely, the "law of the tendential decline of the profit rate." [31] This law states quite
simply that as the capitalist class as a whole invests more
and more heavily in machinery, and proportionally less
in wages, the *rate* of profit will tend to decline. The fact
that Marx assumed competitive market conditions, and
that these no longer are typical today, however, does not
destroy the usefulness of this law as an explanatory concept. What Baran and Sweezy in *Monopoly Capital* have
called the "tendency of the surplus to rise" is not only not
contradictory to Marx's law, but is in fact only another
aspect of it. [32] Marx was quite specific, and repeatedly so,
in stating that the tendential decline in the profit *rate* not
only can but *must* lead to a corresponding rise in the *mass*
of profits, and that a decline in the profit rate *must* tend

[31] *Kapital III, Werke* 25, p. 223.

[32] Paul Baran and Paul Sweezy, *Monopoly Capital* (Monthly Review
Press, New York and London, 1966). The authors of this monumental
study consider the "law of the rising surplus" a *substitution* for Marx's
law of the tendential fall of the profit rate (see p. 72) without however
discussing the fact that the law of the rising surplus is really no substitution at all, but merely another aspect of Marx's law.

to *increase* both the *rate* and the *mass* of the *surplus*.[33]
(The surplus is computed only on the basis of necessary
versus surplus labor time; but the profit is computed on
the basis of investment in machinery also, which explains
the seemingly contradictory movement of profit and surplus.) Thus in the course of capitalist development, Marx
held, the capitalist class tends to realize a smaller profit
rate on its investments, but the volume of profits, as well
as the rate and volume of the surplus which it controls,
tends to grow disproportionately faster. For example, an
eighteenth-century manufacturer employing one thousand workers with hand tools might make a profit of fifty
per cent, for a mass of profit measured in a few thousands
of dollars; but a modern corporation with an equal number of workers, and a multi-million-dollar investment in
machinery, may make only five per cent, but its profits
may also be in the millions.

This tendency has important implications for the relationship between the capitalist class and the working
class. One of them is that the process of advanced capitalist development enables the capitalist class to face workers' demands for higher wages with an unprecedented
degree of flexibility. The small capitalist of an earlier
period sometimes literally could not increase wages without eventually going out of business. For the huge corporation with its voluminous reserves, the refusal to grant
wage increases is less a matter of life-and-death necessity
and more a matter of policy. What happens then, Marx
foresaw, is that the workers' submission to the capitalist
class is clothed

. . . in bearable, or, as Eden says, "comfortable and liberal"
forms. . . . From the workers' own swelling surplus product,

---

[33] This is already stated in *Grundrisse,* p. 649: "Thus the profit rate
stands in an inverse relationship to the growth of relative surplus
value. . . ." More explicitly in *Kapital III:* "As the process of production
and accumulation progresses, the mass of surplus labor that can be and
is appropriated, and thus the absolute mass of the profits appropriated
by the capitalist class, *must* grow." (*Werke* 25, p. 229; also pages 228, 230,
and elsewhere in the same chapter.

a part of which is constantly being converted into additional capital, a greater portion flows back to them in cash, so that they can broaden the sphere of their consumption, equip themselves better with clothing and furniture, etc., and develop a small reserve of savings.[34]

Since a large capital can and does expand faster, although with a smaller profit rate, than smaller capital, wage increases of this sort at this stage of capitalist development may be safely granted, for they in no way hinder the accumulation of capital or its concentration in the hands of the class of big capitalists.[35] Elsewhere, Marx writes that what really matters under capitalism is not the absolute level of wages, but the incomes of the classes relative to one another.[36] Once capital has accumulated a certain volume of surplus, in other words, the absolute impoverishment of the workers becomes a negligible possibility because it is no longer the essential precondition of capitalist accumulation. Exploitation itself becomes a relative term; in *Capital* the rate of exploitation means the ratio of necessary labor to surplus labor in the working day. Thus the rate of exploitation may escalate almost *ad infinitum*, yet at the same time the working class may live more comfortably than ever. The rising surplus makes it possible for the capitalist class to exchange its tyranny for a benevolent despotism.

The saddest victims of capitalist accumulation in its advanced stage, as Marx charted it, are not the workers but the unemployed, the "industrial reserve army." As productivity rises, the demand for productive labor in a

[34] *Kapital I, Werke* 23, p. 646.

[35] *Ibid.*, p. 647.

[36] Karl Marx, *Theorien Ueber den Mehrwert*, Karl Kautsky, editor, (Dietz, Stuttgart, 1919), Volume II, part 1, p. 141. A new edition of this important work is being issued by the editors of the *Werke* series; however, only Volume I of the new edition was available to me, and I have preferred to quote from the Kautsky edition, which seems to be more widely available in libraries. This work, consisting of three volumes in four books, figures in the *Werke* edition as "Volume Four" of *Capital*; it was written in manuscript by Marx in 1861-1862, however, and thus predates the other volumes of *Capital*. I shall refer to it as *"Theorien"* in the notes below.

given industry or in all industries generally may drop
temporarily, or in the long run, will tend to drop permanently. Thus is created a constant stream of under-
employed, unemployed, prematurely used up, obsolete,
or unemployable individuals.[37] When unskilled labor is
the standard mode in the society, as Marx posited in *Capital*, then this reserve army serves to depress the wages of
the employed; but, he might have added, at a certain stage
in the development of productivity only skilled labor can
be used (e.g. the replacement of ditch-digging gangs by
earth-moving machinery), so that the unskilled unemployed lose even their competitive link with the working
class, and as one generation of unemployed begets another,
a permanent welfare class comes into being. At the same
time, the greater volume of surplus makes it possible to
support growing numbers of these people, however mis-
erably. In the advanced stages of capitalist development,
the "exploitation" of the working class appears as prosperity beside the poverty of this never-working subpro-
letariat.

The implications of Marx's theory of the surplus, in
short, destroy the relationship between capital and labor
which the *Manifesto* had foreseen. In the hands of an
intelligent capitalist class bent on its own survival, the
swelling surplus provides a cushion against the more acute
forms of class conflict, and prevents absolute social polarization along the lines laid out by the Hegelian choreography. The specifically capitalist dialectic does not obey
the laws of the great philosopher.

C. THE RISE OF THE SURPLUS CLASS

The rise of the surplus not only alters the relationship
between the capitalist class and the working class, but it
also creates an entirely new class between them. While the

[37] *Kapital I, Werke* 23, p. 673; also *Kapital III, Werke* 25, p. 232.

term "surplus class" to designate this stratum does not to my knowledge occur in Marx's writings, the idea and its implications were clearly seized and expressed by him.

The essential feature of capitalism, Marx says, is to appropriate surplus labor. That is to say, labor is productive for capitalism only insofar as it yields surplus labor; or, as Marx put it succinctly, "labor is productive only insofar as it produces its own opposite."[38] As labor becomes more and more productive, it produces more and more of its own opposite. This tendency yields what may be called the "law of the surplus class" in its most general form: as less and less people are forced to produce more and more, more and more people are forced to produce less and less. As Marx put it:

Given an advance of industrial productivity to the point where only one third of the population takes a direct part in material production, instead of two thirds as before, then one third furnish the means of life for the whole, whereas before two thirds were required to do so. Before, one third was net revenue (as distinct from the workers' income), now net revenue is two thirds. Disregarding the class contradiction, the whole nation would now need only one third of its time for direct production, whereas earlier it had needed two thirds. With equal distribution, everyone would now have two thirds of his time for unproductive labor and for leisure. But in capitalist production, everything appears and is contradictory.[39]

The contradiction resides in the fact that the distribution of disposable time cannot be equal so long as the capitalist system operates by appropriating surplus labor, i.e. so long as it is the capitalist system of production; for if everyone worked only long enough to reproduce the means of life, there would be no surplus for the capitalists to appropriate. What does happen, under capitalism, to the mass of people who are released from direct, productive labor by the advance of productivity? The question is the

[38] *Grundrisse*, p. 212.
[39] *Theorien I*, p. 189; see also p. 199.

same as the question of what happens to the mass of surplus value generated by advanced capitalist production.

Marx divided the surplus value into a number of categories, of which we need distinguish only the broadest, capital and revenue. Capital is that part of the surplus value which the capitalist reinvests in further production. Revenue includes everything the capitalist pays out to himself and others, such as dividends, interest payments, land rent, taxes, and most importantly, payment for services rendered to his enterprise by *other than productive workers*. A great number of people who produce no commodities for profitable sale are essential to the capitalist enterprise and consume a part of its revenue; e.g. bookkeepers, clerks, secretaries, lawyers, designers, engineers, salesmen, etc.—in general, all the people who do not themselves control capital (as bankers do) and who fulfill a function in the vast system of financing, distributing, exchanging, improving and maintaining the commodities produced by the proletariat and appropriated by the capitalist class.[40] From the law of the rising surplus, it follows that except during times of exceptionally heavy capital investment, the mass of disposable revenue must also tend to rise; that is, there must be an increase in that part of the surplus which can be expended for the utilization of unproductive labor.

[40] These are of course the so-called white-collar proletarians, and the fact that this class also works for wages has aroused hopes that it also might in time be stimulated to develop along the classic lines of increasing proletarian militancy. Whatever the merit of this idea, however, it should be clear that to Marx, the proletariat meant *productive* only. If the proletariat is defined to include all those who work for wages, then many corporation executives and managers are proletarians too. Marx's early view of wage labor shows, by contrast, considerable lack of rigor; thus in the *Manifesto* he writes that the bourgeoisie has turned the judge, the parson, the poet, the scientist into its "paid wage laborers" (*Werke* 4, p. 465), which would put these worthy gentlemen into the proletariat, too, or so it would seem. Here again, as mentioned before, Marx sees the transformation of human values into market values as the overriding characteristic of the capitalist epoch, and has not yet become aware of the profounder characteristic, namely the creation and appropriation of surplus by the capitalist class. The shift from the market concept to the surplus concept marks, in my opinion, the central difference between "young" and "mature" Marxist thought. See footnote 25, above.

The surplus not only can, it *must* be expended for unproductive labor, for two reasons.

First, as productivity rises, the number of unproductive laborers required to service and maintain the growing capital establishment also rises. The number of the traditional unproductive workers increases, e.g. clerks, bookkeepers. More significantly, entirely new branches of unproductive work are called into being, of which the banking system, the credit system, insurance empires and advertising are the most obvious examples, but the growth of the scientific and technological establishments, as well as an increase in public education generally, are also in this category. Marx himself pointed to the growth of this requirement for nonproductive services.[41]

The second reason why there must be an increase of nonproductive workers is that an increase in the surplus product requires an increase in the number of people who can afford to consume it. Surplus production requires surplus consumption. The capitalist system is based on the extraction from the laboring class of more commodities than that class is permitted to consume; the system would collapse if there were not also a class which consumed more than it produced. Some excerpts from Marx on this problem will be quoted below.

Together, these two corollaries of Marx's theory of the surplus make up what I have called the "law of the surplus class," that is, the law of the tendential rise of a new middle class.

That Marx formulated precisely such a law may come as something of a surprise to many Marxists. The reasons for this surprise, if my conjecture is correct in that regard, are not difficult to find. First, Marx's theory of the new middle class remained embryonic, though explicit; it was one of the many implications of his economic discoveries which he chose not to develop further, or was prevented

---

[41] *Kapital III*, *Werke* 25, p. 310. The necessary connection between the rising requirement for such auxiliary services and the rise of the middle class is evident, but Marx does not state it at this point.

by time from developing. The phenomenon which this theory describes, after all, had not emerged in its full dominance at the time he wrote. Secondly, the works in which Marx does develop this theory most clearly (the *Grundrisse* and the *Theorien Ueber den Mehrwert*) have not been translated into English (as far as I know), and the originals are not available in every library. Third, the theory of the middle class follows directly from the labor theory of value, the theory of the surplus and the law of the tendential fall in the profit rate, and there seems to be considerable tacit acquiescence on the left in the orthodoxly academic refusal to take these Marxist theses seriously.[42] Finally, there are still some Marxists, particularly in the New Left, who have not taken the trouble to read attentively anything that Marx wrote after the *Manifesto,* or, worse, anything after the *1844 Manuscripts.* There is an amusing tendency, at least in the academic circles known to me, to repeat an experiment Marx ventured when he was twenty-six, namely to try to squeeze the concept of alienated labor hard enough to make all the categories of sociology, politics and economics come dripping out of it, as if this philosopher's touchstone were a lemon. The drippings are flavorful but somewhat lacking in substance.

To make the data on Marx's theory of the middle class more widely available, I should like here to quote a number of excerpts at length, all of them from the untranslated works.

It was apparent to Marx from the beginning of his investigation of the surplus problem that the class of capitalists could not and did not consume all of the surplus which it extracted from the workers. Thus, in the

---

[42] For example, even so sympathetic an economist as Joan Robinson dismisses the labor theory of value as an "incantation" which is insubstantial for the rest of his work, which is a bit like saying that the concept of motion has no relevance for the understanding of Newton's laws. See Joan Robinson, *An Essay on Marxian Economics* (Macmillan, London, 1949), p. 22.

Grundrisse, a few dozen pages after the surplus problem had been raised, we find the following footnote:

> . . . the creation of surplus labor on one side corresponds to the creation of minus-labor, relative idleness (or *nonproductive* labor at best) on the other. That goes without saying as far as the capitalist class itself is concerned; but it also holds for the classes with whom it divides; thus, for the paupers, flunkeys, bootlickers and the whole train of retainers living off the surplus product; the part of the *servant* class which lives not from capital but from revenue. Essential difference between this *servant* class and the *working* class. . . . Thus Malthus is entirely logical when he calls not only for surplus labor and surplus capital but also for surplus idlers, consuming without producing, or the necessity for waste, luxury, ostentatious philanthropy, etc.[43]

Here Marx is thinking only of workers, rather, nonworkers who perform *personal* services for the capitalist, not those who fulfill a necessary unproductive function for the capital establishment. As the following excerpt from the *Theorien Ueber den Mehrwert* shows, he is not entirely clear that there is a difference.

> Although the bourgeoisie is initially very frugal, with the growth in the productivity of its capital, i.e. its workers, it imitates the feudal system of retainers. According to the last (1861 or 1862) Factory Report, the total number of persons employed in the factories of the United Kingdom (managers included) was only 775,534—while the number of female servants in England alone was one million. What a beautiful arrangement, where a factory girl sweats in the shop for 12 long hours so that the factory owner can use a part of her unpaid labor to take her sister as maid, her brother as groom, and her cousin as policeman or soldier into his personal service! [44]

When one sees the individual capitalist as the embodiment of the capitalist class, however, as Marx does consistently, the inclusion of soldiers and policemen together with domestic servants in the single category of *servants* makes more sense. In a relatively well-known section of *Capital,*

---

[43] *Grundrisse,* pp. 304-5, fn.
[44] *Theorien I,* p. 171. See also p. 189.

he measures out his scorn and ridicule impartially to all unproductive workers, including valets, politicians, churchmen, lawyers, soldiers, landowners, rentiers, paupers, vagabonds and criminals,[45] regardless of whether they perform their services for the individual capitalist or for the class as a whole.

His contempt for these people vents itself with particular fury (in the *Theorien*) on the dismal parson, Malthus, who advocated the creation of ever larger masses of these idlers to keep the capitalist economy going by consuming its surplus product. "What a ridiculous idea," Marx writes, "that the surplus has to be consumed by servants and cannot be consumed by the productive workers themselves."[46] Yet, he writes that Malthus is right about the necessity for unproductive consumers in a *capitalist* economy.[47] The fact that Malthus' "remedies" for the evil of overproduction—"heavy taxes, a mass of state and church sinecures, great armies, pensioners, tithes for the churchmen, a heavy national debt and periodic costly wars"[48] —have been in great part adopted by every advanced capitalist system would not have surprised Marx. He writes of Malthus that

His greatest hope—which he himself indicates as more or less utopian—is that the middle class will grow in size and that the working proletariat will make up a constantly decreasing proportion of the total population (even if it grows in absolute numbers). That, in fact, is the course of bourgeois society. [*Das ist in der Tat der Gang der Bourgeoisgesellschaft.*][49]

[45] *Kapital I, Werke* 23, pp. 469-70. See also Engels summarizing Marx in "Zur Wohnungsfrage" *Werke* 18, p. 214, where he speaks of the division of the surplus among unproductive workers, ranging from valets to the Pope, the Kaiser, the night watchman, etc. At one point Marx calls the various strata of civil servants, churchmen, etc., nothing but "elegant paupers." (*Theorien I*, p. 189.)

[46] *Theorien I*, p. 184.

[47] *Ibid.*; see also footnote 43 above.

[48] *Theorien III*, p. 49.

[49] *Ibid.*, p. 61.

Although Marx had nothing but spit and venom for any scheme designed deliberately to foster the growth of an unproductive class, he was repeatedly forced to recognize that the growth of productivity, i.e. the rise of the surplus, created precisely such a class. A few excerpts will make that clear:

> In order to produce "productively" one has to produce in a manner that excludes the mass of the producers from a part of the market demand for the product; one must produce in contradiction to a class whose consumption stands in no relationship to its production—since precisely this excess of production over consumption makes up the profit of capital. On the other hand, one has to produce for classes which consume without producing.[50]

> On a low level of development of the social productivity of labor, where therefore surplus labor is relatively small, the class of those who live off the labor of others will in principle be small in relation to the number of workers. This class can grow to significant proportions to the degree that productivity, i.e. relative surplus value, develops.[51]

> The progressive transformation of a part of the workers into servants is a lovely prospect, just as it is a great consolation for them [the workers] that, as a consequence of the growth of the net product, more spheres open up for unproductive workers who live off surplus labor and whose interests more or less compete with the directly exploiting class in exploiting them.[52]

Marx's consistency in this matter can be tested negatively as well; if he agrees, as we have seen, with economists who predict a growth of the unproductive class in the course of capitalist development, then he should also disagree with economists who think that they can do away with this class without abolishing the capitalist system itself. The bourgeois economist Ramsay advocated the abolition of interest on capital, i.e. the dividends paid by industrialists to investors and coupon-clippers, and the

[50] *Ibid.*, p. 139 fn.
[51] *Theorien II*, part 1, p. 127.
[52] *Theorien II*, part 2, p. 365.

abolition of land rent. Ramsay saw no useful function for either of these groups. Marx's acid comment on this proposal should be read with the phrase about the simplification of class contradictions (from the *Manifesto*) in mind:

> If this bourgeois ideal could really be put into practice, its consequence could only be that the entire surplus value would fall directly into the hands of the industrial capitalists, and all of society would be economically reduced to the simple contradiction between capital and wage labor, a simplification which certainly would hasten the dissolution of this form of production.[53]

Here again is the role of the surplus as a complicator of the simple class antagonisms reckoned with earlier. (A further, minor, example of the distance Marx's theory has carried him comes when he discusses economic crises in Volume II, part two of the *Theoricn*; he writes that his analysis proceeds without dealing with "the real constitution of society, which by no means consists only of the class of workers and the class of industrial capitalists." [54]

The clearest statement of Marx's theory of the middle class known to me occurs in his critique of Ricardo's analysis of the effect of increased productivity on the labor force. Ricardo, like Marx, was a bitter enemy of all forms of unproductive labor, which were to him as to Marx so many *"faux frais de production,"* false production costs; and consequently Ricardo called for the extension of productive labor on a maximal scale. While Ricardo saw that only machinery permits the efficient utilization of vast quantities of industrial laborers, he was troubled by the fact that the growing productivity of machinery tended at the same time to make the worker superfluous. Marx comments:

> One tendency throws the workers onto the pavement and creates a superfluous population. The other tendency absorbs

[53] *Theorien III,* p. 423.
[54] *Theorien II,* part 2, p. 264.

it again and expands wage slavery on an absolute scale, so that
the worker's lot changes constantly but he can never escape it.
That is why the worker correctly considers the development of
the productive capacities of his labor as a hostile tendency,
and why the capitalist treats him as an element to be constantly
eliminated from production. These are the contradictions with
which Ricardo struggles in this chapter. *What he forgets to
emphasize is the constant increase of the middle classes, who
stand in the middle between the workers on one side and the
capitalists and landed proprietors on the other side, who are
for the most part supported directly by revenue, who rest as
a burden on the laboring foundation, and who increase the
social security and the power of the upper ten thousand.*[55]
(Italics mine—MN)

These excerpts represent, as far as I know, the most
explicit statements of Marx's theory of the new middle
class in the entire Marxian opus. It seems entirely possible
to explain why Marx did not carry this theory further,
and it may even be possible for someone to show somehow that this theory does not contradict Marx's prediction of class polarization and proletarian revolution
(although I doubt it); but one thing cannot be done with
Marx's theory of the middle class: it cannot be explained
away. Even if Marx himself had never mentioned the
terms "unproductive class" or "middle class," someone
else would have to draw these implications of his theory,
for the rise of the middle class follows directly from the
law of the tendency of the surplus to rise, which is part
of the law of the tendency of the profit rate to fall, which
arises directly out of the solution of the surplus value
problem, which consists of the labor theory of value. Let
me review this chain of ideas once more. The labor theory
of value holds that the only agency which is capable of
creating more value than it represents is labor; that is,
only labor is capable of creating *surplus* value. The capi-

---

[55] *Ibid.*, p. 368. A part of this excerpt appears in a not-quite-tight translation in T. B. Bottomore and Maximilien Rubel, editors, *Karl Marx,
Selected Writings in Sociology and Social Philosophy* (McGraw-Hill paperback, 1964), p. 191.

talist system of production consists of the appropriation
by the capitalist class of ever greater quantities of this
surplus value. In a developed capitalist system, the capitalist class will concentrate on increasing *relative* surplus
value. That is, it will introduce machinery in order to
decrease that portion of the working day which is necessary to reproduce the workers' labor power, and to increase
that portion which is surplus labor. On the one hand,
increased productivity requires increased investment in
machinery, so that the *rate* of *profit* will tend to fall. On
the other hand, the mass of profit will rise, and both the
rate and the *volume* of *surplus* must rise. What happens
to this swelling surplus? It *enables* the capitalist class to
create a class of people who are not productive workers,
but who perform services either for individual capitalists
or, more important, for the capitalist class as a whole;
and at the same time, the rise of productivity *requires*
such a class of unproductive workers to fulfill the functions of distributing, marketing, researching, financing,
managing, keeping track of and glorifying the swelling
surplus product. This class of unproductive workers,
service workers, or servants for short, is the middle class.
In short, the middle class follows from the central principles which Marx spent the best decades of his life and
his health in elaborating, and which he considered his
historic contribution to the understanding of capitalism.
If one denies, as it seems to me one must, the validity of
Marx's class polarization and proletarian revolution predictions from the *Manifesto,* one does not deny that Marx
was a champion of the proletarian cause; one cuts out of
Marxism only its youthful optimism, the product of excessive captivation with the elegance of Hegelian idealism. But in order to cut out of Marx his theory of the
middle class, one has to overthrow Marxism, scientific
socialism, at its core—and fly in the face of contemporary
reality. There *is* after all a middle class in advanced industrial society; and it must be considered one of Marx's

great scientific achievements (and a great personal achievement, considering where his sentiments lay) to have not only predicted that such a new middle class would arise, but also to have laid down the fundamental economic and sociological principles which explain its rise and its role in the larger class structure. The outlines of what may become an adequate theory to account for the generation, growth, economic function and movement of the middle class have to my knowledge not been contributed by any other social scientist before Marx or after him. Here is a rare accomplishment and a rare challenge.

On Antonio Gramsci

BY *Eugene D. Genovese*

Volume VII, No. 2
March–April 1967

"The real philosophy of every man
is contained in his politics."
—Antonio Gramsci
Il Materialismo storico

*In this essay Eugene D. Genovese discusses the central impor-
tance to socialist movements in advanced industrial countries
of the struggle to build a popular consciousness of the possibility and desirability of an alternative social system. He
stresses here the crucial nature of the question of ideological
hegemony, especially in the Western democracies where the
loyalty of the population is maintained primarily through
ideological means, rather than through direct repression, as in
the colonial world.*

I

That the work and indeed the name of Antonio Gramsci*
remain virtually unknown to the American Left provides
the fullest, if saddest, proof of the intellectual bankruptcy
of "official" Marxism and its parties, old and new. Every
sect, no matter how trivial or tiresome, will spend its first
few dollars to publish some cant labeled theory. After all,
without a revolutionary theory there can be no. . . . Even
more appalling, the franchise holders of what was once a
Communist movement continue to be financially well
endowed if morally and politically moribund, and hardly

* Cammett, John. *Antonio Gramsci and the Origins of Italian Communism.* Stanford University Press, Stanford, California, 1967.

know what to do with their money. Publishing houses, schools and institutes abound, and if my talent for estimating bureaucratic expenditures does not fail me, annually cost tens and hundreds of thousands of dollars. The barely literate party hack has come into his own. Like the associate professor at Useless U. who finds himself in the paperback market, he will be published. All of which would not be without its delights were the price not so dear. As it is, it is nothing short of a disgrace that the greatest Western Marxist theorist of our century remains untranslated, unread, and undiscussed.[1]

Professor Cammett's excellent book brings this shabby game to a close, although not until a significant portion of Gramsci's *Quaderni del carcere (Prison Notebooks)* are in English will the full extent of the shabbiness be appreciated. The few intellectuals surviving in the Communist Party, with an occasional exception, recite from dated texts of minimal relevance to current problems; their counterparts in the leftist sects, who at least have the excuse of youth and of political *élan,* diligently search the writings of recent theorists of societies radically unlike our own. While these charades are being played out, the books of the one theorist of genius who posed and faced Western socialism's most difficult problems lie unopened. It is no accident. Gramsci challenged the best of the bourgeois intellectuals on their own ground, but no less did he challenge their social-democratic imitators and especially their dogmatic, simple-minded and mediocre opponents in the revolutionary camp. Gramsci's thought represents the maturation of Marxism and its restoration to the high level of its founders; as such, it

---

[1] There are two slim and inadequate volumes in English: *The Open Marxism of Antonio Gramsci,* trans. and ed. Carl Marzani (New York, 1957). A brief selection from the *Materialismo storico,* much of which consists of the editor's extrapolations in editorial comments on American problems; *The Modern Prince and Other Writings,* trans. and ed. Louis Marks, consisting of selections from several volumes of Gramsci's *Opere* with inadequate editing.

exposes the degeneracy of much that has passed for Marxism in our day.

Professor H. Stuart Hughes takes some liberties when he writes that compared with the theoretical work of Gramsci that of Lenin appears "crude indeed."[2] The assertion is exaggerated and unjust, but it is not absurd or indefensible. Its plausibility constitutes the highest compliment to the richness and depth of Gramsci's thought. And there is no higher compliment to Lenin's intellectual achievements than that Gramsci sincerely considered himself a Leninist and did not merely strike a Leninist pose to facilitate his leadership of the Italian Communist Party (PCI). For Gramsci, Lenin was the man who revitalized Marxism by purging it of determinism and economism, by restoring the element of will and by grasping the role of consciousness. Gramsci did for European Marxism what Mao Tse-tung did for Asian: he continued Lenin's effort to liberate Marxism from the mechanism that has plagued it from the beginning.

Cammett explores briefly but suggestively the intellectual kinship of Gramsci and Mao. Gramsci early saw the backwardness of Italy and the attendant weakness of its social order as providing especially good soil for a revolutionary movement. He was the first Italian Marxist political leader to stress the agrarian question in general and the question of the *Mezzogiorno* (the underdeveloped South) in particular. If he insisted that only the working class could solve those questions, he also insisted that the success of the proletarian revolution was bound up with them. Cammett sees a parallel between Gramsci's work on the *Mezzogiorno* (1926) and Lin Piao's celebrated thesis as presented in *Long Live the Victory of a People's War!* (1965), "In [Lin's] theory the whole underdeveloped world becomes a vast *Mezzogiorno*. The principal difference is that for the Italian theorist of 1926, the revolutionary impulse originated in the cities, though its success

[2] H. Stuart Hughes, *Consciousness and Society* (New York, 1958), p. 101.

depended on support from the rural areas. For the Chinese theorist of 1965, the revolution has its primary center in the countryside, and support from the cities may even be unnecessary." Cammett examines the relationship between Italian and Chinese Marxism on several levels but stresses the peasant question. This emphasis, although justified by today's most pressing practical questions, should not obscure the deeper link between the two—that concern for the dialectics of historical development which Cammett elsewhere discusses with considerable sophistication. Gramsci's remarks on revolutionary thought represent, although obviously not so intended, the firmest defense of the "Marxism" of a Chinese revolution with a peasant rather than proletarian base: "Revolutionary thought does not see time as a factor of progress. . . . To pass through one stage and advance to another, it is enough that the first stage be realized in thought."

II

Antonio Gramsci came from a petty-bourgeois family in Sardinia—perhaps the most economically and culturally wretched section of Italy. Despite his achievements as a pupil he had to leave school as a boy to help support the family. Supported by the efforts of his mother and sisters he finally managed to study at the University of Turin, which was then beginning to feel the powerful cleansing wind of Crocean idealism and to slough off its superficial positivism. There is much about Gramsci's youth we do not know, but Cammett's painstaking scholarship gives us enough. His biographical sketch shows us a sensitive, physically deformed, brilliant boy who, in his own words, "had known only the most brutal aspects of life." Cammett shows two great and lasting influences in his life: the experience with personal and class harshness, which steeled him for the life of a revolutionary and for an eleven-year confinement in a fascist prison, and the serious study of Hegelian and Crocean thought, from which he proceeded to Marxism and because of which he became implacably hostile to economic determinism and mechanism of all varieties.

The outcome was the making of an unusual Communist, who like his long-time collaborator and successor to the leadership of the PCI, Palmiro Togliatti, remained an intellectual deeply concerned with the quality of man's spiritual and cultural life and who simultaneously had the qualities necessary to win the support of the Comintern and to prepare the PCI to survive the long years of fascist repression. In 1926 the fascist secret police reported that the PCI, alone among the opposition parties, retained links with the masses and had prepared itself for underground struggle. Gramsci himself was arrested and spent the last eleven years of his life in prison, where he read whatever the authorities would let him have and where he wrote his greatest works—prison notebooks on political theory, Italian history and culture, philosophical criticism (most notably his critique of Croce), and on an astonishing assortment of other subjects. Prison, he observed, is a poor place to study, but he made it do and by this act of will alone exemplified that selflessness and heroism which has brought socialism into the world. If the American Left has not appreciated the significance of Gramsci's thought, the Italian fascists were not so backward. This "Sardinian hunchback," remarked Mussolini, "has an unquestionably powerful brain." More to the point were the words of the fascist prosecutor at Gramsci's trial in 1926, "We must stop this brain from functioning for twenty years."

As a party leader Gramsci had a difficult time on two counts. First, he and his fellow students from the University of Turin had to organize their own socialist faction around the journal *L'Ordine nuovo* (*The New Order*). Their position as intellectuals and their concern with cultural questions as well as with bread-and-butter issues made them suspect in the PSI generally and especially in proletarian Turin. It was a long road to leadership first of the Turin proletariat and then of the new Communist Party, in which they were originally only secondary and uncomfortable allies of the ultraleftist Amadeo Bordiga. Their success depended less on factional political maneuvering, for which Gramsci had great distaste, than on the wisdom of their course in the specific circumstances of the Turin labor movement. This side of the story can only be noted here, but its telling is one of Cammett's special achievements. Rarely has the relationship between a man's political thought and action been explored so specifically and shrewdly as is Gramsci's in this indispensable book. The second front on which Gramsci had to fight was against the Comintern itself. His arrest in 1926 might have saved him from being deposed as a party leader. Although he had no special admiration for Trotsky— Cammett even suggests that he had put forward the idea of socialism in one country before anyone in Russia—he spoke up in opposition to excessive and administrative measures against the left opposition and warned of the dangers of bureaucratic degeneration. An early advocate of the united front, he received news of the "Third Period" and its attacks on "social fascism" with foreboding. Had he been a free man and effective leader of the party at the time, his fate would have become problemmatical. The subsequent turn to the popular front, long foreshadowed in his own work, removed the pressure. Gramsci's life's work came to political fruition in the postwar rise of the PCI under the brilliant leadership of Togliatti.

III

The great question absorbing Gramsci's attention and intruding itself into everything else was the nature and role of the party. Even his lengthy and painstaking examination of the historical role of the intelligentsia represents a special case of his more general concern. I suspect that he would have found nonsensical or at least trivial the question of "agency of change" now agitating the American left, and would have found incomprehensible the dispute over the relative merits of class and party as agency. One of his most striking ideas was that a class is hardly worthy of the name until it comes to self-consciousness—an idea that veers dangerously close to idealism and that nonetheless is hard to turn aside. The party of the working class therefore has tasks beyond that of providing leadership in daily battle; it is charged with the transformation of the working class itself into a body worthy to rule. The "cultural" task of the party is to win the working class to a world view capable of absorbing and transcending the culture and accomplishment of the past.

Professor Hughes is mistaken when he writes, "What interested him was the character of the new culture that would develop *after* the proletarian assumption of power."[3] The reverse is true. Gramsci had no faith in the triumph of a working class that had not already begun to think and live in a new way. To the party fell the task of completing that transformation in the working class which was immanent in capitalist society itself. To accomplish this task the party needed to find its own way—to establish an authentic, autonomous world view purged of all fatalism and mechanical determinism. It is in this context that Cammett's penetrating remark on Serrati and Gramsci must be evaluated: "Serrati thought of the possession of power as the culmination of the general elevation of the masses, whereas Gramsci believed that the masses could be elevated only by possessing power. The principal difference between the Second and Third Internationals is contained in this contrast." The posses-

[3] Hughes, *Consciousness and Society*, p. 102. Original emphasis.

sion of power, however, means in the first place the building of an autonomous party and movement; the "elevation
of the masses" therefore begins with the struggle for
control of civil society as well as the state, and reaches
its climax when the state has been conquered and turned
to that purpose.

Nothing irritated Gramsci more than the mechanical
side of Marxism. For him the genuine doctrine of Marx
was one "in which man and reality, the instrument of
labor and the will, are not separated but come together
in the *historical act*. Hence [Marxists] believe that the
canons of historical materialism are valid only after the
fact, for studying and understanding the events of the
past, and ought not to become a mortgage on the present
and future." He scoffed at reliance on such "objective
conditions" as economic depression. The objective conditions for proletarian revolution, he once observed, had
existed in Europe for fifty years or more. It seems to me
that Cammett stresses unduly the relationship between
Gramsci's concern for superstructural problems, in contradistinction to those directly connected with the economic
base, and the post-revolutionary situation in the 1920's
and 1930's. Cammett is correct in pointing out that
Gramsci himself saw the cultural front as especially important during such periods, when the direct confrontation of classes recedes, and that Gramsci, unlike so many
others in the Comintern, understood the defensive character of the period in question. Yet, this emphasis on
superstructure—in Cammett's words, on "the whole complex of political, social, and cultural institutions and
ideas"—had even deeper roots in his awareness of the
dependence of revolution, even in periods of dramatic
confrontation, on consciousness rather than on economics.
(There is in Cammett's book a tendency to avoid a frank
discussion of the markedly idealist cast of Gramsci's
thought, and this tendency, I suspect, accounts for his
insistence on reading Gramsci narrowly on this question.)

Simple as it is, Gramsci's observation that capitalism has been objectively ready for burial since the late nineteenth century—that, if I may put it this way, the Leninist theory of a general crisis in society and not merely the economy deserves to be taken seriously—ought to render permanent the concentration on the ideological struggle. Unlike the simpletons who insist that the desire for liberation flows from the innate qualities of oppressed classes and peoples, Gramsci saw that desire as a function of specific social processes: "Men, when they feel their strength and are conscious of their responsibility and their value, do not want another man to impose his will on theirs and undertake to control their thoughts and actions." It was precisely the struggle to bring the working class to a sense of its strength, responsibility and value that provided his main concern. He obliquely criticized Marx for lapsing on occasion from his own insight and for stressing in an abstract way the predominance of material over ideeological forces. Gramsci pointed out that the principle of unity of form and content calls into question the validity of such a dichotomy. Material forces as "content" and ideologies as "form" necessarily comprise a "historical bloc" since material forces are unthinkable without form and ideologies merely individual chattering when not expressive of such forces.

The instrument favored by Gramsci in the ideological struggle for the working class was the workers' council or soviet. He did not borrow this idea directly from Russian experience. It arose from several sources, not the least of which was the American journal, *The Liberator,* and especially the writings of Daniel De Leon. For Gramsci the socialist state already existed in the potentiality of working-class social institutions. To create such a state the first task is to bring the working class as a whole within such institutions.

Gramsci rejected the trade unions as organs of revolutionary transformation and preparation, and Cammett's account of his critique ought to be required reading for American socialists, especially those in the Marxist parties. The seriousness with which Gramsci viewed the role of the councils may be gleaned from his insistence that the working class must "educate itself, gather experience, and acquire a responsible awareness of the duties incumbent upon classes that hold the power of the state."

For him the worst error committed by the party in relation to the unions was the tendency to regard the economic struggle as an activity essential to the social revolution. The trade union, in its very origins, organized itself in response to hostile and imposed conditions, rather than as an autonomous expression of the working class. The trade union struggle was contingent, not permanent, and its organization was, accordingly, incapable of embodying a revolutionary movement. Unionism, being a form of capitalist society, brings the worker to see labor as a means for gain, not as a productive process, but it is consciousness of the latter that alone can raise the working class to an appreciation of its historic responsibilities. The council, on the other hand, effected the collaboration of skilled and unskilled workers, the technical strata and the clerical personnel within a notion of the unity of the industrial process. Whereas the unions exist to prevent the class war from being unleashed, the council threatens to unleash it at any moment. Long before the corporate state in Italy or the perception by radicals of a growing corporate liberalism in the United States, Gramsci observed that the detachment of the union bureaucracies from their rank-and-file constitutes the movement's strength, not weakness. The detached bureaucracies, isolated from the tumult of the masses, guarantee stability in the negotiation and enforcement of contracts. This guarantee establishes the "legitimacy" of the unions in the eyes of the bourgeoisie and makes possible those union-inspired advances in living conditions which have occurred under capitalism.

Gramsci's thinking on these questions, even apart from his critique of trade unionism, should prove unusually suggestive in our country. In his view the councils could educate the Italian workers in the political process and prepare them to wield state power. The English and American workers, however, have long been practiced in the exercise of political power, at least in the ordinary sense of the word. Certainly, he meant something deeper— the instillation in the working class of a sense that it stands for a culturally, economically, politically and socially superior order. Yet, it does seem to me that as a practical matter the two meanings were necessarily inseparable in the thought of a man concerned with one of the weaker and more backward capitalist states of Europe. Cammett cites the view of the distinguished Marxist historian, Giuliano Procacci, that the backwardness of the Italian labor movement prevented its being trapped like those of the more advanced countries into a primary concern for economic issues. The struggle for democracy and for the reorganization of civil society became indissolubly linked to the economic struggle.

Thus does the Marxism of Italian Communism part company with the superficiality of its official American counterpart. One of the more banal themes of American Marxist historiography has been the allegedly wonderful advantages to the working class provided by the gift of bourgeois democracy. From this philistine viewpoint, the movements associated with St. Thomas of Monticello and Andrew Jackson, our first outspoken presidential expo-nent of genocide and strike-breaking, graciously bestowed upon the working class the full benefit of their battle to broaden the base of American capitalism. The victory of the "people" over Tories, Federalists and Whigs produced a broad franchise; by the time the working class matured it found itself enfranchised free of charge. Those on the Left who have celebrated this circumstance have substi-tuted a vulgar retrospective popular-frontism for Marxian analysis and have thereby missed the duality of the process and its significance. On the one hand this bourgeois-democratic political process did present the working class with extraordinary opportunities for improving its material conditions under capitalism; on the other hand this same process drew the revolutionary teeth of the proletariat and helped extend over it the hegemony of the bourgeoisie. We should let the bourgeoisie do the celebrating. For American socialism it ushered in a debacle, albeit one retaining some long-range positive possibilities. At least it has generated a level of culture and political practice among the workers on which a movement not sterilized by dogmatism or liberal shibboleths may someday build.

Gramsci's central concern with the working class and its changing composition led him to consider the metamorphosis of the bourgeoisie as well. He noted that technological developments were eliminating the master craftsmen and were rendering the workers increasingly capable of carrying on without technical supervision. With a self-disciplined working class the technicians were being "reduced to the level of the producer," connected to the capitalists by a nakedly exploitable relationship. Cammett notes that Gramsci regarded this shift as carrying with it an attendant shift from a petty-bourgeois to a proletarian consciousness. In relatively underdeveloped Italy this attendant shift may well have taken place according to Gramsci's expectations, but in the United States the reverse has apparently occurred: the technicians have shifted from a petty-bourgeois to a bourgeois psychology. They have proceeded from shopkeeper individualism to team-consciousness within the framework of bourgeois values and assumptions; they have proceeded from consciousness of personal economic and social interests to consciousness of class responsibilities, which unfortunately have been the responsibilities of the present rather than the future ruling class. Yet, the potentialities foreseen by Gramsci

remain and provide considerable hope for a future socialist movement; the realization of these potentialities depends in part on a full appreciation of the remainder of
Gramsci's analysis of the problem.

Finance capitalism, Gramsci observed, separates the
owner from the factory and therefore renders him para-
sitic and superfluous; he no longer has a role to play in
production. The consequences of this process, about
which bourgeois theorists talk such self-serving nonsense,
are as ominous as they are ludicrous:

> The owner of capital [writes Gramsci] has become a dead
> branch in the field of production. Since he is no longer indis-
> pensable—since his historical functions have atrophied—he
> has become a mere agent of the police. He puts his interests
> immediately in the hands of the state, which will ruthlessly
> defend them.

These circumstances—increasing parasitism and increasing reliance on an authoritarian state—create favorable
conditions for a working-class movement sufficiently broad
to include the technical strata and the so-called new
middle class. The rationalization of the economy proceeds
hand-in-hand with the intensification of the system's
higher-level irrationalities, which have their primary manifestations in war, racism, ghetto poverty and moral decay.
The process as a whole threatens to destroy the very security it offers the affluent sections of the upper and middle
echelons of the technical and proletarian strata. When
Staughton Lynd told the First Annual Socialist Scholars
Conference in 1965 that the irrationalities of capitalism
might soon force the American people as a whole to consider a socialist alternative as a matter of survival, he
departed less from a class analysis than would appear on
the surface.

Gramsci's popular-frontism must be understood in this
context. Early in his career he stressed the national character of the proletarian revolution and spoke of the need
to explain the advantages of socialism to the middle

classes. At the same time he had the utmost contempt for the revisionists and would have roared with laughter at the slogan, "Socialism is not on the agenda." The autonomy of the party and the unceasing agitation among the masses for socialism were among his lifelong themes. For him tactical alliances with other parties and classes, especially defensive ones, could never be an excuse for hiding the face of the party, or for advancing only bourgeois-democratic demands, or for sowing illusions about "progressive" sections of the bourgeoisie.

Gramsci initially fought for unity in the PSI, although he sharply criticized the reformists, but the failure of the party's nerve during the revolutionary crisis of 1919-1920 convinced him of the need for a split. He may have been influenced in this course by his assessment of the rise of fascism, which he analyzed with a depth and clarity setting him apart in Italy and, with the exception of Trotsky and a few others in the Comintern as well. After the split in 1921 he worked unceasingly to win the new Communist Party away from Bordiga's ultraleftism and to create an apparatus capable of guiding the workers through a rapid ideological transformation.

In Gramscian terms a political party is an agent of education and civilization—a school in which one studies the life of the state. Parties represent the adherence of élites to particular forms of class rule; they educate their followers in the principles of moral conduct, the duties and the obligations appropriate to that social order. A party justifies its historical existence when it develops three strata: (1) a rank-and-file of ordinary men whose participation is characterized by discipline and faith; (2) a leadership, which provides cohesion; and (3) cadres, which mediate morally, physically and intellectually between the other two. Of these three strata he stressed leadership:

We speak of captains without an army, but in reality it is easier to form an army than to find captains. It is surely true that an already existing army will be destroyed if it lacks captains, whereas a group of captains, cooperative and in agreement on common ends, will not be slow in forming an army where none exists.

To this view he added two observations. Contrary to the Social Democrats he argued that a socialist party must be an autonomous entity, not one dependent on the larger movement of bourgeois democracy; it must reject the existing order and work relentlessly for its overthrow. It must also be monolithic in the sense that it is formed on principle and essentials, not on secondary considerations. As in so many cases, his verbal acquiescence in the line of the Stalinist Comintern hid fundamental differences. A monolithic party, to Gramsci, meant one without factional organizations but with room for dissent. A socialist party must have enthusiasm and good will from its members, neither of which can be coerced ideologically or by administrative measures. To grasp the full significance of his ideas on these subjects we need to consider his groundbreaking work on the role of the intellectuals.

IV

Critical self-consciousness, wrote Gramsci in *Il Materialismo storico,* means historically and politically the formation of an intellectual élite, for the masses cannot achieve ideological independence through their own efforts. They first must be organized, but there can be no organization without intellectuals. By intellectuals Gramsci meant more than artists and scholars; he meant also technicians, industrial managers and administrative personnel. The first he called "traditional intellectuals"; the second he called "organic intellectuals." Cammett's last chapter summarizes concisely and impressively the ideas on both strata that Gramsci scattered in the *Quaderni.*

The outstanding feature of the traditional intellectuals is their sense of representing, in Gramsci's words, "historical continuity uninterrupted even by the most radical and complicated changes of social and political systems." These men consequently consider themselves an autonomous group, independent of the ruling class. They are tied to the Establishment indirectly and in ways sufficiently subtle to permit them to maintain illusions. If this indirection fosters illusions, it also creates room for independent thought and action.

The organic intellectuals, being more directly bound to the Establishment, rarely escape awareness of their place in the economic process. These men share the interests of the ruling class. For this reason the working-class movement must create its own organic intellectuals— must train its own technical strata. Here again the party looms as the indispensable instrument. Gramsci apparently had in mind primarily one section of the organic intellectuals—the administrative personnel capable of commanding the state and the organs of political society. The changes of the last few decades have not lessened the urgency of this task, but the growing importance of technical strata capable of commanding the economy cannot be ignored. In Gramsci's day it was still possible, if not wholly realistic, to urge the technical training of workers under autonomous auspices in order to prepare them for the tasks of class rule. The technological revolution through which we are passing has enormously widened the gap between these organic intellectuals and the most intelligent, skilled and politically advanced workers. It appears, therefore, that our tasks are today much more complex and include a determined effort to break the hegemony of the bourgeoisie over these, its most pampered, servants.

The two groups of intellectuals parallel those two aspects of society which Gramsci analyzed in terms reminiscent of Vico and Hegel. The organic intellectuals, as part

of the ruling class, provide the personnel for those coercive organs constituting "political society." The traditional intellectuals, in contrast, staff the organs of "civil
society"—the church, schools, social clubs, political parties, etc. Their task is to reason with the masses, to persuade, to convince; they are the essential element in the
hegemony of the ruling class.

Gramsci's notion of hegemony is perhaps his most important contribution to Marxian political theory and
forms a necessary counterpart to Lenin's development of
the Marxian theory of the state. Gramsci's notion has
been summarized by Gwynn Williams:

[Hegemony is] an order in which a certain way of life and
thought is dominant, in which one concept of reality is dif-
fused throughout society in all its institutional and private
manifestations, in forming with its spirit all taste, morality,
customs, religious and political principles, and all social relations, particularly in their intellectual and moral connota-
tions.[4]

Hegemony, therefore, is achieved by consent, not force,
through the civil and ostensibly private institutions of
society. Marxists, as Cammett observes, usually think of
"the state" simply as political society, whereas, he argues,
the state (or as I should prefer to say, the system of class
rule) ought to be understood more broadly as an equilib-
ium between political and civil society. Cammett observes
further, "In its general sense, hegemony refers to the
'spontaneous' loyalty that any dominant social group ob-
tains from the masses by virtue of its social and intellectual prestige and its supposedly superior function in the
world of production."

It follows that hegemony depends on much more than
consciousness of economic interests on the part of the
ruling class and unconsciousness of such interests on the
part of the submerged classes. The success of a ruling
class in establishing its hegemony depends entirely on its

[4] Gwynn Williams, as quoted by Cammett, *Antonio Gramsci,* p. 204.

ability to convince the lower classes that its interests are those of society at large—that it defends the common sensibility and stands for a natural and proper social order. It is nonsense to think that an economic depression or devastating war could alone revolutionize consciousness. For the masses to be able to attribute their particular woes to the social system they must be more broadly convinced that the interests of the ruling class are at variance with those of society in general and of their own class in particular. To bring the masses to such a point we need to face the fact that such an identification between bourgeois and general interests exists and has existed, with the exception of the autebellum South, throughout American history. Too often our Marxists have assumed that economic deprivation, political repression or socially retrogressive actions could rouse the exploited classes to anger and resistance. Even today we witness the absurdity of allegedly "vanguard" movements tying their hopes to some future depression or alternative catastrophe. Apathy, however, is not necessarily a product of fear, much less of indifference to discomfort and oppression; it may flow from a failure to identify the source of the discomfort and oppression. Every organ of civil society labors to cloud the issue, to misdirect the anger and to produce resignation. If all we had to contend with was the force of political society, as so many of our ultra-leftists as well as dogmatic revisionists like to believe, our prospects would now be much brighter. If, as is the case, we have to contend with a pervasive world view that identifies exploitation and social injustice as minor concommitants of the defense of a proper order, of religious and moral truth and of elementary decency in human relationships, then we had better begin doing our homework in philosophy, sociology, political theory and even theology. It is the totality of the bourgeois world view—the enormous complex of prejudices, assumptions, half-thought-out notions and no small number of profound ideas—that infects the victims of bourgeois rule, and it is the totality of an alternative world view that alone can challenge it for supremacy.

Socialists, as Gramsci said, must overcome the reluctance of the masses to risk the chaos inevitably accompanying the transition to a new society, but one of our hardest tasks seems to be to convince our own ultras that the masses, even the most wretched and desperate sections of them, normally do fear such chaos and must be made to see order and discipline during the most tumultuous transformations. The only elements that welcome chaos are those among the masses whom the bourgeoisie has degraded into nihilism or those among our most dedicated and courageous cadres who have been tragically misled into desperation. In bourgeois-democratic societies the hegemony of the bourgeoisie masks its dictatorship. As Gramsci noted,

> In countries where open conflicts do not take place, where fundamental laws of the state are not trampled on, where arbitrary acts of the dominant class are not seen, the class struggle loses its harshness, the revolutionary struggle loses its drive and falters. . . . Where an order exists, it is more difficult to decide to replace it with a new order.

Fascism, therefore, is a sign of great weakness on the part of the bourgeoisie, and it is exasperating inanity to speak, as so many of our official Marxists do, of the "drive" of the bourgeoisie toward fascism.

The trouble with those who anxiously pore over the lessons of China and Cuba, or of Russia for that matter, is not that all those great revolutions do not have much to teach us, but that the gulf separating all of them from the experience of Western Europe must always be kept in the forefront. In each of those societies civil society had come apart and hardly existed as a hegemonic force any longer; the struggle could therefore be opened on the terrain of political society. The central fact of our own experience has been the enormous power of civil society even when the state power has faltered momentarily; we cannot hope to topple the state until we have fought and won the battle for civil society. In the Western capitalist countries the hegemony of the bourgeoisie creates especially painful difficulties. Gramsci noted the contrast to Russia: "In the East the state was everything, and civil society was primordial and gelatinous; in the West there was a correct relationship between the state and civil society." A robust civil society can support an apparently shaky state and can carry it through difficult moments. Under this condition the seizure of power is unlikely until civil society has been substantially transformed. The war for position on the cultural front and the allegience of the intellectuals is consequently vital to the struggle for socialism. As Cammett adds,

The fundamental assumption behind Gramsci's view of hegemony is that the working class, before it seizes power, must establish its claim to be a ruling class in the political, cultural, and 'ethical' fields. 'The founding of a ruling class is equivalent to the creation of a *Weltanschauung.*' . . . For Gramsci, a social class scarcely deserves the name until it becomes *conscious* of its existence as a class; it cannot play a role in history until it develops a comprehensive world-view and a political program.

Bourgeois sociologists are, from this point of view, not entirely wrong to deny the existence of a working class in the United States. Leftist dismissal of the working class as "corrupt," or "irrelevant" or "just another part of the Establishment" nonetheless constitutes a superficial response to a problem that may be defined as the search for ways to develop such consciousness among those strata of the population capable, immediately or potentially, of forming a new ruling class.

V

I have tried in the foregoing sections to present Gramsci's ideas, as outlined by Cammett, with a minimum of extension and interpretation; at least I hope that it is clear where Gramsci ends and Cammett begins and where Cammett ends and Genovese begins. The following section is, however, wholly interpretive and polemical and consists of loosely related thoughts suggested by Cammett's book and Gramsci's voluminous writings, parts of which I have studied carefully, parts casually and parts not at all.

THE ROLE OF THE WORKING CLASS

Pretense aside, the great Communist revolution in China has been based on the peasants. Admitting some exaggeration, we might say that instead of the proletariat's making the revolution, the revolution has been making the proletariat. For a revolution to pass from one stage to another, to recall Gramsci's dictum, it is enough to realize the first stage in thought. Socialism traditionally has been a proletarian demand and program; as a major political movement it was the creation of the working class, defined to include those intellectuals openly attached to it. For more than one hundred years socialism has been a living idea; as such it has embraced the aspirations of all who value the humane and egalitarian traditions of Western society but who recognize that capitalism is unable to preserve the best in its own revolutionary heritage. If the idea of socialism, with its proletarian origins and its intention of raising the working class to power, could seize hold of the peasants of China, there is no reason that it cannot seize hold of the "new middle class" in the United States. The Chinese revolution was prevented from degenerating into a peasant-based social order by the commanding position of the party. With a small working class with which to staff the organs of political society, the party has to create a civil society of its own—to persuade, to convince, to win the battle for the minds of the peasant

masses. The "proletarian" character of the Chinese revolution has rested on its commitment to a socialist order
and has been determined in the realm of ideology—of
thought. The assertion that only the working class can
establish socialism is dogmatic nonsense.

I do not suggest that American socialism turn away from
the working class, for I cannot imagine to what else it
could turn. I do suggest that we recognize the extent to
which the question of socialism has become a matter of
urgency for our people as a whole, and the extent to
which the psychology of our workers, at least of our organized workers, has become indistinguishable from that of
the "new middle class" of which so many of them in fact
form a part. In view of the unprecedented strength of
American capitalism, the power center of world imperialism, the prospects for resolving the old class questions—
depression levels of unemployment, hunger, acute deprivation, insecurity in old age—within the present system
are excellent. Capitalism's inherent irrationality and
immanent contradictions have not been overcome, but
their social and phenomenal manifestations have changed
drastically. The great issues facing the working class today
are only indirectly those suggestive of economic exploitation. Principally they are the issue of survival (war or
peace), elementary security to enjoy those material advantages which high capitalism has generated (protection
against race riots, urban congestion, rampant hooliganism
and crime and the rest of the familiar items from Senator
Goldwater's demagogic but by no means irrelevant
speeches), the preservation of an adequate degree of stability in the face of pressures to dissolve the family without providing an adequate replacement, and in general
the crisis in ideals and values that has descended in personal as well as social relationships. These are problems
facing society as a whole; they grip all social classes, although not to the same degree, and are not class questions
in the traditional sense. The solution, however, is very

much a class question, for nothing short of the hegemony of the working class, broadly defined to include most of the producing elements of our society, can establish a viable alternative social order.

Two conclusions follow. First, the most oppressed sections of our society can, in various ways too complicated for summary discussion, play an important part in the formation of a new revolutionary movement but cannot serve as its basis since they cannot possibly form the basis of a new ruling class. Second, under present conditions the working class can be won and the hegemony of the bourgeoisie broken only through a struggle that includes but does not rely on the bread-and-butter issues. The measures necessary to win the workers are essentially the same as those necessary to win the technical strata and the intelligentsia as a whole. To reach the workers, especially the most socially conscious workers, we need to frame appeals to a much broader section of our population. The spectacle of dock workers refusing to load ships that trade with Communist countries is especially instructive. These workers are not motivated primarily by the desire for personal gain; such stoppages might even cost them a good deal of money. However much we may deplore their reactionary stance, we ought to realize that their action connotes a strong social consciousness and a sense of their responsibility as workers in the formulation of social policy. Their willingness to move from economic to political and social issues opens the way to their radicalization and provides a suitable terrain on which to struggle for their ideological allegiance.

The position of the new technical and administrative strata may be approached in one of two ways. We might, with some justice, place them in the bourgeoisie, which certainly holds their allegiance at present. In this case, we would, even under the best of circumstances, have to concentrate on winning the working class alone since the agrarian classes no longer are numerically significant.

Among the several objections to such an approach is the obvious one that a large and perhaps decisive section of the working class itself shares the outlook of these strata for the good reason that its social and economic position is only quantitatively distinct. The second approach would be to consider these technical and administrative strata as part of the working class, and in traditional Marxian terms a good case can be made out for the identification. This solution would, however, be mere sleight-of-hand and deep-deception were it not for that degradation of all these strata alluded to by Gramsci. The technicians and administrators are well paid servants, but they in fact run the plant and have usurped the functions of the capitalists. As a result the system hardly gives full rein to their talent or, worse, prostitutes it. They are, moreover, victims of the same general insecurities plaguing the population as a whole. If the working class has become part of the middle class, in a psychological sense and even to some extent as an income stratum, it is no less true that the new middle class is part of the working class. As such, its members have personal bourgeois interests but not a bourgeois class interest. Together with the traditional working class, they are the ones most capable of ruling society and of undergoing a revolution in consciousness. The ghetto populations may prove to be invaluable allies, but the construction of a new ruling class must come from the stable elements of our society.

THE STRUGGLE FOR HEGEMONY

If we were to pose the question of hegemony in Gramscian terms and ask which sections of the American left have addressed themselves to it, we should have to confess that the answer would be the New Left. In a country and at a time when the idea of workers' councils and a mass party seems remote, the New Left's notion of counter-communities and counter-institutions has considerable plausibility. Measured against this notion the traditional insistence of the Communist Party and other groups on working within existing institutions might seem not only old-fashioned but counter-revolutionary. Would that life were so simple! The overwhelming fact is that all attempts to replace the universities, for example, with "free universities" or "people's schools" are doomed to failure. The concentration of wealth and the level of institutional integration and sophistication being what they are, the most we could hope to accomplish would be supplementary activities, which might prove politically invaluable but only within narrow limits. Free universities can do important work in helping to train political and intellectual cadres, but can hardly be expected to replace the academic institutions.

The problem we face is how to steer between two equally futile courses. To orient ourselves to work in existing universities, unions and political organizations in the way in which the Communist Party urges would merely repeat past defeats and add up to the pathetic efforts of well meaning individuals who objectively work to strengthen the hegemony of the bourgeoisie. To withdraw, to go it alone, to spend our strength trying to build counter-institutions would be to surrender the possibilities of practical and meaningful work and to replace it with activities designed to save our individual souls from sin and corruption. The course demanded is to work within the institutions of civil society openly as socialists, despite the risks, with the avowed aim of transforming them into organs of transition to socialism. They must be made the battleground on which we transform the consciousness of the intelligentsia and the masses and therefore instruments for the structural reform of society. What separates a revolutionary from a reformist notion of structural reform, as Togliatti pointed out in his brilliant post-war articles in *Rinascita,* is the commitment to the socialist goal—the insistence that every advance must be integrated into the life of the party, the incessant struggle against bourgeois ideology, the adherence to the responsibilities of internationalism and the unfailing attention to the conquest of state power.

The state of and prospects for international relations present favorable opportunities for a struggle within the existing institutions—within civil society. So long as the world movement, even in its present state of crisis and disunity, remains sufficiently powerful and responsible to prevent the United States from unleashing a general nuclear war, the prospects for American imperialism's retaining its informal empire are not bright. The retreat from a position of worldwide looting must necessarily bring the United States face to face with itself. Even if armaments expenditures have largely usurped the place previously held by capital exports in the structure of imperialist economics, the bourgeoisie is headed for trouble. The Cold War is needed more and more to support domestic war programs, instead of vice versa, but the imperialists' growing difficulty in maintaining a Cold War psychology threatens them on all fronts. There is no reason, except one, to assume that our people will forever tolerate a régime which cannot cope satisfactorily with the most pressing problems of the day despite unprecedented resources. The one reason, of course, is the continued absence of a movement capable of advancing alternatives.

If the primary task at the moment must be a Gramscian "war for position on the cultural front" and if that war must be fought within the existing unions, universities and social organizations, a variety of problems present themselves for urgent attention. Without attempting here even a suitable preliminary analysis of these complex problems, we may for the moment restrict ourselves to a few questions posed in the universities.

As the citadels of the traditional intellectuals, the universities are probably the institutions most convinced of their own autonomy, independence and freedom of thought. Let us grant that the reality has always been something less; the fact remains that the myth of a community of disinterested scholars and the tradition, however often violated, of academic freedom ought to be central concerns for socialists. We may bypass for the present the problem of disinterestedness and partisanship in scholarship. It ought to be clear that the development of a humane and just social order requires maximum freedom of thought and expression, and that the universities are the institutions in which the greatest latitude possible must be maintained. Our task, accordingly, is not to cry over the prevalence of bourgeois sterility, much less to dream of the day when we will have control of these institutions and can settle old scores. The ideal of the university as a community of scholars constitutes one of the finest features of the civilization we inherit from the past. If the reality falls far short of the ideal, socialists ought to be the staunchest champions of the ideal; they ought to be easily identified as men who advance specific programs for bringing the reality closer to the ideal and who have definite ideas for narrowing the gap in a future society. The university as ideal is already a quasi-socialist institution; the struggle to uphold the ideal is or could be a struggle to educate its personnel and the people generally in socialist ethical and political standards.

An object lesson in what not to do came out of Stanford University recently. A remarkable young man—serious, dedicated, intelligent and morally responsible—undertook to campaign for the presidency of the Student Council on a radical New Left platform that included hostility to America's imperialist war in Vietnam. To everyone's surprise in so conservative a university he won. After a while he resigned, arguing that he had made his point through the campaign and had no desire to be caught up in the Establishment's bureaucracy, in which he could only function more or less like everyone else. I cannot imagine a greater exercise in futility; enough such abdications and the Left will lose, and deserve to lose, whatever audience it has. I intend no personal criticism of this young man, for what else could he have done in a political vacuum? We have no party or organized movement to provide direction and purpose; we have no general strategy to apply to specific situations. Quite possibly he was, in a narrow sense, right: had he remained in office under such circumstances, he might have become merely another functionary.

The frustration and confusion with which we must contend are exemplified by the tendency to nihilism among some of our best young people in the universities. Unable to influence society as a whole and overcome with a sense of powerlessness, they confront the universities with unreasonable and dubious demands and charges: all administrations are necessarily class enemies; the professors are generally finks, sell-outs, and prigs; the students ought to control the curricula; students and professors have equal rights in the classroom; and only the Good Lord knows what else.[5] Nothing will come of all this thrashing because nothing can come of it. Certainly, students' opinions on most matters of educational policy ought to be sought; and with equal certainty, no professor worthy of the name would surrender his prerogative to teach his course as he and he alone sees fit. The university cannot supply the student with the sense of power and relevance that society denies him. It is an institution with

[5] Let me make clear that these remarks are no veiled criticism of student behavior at Berkeley or elsewhere, where complicated issues require specific analysis. I speak here only of a mood that prevails over too large a section of our student radicals.

specific purposes, not society in microcosm. Its administrators are generally weak, frightened careerists rather than conscious servants of a hostile power; it does them too much honor in most cases to regard them as class enemies.

It is, of course, easier to provoke a bitter quarrel with an administration than to organize a movement for peace and socialism—the students will support you much more readily—but this is the essence of opportunism. The only administration worthy of being treated as enemies are those which deny the right of the faculty or the student body to pursue its legitimate intellectual interests and to organize itself politically. In a period in which the financial control of the universities is passing into the hands of the state, students and professors have a double duty: to organize opinion and action against the foreign and domestic policies of imperialism and to defeat every encroachment against traditional liberties on the campus. What might a president of a student council do? He might, among other things, lead a movement to drive off the campus every agency threatening the institution's autonomy, and he might lead an effort to make his university an ideological battleground in which the problems of our society are debated and the outlines of a better society are explored. To do this does not require usurping the prerogatives of professors or destroying the structure of the classroom. Much of the theoretical work of the international socialist movement came out of the universities, as the experience of Gramsci and his circle reminds us. They must be kept free to permit that work to continue and expand. The fight for the preservation of their freedom and for their transformation, through ideological work and persuasion, not self-defeating bullying and totalitarian measures, into authentic communities of scholars is the fight to prepare them for their place in a new socialist order. It is one of many battles that must be waged to overthrow the hegemony of the bourgeoisie.

THE PARTY

Those on the left who today call for a new socialist party generally stress the urgent need for a center to coordinate political action and provide ideological and organizational continuity. The editorials in *Studies on the Left* may be cited as a good example. That we do face such urgency and do need a party to cope with it could hardly be denied. The case for a new party rests, however, on a broader base, as the experience of the New Left makes clear.

The New Left has been primarily a moral rather than political (in the narrow sense of the word) movement. It has been a protest against a society wealthy and cynical enough to buy the silent acquiescence of its people in worldwide plunder and various forms of domestic barbarism. The answers to the New Left have been thin and sometimes so utopian or undesirable as to call forth ridicule and even contempt. This reaction, of which I among others have sometimes been guilty, has missed the most politically important contribution that the New Left has made: in its own terms it has raised the question of cultural hegemony and has insisted on its centrality. Its answers have been poor, and in some ways worse than nothing, but its instinct for the enemy's vulnerability and its sense of what constitutes a proper battleground have been much more impressive than anything coming from Marxist sources, old or new, official or independent.

The New Left has nonetheless been unable to proceed from its insights to a position from which it could effectively challenge the régime. The reasons are familiar, and the most thoughtful elements in the new movements have provided as good an analysis as have their critics. Those who have criticized them from a Marxist viewpoint have failed to impress them with the arguments for a new party because that demand has been advanced as a political-administrative solution to what seems to them, quite correctly, to be a moral and broadly social problem. They deny a hostility to theory, but insist they have seen no theory worthy of their commitment. Marxists have been irritated and puzzled by this taunt because they know that Marxism, for all its roughness and incompleteness, offers a perfectly sound starting point for theoretical work, and they cannot understand the lack of attention from the New Left. There are many reasons for this lack, not all of which are flattering to the New Left, but there can be no question about the intelligence, sincerity and seriousness of many who have remained aloof. In part the problem has been the unwillingness of the Marxist parties and tendencies to accept responsibility for waging a Gramscian struggle on the cultural level. The most profound questions have been reopened in the light of the negative side of the experiences of the Eastern socialist countries: questions about the nature of man, of his responsibility to himself and to society, of a new and higher morality and of the proper relationship among students and workers, leaders and led, men and women. Our Marxists have given no answers, or answers the banality of which ought to embarrass them.

The New Left's indifference to Marxism may, with supreme irony, finally do what the sterile Marxist parties have failed to do—lead to the restoration of Marxism to its rightful place in American intellectual and political life. By rejecting the mechanism and determinism of official American Marxism, not to mention its totalitarianism, the New Left may finally force American Marxists to come to terms with Gramscian thought and to prepare to make its own departure. American Marxists cannot hope to advance until they meet the ideologies of the New Left on their own ground; the thought of Antonio Gramsci does not provide ready-made answers but does provide the starting point for which we have been searching.

The need is for more than a dialogue; it is for a body of common experience in action. Until socialists have a party within which to test their doctrines, the doctrines must remain abstract and undeveloped. Until we have an organization capable of demonstrating that we can live and work as well as think in ways foreshadowing a better society, there is no reason for any skeptic, no matter how honest and conscionable, to believe us. The question of building a party can no longer be avoided. If the careful study of Gramsci's life and work does not guarantee our success, it will at least help us shape the kind of party in which we and our potential allies on a fragmented Left can live together.

VI

We may hope that Cammett's book receives the wide reading it deserves; it is a model of meticulous scholarship and clarity of exposition. We might regret that Cammett does not develop his criticisms of Gramsci and that he restricts himself so much to the task of presenting Gramsci's case, but he is right in believing that the main problem at the moment is to tell the story. He will be writing other books in which the job of developing his critical insights, largely implicit or in passing in this book, can be undertaken. Until Gramsci's works are made available in English it will be difficult to exploit his accomplishment. Even then they would be incomprehensible without an understanding of their historical and political context. To provide this context Cammett had to proceed with painstaking care with the biography, the factional struggles in the PSI, PCI and the Comintern and the intellectual origins of Gramscian Marxism. He has accomplished this task, to which he has selflessly devoted himself for more than a decade, with admirable intellectual depth, political judgment and scholarly responsibility. It now becomes possible to raise significantly the level of our theoretical work through the study of Gramsci's contributions, and for this we owe Cammett an immeasurable debt.

Socialism
and the New Left

BY *Martin J. Sklar* AND *James Weinstein*

Volume VI, No. 2
March–April 1966

This essay is an attempt to explain the reasons for the failure of the old left to come to grips with the changed nature of advanced corporate capitalism, particularly in the United States, over the past fifty years.

Underlying much of the activity of New Left groups—whether it be repeated demonstrations against the war or organizing projects among the poor—is a shared sense that their activity will change American society fundamentally. In the ghettos the specific content of the political programs seldom goes beyond the standard demands of liberal pressure groups, and is consistent with the "pluralist" idea that if an "excluded group" organizes and makes enough noise it will receive some rewards within the system as it is now constituted. In the peace movement repeated demonstrations increasingly serve to bolster the system by proving that it permits ritualistic dissent, and by allowing the demonstrators to believe that they have discharged their responsibilities by publicly taking a stand (or by demoralizing them as they witness their own impotence). In New York, for example, the peace organizations planned, *in advance of the resumption of bombing* North Vietnam, to demonstrate the following day—a procedure that could not prevent the bombing, but that would show the world that some Americans are more moral than others.

Of course, many activists in the movements recognize these circumstances. The failure to change them is perhaps most commonly attributed to the power and flexibility of America's great corporations and their political representatives. We do not raise these questions to be carping. But we suggest that the reasons lie closer to home. In view of the state of radical politics inherited by the New Left in the late 1950's, its accomplishments are impressive. Yet it is becoming clear that the new movements are at, or are fast approaching, states of crisis, that the initial usefulness and success of their anti-ideological stances have worn thin, and that the need now is to search for theoretical clarity about revolutionary politics in the United States.

Before we can do that some questions have to be answered about the old left and its failures. This is necessary because many old left concepts operate under New Left trappings, and because many of the arguments against ideology (in the sense of theory) are the result of unthinking equations of Marxism or socialism with the organizational and political concepts of the communist and socialist left in the United States between 1920 and 1965.

In 1962 we wrote that although *Studies on the Left* had been called a theoretical organ for the New Left in the United States, we could not identify a movement that could call itself *the* New Left. Almost four years later there is still a great deal of confusion over what and who the New Left it; but it is clear that there is a new ideological framework of left politics and within that, as Hal Draper has recently pointed out, a new left type.[1] Unfortunately, the most usable definitions of the New Left, both of its encompassing framework and of its organizations and leaders, are negative. We know what the New Left is against, what it rejects, at least at any given moment; no one knows what it is for.

[1] Hal Draper, "In Defense of the 'New Radicals,'" *New Politics,* IV, 3 (Summer, 1965), 5-28.

The New Left is essentially a student movement. Most of its members and activists are from middle class families, many from upper middle class families. They come to radicalism out of a feeling that American society has failed to live up to its potentials and to its articulated values. That is, the rhetoric of democracy and liberalism is seen as fraudulent, as a mask behind which the large corporations carry on neo-colonial wars and manipulate public tastes, opinions and perceived needs so as to create vast new markets for products that degrade as much as they satisfy. These new radicals are not motivated, as many who grew up in the 1920's and 1930's were, by a notion that American capitalism's failure consists of its inability to satisfy the material needs of most Americans despite a great unused productive capacity. They see poverty, and they react to it as something immoral. Their radicalism is not created by a consciousness of material poverty, however; they are more concerned about the poverty of human relationships and values. In other words, the new radicals become radicals first, then organizers in the ghetto, or in anti-war activity.

Marx, himself, was no less aware of poverty, but his critique of capitalism was not based on its inability to produce material goods. Marx saw capitalism as inexorably driven to expanding production for production's sake in the incessant creation and appropriation of surplus value. The ultimate social result that Marx foresaw was that this process, fed by and nourishing personal desires for enrichment and power, would create those material conditions "which alone can form the real basis of a higher form of society, a society in which the full and free development of every individual forms the ruling principle." [2] That higher form of society would be post-industrial in the sense that the process of accumulation, or industrialization, was a necessary prerequisite to it. Socialism, Marx believed, would be truly liberating because,

[2] *Capital,* I (New York: Modern Library, 1936), 649.

having achieved complete industrialization, society would
no longer be concerned with imposing discipline on the
work force, of extracting from the workers the social
surplus needed for reinvestment in further expansion.
That meant that under socialism the former working
class could do what it wanted with its time—work in the
old sense would become marginal to man's life, rather
than central: the proletariat would be abolished as a class.
(Perhaps, for example, everyone would spend two years
of his life doing the remaining necessary labor. In such a
case society's necessary work would be done without a
class of workers.)

Marx's theory assumed that the revolution would occur
in the most industrialized capitalist countries, that socialism would be the form of a post-industrial society. In fact
things did not work out that way. The avowedly socialist
revolution came first in Russia, a country still only on the
threshhold of industrialization. Since the process of accumulation, the necessary condition for industrialization,
had not taken place under capitalist auspices in Russia,
it had to be done under socialist auspices. The Communist
Party had to lead Russia through the process of industrialization, just as the capitalists had done in Western
Europe and the United States. Instead of individual capitalists extracting surpluses from the workers, enabling
the capitalists to live in relative luxury, but also providing
the funds for reinvestment in industrial expansion, it became necessary for the party in control of the state to play
this role. This meant that the working class in Russia
could not be liberated in the sense that Marx foresaw.
It also meant that the party had to be the instrument of
accumulation, exploiting and disciplining the workers,
rather than being, in the full sense, a party of the liberation of the working class. It further meant that an entire
bureaucracy designed to serve this purpose—to keep the
workers in line and on the job—had to be set up.

If the Soviet Union were to industrialize, if the Communist régime were to survive, this process was inevitable. The point here is not whether it was good or bad, desirable or undesirable, carried out with a minimum of suffering or not. What was most damaging to Western socialism and most corrupting in Russia was not necessarily that this process had to take place, but that the Communist Party did not say frankly what it was doing. Instead, it put the process forward not as a preliminary stage to socialism (although in the early period this was done), but as the real article. It did not explain why it had to do what it was doing, but glorified a process that whether done under capitalist competition or socialist planning was costly in human terms, was tough and sometimes brutal.

The failure of Western socialism since 1925—both communist and anti-communist—derived decisively from its acceptance of this pre-socialist phase as fully developed socialism because that was what the Russians said it was. The impact of this failure has been particularly great in the United States, where a radical intellectual tradition has been weakest. Here, where the question of how socialism in an industrialized country would be different and better was most relevant, there was the least confrontation. Instead the argument has been over whether what the Russians were doing was truly ideal (which the Communists asserted), or a betrayal and perversion of socialism and its ideals (which the anti-communist socialists asserted).

The entire argument was off the point; much worse, it led socialists in the West away from their primary responsibility of working out their own roads to socialism and their own visions of post-industrial society. Some socialists went so far as to align themselves with "democracy" as an abstract principle, and then made themselves available as agents of the anti-revolutionary policies of Woodrow Wilson, Franklin D. Roosevelt, Harry Truman, John F. Kennedy and Lyndon B. Johnson.

This central concern with socialism in the East led to a polarization of attitudes and inquiries that was only superficially related to the consciousness of those disaffected by the failures of capitalism—both those who experienced material plenty but rejected the loss of human dignity that was its price, and those who saw affluence around them but were excluded because of their race or class. The communist movement in the Western industrialized countries, mimicking the Russians in mindless admiration and deference, adopted attitudes, programs and even forms of Party organization that had been developed to achieve revolution in a pre-industrial country under wartime conditions, and that was later adapted to the needs of the process of "primitive socialist accumulation"—that is, to accelerated, forced-march industrialization under Communist Party direction. One result was an entire set of attitudes toward politics that glorified centralization and control by a small elite—the vanguard. Another was an equation of revolutionary politics with rigidly disciplined, bureaucratic ("monolithic") party organizations.

For our present purposes, two points must be made about the American Communists. First, they never applied Marxist theories to a serious analysis of American society. During their "left" periods they mimicked the pre-revolutionary Russians. During their united front period (essentially from 1935 to the present) they mimicked American liberalism, except in foreign policy where they mechanically followed the Russians. Second, their concepts of organization were copied from the Russian experience, despite the basically different conditions and problems facing American socialists. The effect of this in isolating them from traditional American radicalism and from the New Left can be seen in its effects on the Progressive Labor Party. Although it is part of the new insurgency, PLP's style of work and concepts of party organization (what it calls the Leninist party) have created a gulf between it and the new radicals almost as wide as that separating the New Left from the Communist Party.

Anti-communist socialists fare no better with the New Left, despite (maybe because of) their tireless reiteration that they are the "democratic left." This is in part because they lack any convincing intention of transforming American society, a condition which flows from their gradual acceptance of American democratic capitalism as preferable to communism as it has developed in Russia. This attitude toward communism in Russia and the United States was facilitated by the unceasing attacks of communists on socialists even before the socialists had adopted the attitudes they now have; however, it also reflects an inability to understand social development in its specific historical context. That is, it is the result of an identification of post-industrial socialism with the process of industrialization under socialist auspices that has gone on in Russia, China, Eastern Europe and Cuba. But it is not this that creates the near contempt of so many New Leftists for men like Irving Howe and others of the League for Industrial Democracy. That view comes from the role that "socialists" have played since 1946 as ideologues for the Cold War, which is to say, as the ideological defenders of American neo-colonialism. It was, after all, the right wing socialists who laid the ideological basis of McCarthyism.

The ideological framework in which the New Left has developed is socialist, but it is not part of the old debates described above. This is not to say that the archetypical New Leftist is a socialist; he is not necessarily that, although he is anti-capitalist in the sense that he is opposed to the values which sustain the capitalist system. But there is a set of attitudes, an intellectual milieu, within which the New Left germinated. The earliest enunciation of these views was made by *Monthly Review,* the first socialist journal that was non-communist, but not anti-communist. That is, it was committed to socialism, critical of the Soviet Union but against the Cold War, and on the side of the social revolutions throughout the world that were and are the main victims of Cold War policies. Before 1956 that position was novel and difficult to take and maintain. After the Twentieth Congress in the Soviet Union, which exposed Stalinist terror even for Communists to see, and after the Cuban revolution, which proved that revolution could occur and be successful under non-Communist auspices, the need for a new look at revolutionary politics became much more readily apparent. In that atmosphere, *Studies on the Left, New University Thought, Root and Branch* and many other small magazines came into being.

It would be difficult to trace the connections between these ideological predecessors and what we now know as the New Left. Yet in the origins of SLATE, FSM and the Vietnam Day Committee at Berkeley, of TOCSIN at Harvard, of SNCC and of the Students for a Democratic Society, there are many direct connections, in addition to the more important general framework of ideas reflected in *Studies* and the other journals.

Unfortunately, the archetype new radical defined by Hal Draper has chosen to remain unconscious of all this. He would prefer not to think of theory. He chooses, not as a temporary necessity but as a positive good, to be uncommitted to any system of ideas about the transformation of society. One of the reasons he does so is outlined above: there are no immediately usable alternative theories. Another reason is that present prospects appear so bleak: the system seems to be infinitely flexible and impenetrable. A third reason is that few of the new radicals are willing to make the kind of commitment required to build a revolutionary movement and party. To spend a year or two working full time in the movement between graduation and settling down to life's work is one thing. To commit oneself to the lifetime job of slowly building a new theory and revolutionary party is another. The first has a glamour and sense of immediacy and fulfillment that the second does not. It is easier to feel radical by rejecting everything about middle class life, to wear the old clothes of the ghetto and live in mock poverty, than it is to accept who and what you are and still try to revolutionize society.

But there is among the new radicals a growing awareness that *activity,* although essential within a worked-out political perspective, leads nowhere by itself. This is a result of the increasing frustrations experienced by organizers in the South, in ghetto projects and in the peace movement. Demonstrations never change power relationships, at best they cause those in power to grant concessions. On the war in Vietnam they do not even do that. The repeated and increasingly large demonstrations against the war have produced few lasting gains because there is no political movement of opposition which can recruit from the demonstrators and continue their education as radicals. In recognition of this and in the hope of moving toward a new socialist politics, some groups are beginning to search for new theory and are beginning to study the American past. Others, swinging from an extreme anti-electoral bias, are becoming fully involved in political campaigns, but in so doing they are reliving the patterns of old left popular front electoral action. Instead of viewing electoral activity as an educational and organizing device, so that after the election independent, self-conscious radical constituencies have been created, this activity is designed to win. That means that programs are but partially developed, that large territories are tackled without attention being given to continuing relationships with groups of voters, that compromises are made to get votes. In other words, that the mindless living for the moment of the united front is being repeated.

The essential work now involves developing in outline, and to a degree programmatically, a view of the new post-industrial society posited by present-day capitalism, and to begin building a new movement around this view. William Appleman Williams has taken a first step in this direction in suggesting that socialists should reject programs of further consolidation and centralization. These, Williams argues, are more in line with the needs and values of the liberal guardians of the large corporations. Socialist ideals of community, equality, democracy and free individual development require not only social ownership and control of the nation's industrial plant, not only planning, but also units of government and of economic organization small enough to encourage and permit anyone to participate in the decisions that establish the framework of his life. These suggestions, of course, only indicate a direction in which socialists should look as they work out new programs and visions. To assess and go beyond these suggestions is the intellectuals' part in the process of building a new revolutionary movement.

The easiest and least useful thing one can do is to decry the deficiencies of others; the difficult and most urgent task is to determine where we go from there. The first step is for New Leftists to examine the content of their radicalism and determine if they are committed to a transformation of American capitalism into that higher form of society envisaged by Marx. If they are, then all of their activities should be consciously determined by an intention to build a revolutionary movement and then a party that has the perspective of gaining power in the United States. Such an outlook requires taking the long view as well as the short, thinking ten, fifteen, maybe twenty-five or fifty years as well as ten days, weeks or months ahead.

Assuming that liberalism will remain the dominant political ideology of the large corporations—that is, that the basic commitment to formal democracy will be maintained and the socially disruptive programs of the ultra-right will continue to be rejected—then electoral politics will continue to be central to the political consciousness of Americans. This will mean that the electoral arena will be entered. But electoral politics will make sense only if they are utilized in such a way as to build growing, solidly based constituencies that understand the way in which society might be reorganized in the same way as do the organizers. That is, the purpose of all such activity should be what Eugene V. Debs always insisted it should be: to make socialists, not merely votes. Success cannot be measured by adding up the numbers who demonstrate or get arrested or vote in a particular election. Whatever the form of radical activity, its value to us and to those who share our long-range perspective can be estimated finally in terms of how many new, consciously socialist individuals emerge and organize within a developing movement.

Notes on the Need
For a Socialist Party

BY *James Weinstein*

Volume VII, No. 1
January–February 1967

These notes were prepared for a conference on the need to develop a new socialist politics in the United States, sponsored by Studies *in New York City, December 1966. They were printed as notes rather than as a formal essay in the hope of stimulating discussion.*

I

My approach to socialist politics in the United States starts with an estimate of the dominant political ideology of the corporations and the nature of the liberal state. Most *Studies on the Left* readers accept the concept of corporate liberalism as the ideology of big business, so there is no need for elaboration of that here. But it is important to know, and to remember, that this concept is almost totally at variance with the thinking not only of ordinary liberals, who form the great majority of politically conscious Americans, but also of Communists and of many others who call themselves socialists. Both the Communist and Socialist Parties for the past thirty years or more have accepted the myth created in the Progressive Era and perpetuated by Democratic Party ideologues that liberalism is a political movement against the power of business. It is, therefore, necessary to reassert our understanding of this and to make clear that liberalism is not a neutral system of political thought but an ideology that sustains and strengthens the existing social structure.

If this is not understood by most radicals today, it was clearly perceived by many socialists over fifty years ago. Like so much else in American socialism, there has been a regression here since the collapse of the old Socialist Party. In 1912, Robert Rives LaMonte, a left wing Socialist, explained that "no matter whether the Republicans or the Democrats win the Presidency we shall get more workmen's compensation acts, more and more restrictions upon child labor, more and more regulation of women in industry" as well as the suffrage, reduction of unemployment and old age pensions.

"Very soon," LaMonte argued, "there will cease to be any real opposition to reforms that aim at preserving your health and efficiency.

"Old age pensions, insurance against sickness, accident and unemployment are cheaper, are better business than jails, poor houses, asylums, hospitals, etc., to care for the unemployables.

"They are even learning that too widespread joblessness and a wage too far below a decent subsistence level leads to agitation that threatens the whole fabric of capitalism."

Beyond that, the rich "know more about the poor today than ever before." "And this increased knowledge begets increased sympathy." "The rich, altogether apart from self-interest, want to help the poor. And this kindly desire is a factor in all modern social legislation. But the rich are so placed that they can afford to help the poor only when by so doing they help themselves still more."

Reforms, LaMonte concluded, were therefore the business of progressives. The speed of reform would depend on the size of the Socialist vote. Socialists should demand only impossible reforms—those which embodied truly socialist principles and which educated the public to the ethical and social superiority of socialism.

Other socialists understood the role of the state in a way

that Communists and socialists since have either forgotten or submerged for "tactical" reasons.

"The clearest thinkers among the capitalists and their politicians," the *International Socialist Review* wrote in 1912, "realized that if American manufacturers were to compete with Germany in the world market," the "next step" might be for the businessman "to act on the discovery that he can carry on certain portions of the productive process more efficiently through *his* government than through private corporations." "Some muddleheads may think that will be socialism," the *Review* added, "but the capitalist knows better." "The right of wage workers to organize and to control the conditions under which they work—that is the issue that must be fought out between the two great opposing classes."

II

The second assumption, which is explicitly rejected by most of the New Left and implicitly rejected by the old left of the Communist and Socialist Parties, is (to quote Kenneth McNaught in the December, 1966 issue of *The Journal of American History*) that "the collapse of American socialism, and thus of all twentieth-century attempts to organize a political basis of ideological dissent outside the major parties, could scarcely be more crucial as a determinant of the nature of the present Great Society." Put another way, activity that does not explicitly lead toward the emergence and development of a popular socialist party as a rallying point for anti-capitalist dissent can only lead to the strengthening of the dominant liberalism. This, too, is nothing new. In 1919 Harold Laski, complaining about the lack of a socialist commitment on the part of the New Leftists of that day, wrote that "the worst of it is that the liberals [new left] have no program beyond specific protest. . . . There is interest in the teachers' sufferings one day and it dies before the strike at Lawrence the next which, in turn, gives way to riots on May Day. . . . The most hopeful thing I see is twofold in aspect—the movement toward a labor party and the restlessness of the undergraduates."

Today, as in 1919, we have a move toward independent politics and we have restless undergraduates. And, indeed, in the forty-six years since 1919 that situation has been repeated more than once, but the result has always been what it is today: activity that leads to despair or desperation. The reason for that should be clear: to be meaningful activity must either lead to immediate change of a significant nature, or it must lead to the strengthening of a visible organization that has a long-range commitment to transform society in a specific manner, that is, a party with a program and a strategy. In this society the first alternative is rarely possible, partly because the state has come to understand the efficacy of what Veblen called "patient ambiguity and delay," and partly because those in power realize that sporadic, ad hoc, or single-issue movements represent no challenge to their power—that to move beyond protest and dissent, which in the end can lead only to dropping out of the system, requires a permanent rallying point that has a serious and public intention to replace those in control. Dropping out, of course, is frowned upon by some conscious radicals and appreciated by others, but whatever it may signify about the state of mind in the drop-outs, and, therefore, of their potentially revolutionary character, it is clear that if all dissenters dropped out there would be no one left to run things but those who now do so.

To advocate the formation of a popular socialist party in the United States is to evoke two responses, each of which in its true nature is a criticism of the *internal* and *fundamental* failure of twentieth-century Western socialism, and of American socialism more than any other. One criticism is that ideological politics is a dead end. That criticism, although few realize it, is exactly upside down. What is seen as ideological politics, namely the disputes between Communists, Socialists and Trotskyists in the 1930's and since, is ideological only in the sense of ideology as false consciousness. What this "ideological" politics really represents is what Daniel Bell correctly calls the end of ideology, only where Bell means to apply this to politics in general, it has been true only of the left. Liberalism, consensus, the politics of negotiated social reform, is the most highly ideological of all American politics. It is precisely with Theodore Roosevelt and Woodrow Wilson that the dominant politics becomes highly and *consciously* ideological at the center. And it is since Wilson that the socialists have become absorbed by the dominant ideology, while retaining their differences about the nature of Soviet society. The need is to discard the falsely ideological politics of the left of the last forty years and to resume the job of developing a socialist ideology for the United States.

The other criticism is that which appears to some to be a put-down of Marx—Ronald Aronson's insistence that Marxism is no longer useful because its central thesis, the working class as revolutionary agent, has been proved invalid. This, too, is really a criticism of the American socialists above all, although, as I will explain below, I think it is also a misreading of Marx. On this point it is interesting to see that the new socialists in Europe, those that put out the *International Socialist Journal,* are already more advanced in their analysis and consciousness of what they call neocapitalism than are traditional socialists in the United States of corporate liberalism—even though American corporate liberalism dates back to before the First World War, whereas European neocapitalism is a post-World War II phenomenon.

Aronson, and many others, view the call for a new socialist party simply as an act of faith, since the "agent" has disappeared. There seem to me to be three things

wrong with this, or, at least two and one half. 1) Although
Marx did speak of the working class as the agent of change,
in fact he acted, and all socialists since him have acted,
on the understanding that the *agent* of change is the party
—the self-conscious socialists—which has always been made
up of several classes, and has always been led by what we
call middle-class intellectuals (at least in those countries
with successful parties). 2) Marx's concept of the proletariat and proletarianization went beyond the industrial
working class, although his stress was on this section of
workers because he was describing an emergent industrial
system. Indeed, the true inner logic of *Capital,* which is,
above all, a theory of capital accumulation, leads inevitably to the disappearance of the industrial working
class as the largest social grouping. This is implicit in the
theory of the falling tendency of the rate of profit. Marx
does assert that the law does not mean a decrease in the
total number of workers, even though it operates through
a steadily increasing proportion of fixed capital (machinery) to variable capital (labor power). But Marx was describing the early stages of industrial expansion, when
capitalism was still restricted to relatively narrow spheres
of activity. At one point he does recognize that "a development of the productive forces which would diminish the
absolute number of laborers, that is, which would enable
the entire nation to accomplish its total production in a
shorter time, would cause a revolution because it would
put the majority of the population on the shelf." (The
point here is not whether such a situation would, by itself,
cause a revolution, but that Marx saw such a development
as coming at some time as a result of the operation of the
process of accumulation he described.) "In this," Marx
continued, "the specific barrier of capitalist production
shows itself once more, proving that capitalist production
is not an absolute form for the development of the productive powers and creation of wealth, but rather comes
in collision with this development at a certain point" [*Cap-*

ital, Volume III, page 309, Kerr edition]. I will come
back to this. 3) The working class has not yet disappeared
in the United States. In fact, the industrial work force is
today approximately the same size as it was fifty years ago.
It has declined relatively, but unlike the agricultural
work force, which has shrunk from fifty per cent of the
population to seven per cent, its decline has been slight.

All three of these questions need to be examined in
depth and given serious thought (not just offhand remarks,
such as these); I do not mean to belittle the importance
of them. But Aronson's pronouncement that "by mistak-
ing his personal commitment to socialism for a real historical trend, the Marxist can view his role as making
Americans 'see the relevance' of socialism, as working to
bring about 'socialist consciousness'—whatever that might
mean at a time when proletarian consciousness no longer
exists," misses the mark. In the first place, there never
was "a real historical trend" toward socialism, except to
the extent that a self-conscious *party* worked to create
socialist consciousness among certain social groupings
(industrial workers, skilled workers, tenant and family
farmers and intellectuals in the United States). Indeed, in
the last issue of *Studies on the Left,* along with Aronson's
piece, Gabriel Kolko pointed out that the main weakness
of socialists in the United States was their mistaken belief
in the inevitability of socialist development—that is, in
"real historical" social trends as something that existed
outside of the conscious and purposeful intervention of
committed individuals. No class or group of classes has
ever spontaneously developed its class consciousness, but
only an interest consciousness. As Marx asserts, this interest consciousness, or immediate interest, may often run
counter to a class's real or historical interest. The success
of the corporations, in fact, has rested largely in their
great sophistication and ability to transcend their immediate interests when necessary in the pre-World War I

days and to have developed and accepted what we call corporate liberalism as in their true class interest, even though at some points such social reforms as were instituted violated the more narrow interests of those sponsoring them. But this development did not occur spontaneously in response to historical trends without conscious intervention by individuals.

The same was true of working-class consciousness where it existed, or of socialist consciousness; it was always the result of the willful action of parties.

Now, of course, this begs the question of the role of the working class, and I will come back to that, too. But it does indicate that a personal commitment to socialism on the part of intellectuals is, indeed, the first prerequisite of a popular socialist movement. If there is to be such a movement there must first be a group of people committed to social transformation, capable of developing a vision of a better society and then of working out a strategy for its attainment. Neither task can be done except through the existence of a rallying point for those who would move in that direction: a party. The intellectual work that Aronson calls for cannot be done outside such a framework, since outside it there is no need for the work. It is, of course, true that the working out of these ideas and this strategy have not gone very far. The question is how far they can go without a collective, willful commitment to, and need for, their further development. Sociological arguments such as Aronson uses are self-fulfilling, since no judgment can be made about the possibilities of socialist politics and the development of socialist consciousness in the absence of an attempt. As long as there is no socialist program, no socialist alternative presented to workers and other classes, it is impossible to say that they cannot accept such ideas. The ideas will not develop out of the masses spontaneously. A party is needed if only to test the possibilities of socialist politics.

Until such a test is made the only conclusion that one can draw is that proletarian consciousness does not develop unaided.

III

I have already indicated that the agent of social change is a conscious group of individuals committed to transforming society in a specific direction or manner, and organized to do so. If such a party is to be taken seriously it must solve two theoretical problems. It must develop both a vision of a new society, and the theoretical and technical competence to plan for and run such a society. As Veblen put it in 1919, "No movement for the dispossession of the Vested Interests in America can hope for even a temporary success unless it is undertaken by an organization which is competent to take over the country's productive industry as a whole, and to administer it from the start on a more efficient plan than that now pursued" by those in power. Veblen pointed out that the problem of revolution in an advanced industrial society was different from that in Soviet Russia. "As compared with America and much of Western Europe," he wrote, "Russia is not an industrialized region, in any decisive sense," and this was in part responsible for the "astonishing measure of success" she had achieved. "They have been able to fall back on an earlier, simpler, less close-knit plan of productive industry: such that any detailed part of this loose-knit Russian community is able, at a pinch, to draw its own livelihood from its own soil by its own work, without that instant and unremitting dependence on materials and wrought goods drawn from foreign ports and distant regions. that is characteristic of" the United States [*Engineers and the Price System,* page 95].

Veblen's stress was on competence and efficiency, and his vision was somewhat distorted by this emphasis. But he saw also that "management of industry by business methods" had become highly wasteful and was bound increasingly "to run more and more consistently at cross purposes with the community's livelihood." "With every further increase in the volume and complexity of the industrial system, any businesslike control is bound to grow still more incompetent, irrelevant and impertinent" [pages 100-101]. Veblen, however, did not talk about the uses to which this industrial capacity should be put, although he clearly implied a rejection of the imperatives of the market economy as a determinant. Since he was concerned primarily with competence and efficiency, he looked to the engineers and technicians as the group to rely upon for the reorganization of industry and society. We need to go beyond this, but we should also recognize the importance of the above.

IV

It seems to me that those of us who assert the need for a socialist transformation do so not as an act of faith, as Aronson implies, but out of a real need for a better life and because we can see that under capitalism things are organized both irrationally and inhumanly. The large number of socialists like ourselves and the widespread dissatisfaction with material comforts as a substitute for human relationships and meaningful activity indicates something about the potential constituency for a socialist movement. It is related to and an outgrowth of Marx's insistence on increasing proletarianization under capitalism. "Within the capitalist system," Marx wrote, "all means for the development of production transform themselves into means of domination over, and exploitation of, the producers . . . they transform life-time into working-time. . . . In proportion as capital accumulates, the lot of the worker, be his payment high or low, must grow worse" [*Capital,* Volume I, pages 708-709, Modern Library edition]. Marx, of course, was writing about industrial capital; in his day there was still much room for new investment in manufacturing industry. Since then, with the constant growth of surplus capital, corporate investment and control has spread beyond manufacturing to the realm of distribution and service industries. The result has been a rapid decline in the number of individual entrepreneurs. Formerly independent entrepreneurs, urban and rural, have become and are becoming the wage or salaried employees of corporations. These people are deprived of economic independence, not only in the former sense that they were dependent on general market conditions, but also in the sense that their very jobs depend on the needs of other people's enterprises. Beyond this, the universities, both private and state, are increasingly converted to training grounds and service operations for the corporations, and faculty and students into appendages of the market economy.

William A. Williams has made this point strongly in his *The Great Evasion* (pages 114-122). He emphasizes the loss of any participating role in the principal decisions of the capitalist marketplace due to the loss of control over any private property which plays a part in the productive activities of the system. The overt sign of proletarianization, as Marx defines it, is the change from entrepreneurial standing to that of wage or salaried work. As Williams puts it, in a political economy based upon the control of private property, with its law codified in that framework, the loss of productive private property also involves a fall into second-class citizenship. It is the consciousness of this that has created the popularity of the SDS slogan of participatory democracy, not among the poor, but among the students.

What this process implies to me is that increasingly the real interests of the great majority of the population, including the poor, the industrial workers, service workers and large sections of what we mistakenly call the middle class, run counter to those of the corporations and the further extension of the market economy.

It would seem most useful to view the potential constituency for a socialist movement—that is, a party with an intention to take power and transform society—as having to include large numbers from all those classes whose real interests are violated by the corporations and who are not a part of the governing system. This includes those that we know as the poor, the workers and the middle classes. It also includes racial minorities.

But the process of building a socialist movement will go through many stages. The problem at the beginning— which is where we are—is how to bring together those who already think of themselves in some way as socialists into a coherent and self-conscious grouping so that the work of developing a vision of a new society and an initial organizing strategy can be done consistently. We know that there are hundreds of thousands, maybe a million or two persons in this country that consider themselves socialists in some sense or other, but who are unaffiliated and unorganized. We know these people are largely of the so-called middle class, that is, intellectuals, students, teachers, technicians, white-collar workers of various kinds. In the absence of a meaningful left many are beats and hippies. We ourselves are from these groups. Many of these people already reject the dominant values of American business society. Many are immune to cooptation through material payoffs. Many understand the idea of socialism as a prerequisite for the good society. It seems self-evident that the first steps toward a socialist party should be to bring these people into a dialogue about transforming the United States, so that we can find those among them who will be serious revolutionaries.

The poor, who in classical Marxist thought are not working class but an unorganizable *lumpenproletariat,* are not now a likely source of recruitment for a new

socialist movement, nor are they likely to contribute substantially to its development in the initial stages. The
primary social goal of most poor people—those who are
not totally demoralized—is to make it, to enter the "middle class," or to have their children do so. They have, as
a class, neither the leisure nor the education to do the
work of revitalizing the concept of socialism or to work
out a strategy for a socialist transformation of society.
Their immediate interest is to improve their material
conditions, and on an individual basis this can be done in
the context of the existing social order. This does not
mean that the poor will not be part of a socialist constituency if a party emerges. But they will become that
only after we have a visible, relevant, substantial party
with which they can identify from the beginning of their
association with us.

The white working class is inaccessible to socialists
through its places of work at present because we have no
public identity. In the past socialists have been influential
among workers in the shops because they were in the
forefront of union organization. Now the trade-union
movement is tightly controlled by supporters of the dominant liberalism, and is inaccessible to individual radicals
or socialists unless they totally submerge their ideology.
Our views of American society are relevant to industrial
workers, but we will have no influence on them in their
work places until we have a visible party with a public
presence and program.

That leaves us with the need first to bring together those
who share in a general way our view of the existing society
and our incipient views of the alternative. Those people
are mostly young students and intellectuals, but also include numbers of older unaffiliated socialists.

The immediate job is not organizing in the sense that
term has been used on the New Left in recent years, or,
for that matter, by Communists for decades. Every debate
on the left, in SNCC, SDS, CIPA, certainly in the sects,

makes it clear that the lack is in the realm of ideas, in our knowledge of American society and how it got to be what it is, in beginning to be able to talk about what we mean by the good society. We must begin to be able to say not simply that socialism is the answer, but to define what socialism could mean in the United States. Our demands and program must develop out of such a framework of thought, otherwise we will put together nothing more than another competing organization.

PART III

BLACK
NATIONALISM

Revolutionary Nationalism and the Afro-American

BY *Harold Cruse*

Volume II, No. 3
Summer 1962

Harold Cruse is a black critic and historian, and the author of The Crisis of the Negro Intellectual *(1967). This essay was his first published on the subject of revolutionary nationalism. It is primarily a critique of old left and liberal attitudes toward black liberation. His article elicited numerous responses; two are reprinted here together with his replies.*

REVOLUTIONARY NATIONALISM
AND WESTERN MARXISM

Many of Western Marxism's fundamental theoretical formulations concerning revolution and nationalism are seriously challenged by the Cuban Revolution. American Marxism, which, since World War II, has undergone a progressive loss of influence and prestige, is challenged most profoundly. For, while most American Marxists assert that the Cuban Revolution substantiates their theories of nationalism, national liberation and revolution, in fact, the Cuban success is more nearly a *succès de circonstance*. Orthodox Marxists were unable to foresee it, and, indeed, they opposed Castro until the last minute. One would hope that such a development might cause American radicals to re-evaluate their habitual methods of perceiving social realities, but in the spate of written analyses of the Cuban Revolution one looks in vain for a new idea or a fleeting spark of creative theoretical inspiration apropos of the situation in the United States.

The failure of American Marxists to work out a meaningful approach to revolutionary nationalism has special significance to the American Negro. For the Negro has a relationship to the dominant culture of the United States similar to that of colonies and semi-dependents to their particular foreign overseers: the Negro is the American problem of underdevelopment. The failure of American Marxists to understand the bond between the Negro and the colonial peoples of the world has led to their failure to develop theories that would be of value to Negroes in the United States.

As far as American Marxists are concerned, it appears that thirty-odd years of failure on the North American mainland are now being offered compensatory vindication "ninety miles from home." With all due respect to the Marxists, however, the hard facts remain. Revolutionary nationalism has not waited for western Marxist thought to catch up with the realities of the "underdeveloped" world. From underdevelopment itself have come the indigenous schools of theory and practice for achieving independence. The liberation of the colonies before the socialist revolution in the West is not orthodox Marxist (although it might be called Maoism or Castroism). As long as American Marxists cannot deal with the implications of revolutionary nationalism, both abroad and at home, they will continue to play the role of revolutionaries by proxy.

The revolutionary initiative has passed to the colonial world, and in the United States is passing to the Negro, while Western Marxists theorize, temporize and debate. The success of the colonial and semi-colonial revolutions is not now, if it ever was, dependent upon the prior success of the Western proletariat. Indeed, the reverse may now be true, namely, that the success of the latter is aided by the weakening of the imperial outposts of western capitalism. What is true of the colonial world is also true of the Negro in the United States. Here, the Negro is the

leading revolutionary force, independent and ahead of
the Marxists in the development of a movement towards
social change.

THE AMERICAN NEGRO:
A SUBJECT OF DOMESTIC COLONIALISM

The American Negro shares with colonial peoples many
of the socioeconomic factors which form the material basis
for present day revolutionary nationalism. Like the peoples of the underdeveloped countries, the Negro suffers in
varying degree from hunger, illiteracy, disease, ties to the
land, urban and semi-urban slums, cultural starvation,
and the psychological reactions to being ruled over by
others not of his kind. He experiences the tyranny imposed
upon the lives of those who inhabit underdeveloped
countries. In the words of a Mexican writer, Enrique
Gonzales Pedrero, underdevelopment creates a situation
where that which exists "only half exists," where "countries are almost countries, only fifty per cent nations, and
a man who inhabits these countries is a dependent being,
a sub-man." Such a man depends "not on himself but on
other men and other outside worlds that order him
around, counsel and guide him like a newly born infant."[1]

From the beginning, the American Negro has existed
as a colonial being. His enslavement coincided with the
colonial expansion of European powers and was nothing
more or less than a condition of domestic colonialism.
Instead of the United States establishing a colonial empire in Africa, it brought the colonial system home and
installed it in the Southern states. When the Civil War
broke up the slave system and the Negro was emancipated,
he gained only partial freedom. Emancipation elevated
him only to the position of a semi-dependent man, not
to that of an equal or independent being.

[1] Enrique Gonzales Pedrero, "Subdesarollo y Revolución," *Casa de las
Americas,* (August-September, 1960).

The immense wealth and democratic pretensions of the American way of life have often served to obscure the real conditions under which the eighteen to twenty million Negroes in the United States live. As a wage laborer or tenant farmer, the Negro is discriminated against and exploited. Those in the educated, professional, and intellectual classes suffer a similar fate. Except for a very small percentage of the Negro intelligentsia, the Negro functions in a sub-cultural world made up, usually of necessity, only of his own racial kind. This is much more than a problem of racial discrimination: it is a problem of political, economic, cultural, and administrative underdevelopment.

American Marxists, however, have never been able to understand the implications of the Negro's position in the social structure of the United States. They have no more been able to see the Negro as having revolutionary potentialities in his own right, than European Marxists could see the revolutionary aspirations of their colonials as being independent of, and not subordinate to, their own. If Western Marxism had no adequate revolutionary theory for the colonies, it is likewise true that American Marxists have no adequate theory for the Negro. The belief of some American Marxists in a political alliance of Negroes and whites is based on a superficial assessment of the Negro's social status: the notion that the Negro is an integral part of the American nation in the same way as is the white working class. Although this idea of Negro and white "unity" is convenient in describing the American multi-national and multi-racial makeup, it cannot withstand a deeper analysis of the components which make American society what it is.

Negroes have never been equal to whites of any class in economic, social, cultural, or political status, and very few whites of any class have ever regarded them as such. The Negro is not really an integral part of the American nation beyond the convenient formal recognition that he lives within the borders of the United States. From the white's point of view, the Negro is not related to the "we," the Negro is the "they." This attitude assumes its most extreme expression in the Southern states and spreads out over the nation in varying modes of racial mores. The only factor which differentiates the Negro's status from that of a pure *colonial status* is that his position is maintained in the "home" country in close proximity to the dominant racial group.

It is not at all remarkable then, that the semi-colonial status of the Negro has given rise to nationalist movements. It would be surprising if it had not. Although Negro Nationalism today is a reflection of the revolutionary nationalism that is changing the world, the present nationalist movement stems from a tradition dating back to the period of the first World War.

Negro Nationalism came into its own at that time with the appearance of Marcus Garvey and his "Back to Africa" movement. Garvey mobilized large sections of the discontented urban petit-bourgeois and working class elements from the West Indies and the South into the greatest mass movement yet achieved in Negro history. The Garvey movement was *revolutionary nationalism* being expressed in the very heart of Western capitalism. Despite the obvious parallels to colonial revolutions, however, Marxists of all parties not only rejected Garvey, but have traditionally ostracized Negro Nationalism.

American Marxism has neither understood the nature of Negro Nationalism, nor dealt with its roots in American society. When the Communists first promulgated the Negro question as a "national question" in 1928, they wanted a national question without nationalism. They posed the question mechanically because they did not really understand it. They relegated the "national" aspects of the Negro question to the "black belt" of the South, despite the fact that Garvey's "national movement" had been organized in 1916 in a northern urban center where the Negro was, according to the Communists, a "national minority," but not a "nation," as he was in the Southern states. Of course, the national character of the Negro has little to do with what part of the country he lives in. Wherever he lives, he is restricted. His "national boundaries" are the color of his skin, his racial characteristics, and the social conditions within his sub-cultural world.

The ramifications of the national and colonial question are clear only if the initial bourgeois character of national movements is understood. However, according to American Marxism, Negro movements do not have "bourgeois nationalist" beginnings. American Marxists have fabricated the term "Negro Liberation Movement"—an "all-class" affair united around a program of civil and political equality, the beginnings of which they approximately date back to the founding of the National Association for the Advancement of Colored People in 1909. True, the NAACP was, from its inception, and is still, a bourgeois movement. However, it is a distortion to characterize this particular organization as the sole repository of the beginnings of the Negro bourgeois movement. For, such a narrow analysis cannot explain how or why there are two divergent trends in Negro life today: pro-integration and anti-integration. That is to say, it does not explain the origins of the Nationalist wing, composed of Black Nationalists, Black Muslims, and other minor Negro Nationalist groupings, as an outgrowth of basic conflicts within the early bourgeois movements (circa 1900), from which also developed the present day NAACP-Martin Luther King-Student coalition.

Furthermore, the Marxian version of the NAACP's origins does not explain why the Nationalist wing and the NAACP wing oppose each other, or why the overwhelming majority of Negroes are "uncommitted" to either one. There is widespread dissatisfaction among various classes of Negroes with the NAACP's approach to racial problems. On the other hand, in recent years, the Nationalists have been gaining support and prestige among "uncommitted" Negroes. This is especially true of the Muslims, the newest Negro Nationalist phenomenon.

The rise of free African nations and the Cuban Revolution have, without a doubt, stirred up the latent nationalism of many Negroes. The popular acclaim given Fidel Castro by the working class Negroes of Harlem during his visit in the fall of 1960 demonstrated that the effects of the colonial revolutions are reaching the American Negro and arousing his nationalist impulses. Many Negroes, who are neither Nationalists nor supporters of the NAACP, are becoming impatient with the NAACP-Martin Luther King-student legalistic and "passive resistance" tactics. They suspect that the long drawn out battle of attrition with which the NAACP integration movement is faced may very well end in no more than pyrrhic victories. They feel that racial integration, as a goal, lacks the tangible objectives needed to bring about genuine equality. After all, "social" and "racial" equality remain intangible goals unless they are related to the seizure and retention of objectives which can be used as levels to exert political, social, economic, and administrative power in society. Power cannot be wielded from integrated lunch counters, waiting rooms, schools, housing, baseball teams, or love affairs, even though these are social advances.

There emerges from this dilemma a recognizable third trend, personified in the case of Robert F. Williams. Williams was forced to take an anti-NAACP position, but he was not a Nationalist and was critical of the "Marxists." As a rebel, Williams' objectives were the same as those of the NAACP; he differed only in his *approach*. However, his seemingly "revolutionary" stance is thwarted by the same lack of substance that makes a program of "racial integration" unsatisfactory to many Negroes. Williams resorted to arms for *defense* purposes—but arms are superfluous in terms of the objectives of racial integration. Arms symbolize a step beyond mere "racial integration," to the seizure of actual centers of social power. The adherents of this third trend—young social rebels who are followers of Williams' Monroe Movement—are faced with this predicament. They are neither avowed Nationalists nor NAACPers. They consider themselves "revolutionary," but are shy of having revolutionary objectives.

However, they are not a force as yet, and their future importance will rest, no doubt upon how much influence the Nationalist wing will exert in the Negro community. In short, the main trends in Negro life are becoming more and more polarized around the issues of pro and anti-integration.

INTEGRATION VS. SEPARATION: HISTORY AND INTERPRETATIONS

Negro historiography does not offer a very clear explanation of how the Negro has become what he is today. As written, Negro history appears as a parade of lesser and greater personalities against a clamor of many contending anonymous voices and a welter of spasmodic trends all negating each other. Through the pages of Negro history the Negro marches, always arriving but never getting anywhere. His "national goals" are always receding.

Integration vs. separation have become polarized around two main wings of racial ideology, with fateful implications for the Negro movement and the country at large. Yet we are faced with a problem in racial ideology without any means of properly understanding how to deal with it. The dilemma arises from a lack of comprehension of the historical origins of the conflict.

Furthermore, the problem is complicated by a lack of recognition even that it exists. The fundamental economic and cultural issues at stake in this conflict cannot be dealt with by American sociologists for the simple reason that sociologists never admit that such issues should exist at all in American society. They talk of "Americanizing" all the varied racial elements in the United States; however, when it is clear that certain racial elements are *not* being "Americanized," socially, economically, or culturally, the socioligtsts proffer nothing but total evasion, or more studies on the "nature of prejudice." Hence the problems remain with us in a neglected state of suspension until they break out in what are considered to be "negative," "anti-social," "anti-white," "anti-democratic" reactions.

One of the few attempts to bring a semblance of order to the dominant trends in the chaos of Negro history was made by Marxist historians in the 1930's and 1940's. However, it proved to be a one-sided analysis which failed to examine the class structure of the Negro people. Viewing Negro history as a parade from slavery to socialism, the Marxist historians favor certain Negro personalities uncritically while ignoring others who played vital roles. Major figures, such as Booker T. Washington and Marcus Garvey, who do not fit into the Communist stereotype of Negro heroes are ignored or downgraded. In the process, Marxist historians have further obscured the roots of the current conflict in racial ideology.

Under the aegis of other slogans, issues and rivalries, the pro-integration vs. anti-integration controversy first appeared at the turn of the century in the famous Booker T. Washington-W. E. B. DuBois debate. Washington's position was that the Negro had to achieve economic self-sufficiency before demanding his political rights. This position led Washington to take a less "militant" stand on civil rights than did other Negro leaders, such as DuBois, who accused Washington of compromising with the racists on the Negro's political position in the South.

It is not sufficient, however, to judge Washington purely on the political policies he advocated for the Negro in the South. For Washington gave voice to an important

trend in Negro life, one that made him the most popular
leader American Negroes have had. The Washington-
DuBois controversy was not a debate between representatives of reaction and progress, as Communist historians
have asserted, but over the correct tactics for the emerging
Negro bourgeoisie.

From the Reconstruction era on, the would-be Negro
bourgeoisie in the United States confronted unique difficulties quite unlike those experienced by the young bourgeoisie in colonial areas. As a class, the Negro bourgeoisie
wanted liberty and equality, but *also* money, prestige, and
political power. How to achieve all this within the American framework was a difficult problem, since the whites
had a monopoly on these benefits of western civilization,
and looked upon the new aspirants as interlopers and
upstarts. The Negro bourgeoisie was trapped and stymied
by the entrenched and expanding power of American
capitalism. Unlike the situation in the colonial areas, the
Negro could not seize the power he wanted or oust "foreigners." Hence, he turned inward toward organizations
of fraternal, religious, nationalistic, educational and political natures. There was much frustrated bickering and
internal conflict within this new class over strategy and
tactics. Finally the issues boiled down to that of *politics
vs. economics,* and emerged in the Washington-DuBois
controversy.

In this context, it is clear that Washington's program
for a "separate" Negro economy was not compatible with
the idea of integration into the dominant white economy.
In 1907 DuBois complained of Washington that:

He is striving nobly to make Negro artisans business men and
property owners; but it is impossible, under modern competitive methods, for workingmen and property-owners to defend
their rights and exist without the right of suffrage.

Yet, Washington could not logically seek participation
in "white" politics in so far as such politics were a reflection of the mastery of whites in the surrounding econ-

omy. He reasoned that since Negroes had no chance to take part in the white world as producers and proprietors, what value was there in seeking political rights *immediately?* Herbert Aptheker, the leading Marxist authority on Negro history, quotes Washington as saying:

> Brains, property, and character for the Negro will settle the question of civil rights. The best course to pursue in regard to a civil rights bill in the South is to let it alone; let it alone and it will settle itself. Good school teachers and plenty of money to pay them will be more potent in settling the race question than many civil rights bills and investigation committees.

This was the typical Washington attitude—a bourgeois attitude, practical and pragmatic, based on the expediencies of the situation. Washington sought to train and develop a new class. He had a longer range view than most of his contemporaries, and for his plans he wanted racial peace at any cost.

Few of the implications of this can be found in Marxist interpretations of Negro history. By taking a partisan position in favor of DuBois, Marxists dismiss the economic aspects of the question in favor of the purely political. However, this is the same as saying that the Negro bourgeoisie had no right to try to become capitalists—an idea that makes no historical sense whatsoever. If a small proprietor, native to an underdeveloped country, should want to oust foreign capitalists and take over his internal markets, why should not the Negro proprietor have the same desire? Of course, a substantial Negro bourgeoisie never developed in the United States. Although this fact obscured and complicated the problems of Negro Nationalism, it does not change the principles involved. Washington sought to develop a Negro bourgeoisie. He failed. But his failure was no greater than that of those who sought equality through politics.

Washington's role in developing an economic program to counteract the Negro's position is central to the emergence of Negro Nationalism, and accounts for much of his popularity among Negroes. Yet Aptheker makes the error of assessing Washington purely on political grounds. On this basis, of course, Aptheker finds him not "revolutionary" or "militant" in the fashion that befits a Negro leader, past or present. He rejects the historico-economic-class basis of Washington's philosophy, although these are essential in analyzing social movements, personalities, or historical situations. Aptheker has not seen Washington in the light of what he was: the leading spokesman and theoretician of the new Negro capitalists, whom he was trying to mold into existence. All that Aptheker has to say about Washington is summed up by him as follows:

> Mr. Washington's policy amounted objectively to an acceptance by the Negro of second class citizenship. His appearance on the historical stage and the growth of his influence coincided with and reflected the propertied interests' resistance to the farmers and workers' great protest movements in the generations spanning the close of the nineteenth and the opening of the twentieth centuries. American imperialism conquers the South during these years and Mr. Washington's program of industrial education, ultra-gradualism and opposition to independent political activity and trade unionism assisted in this conquest.

Thus is the Marxian schema about the "Negro people" projected back into history—a people without classes or differing class interests. It is näive to believe that any aspiring member of the bourgeoisie would have been interested in trade-unionism and the political action of farmers. But American Marxists cannot "see" the Negro at all unless he is storming the barricades, either in the present or in history. Does it make any sense to look back into history and expect to find Negroes involved in trade unionism and political action in the most lynch-ridden decade the South has ever known? Anyone reading about the South at the turn of the century must wonder how Negroes managed to survive at all, let alone become involved in political activity when such politics was dominated by the Ku Klux Klan. According to Aptheker, however, the Negroes who supported Washington were wrong. It was the handful of Negro militants from above the Mason-Dixon line who had never known slavery, who had never known Southern poverty and illiteracy, the whip of the lynch-mad KKK, or the peasant's agony of landlessness, who were correct in their high-sounding idealistic criticism of Washington. These were, Aptheker tells us, within a politically revolutionary tradition—a tradition which had not even emerged when Washington died!

After the Washington-DuBois debate, DuBois went on to help form the NAACP in 1909. Washington died in 1915. The controversy continued, however, in the conflict between the NAACP and the Garvey movement.

In 1916, Marcus Garvey, the West Indian-born Nationalist, organized his "Back to Africa" movement in the United States. Garvey had, from his earliest years, been deeply influenced by the racial and economic philosophies of Booker T. Washington. Adopting what he wanted from Washington's ideas, Garvey carried them further—advocating Negro self-sufficiency in the United States linked, this time, with the idea of regaining access to the African homeland, as a basis for constructing a viable black economy. Whereas Washington had earlier chosen an accommodationist position in the South to achieve his objectives, Garvey added the racial ingredient of Black Nationalism to Washington's ideas with potent effect. This development paralleled the bourgeois origins of the colonial revolutions then in their initial stages in Africa and Asia. Coming from a British colony, Garvey had the psychology of a colonial revolutionary and acted as such.

With the rise of Nationalism, DuBois and the NAACP took a strong stand against the Garvey Movement and against revolutionary nationalism. The issues were much deeper than mere rivalry between different factions for the leadership of Negro politics. The rise of Garvey Nationalism meant that the NAACP became the accommodationists and the Nationalists became the militants. From its very inception, the Negro bourgeois movement found itself deeply split over aims, ideology and tactics, growing out of its unique position of contending for its aims in the very heart of Western capitalism.

Neither the nationalist side of the bourgeois movement nor the reformist NAACP wing, however, were able to vanquish the social barriers facing Negroes in the United States. The Garvey Movement found its answer in seeking a way out—"Back to Africa" where the nationalist revolution had elbow room, where there was land, resources, sovereignty—all that the black man had been denied in the United States.

The Garvey era manifested the most self-conscious expression of nationality in the entire history of the Negro in the United States. To refrain from pointing this out, as Aptheker does in his essays on Negro history, is inexcusable. In his essay, "The Negro in World War I," Aptheker says: "What was the position of the Negro People during the years of Wilson's 'New Freedom'?" He then mentions the activities of the NAACP, the National Race Congress of 1915, and the formation in 1915 of the Association for the Study of Negro Life and History. But in discussing the racial unrest of the time, Aptheker fails to mention the Garvey movement, despite the fact that it had organized more Negroes than any other organization in the three years following its establishment in 1916. The causes for these omissions are, of course, apparent: orthodox Western Marxism cannot incorporate nationalism into its schema.

With the NAACP and the Garvey Movement growing apace, the "Negro People" had two "Negro Liberation Movements" to contend with. Never was an oppressed people so richly endowed with leadership; the only difficulty was that these two movements were at bitter odds

with one another. Furthermore, within the Negro community, prejudice about lighter and darker skin coloring
also served as a basis for class stratification. Thus, when
retaliating against DuBois' criticisms of his movement,
Garvey attacked him on the basis of his skin color, and
assailed the assimilationist values of the upper class Negro
leadership. In addition, the Garvey "blacks" and the
NAACP "coloreds" disagreed as to which was the true
"motherland"—black Africa or white America.

During the period when the Communists looked upon
the Negro question as a national question, some Communist writers perceived the positive, as well as the negative, aspects of Garvey's appeal. Harry Haywood, for
example, wrote that the Garvey movement "reflected the
widening rift between the policies of the Negro bourgeois reformism and the life needs of the sorely pressed
people." He sees in Garvey's "renunciation of the whole
program of interracialism" a belief that the upper class
Negro leadership was "motivated solely by their desire for
cultural assimilation," and that they "banked their hopes
for Negro equality on support from the white enemy."
Haywood sympathized with this position, seeing in the
"huge movement led by Garvey" a "deep feeling for the
intrinsic national character of the Negro problem."

In 1959, the Communists withdrew the concept of "self-
determination" in the black belt, and side stepped the
question of the Negro's "national character." Instead, they
adopted a position essentially the same as the NAACP.
Their present goal is to secure "with all speed" the "fullest
realization of genuinely equal economic, political and
social status with all other nationalities and individual
citizens of the United States"—this to be accompanied
by "genuinely representative government, with proportionate representation in the areas of Negro majority
population in the South." This position is essentially no
different from that supported by the NAACP.

Thus, it is not surprising that it is difficult to under-

stand the present conflict within the Negro movement;
the roots of the conflict have been obliterated. While most
historians do not attempt at all to bring order to the chaos
of Negro history, those that have—the Marxists—find it
convenient from a theoretical standpoint to see Negroes
in history as black proletarian "proto-types" and forerunners of the "black workers" who will participate in the
proletarian revolution. This Aptheker-Communist Party
mythology, created around a patronizing deification of
Negro slave heroes (Denmark Vesey, Nat Turner, So-
journer Truth, Frederick Douglass, etc.), results in
abstracting them from their proper historical context and
making it appear that they are relevant to modern reality.
Of course, there will be those Marxists who will argue
that their inability to come to terms in theory with Negro
Nationalism does not arise from an error in their interpretations of the role of the Negro bourgeoisie, of Washington, or of DuBois. They will defend all the historical
romanticism and the sentimental slave hero worship of
the Aptheker Cult. They will say that all this is "past
history" and has no bearing on the "new situation." But
if one takes this position, then of what value is history
of any kind, and particularly, of what value is the Marxist
historical method? The inability to view Negro history
in a theoretical perspective leads to the inability to cope
with the implications of Negro Nationalism.

NEGRO NATIONALISM AND THE LEFT

To the extent that the myth of a uniform "Negro People"
has endured, a clear understanding of the causes of Negro
Nationalism has been prevented. In reality, no such uni-
formity exists. There *are* class divisions among Negroes,
and it is misleading to maintain that the interests of the
Negro working and middle classes are identical. To be
sure, a middle class NAACP leader and an illiterate farm-

hand in Mississippi or a porter who lives in Harlem, all want civil rights. However, it would be far more enlightening to examine why the NAACP is not composed of Negro porters and farmhands, but only of Negroes of a certain "type."

What we must ask is why these classes are not all striving in the same directions and to the same degree of intensity. Why are some lagging behind the integration movement, and still others in conflict with it? Where is the integration movement going? Into what is the integration movement integrating? Is the Negro middle class integrating into the white middle class? Are integrated lunch counters and waiting stations commensurate with integration into the "mainstream of American life"? And what exactly *is* the "mainstream of American life"? Will the Negro ten per cent of the population get ten per cent representation in the local, state, and national legislatures? —or ten per cent representation in the exclusive club of the "Power Elite"?

Why are some Negroes anti-integration, others pro-integration, and still others "uncommitted"? Why is there such a lack of real unity among different Negro classes towards one objective? Why are there only some 400,000 members in the NAACP out of a total Negro population of some eighteen to twenty million? Why does this membership constantly fluctuate? Why is the NAACP called a "Negro" organization when it is an *interracial* organization? Why are the Negro Nationalist organizations "all Negro"? Why do Nationalist organizations have a far greater proportion of working class Negro membership than the NAACP? Finally, why is it that the Marxists, of all groups, are at this late date tail-ending organizations such as the NAACP (King, CORE, etc.), which do not have the broad support of Negro workers and farmers? We must consider why the interests of the Negro bourgeoisie have become separated from those of the Negro working classes.

Tracing the origins of the Negro bourgeoisie back to the Booker T. Washington period (circa 1900), E. Franklin Frazier, a Negro sociologist and non-Marxist scholar, came to the enlightening conclusion that "the black bourgeois lacks the economic basis that would give it roots in the world of reality." Frazier shows that *the failure of the Negro to establish an economic base in American society served to sever the Negro bourgeoisie, in its "slow and difficult occupational differentiation," from any economic, and therefore cultural and organizational ties with the Negro working class.* Since the Negro bourgeoisie does not, in the main, control the Negro "market" in the United States economy, and since it derives its income from whatever "integrated" occupational advantages it has achieved, it has neither developed a sense of association of its status with that of the Negro working class, nor a "community" of economic, political, or cultural interests conducive for cultivating "nationalistic sentiments." Today, except for the issue of "civil rights," no unity of interests exists between the Negro middle class and the Negro working class.

Furthermore, large segments of the modern Negro bourgeoisie have played a continually regressive "non-national" role in Negro affairs. Thriving off the crumbs of integration, these bourgeois elements have become de-racialized and de-cultured, leaving the Negro working class without voice or leadership, while serving the negative role of class buffer between the deprived working class and the white ruling elites. In this respect, such groups have become a social millstone around the necks of the Negro working class—a point which none of the militant phrases that accompany the racial integration movement down the road to "racial attrition" should be allowed to obscure.

The dilemma of the Negro intellectual in the United States results from the duality of his position. Detached from the Negro working class, he tries to "integrate" and to gain full membership in a stagnating and declining

Western society. At the same time, failing to gain entry to the status quo, he resorts to talking like a "revolutionary," championing revolutionary nationalism and its social dynamism in the underdeveloped world. But this gesture of flirting with the revolutionary nationalism of the non-West does not mask the fact that the American Negro intellectual is floating in ideological space. He is caught up in the world contradiction. Forced to face up to the colonial revolution and to make shallow propaganda out of it for himself, the American Negro intellectual is unable to cement his ties with the more racial-minded sections of the Negro working class. For this would require him to take a nationalistic stand in American politics—which he is loath to do. Nevertheless, the impact of revolutionary nationalism in the non-western world is forcing certain Negro intellectuals to take a "nationalist" position in regard to their American situation.

Although Frazier does not delve into the nature of Nationalism or connect the rise of Nationalism with the failure of the Negro bourgeoisie to establish the "economic basis" of which he writes, it can be seen that the sense of a need for "economic self-sufficiency" is one of the causes for the persistence of nationalist groupings in Negro life. The attempt to organize and agitate for Negro ascendency in and control of the Negro market is expressed in such racial slogans as "Buy Black." The Negro Nationalist ideology regards all the social ills from which Negroes suffer as being caused by the lack of economic control over the segregated Negro community. Since the Nationalists do not envision a time when whites will voluntarily end segregation, they feel that it is necessary to gain control of the economic welfare of the segregated Negro community. Moreover, many Negro Nationalists, such as the Black Muslims, actually believe that "racial separation" is in the best interests of both races. Others maintain this separatist position because of the fact of the persistence of segregation.

Thus, when Communists and other Marxists imply that

"racial integration" represents an all class movement for liberation, it indicates that they have lost touch with the realities of Negro life. They fail to concern themselves with the mind of the working class Negro in the depths of the ghetto, or the nationalistic yearnings of those hundreds of thousands of ghetto Negroes whose every aspiration has been negated by white society. Instead, the Marxists gear their position to Negro middle class aspirations and ideology. Such Marxists support the position of the Negro bourgeoisie in denying, condemning, or ignoring the existence of Negro Nationalism in the United States—while regarding the reality of Nationalism in the colonial world as something peculiar to "exotic" peoples. The measure of the lack of appeal to the working classes of the Marxist movement is indicated by the fact that Negro Nationalist movements are basically working class in character while the new Negroes attracted to the Marxist movement are of bourgeois outlook and sympathies.

Ironically, even within Marxist organizations Negroes have had to function as a numerical minority, and were subordinated to the will of a white majority on all crucial matters of racial policy. What the Marxists called "Negro-white unity" within their organizations was, in reality, white domination. Thus, the Marxist movement took a position of favoring a "racial equality" that did not even exist within the organization of the movement itself.

Today, the Marxist organizations which advocate "racial integration" do not have a single objective for the Negro that is not advocated by the NAACP or some other reform organization. It is only by virtue of asserting the "necessity of socialism" that the Marxist movement is not altogether superfluous. It could not be otherwise. For Marxism has stripped the Negro question of every theoretical concern for the class, color, ethnic, economic, cultural, psychological, and "national" complexities. They have no program apart from uttering the visionary call for "integration plus socialism" or "socialism plus integration."

However, when Marxists speak of socialism to the Negro, they leave many young Negro social rebels unimpressed. Many concrete questions remain unanswered. What guarantee do Negroes have that socialism means racial equality any more than does "capitalist democracy"? Would socialism mean the assimilation of the Negro into the dominant racial group? Although this would be "racial democracy" of a kind, the Negro would wield no political power as a minority. If he desired to exert political power as a racial minority, he might, even under socialism, be accused of being "nationalistic." In other words, the failure of American capitalist abundance to help solve the crying problems of the Negro's existence cannot be fobbed off on some future socialist heaven.

We have learned that the *means* to the *end* are just as important as the end itself. In this regard, Marxists have always been very naïve about the psychology of the Negro. It was always an easy matter for Marxists to find Negro careerists, social climbers, and parlor radicals to agree with the Marxist position on the Negro masses. However, it rarely occurred to Marxists that, to the average Negro, the *means* used by Marxists were as significant as the ends. Thus, except in times of national catastrophe (such as in the depression of the 30's), Marxist means, suitable only for bourgeois reform, seldom approximated the aspirations of the majority of Negroes. Lacking a working class character, Marxism in the United States cannot objectively analyze the role of the bourgeoisie or take a political position in Negro affairs that would be more in keeping with the aspirations of the masses.

The failure to deal adequately with the Negro question is the chief cause of American Marxism's ultimate alienation from the vital stream of American life. This political and theoretical deficiency poses a serious and vexing problem for the younger generation who today have become involved in political activity centered around the defense of Cuba. Some accept Marxism; others voice criticisms of Marxist parties as being "conservative," or otherwise limited in their grasp of present realities. All of these young people are more or less part of what is loosely called the "New Left" (a trend not limited to the United States).

It is now the responsibility of these new forces to find the new thinking and new approaches needed to cope with the old problems. Open-minded whites of the "New Left" must understand that Negro consciousness in the United States will be plagued with the conflict between the compulsions toward "integration" and the compulsions toward "separation." It is the inescapable result of semi-dependence.

The Negro in the United States can no more look to American Marxist schema than the colonials and semi-dependents could conform to the Western Marxist timetable for revolutionary advances. Those on the American left who support revolutionary nationalism in Asia, Africa, and Latin America, must also accept the validity of Negro Nationalism in the United States. Is it not just as valid for Negro Nationalists to want to separate from American whites as it is for Cuban Nationalists to want to separate economically and politically from the United States? The answer cannot hinge merely on pragmatic practicalities. *It is a political question which involves the inherent right accruing to individuals, groups, nations and national minorities, i.e., the right of political separation from another political entity when joint existence is incompatible, coercive, unequal, or otherwise injurious to the rights of one or both.* This is a principle that must be unheld, all expedient prejudices to the contrary.

It is up to the Negro to take the organizational, political and economic steps necessary to raise and defend his status. The present situation in racial affairs will inevitably force nationalist movements to make demands which should be supported by people who are not Negro Na-

tionalists. The Nationalists may be forced to demand the
right of political separation. This too must be upheld
because it is the surest means of achieving Federal action
on all Negro demands of an economic or political nature.
It will be the most direct means of publicizing the fact
that the American government's policy on "underdeveloped" areas must be complemented by the same approach to Negro underdevelopment in the United States.

It is pointless to argue, as many do, that Negro Nationalism is an invalid ideology for Negroes to have in
American life, or that the Nationalist ideas of "economic
self-sufficiency" or the "separate Negro economy" are unrealistic or utopian. Perhaps they are, but it must be
clearly understood that as long as racial segregation remains a built-in characteristic of American society, Nationalist ideology will continue to grow and spread. If
allowed to spread unchecked and unameliorated, the end
result can only be racial wars in the United States. This
is no idle prophecy, for there are many convinced Negro
Nationalists who maintain that the idea of the eventual
acceptance of the Negro as a full-fledged American without regard to race, creed, or color, is also utopian and
will never be realized. These Nationalists are acting on
their assumptions.

Can it be said, in all truth, that Nationalist groups such
as the Black Muslims are being unrealistic when they
reject white society as a lost cause in terms of fulfilling
any humanistic promises for the Negro? For whites to
react subjectively to this attitude solves nothing. It must
be understood. It must be seen that this rejection of white
society has valid reasons. White society, the Muslims feel,
is sick, immoral, dishonest, and filled with hate for nonwhites. Their rejection of white society is analogous to
the colonial people's rejection of imperialist rule. The
difference is only that people in colonies can succeed and
Negro Nationalists cannot. The peculiar position of Negro
Nationalists in the United States requires them to set

themselves against the dominance of whites and still manage to live in the same country.

It has to be admitted that it is impossible for American society as it is now constituted to integrate or assimilate the Negro. Jim Crow is a built-in component of the American social structure. There is no getting around it. Moreover, there is no organized force in the United States at present, capable of altering the structural form of American society.

Due to his semi-dependent status in society, the American Negro is the ouly potentially revolutionary force in the United States today. From the Negro, himself, must come the revolutionary social theories of an economic, cultural and political nature that will be his guides for social action—the new philosophies of social change. If the white working class is ever to move in the direction of demanding structural changes in society, it will be the Negro who will furnish the initial force.

The more the system frustrates the integration efforts of the Negro, the more he will be forced to resolve in his own consciousness the contradiction and conflict inherent in the pro and anti-integration trends in his racial and historical background. Out of this process, new organizational forms will emerge in Negro life to cope with new demands and new situations. To be sure, much of this will be empirical, out of necessity, and no one can say how much time this process will take to work itself towards its own logical ends. But it will be revolutionary pioneering by that segment of our society most suitable to and most amenable to pioneering—the have-nots, the victims of the American brand of social underdevelopment.

The coming coalition of Negro organizations will contain Nationalist elements in roles of conspicuous leadership. It cannot and will not be subordinate to any white groups with which it is "allied." There is no longer room for the "revolutionary paternalism" that has been the hallmark of organizations such as the Communist Party. This is what the "New Left" must clearly understand in its future relations with Negro movements that are indigenous to the Negro community.

Reply:
Studies on the Right?

BY *Richard Greenleaf*

Volume III, No. 1
Fall 1962

The last thing I expected to see in *Studies on the Left* was an article favoring racial segregation. Or maybe that was the next-to-the-last-thing. The last thing I expected to see was an attack on Marxism for not favoring segregation.

But even this is not the most puzzling thing about the piece by Harold W. Cruse. American Communists were guilty for several decades of sponsoring a formulation which might well have been called a policy of segregation. More recently they have dropped this formulation. But Mr. Cruse takes it up. What's more, he insists that his segregated Negro nation shall be a bourgeois state and not a proletarian state. And to cap everything, he puts forward his ideas as an appeal to the Negro working class, and castigates the Marxists for attempting (he charges) to appeal to the Negro bourgeoisie.

A more contradictory set of ideas on racial matters in the United States could hardly be imagined. Yet I believe that the summary I have given of the Cruse essay is a fair one.

"The failure of American Marxists to understand the

bond between the Negro and the colonial peoples of the world has led to their failure to develop theories that would be of value to Negroes in the United States" (p. 12). The main theory American Marxism has put forward to meet this need is as follows:

The exploitation of the American Negro is but a refinement and extension of capitalism's exploitation of the American worker. The best way to end the first is to end the second.

Cruse feels that this idea is of no value to the United States Negro. He feels, further, that its lack of value springs from the failure of the Marxists to comprehend the bond between the Negro and the colonial peoples.

That there is such a bond no Marxist would deny. At the present hour of world history, the bond between colonial peoples and the workers of the imperialist nations is especially vivid and especially vital to the cause of peace, freedom and equality. French workers have a bond with Algerians; Portuguese workers have a bond with Angolans; above all, United States workers have a bond with Cubans. The United States Negro is a part of the United States working class.

But Cruse means more than a bond. He is saying that the plight of the United States Negro is the same as that of the Cuban—that the Negro's battle is one for national independence and ultimate sovereignty (within what territory Cruse does not say).

Certainly Marxism affords no basis for such a view. As I look back now, the Communist Party formulation of a separate Negro nation in the Black Belt seems not only archaic but fundamentally erroneous from a Marxist viewpoint. I have not recently reviewed any of the literature, but it is hard to believe that professed Marxists could have seen in the United States Negro any of the characteristics of a nation as that term is defined in Marxism.

Cruse, however, carries that error much farther than the Communists did. "This is much more than a problem of racial discrimination: it is a problem of political, economic, cultural, and administrative underdevelopment," he writes (p. 14). And further: "The Negro is not really an integral part of the American nation beyond the convenient formal recognition that he lives within the borders of the United States" (p. 14).

From these premises Cruse hurries along to his central conclusion: "The ramification of the national and colonial question are clear only if the initial bourgeois character of national movements is understood" (p. 15).

If the United States Negro constitutes a nation in a colonial status, and if all national liberation movements are necessarily bourgeois in origin, then the first indispensible step toward Negro liberation in the United States is the formation and hegemony of a Negro bourgeoisie. This, so far as I am able to follow it, is Cruse's basic reasoning.

But such a conclusion can be put much more simply: If we are to end the exploitation of the Negro, we must first make sure that the Negro worker is exploited by other Negroes. Of course, when the conclusion is put as simply as this its absurdity becomes obvious.

However, let us pursue this absurdity somewhat further. There has been no lack of Negroes who aspired to exploit their fellow Negroes. But, writes Cruse, "From the Reconstruction era on, the would-be Negro bourgeoisie in the United States confronted unique difficulties quite unlike those experienced by the young bourgeoisie in colonial areas. . . . Unlike the situation in the colonial areas, the Negro could not seize the power he wanted or oust 'foreigners'" (p. 17). Despite these difficulties, the bourgeois orientation of Booker T. Washington and his followers was, Cruse believes, "practical and pragmatic, based on the expediencies of the situation" (p. 18). The implication is that any joint effort of Negro and white workers to put an end to *all* exploitation would have been impractical and inexpedient.

The sin of the Marxists, says Cruse, was that they held

"that the Negro bourgeoisie had no right to try to become capitalists—an idea that makes no historical sense whatsoever" (p. 18). Just what Cruse means by his phrase "historical sense" is not altogether clear, but his own obligation, which he assumed at the beginning of his essay, is not merely to make sense but to "develop theories that would be of value to Negroes in the United States" (p. 12). We have two theories between which to choose: First, that some Negroes have a right to exploit other Negroes; second, that nobody has a right to exploit anybody. The choice does not seem difficult.

Marxism, it is true, holds that capitalism was once a progressive system whose emergence represented a great step forward for humanity from the feudalism which had preceded it. It was, in other words, *less unjust* than feudalism, though capitalism contained intrinsic injustices which were destined to become sharper as capitalism developed.

But the world in which we are now trying to provide the Negro with theories useful to him is a world in which capitalism, wherever it exists, has developed beyond its point of maximum helpfulness and has become only a hindrance to human aspirations for peace, freedom and equality. True, there are still parts of the world where domestic capitalism has not yet emerged, or where it has been retarded by colonial pressures from foreign capitalisms. If, just for the momentary purposes of argument, we choose to regard the United States Negro as constituting a nation, then it is certainly one of those nations whose own capitalisms have not been permitted fully to emerge. But do such nations have to become capitalist nations when they attain sovereignty? Cuba answers this question in the negative, and so, I believe, will many of the new nations of Africa, Asia and Latin America.

But the United States Negro does not constitute a nation. He constitutes instead the most thoroughly proletarianized section of the United States working class. The "unique difficulties" placed in the way of the Negro who was trying to enter the bourgeoisie were the devices of race-handicap which we usually and inaccurately refer to as "discrimination." The same devices have been employed to exclude the Negro from the benefits of trade-unionism, and there they have contributed even more greatly to the prolongation and intensification of his proletarian status.

Is the Negro's path to freedom, then, to be found by passing from subjection under white men to subjection under other Negroes? Or is it to be found by joining with white proletarians to end the mastery of man over man? This question, too, answers itself.

But what seems to me an obvious answer is to Cruse a "mythology, created around a patronizing deification of Negro slave heroes" (p. 20). It is "historical romanticism." It would be interesting to learn how it is possible to deify and patronize someone at the same time; for my part, I regard Nat Turner and Frederick Douglass neither as boys nor as gods, but as good and courageous men. If it is romanticism to invoke their names in Little Rock and Montgomery and Detroit and New York, then let us have more of this kind of romanticism.

Harold Cruse's article is a study on the right. Would it be impertinent to ask what it is doing in *Studies on the Left?*

Reply

BY *Harold Cruse*

Volume III, No. 1
Fall 1962

Richard Greenleaf's reply to my article on "Revolutionary Nationalism" must be put down as nothing more than a sophomoric exercise in dogmatic evasion of some salient issues raised by it. His response is typical of the doctrinaire obtuseness American Marxism has inculcated into the thinking processes of its exponents, rendering them unable to transcend a closed world of outmoded concepts.

To take Greenleaf's reply at face value, however, presents a difficulty. To answer him is comparable to trying to explain calculus to a high school student who has flunked algebra. Apparently, Mr. Greenleaf is not even superficially acquainted with much of what American Communism has presented theoretically on the Negro "for several decades." For example, his ideas about the Communist Party's previous formulations which he says "might well have been called a policy of segregation" (*i.e.* self-determination in the black belt of the South) obviously do not derive from Communist writings on the subject, but from other sources which have perennially distorted the Communists' original distortion of Negro reality. But this is an old story, and Greenleaf's total lack of originality in reiterating this issue shows that he has little conception of why the Communist Party presented this formulation in the first place and why it retreated from this position under Browder, adopted the position again in 1946, only to drop it finally in 1959.

It is no longer important whether the Communist Party was right, wrong, or in between, when it put forth "self-determination" in 1928. What is important is that the same sociological trends that gave rise to Communist formulations in earlier years are still in evidence, but on a dialectically higher phase of maturity. Greenleaf, who has undoubtedly read a few Marxist pamphlets and heard some primer lectures, understands what terms like "proletariat," "bourgeois state," "nation," "left," "right," "national independence," etc., mean for other times and other places, but is rather innocent as to what these concepts might mean for the United States in 1962 or ten years hence. For lack of anything more novel, he has to fall back on the hackneyed, sing-song recitative about

"Negro-Labor unity," "peace, freedom and equality" and all the other catch-phrases in the lexicon of the Old Left. Thus, it is necessary to attempt to divest Greenleaf of certain misconceptions he entertains about the meaning and intent of my article.

Judging from the tone of his reply, it seems that Greenleaf believes my article is meant to be the opening statement of an intended debate between the Marxists and the trend of Negro thinking I represent. If so, he is thoroughly mistaken and is not in tune with the temper of the time. My article is meant to inform Marxists of a particular Negro trend in the U.S. these days. If Marxists and their supporters (Negro or white) are not inclined to approve of what this trend implies politically, we are not the least bit impressed. *We are laying down a new Afro-American political line which will be developed as we go along, and this line will be developed independently of and without interference from Marxist groupings.* If Greenleaf was disturbed by the tone of my piece, it is well that he realize that the article was edited by *Studies on the Left* to keep its polemic within the bounds of a certain decorum. There are many within my trend who would not be half so polite. There are others who agree with everything I said, but who insist that the article did not go far enough and that *Studies* was too stringent in the space allotted. I emphasize this because Greenleaf does not seem to be aware of the fact that whereas Marxist theory qua *theory* may be sacred to some people who have become accustomed to thinking that it is their sole, exclusive, intellectual property, there are many other people who judge the worth of Marxist theory solely on its practices. On these grounds, Marxism has had a sorry record in the Negro community and has, therefore, forfeited its right to pose as a guide to lead anyone, black or white, out of the American morass.

Thus, when Greenleaf restates what is alleged to be the

"main theory of American Marxism" on the Negro and underscores it,

> The exploitation of the American Negro is but a refinement and extension of capitalism's exploitation of the American worker. The best way to end the first is to end the second.

I am prompted to inquire of him in the old army manner: is this a command or a request? Further, when does he anticipate the (American) worker to act to end capitalism's exploitation? Before or after the bomb falls? If the (American) worker does not act before the holocaust, should the (Negro) worker as worker fold his arms in hopes of "unity" or attempt to act independently on his own behalf? But even this is an oversimplification. Actually, Greenleaf is saying that the exploitation of the American Negro (as worker or bourgeois) can be ended only by ending the exploitation of the American worker (as Negro and white), understanding, of course, that the working class is overwhelmingly white. Now this is *theoretically* acceptable from a certain point of view, but, for a long time now, it has had very little practical application in life because the Negro (as worker and bourgeois) has always been most keenly aware of *racial* exploitation.

The belief in the revolutionary potentialities of white workers is a carry-over from nineteenth century classic Marxism. In my opinion, the changes that have taken place both in the structures and relationships of western capitalism and the underdeveloped world have rendered nineteenth century Marxian concepts obsolete. This presents a challenging problem for those who want to deal seriously with social reality. Yet Western Marxists, particularly Americans who are theoretically inept, cannot afford to let go the illusion that orthodox Marxian concepts still have validity. To abandon these concepts in the face of proletarian complacency would mean the passing off the scene of Marxist parties in the western world.

Hence, in order to stay alive, Marxists adopt the very reformist tactics of the Bernstein philosophy they once condemned, behind revolutionary phraseology. Marxists in the West cannot exist without the dogmas.

In the United States, where the Negro (as worker and bourgeois) is more keenly aware of his peculiar racial exploitation than is the white worker of his class position, the Negro is relegated by Marxist theory to a position which is actually subordinate to that of the predominantly white working class. The Negro is advised by Marxists that he cannot make effective or decisive political efforts unless he is in union with white workers. However, as Greenleaf points out, the Negro has made effective efforts in recent years toward racial equality goals—in Montgomery, Alabama, for example. But without the white working class. True, these struggles were not in themselves revolutionary, but they are indicative of the absence of Negro-labor unity that Marxists keep conjuring up as a *sine qua non* of Negro social endeavor. If Marxists find it a matter of life and death for the dogma that they maintain abiding faith in the revolutionary promise of white workers, that is their problem. Most Negroes, however, have long ago learned the futility of believing that the white worker would jeopardize his favored position in the labor market by aiding and abetting Negro struggles. Hence, Negroes, generally, comprehend that Marxist theory about the American proletariat is very remote from reality.

Faced, as we are, with a very complex social reality which Marxism does not comprehensively embrace, then a little (Marxist) learning like that of Greenleaf is a dangerous thing. So pitifully insufficient is his grasp of the world that he is worried about my views on the Negro bourgeoisie. This very idea of the Negro bourgeoisie in the role of exploiters of Negro workers before the capitalist jig is up comes like a nightmare in the dream world

of official dogma. Heresy of Heresies! Now we shall have
to "proletarianize" the black bourgeoisie to make them
fit the Marxist schema today so as to make sure they will
not become counter-revolutionaries when the millenium
arrives. However, Greenleaf at least admits we *do* have a
Negro bourgeoisie to contend with even though he obviously wishes this were not so. This is progress. Heretofore,
American Marxists were content to beguile us into believing that any Negro was simply one of the "Negro
people" whether a cotton-picker, a showgirl, a steel-
worker, a political appointee of the party in power, or the
editor and publisher of *Ebony* magazine. But having admitted the existence of the Negro bourgeoisie, Greenleaf
proceeds to avoid any discussion or definition of the
peculiar role this class stratum plays or could play in
Negro affairs. Such evasion, however, is not permissible
when the Negro bourgeoisie is the most vocal and articulate class in the matter of racial relations.

When one discusses Negro-white relations in the United
States, from a Marxist or any other point of view, very
little sense is made unless the question is discussed in
terms of two parallel bourgeois developments. One—the
dominant white bourgeois development—has long reached
its apex, while the other—the minor Negro bourgeois
development—is distorted and stunted. The Negro bourgeoisie never completed its own economic, political and
administrative revolution within the social structure of
American society. In this sense, it is a backward bourgeoisie and it follows that the Negro as a people is condemned
to backward economic, political and cultural conditions:
to social underdevelopment pure and simple.

The reasons Marxists cannot deal with these facts and
their immense corollaries are many. But the chief one is
that Western Marxists have a split personality over their
dual allegiance to Marx and Lenin. In their approach to
the (American) working class they invoke Marx's proletarian vision where it is no longer relevant, while pay-

ing homage to Lenin only insofar as Lenin rationalizes
his revisions of Marx in the name of Marx. But when
Marxists attempt to apply this schema to include the
Negro (as worker and bourgeois) they run afoul of the
formal contradiction in the concept of "Marxism-Lenin-
ism." Leninism as a world-view has more meaning for
Negroes within American society than does classical Marxism. But wherever the theoretical and political innova-
tions of Leninism run counter to the classic proletarian
concepts of Marx, the Marxists disregard Lenin. In a
country like the United States, Marxian theory is unable
to embrace a social reality whose structural and ideological
contours have developed dialectically beyond the scope of
the theory which is constantly retreating into the shell of
its doctrinal origins. It cannot see that the "class struggle"
is no longer a reality between capitalist and proletariat
within Western nations. The "class struggle" is now
supra-national—a struggle between Western nations and
the colonial and semi-colonial world. It is a struggle between blocs and developing blocs—Common Market *vs.*
Africa; U.S. *vs.* Latin America; U.S.S.R. and China *vs.*
the West. In other words, it is a struggle between the
"have" and "have-not" peoples, the world of super-
developed capitalism *vs.* the underdeveloped world. In this
world-wide struggle, the United States is the key super-
developed nation and exerts a tremendous political,
military and economic influence towards the ultimate
outcome of this world-wide struggle. However, the United
States has within its social structure a key racial minority
—eighteen to twenty million in number—which is larger
than many sovereign nations both in Europe and elsewhere. This Negro minority is not a nation in the formal
sense of the term, but it is in every sense of the term a
national minority. Since both nations and national minorities under varying conditions are capable of developing
nationalistic ideologies, both social and political science
must deal with these ideologies as they appear and trace

them to their roots in the social structure out of which they arise. In our society, just as long as the American Negro (as worker and bourgeois) is not amalgamated socially, politically and economically, Negro Nationalism will develop. This reality has to be dealt with despite Marxist objections.

No social problem can be dealt with unless it is first analyzed, however. Today, the Negro problem can only be analyzed in terms of its relationship to the world situation as it has developed dialectically—not in terms of Marx's proletarian vision. American race relations must be seen in terms of a struggle involving the politics of super-developed capitalism *vs.* the politics of American Negro underdevelopment (as worker and bourgeois). It is but a reflection within the American milieu of the reality of the struggle beyond American borders. Hence, the United States can not separate its policy towards the backward areas of the world from its policies towards the American Negro. Ultimately, the United States must deal with the politics of Negro underdevelopment as Negro Nationalism emerges into a coherent political, economic and cultural philosophy. That this has not developed as yet is due to the backwardness of the Negro bourgeoisie, which although very vocal and articulate on such matters as "integration," cannot carry through its bourgeois revolution to completion within American society. This class, then, "owes a debt" to history of which, for the most part, it is not even cognizant.

Although the implications of this are not generally understood, the American Negro is one of most crucial racial minorities in international affairs. Only in this sense is there a "bond" between the Negro and the colonial world. However, Greenleaf, who admits that "no Marxist would deny" such a bond, has not kept pace with the dialectical outcome of this historical bond as first expressed in the Leninist thesis. He wants the question solved within the theoretical context of Marx's proletarian vision which is historically obsolete, and which went out of vogue at the moment Lenin was forced by historical circumstances to revise it in order to deal with Western capitalism at the focal point of its imperialist designs. It is the Marxists who try to be "Marxists" and "Leninists" at one and the same time who have, in Greenleaf's words, a "contradictory set of ideas on racial matters." The attempt to tie the fate of the Negro worker to that of the white worker in theory is to pursue a myth with no precedent in Western society. For how can a white worker in the United States, a product and appendage of capitalist affluence, have the revolutionary compulsions associated with social backwardness? From the American standpoint of relative positions in social status it is the Negro who is the product of social backwardness. For these reasons the Negro (as worker and bourgeois) has revolutionary potential.

A growing number of Negroes today recognize, in one degree or another, the implications of their position in American society. Those who articulate the trend I am voicing cannot write off the Negro bourgeoisie even though they are critical of its politics and world outlook. We understand clearly the bourgeois aspirations behind the "integration" movement, and why a movement like that of Montgomery, Alabama, was merely a dress rehearsal that had to be shunted off into safer "passive resistance" tactics—a symbol of bourgeois incapacity to pursue militantly its own bourgeois democratic revolution. Realizing that the Negro bourgeoisie has not gone through the process of fulfilling its aspirations in American society, we perceive that "integration" becomes a bourgeois means of achieving bourgeois goals, the "liberation" of the Negro working class being purely incidental. If there are Marxists who are superficial enough to confuse Negro bourgeois goals through integration with what Greenleaf refers to as the Marxist goal, i.e. "joint effort of Negro and white workers to put an end to all exploitation . . ." then it is the Marxists who are confused about Negro class divisions and class aspirations. It is the Marxists who support the Negro bourgeois reform wing of the Negro movement (NAACP, etc.) claiming, thereby, that they are proving Marx's proletarian vision for the Negro working class, although the Negro working class does not support the NAACP. At the same time, most Marxists ignore or condemn the Nationalist wing of the Negro movement for having ideologies contrary to their idea of Marx's proletarian vision, despite the fact that the Nationalists have a predominantly working class membership. The attitude toward Nationalism proves that most Marxists in this country have defaulted on the Leninist legacy. For Negro Nationalism is an ideology that, in part, takes up the issues and problems that the Negro bourgeoisie has abandoned, *i.e.* the completion of the bourgeois democratic revolution.

Hence, it is not a question of demanding that the Negro bourgeoisie have the right to "exploit" other Negroes, but a recognition of the fact that when the bourgeois leadership of a national minority is historically beset with the incapacity to play out its historical role in society, then the working class of that national minority is in serious trouble. Moreover, social theories which do not take these factors into account are of no value to the working class in question. True, the whole question is most complex, and what to do about the Negro bourgeoisie is a serious problem. However, those who are disturbed by my point of view should put aside their preconceived notions about the formal meaning of the "nation" concept and the facile equating of political separation with "segregation." There *is* Nationalism in Negro ideology just as there was Nationalism in Jewish ideology long before the establishment of the State of Israel. But the dialectic of each and every group national-

ism does not necessarily lead to either formal nationhood
or geographical separation. The problem is how to deal
with this Nationalism as a tendency when the material
basis from which it derives gives it political justification.
For, if the Negro bourgeoisie does not win the full membership it is seeking in the Great American nation, this
class will be eventually caught between two opposing pressures—the Negro masses from below and the resistance of
the Power Elite from above. Such a development would
signal an open counter-revolutionary turn in American
foreign policy towards the underdeveloped world, being
reflected on the home front against the vulnerable Negro
and other democratic groups. There is no guarantee that
the white working class will not shift with the prevailing
winds in such an eventuality and go in for "super-
patriotism." In this regard, Greenleaf, who avers that:
"French workers have a bond with Algerians; Portuguese
workers have a bond with Angolans; above all, United
States workers have a bond with Cubans. The U.S. Negro
is a part of the U.S. working class," is indulging in wish-
fulfillment rather than facing facts. If he has been reading
the newspapers he knows that there are French workers
in Algiers and Oran, and Portuguese workers in Angola,
and that the American working class does not care a hoot
about the fate of Cuba. But in the event of an extreme
right-wing turn of the white working class on cue from
such a shift in American foreign policy, I do not visualize
the Negro workers joining in. The very nature of the
Negro's marginal relationships to society would obviate
this. Here, the Great American nation would be thrown
into direct confrontation with the unsolved reality of its
own domestic colonialism. If by that time the Marxian
proletarian vision is not shattered, it really won't matter.
If all this still makes no sense to Greenleaf, all I can do is
to quote a line from a well-known Negro church hymn:
"You will understand it by and by."

Reply:
In Defense of
Robert F. Williams

BY *Clark H. Foreman*

Volume III, No. 1
Fall 1962

Agreeing with Harold Cruse that the American Marxists have not understood the struggle of the American
Negroes, I must nevertheless object to his treatment of the
position of Robert F. Williams.

After saying that Williams personified a "third trend"
as distinguished from the NAACP approach and that of
the Black Nationalists, he more or less dismisses the trend.

It would seem to me from what I know of Williams
personally, and from his very interesting answers published in the same number of *Studies* ("An Interview with
Robert F. Williams"), that he represents the most practical
approach for the Negro who considers himself entitled to
be a full-fledged American.

Cruse is right that Williams is critical of Marxists and
Nationalists as well as of the NAACP, but he does not do
justice to the positive position which Williams represented, at least until the unfortunate circumstances that
made him flee to Cuba. I would like to present what I
understand to have been Williams' program:

1) Williams determined that even a Negro living in
North Carolina had a right to full American citizenship.
Cruse says that the program has no substance, but that
seems to me to be very substantial indeed. Williams in

his answers which you published says "The only thing I care about is justice and liberation" (p. 62).

2) In setting about in Monroe to accomplish his goal, there was at first no suggestion of violence. In fact Williams became president of the local NAACP and resorted to the unusual practice of inducing the rank and file of the Negro population to join up. As he proceeded with their backing to work for justice and liberation, he and his supporters were threatened by the Ku Klux Klan. He saw gross miscarriages of justice and he decided that if he were to win out he would have to be prepared to defend himself and his group against the vigilantism that had for so many years intimidated others. It is true, as Mr. Cruse writes, that "Williams resorted to arms for *defense* purposes" but the rest of that sentence seems to be incorrect: namely, "but arms are superfluous in terms of the objectives of racial integration." They certainly were not superfluous in terms of Williams' program—they were essential to his survival.

3) Mr. Cruse writes that "Arms symbolize a step beyond mere racial integration, to the seizure of actual centers of social power." They may of course, as they did in Cuba, but they can be used, as in Williams' case, to protect one's self and group against illegal oppression—or in Williams' words, for "justice and liberation."

4) Mr. Williams declares his loyalty to the U.S. government but he also bluntly states, "A government should see to it that all the people fare well. When a government fails to do these things, it forfeits its right to exist" (p. 55). Mr. Cruse says of Williams and his group, "They consider themselves 'revolutionary,' but are shy of having revolutionary objectives." (The Communist Party is now outlawed in this country for avowing similar objectives.) And Mr. Williams makes his own views very clear when he adds, . . . "it's only logical that this country must turn to socialism" (p. 62).

5) Mr. Williams does not have much faith in white peo-

ple, and who can say he should? But he does say that
some white people have helped him, some in the NAACP
of Monroe as well as some in the North (p. 58). This
seems to me to be crucial in the development of his plans
for there are few political units in the country in which
the Negroes have a majority.

In Atlanta strong Negro leadership has been able to
win political victories by finding allies among the decent
white people. And conditions there are far ahead of those
cities in which the two groups have no politics that can
bridge the color line. In the South, since the Civil War,
almost all progressive steps have been accomplished with
the aid of Negro voters, and as more and more Negroes
adopt the program of Robert Williams, more and more
white people are going to be willing to join them.

Reply

BY *Harold Cruse*

Volume III, No. 1
Fall 1962

Clark H. Foreman's comments on my approach to Robert F. Williams' movement are very instructive of the
theoretical understanding of leading exponents of American liberalism on the question of the Negro civil rights
movement. My article was not focussed on Williams, but
it is appropriate to explore Williams' relationship to
Negro nationalism, and, at the same time, to examine
some of the shortcomings of liberalism in its approaches
to Negroes as a people.

Mr. Foreman feels that I have treated Williams' "third
trend" too lightly. This is true, however, only insofar as

I have made no attempt to analyze this trend fully. Williams is important as an example of an incipient tendency standing to the "left" of the NAACP-King-CORE-students' alliance. But ideologically and tactically this trend has shown no development; it has merely replaced "passive resistance" with "militant resistance." This catches hold of the imagination, and for many is preferable, but it is still only resistance. Some leftwingers see in Williams' use of arms a symbol of revolt similar to that in revolutionary colonial movements elsewhere. But this is mostly illusory not only because there is considerable difference between armed defense and armed offense, but also because armed revolt (which implies armed offense) is incompatible with Williams' avowed integrationist aim. Armed integration is very unlikely to occur. For any Negro group in the United States to take up arms other than for defense implies a break with the prevailing social order which exerts political, economic and police oppression. Resorting to arms for a break with the prevailing order would be in contradiction to Williams' aims as an integrationist and would put him within the separatist orbit of the Nationalists, which he rejects. To move over into armed offense would not only invite certain annihilation but would imply that there are tangible objectives of a political, economic or military nature in the surrounding social order to be seized for the purpose of altering political, economic, military and class relationships. For Williams, the latter is as unfeasible as armed separation. Foreman seems to think that I am in error when I conclude that "arms are superfluous in terms of the objectives of racial integration." He points out that arms "were not superfluous in terms of Williams' program—they were essential to his survival." But this is non-sequitur reasoning. "Survival" cannot be considered a "program" since Negroes have been practicing "survival" in the South since time immemorial. It is certainly true that arms were essential for Williams' survival under the circumstances, but this does not mean that his "program" was unique in that it had other aims that were not common to the racial integration movement as a whole. For liberals or Marxists to support Williams for political reasons is one thing, but to attempt to prove thereby that Williams had a "program" is dubious. *Williams had no program beyond "survival" because the limitations, both ideological and political, of the racial integration movement as a whole prevented him from having one.* Williams has not even brought about token integration in Monroe, but racial stalemate from which Williams had to flee as a result of certain highly adventuristic acts his movement was maneuvered into committing. In fact, the Monroe movement is symbolic of the dead end towards which the whole integration movement is headed unless it receives from its leadership a completely new orientation. Armed defense is not going to open the road to constitutional guarantees of racial equality. As was demonstrated in Little Rock, only the armed intervention of the state can enforce integration. And even here it has to be integration ordered by government mandate. This, however, is a superficial kind of integration when stacked beside the intricacies inherent in the problems of interracial amalgamation which is what integrationists imply. In short, the kind of integration about which there is so much contention (schools, housing, public facilities, etc.) only begins to dent the barriers that fix the Negro minority in the status of an excluded and exploited sub-cultural group.

One cannot deny that every civil rights gain in the South *is* a gain, however limited, and every action towards this end is positive including the militant armed defense of Williams. What is apparently overlooked, however, is that Negro leadership in the South is, at this late date, struggling for the same level of human rights that the Negro in the North has already achieved, in varying degrees, in housing, public facilities, schools, the franchise, etc. But having achieved these rights in the North has not eradi-

cated that salient symbol of American race discrimination
—the Northern segregated Negro ghetto. The question
liberals should answer when they use the Southern states
as whipping boys on civil rights, is—why these same civil
rights (particularly the vote) have not made it possible
for Negroes in the North to win full citizenship?

This should indicate that the civil rights movement as
now constituted does not deal with all the aspects, nor
with the deeper implications of the problem. In this
regard, liberals and Marxists, in failing to clarify and
publicize the sociological factors inherent in the problem,
are more responsible than the conservatives for the perpetuation of popular confusion. Liberals make the civil
rights question a moral and constitutional issue, and a
political football in election years. But behind all this lies
the reality that civil rights is more fundamentally an
economic and class question. Most civil rights supporters
shrink from admitting that full racial equality cannot be
achieved under the American system as it is now constituted. Conservatives are well aware of this and thus have
little to say about civil rights for fear of dangerously rock-
ing the boat. But liberals spread the illusion that the
ideals of the Constitution can be enforced for the Negro
minority within the present capitalist system, the class
character of which functions outside the purview of the
Constitution. Ideals about human rights are mere words
in modern society when not permitted the kind of economic context in which such ideals can be practiced. In
this regard, when one speaks on "human rights" and the
American Negro, it must be admitted that the present
nature of the American economic system makes it impossible to achieve full integration, or civil rights in the
South, or the kind of social equality vouchsafed by the
ideals of the Constitution. More far-reaching economic
reforms than have ever been instituted in the United
States will be required to achieve such ends. The civil
rights movement, in order to succeed, must extend its

objectives into the economic spheres of private enterprise
vs. government intervention into the economy, wherever
such intervention is deemed necessary in order that the
social and constitutional implications of the civil rights
movement shall have material reinforcements. There
must be developed the kind of economic context which
will enable the Negro to breach the most formidable
barrier of all—that which fixes him in the trap of economic exploitation and exclusion. Unless this barrier is
irrevocably breached, complete racial equality can never
be achieved in the United States. It is sheer illusion to
believe otherwise. And unless the civil rights movement
adopts some kind of economic orientation to buttress its
social and racial demands, the movement can only bog
down in the complete impasse of racial stalemate that is
already developing in the Southern states.

This crucial economic question is, of course, implicit
in the fundamental *class* nature of the civil rights movement. The Negro civil rights movement is essentially a
bourgeois movement. Its articulate leadership is bourgeois,
not working class. Such working class support as is given
this movement is based on the practical necessities of racial
self-interest, not on any essential accord between the two
class ideologies. The breach between Robert F. Williams
and the NAACP was one indication of this fact. However,
the Negro working class must either follow the Negro
bourgeoisie when it leads on civil rights, or swing to the
(bourgeois) Nationalist wing. It has no other perspective
except racial apathy or stalemate. This is true because the
Negro bourgeoisie, as a whole, does not have the political
and economic orientation that could give the civil rights
movement anything resembling a "revolutionary" character which the Negro working class could support without the reservations now evident. The fault here is not
that of the Negro working class but of the Negro bour-
geosie, which pretends to be carrying out its historical
responsibilities in "uplifting" the masses by its vocal de-

mands for "social equality" and "liberation." In modern times, however, there has been no liberation movement of oppressed peoples anywhere in the world that did not espouse far reaching economic demands along with its social, political, cultural or administrative objectives. It is for this reason that the Nationalist wing of the Negro movement is correct in its criticisms of the bourgeois reform wing (NAACP, King, etc.) The reformist leadership is politically backwards and does not measure up to the demands of the situation. The Nationalist wing is politically more advanced in its fundamental estimate of the racial situation, but its potential is also limited. In many respects, its "separatism" can be construed as a negative means of settling the very economics of the racial situation which the Nationalists understand and confront more readily than the reformist wing. What is required here is the adoption of positive economic demands to complement the positive social and constitutional goals of the civil rights movement.

Herein lies the rub. The Negro bourgeoisie cannot project any far reaching economic reforms either in terms of its own class interests or in the interest of the working class Negro without coming into conflict with the entrenched class interests of the ruling American "Power Elite" and the lower echelons of the white middle classes. This is why the NAACP, for example, keeps its economic program keyed to the issue of job discrimination, fair employment practices, and other objectives which have long had the official sanction of local, state and federal agencies. The NAACP, which would readily protest discrimination against Negroes in businesses owned by whites *within the Negro community, does not (and probably never will) challenge the fact that Negro communities are, for the most part, owned lock, stock and barrel by white absentee proprietors. These are the crucial areas in which the economic exploitation of the Negro is focused.* For the Negro bourgeoisie to oppose this would be historically justified, and would be a *legitimate bourgeois demand*. However, it is only the Nationalist wing of the Negro movement which vocally objects to this exploitative situation. *And it was not the NAACP but the Nationalist wing which first fought against discriminatory hiring policies in the large Negro communities and forced white proprietors to hire Negroes in Harlem*. It is in this area that the most crucial American class struggle lies.

It is only in the economic sphere of race relations that the demands of the reformist Negro bourgeoisie for civil rights immediately become radical. Hence, it is along this ideological route that the civil rights movement must progress. Only through this general development can the civil rights movement avoid lapsing into a nationwide racial stalemate, since no one, Negro or white, can solve a problem without the ideological, political or organizational means of doing so.

It should be clear that movements like that of Robert F. Williams in Monroe cannot be considered as having programs that can even begin to cope with the implications of the civil rights movement as a whole. Movements like Williams' can only lead to stalemate, dispersal and martyrdom because they are delimited to the role of armed defense or militant resistance. Foreman is certainly correct in saying that Williams was being "positive" in defending himself against attacks, but it does not follow that Williams "represents the most practical approach for the Negro who considers himself entitled to be a full-fledged American." If Foreman upholds Williams' belief in the necessity of "socialism" (whatever "socialism" is supposed to mean in this context), this implies structural changes. But Foreman has not suggested what path Williams should pursue from armed defense to structural changes. He merely upholds Williams' right to be a rebel without orientation or direction, after the fashion of those who revere John Brown as a martyr for a cause that was eventually won by other means.

The accumulated experience of the twentieth century has shown that it is *social underdevelopment* that gives rise to movements for social change. Moreover, these movements usually manifest bourgeois stages of political and economic consummation whether of short or long duration. In the case of the Negro, integration is a progressive idea only in terms of the dialectical process it initiates among opposing trends and conflicting class interests. For the Negro cannot leap from a segregated status to a fully integrated status without going through a many sided class struggle both within and without the Negro group itself. Until this dialectical process is understood the Negro movement will be worn down by racial attrition.

The Legacy of Slavery and the Roots of Black Nationalism

BY *Eugene D. Genovese*

Volume VI, No. 6
November–December 1966

Eugene D. Genovese is the author of The Political Economy of Slavery *(1965) and of the forthcoming* The World the Slaveholders Made. *In this article he synthesizes the slave experience and the emergence of the modern Nationalist trend among blacks. It was originally delivered as a paper at the Second Annual Socialist Scholars Conference, New York, September 1966.*

American radicals have long been imprisoned by the pernicious notion that the masses are necessarily both good and revolutionary, and by the even more pernicious notion that, if they are not, they should be. The principal task of radical historians therefore has too often been to provide the masses with historical heroes, to make them aware of their glorious tradition of resistance to oppression, and to portray them as having been implacably hostile to the social order in which they have been held. This viewpoint now dominates the black liberation movement, which has been fed for decades by white radical historians who in this one respect have set the ideological pace for their liberal colleagues. It has become virtually sacrilege—or at least white chauvinism—to suggest that slavery was a social system within which whites and blacks lived in harmony as well as antagonism, that there is little evidence of massive, organized opposition to the regime, that the blacks did not establish a revolutionary tradition of much significance, and that our main problem is to discover the reasons for the widespread accommodation and, perhaps more important, the long-term effects both of the accommodation and of that resistance which did occur.

In 1831 Nat Turner led a slave revolt on which has hung most of the legend of armed black resistance to slavery. Of the two hundred fifty or so revolts chronicled and analyzed in Herbert Aptheker's *American Negro Slave Revolts*,[1] Turner's has pride of place and was described by Aptheker as a "cataclysm." Yet, when we look closely, this revolt, like the total history of such revolts, recedes in importance and magnitude. As many of Aptheker's critics have pointed out, most of the two hundred fifty revolts probably never happened, being the imagination of hysterical or self-serving whites, insignificant plots that never matured, or mere local disturbances of a questionable nature. Of the three major revolts, one, Denmark Vesey's, was crushed before it came to fruition; only Gabriel Prosser's in 1800 and Turner's reached impressive proportions. Even so painstaking and thorough a scholar as Aptheker has been unable to discover firm evidence of a major revolt between 1831 and 1865. As for Turner's, less than one hundred slaves joined. A revolt of this size would rate little more than a page or two in a comprehensive work on slave revolts in Brazil. To cite only two outstanding examples, runaway slaves in the Brazilian Northeast organized their own colony, Palmares, and waged a sixty-five-year struggle for autonomy with as many as twenty thousand people.[2] During the first four decades of the nineteenth century there were a series of violent

---

[1] Aptheker, Herbert, *American Negro Slave Revolts* (New York, 1943, 1963).

[2] Carneiro, Edison, *O. Quilombo dos Palmares, 1630-1695* (Sao Paulo, 1947).

and extensive risings in Bahia, culminating in the great Muslim-led holy war of 1835.[3] We need not dwell on Haiti,[4] as the record of Jamaica, Cuba and other countries is also impressive. Even if, as Aptheker suggests, news of many smaller risings was suppressed, the effect would have been to prevent the accumulation of a tradition to encourage and sustain revolt-prone slaves. On balance, we find the absence or extreme weakness of such a tradition.

There were many reasons for this extreme weakness. First, we need to consider the kind of Africans brought here. It has long been falsely assumed that, since slave traders mixed their cargoes, all parts of the hemisphere received similarly mixed bags. But Brazil, for example, received large numbers of Angolans and Congolese, whose military, religious and cultural traditions made them especially difficult to control.[5] Brazil also received a large number of Muslim slaves from Upper Guinea who proved intractable everywhere in the hemisphere. The United States, on the other hand, largely drew its slaves from those portions of Lower Guinea which had a population previously disciplined to servitude and domination. Ironically, these Africans were, in some respects, among the most advanced in technical culture.

Second, the slave trade to the United States came to an end in 1808, although illegal importations continued to trickle in; in contrast, the trade to Cuba and Brazil continued well into the nineteenth century. The presence of large numbers of newly imported Africans can generally be correlated with incidence of revolt. In the United

---

[3] Cf., Abbé Ignace Etienne, "La Secte musulmane des Malès du Brésil et leur révolte en 1835," *Anthropos*, IV (1909), 99-105; 405-415.

[4] Cf., esp. C.L.R. James, *The Black Jacobins: Toussaint L'Ouverture and the San Domingo Revolution* (2nd ed., rev.; New York, 1963), which deserves to rank as a classic of Marxian historiography but has been largely ignored, perhaps because of the author's Trotskyist politics.

[5] For example, Palmares was established by Angolans. See "Carta do Governador Fernao de Souza Coutinho . . ." in Ernesto Ennes, *As Guerras nos Palmares* (Sao Paulo, 1938), pp. 133-138, Nina Rodrigues, *Os Africanos no Brasil* (3rd ed., Sao Paulo, 1945), Ch. III.

States the great majority of slaves during the antebellum period had been born and raised on Southern plantations. Their ranks received little reinforcement from newly enslaved and aggressive Africans.

Third, a review of the history of Brazil and the Caribbean suggests that an important ingredient in the development of revolts out of local disturbances was the division of the whites into warring factions and the general weakness of the state apparatus. Together with these conditions went the general influence of geography in relation to state power. Where suitable terrain was combined with a weak state, runaway slaves could and did found maroon colonies, which directly fomented revolts and kept alive a tradition of armed resistance. With minor qualifications, these conditions did not exist in the United States.

Fourth, a substantial revolt presupposed the formation of ideology and leadership. In Brazil and the Caribbean two circumstances combined to encourage both: the cultivation of sugar led to the establishment of plantations averaging perhaps two hundred slaves or more, and the size of the white population was small. As a result the blacks could keep alive much of their African culture or could develop a syncretized Afro-Brazilian or Afro-Cuban culture, which militated against the loss of identity and which could, under proper conditions, nurture resistance movements. Apart from Islam, non-Christian religious cults, generally of a syncretized type, played a great role in hemispheric slave revolts. In the United States an imposed Protestantism, when effective, generally kept the slaves docile.

Half the slaves in the United States lived on units of twenty or less; most of the others lived in plantations of fifty or less. Although blacks heavily outnumbered whites in large areas of the South, they were, in general, floating in a white sea. The white planters were residents, not absentees; the non-slaveholders were loyal, armed and disciplined; the country immediately beyond the plantation areas was inhabited by armed whites completely hostile to the blacks. Death, not refuge, lay beyond the plantation. For this reason, among others, blacks often looked to their masters to protect them against the depredations and viciousness of the poorer whites. We may therefore understand how, during race riots like that in Atlanta in 1906, blacks reportedly ran to whites—or at least to some whites—for protection.

The residency of the planters and their hegemony across the South gave American slavery its particular quality and especially set it off from Caribbean slavery. Between the Revolutionary War and the War for Southern Independence the treatment of slaves, defined as day-to-day conditions of life (housing, food, rigor of work routine, leisure time, incidence and character of corporal punishment) improved steadily and perceptibly. Although manumission was made increasingly difficult and escape from the system was sealed off, the harsh slave codes were steadily tempered by community sentiment and the interpretations of the state supreme courts. During the late antebellum period steady pressure built up to reform the slave codes in order to protect slave family life and to check glaring abuses of the slave's person. The purpose and effect of this amelioration in practice and at law was not to pave the way to freedom, but to consolidate the system from within and without. Like all liberal reformism it aimed to strengthen the social system.

For the planters these trends formed part of a developing world view within which paternalism became the specific manifestation of class consciousness. Paternalism did not mean kindness or generosity or love, although it embraced some of each; essentially it meant a special notion of duty and responsibility toward one's charges. Arbitrary power, harshness toward disobedience, even sadism, constituted its other side. For our immediate purposes, paternalism and the trend of treatment are especially noteworthy in confronting the slave with a world in which resistance could be quickly, severely and legitimately punished, whereas obedience placed him in a position to benefit from the favor of a master who more often than not had a genuine interest in his welfare. The picture of the docile and infantilized Sambo, drawn and analyzed so brilliantly by Stanley M. Elkins, is one-sided, but he is not far from the mark when he argued that the Southern régime greatly encouraged acceptance of and dependence upon despotic authority.[6] Elkins errs in thinking that the Sambo personality arose only in the United States, for it arose wherever slavery existed. He does not err in thinking that it was especially marked and extentive in the United States, where recourse to armed resistance was minimal and the tradition of paternalism took such firm root.

To say that slaves generally accommodated is not to say that they were so dehumanized as to be incapable of all forms of protest. Historians are quick to claim rebelliousness every time a slave broke a plow or stole a hog, but at least some room might be left for lack of initiative, thoughtlessness, stupidity and venality. Yet, we do know of enough instances of deliberate acts of day-to-day resistance to permit us to speak of a strong undercurrent of dissatisfaction and hostility, the manifestations of which require analysis.

One of the most prominent and irritating habits of recalcitrant slaves was stealing. Plundering the hog pen and the smokehouse was an especially happy pastime. Radical and liberal historians have taken particular delight in insisting that slaves might "steal" from each other but only "took" from their masters. After all, their labor being unpaid, they only took that which was rightfully theirs. I can understand this viewpoint from liberals because I can understand almost anything from liberals; I cannot understand it from Marxists. Since Marxists regard all surplus value as deriving from unpaid

---

[6] Elkins, Stanley M., *Slavery: A Problem in American Institutional and Intellectual Life* (Chicago, 1959), esp. Ch. III.

labor time, we ought, by the same logic, to be delighted every time a worker commits robbery at his plant. I do not wish to discuss the general problem of ethics in relation to class oppression, but I do insist that the encouragement given by the slave system to thefts had dangerous effects on the slaves themselves. The slaves understood the link between conventional morality and the civilized behavior of the whites; by rejecting that morality they registered a protest, but they simultaneously underscored their own isolation from that standard of civilization. Few masters got upset over slave thefts. They expected their slaves to steal, and by doing so, the slaves accepted their master's image of themselves.

Southern folklore abounds with charming stories of slaves outwitting masters by behaving like black versions of the Good Soldier Schweik. The trouble is that too often the masters enjoyed being outwitted in the same way that a tyrannical father sometimes enjoys being out-witted by a child. Every contortion necessary to the job implied inferiority. It proved the slave a clever fellow; it hardly proved him a man. It gained a few privileges or crumbs but undermined self-respect and confirmed the master's sense of superiority. The postslavery tradition of obsequiousness, indirection and the wearing of a mask before white men has played a similar role in the South ever since.

Arson and the mishandling of tools stand out as more positively rebelliousness acts. As expressions of frustration and resentment they are understandable, and might, in a general context of rebellion, have had considerable social value. As it was, they amounted to individual and essen-tially nihilistic thrashing about. With luck a few slaves might do enough damage to ruin a planter, in which case he would be forced to sell out and perhaps have to break up slave families and friendships. Advocates of the philosophy of "burn-baby-burn," whether on a Mississippi plantation in the 1850's or in a Northern ghetto in the

1960's, would do well to bear in mind that of necessity it is primarily the blacks who get burned. On occasion a slave took direct action against a particularly unpleasant master or overseer and killed him. For that manly act he would, if lucky, be hanged.

As we review these actions, which by no means exhaust the range, we find the formation of a tradition of recalcitrance but not revolution, action but not politics, dim awareness of oppression but not cumulative, ideological growth. Thus, whereas most slaves came out of slavery with a psychology of dependence conditioned by paternalism, the most active spirits came out having learned little more than that they could get away with individual acts of undirected, misdirected or naïvely directed violence. What was missing was that sense of group consciousness, collective responsibility and joint political effort which is the essence of a revolutionary tradition.

The formation of class leadership presents another side of this development. Legend has it that house slaves and drivers, by virtue of their special positions, arrayed themselves on the side of the master against the field hands, who as the most oppressed were of course the most revolutionary and pure. Examination of plantation documents casts grave doubts on this legend. Few plantations were big enough to carry a staff of servants large enough to constitute a separate caste. Even then the social life of the plantation proved too enticing for them to maintain total separation. With much of their everyday world conditioned by contacts with field slaves, they could ill-afford to be wholly on the side of the whites. The range of behavior was wide, but there were many instances of identification and sympathy.

The drivers, or slave foremen, present an even clearer case. These men often dominated the everyday life of the plantation. On the whole masters trusted them more than they trusted their white overseers; overseers came and went after a year or two, but drivers usually stayed on in

positions of authority for many years. Masters relied on
their drivers to tell them if an overseer was too lax or
too harsh and if the hands respected him. Rarely did a
planter take his overseer's word against that of a trusted
driver. Some drivers undoubtedly were themselves severe
taskmasters who lorded it over their fellow slaves, but
drivers, too, had no social life apart from that of the slave
quarters and had to live with the others. In general, they
compromised as best they could between the master to
whom they had pledged loyalty and to whom they were
indebted for special favors, and the slaves who constituted
their everyday fellows. Often the driver stood as a protector or interpreter between slave and master or overseer. Drivers and house slaves often, although certainly
not always, comprised a leading stratum in the eyes of
the blacks as well as in the eyes of the whites.

In the Caribbean these privileged slaves led revolts; in
the United States they served as agents of accommodation.
Toussaint L'Ouverture was only the most prominent of
insurrectionary leaders who had been trained to leadership
within the system. The problem in the United States was
not that the system did not create such privileged strata,
nor that these strata were more docile or less courageous
than those in the Caribbean. The problem was that the
total environment reduced the possibilities for successful
insurrection virtually to zero, and therefore made accommodationists out of the most high-spirited slave leaders.
When the mass exodus from the plantations took place
during the War for Southern Independence, drivers and
house slaves often led their people to the Union lines.
Not docility but lack of a tradition of armed resistance
conditioned their leadership.

Potential recruitment of insurrectionary leaders was
hampered by many other circumstances, of which three
are especially noteworthy. For reasons already indicated
little anti-Christian religious sentiment could develop. Religion (Islam, voodoo, or Afro-Catholic syncretisms)
proved to be an essential ingredient in slave cohesion and

organized resistance throughout the hemisphere, but in the United States the enforced prevalence of Protestant Christianity played an opposite role. The second group of potential leaders recruited from all strata were those who had sufficient strength, daring and resourcefulness to flee. The runaways are black folk heroes, with good reason, but they also drained the best elements out of the slave class. In much of Brazil and the Caribbean runaways had nowhere to go except into the back country to form maroon colonies, the existence of which encouraged slave disorder and resistance. Finally, the free blacks and mulattoes in the United States had little opportunity for self-development and rarely could or would provide leadership to slaves. Elsewhere in the hemisphere, where whites were relatively few, these free blacks and mulattoes were needed to fill a wide variety of social and economic functions. Often they prospered as a middle class. In some cases, feelings of racial solidarity, or, as in Haiti, the racist stupidity of the whites, led them into partial identification with the cause of black freedom. Thus, with the exception of a rare Nat Turner, black leadership fell to those whose position within the plantation itself encouraged accommodation and negated the possibilities of effective political organization.

The War for Southern Independence brought these tendencies to a head. The staggering truth is that not one full-scale slave revolt broke out during a war in which local white police power had been drastically reduced. In only a few isolated cases did slaves drive off their masters and divide the land among themselves. Many, perhaps most, struck for freedom by fleeing to Union lines at the first opportunity. The attitude of the slaves toward the federals varied, but the great majority welcomed them with an adulation, trust and dependence that suggests the full force of the old paternalism.[7] Many blacks, free and slaves, Northern and Southern, entered the Union Army,

---

[7] Wiley, Bell Irvin, *Southern Negroes, 1861-1865* (New Haven, 1965; first pub., 1938), esp. pp. 14-15.

where despite humiliating discrimination they gave a creditable account of themselves in action.

For all that, the record of the slaves and ex-slaves during the war constituted a disaster. Having relied previously on the protection and guidance of their masters, they now threw themselves on the mercies of the Union Army. As might be expected, untold thousands died in and out of virtual concentration camps, countless women were raped by Union troops, black soldiers generally found themselves used as menials or cannon fodder. Many decent and selfless white and black abolitionists accompanied the Union Army South and earnestly worked to educate and organize the freedmen; they deserve all the praise and attention historians are now heaping on them. The fact remains that no black movement and only a weak black leadership emerged from the war.

As the war years passed into the period of Reconstruction, these patterns were reinforced. The blacks could and did fight for their rights, but rarely under their own leadership. When they offered armed resistance under competent leadership they did well enough, but mostly they relied on the leadership of white politicians, or on the protection of federal troops, or on the advice of their own inexperienced leaders who in turn relied on whites. As Vernon Lane Wharton has observed, "The lesson learned was that the Negroes, largely unarmed, economically dependent, and timid and unresourceful after generations of servitude, would offer no effective resistance to violence."[8] When Whitelaw Reid asked black school children what they would do if someone tried to reenslave them, most responded that the troops would not permit it. No wonder Northern public opinion asked contemptuously in 1875 why a black majority in Mississippi constantly had to call for outside help.

The blacks sealed their own fate by relying on the

[8] Wharton, Vernon Lane, *The Negro in Mississippi, 1865-1900* (New York, 1965; first pub. 1947), p. 190.

protection of others. The Republican Party, the Union Army and the Freedman's Bureau all took on the role of protectors, but, if anything, the new paternalism proved much more flimsy and more insincere than the old. The best illustration may be found in the history of the Republican-sponsored, largely black militias. Ex-slaves, urged on and even threatened by their women, who were generally more militant than the men, responded to the calls of Republican governors and filled the ranks of state militias, which were put to effective use in guaranteeing Republican electoral victories. In several instances, especially toward the end of Reconstruction, militia units opposed each other on behalf of rival Republican factions. In the most appalling of these instances, the so-called Brooks-Baxter War in Arkansas in 1874, the Republican machine so discredited itself that the Democrats soon rode back to power. As Otis A. Singletary has sardonically observed, "The Negroes had been called to arms to fight in behalf of two white claimants for the governorship, as a consequence of which the Negro was eliminated as a political factor in Arkansas."[9] In Mississippi the radical governor, Adelbert Ames, called the blacks to arms in 1875 to counter Democratic violence, and then lost his nerve and disarmed them in return for a worthless pledge from the opposition. Significantly the black politicians in his party almost unanimously opposed using the black troops in a showdown. The militia movement failed because it faced greater force, but no less because its leaders were never willing to see it steeled in battle, especially in defense of specifically black interests.

In other respects the Reconstruction experience followed parallel lines. In the famous Sea Island experiment the blacks placed their trust in white generals, some of whom meant well and tried hard but could not prevail in the face of Washington's duplicity. When the old

[9] Singletary, Otis A., *Negro Militia and Reconstruction* (Austin, 1952), p. 65.

plantation owners returned with federal support, the blacks protested but ultimately accepted defeat without recourse to arms. Here, as with the militias, the masses seem to have been well ahead of their leaders. Demands for resistance were heard, anti-white feeling was manifest and the desire for land grew apace, but the leadership proved timid or mortgaged, and action independent of whites was deemed impractical. Black congressmen and state legislators rarely fought for basic black interests and even opposed disfranchisement of ex-Confederate whites. With no powerful separate organizations and paramilitary units, without experience in leading their masses, they temporized and collapsed. Their fault did not lie in having coalesced with Northern whites, but in having coalesced from a position of weakness, without independent demands, organization and force. The masses moved sharply to the left and expressed an intense desire for land, but the old pattern persisted; they could not cut loose from accommodating leaders and from dependence on the ultimate authority of the whites. They did not so much demand, much less fight for, land, as they hoped it would be given them as a Christmas present.

The black leaders saw the duplicity of their white Republican allies, but had nowhere to go. Most had been Northerners or privileged Southern mulattoes; their links with the masses had never been firm. When election time arrived they swallowed their doubts and frustrations and, with the best of intentions, lied to their people. Without adequate traditions and without confidence in their masses they made the best deals they could. This lying carried on an old habit. Every slave, at some time or other, would outwit the white folks by pretending to be stupid or docile; unfortunately too often he simultaneously outwitted himself. When carried into slave leadership, it was generally impossible to outwit the whites without also outwitting the blacks. During the war, for example, the respected black pastor of a Baptist Church in Virginia offered a prayer for the victory of Confederate arms. Subsequently he was berated by his deacons for betraying the cause of the slaves, but he pacified them by saying, "Don't worry children; the Lord knew what I was talking about." [10] Undoubtedly, the Lord did, but the good pastor apparently never wondered whether or not his flock did also.

Some of the Reconstruction leaders simply sold out. As a distinguished South Carolina planter noted, they promised their people land and mules at every election but delivered only offices and jobs for themselves and their friends."[11] (Any resemblance to the War on Poverty is not of my making.)

Slavery and its aftermath left the blacks in a state of acute economic and cultural backwardness, with weak family ties and the much-discussed matriarchal preponderance. They also left a tradition of accommodation to paternalistic authority on the one hand, and a tradition of nihilistic violence on the other. Not docility or infantilization, but innocence of organized effort and political consciousness plagued the black masses and kept plaguing them well into the twentieth century. As a direct result of these effects and of the virtually unchallenged hegemony of the slaveholders, the blacks had little opportunity to develop a sense of their own worth and had every opportunity to learn to despise themselves. The inability of the men during and after slavery to support their families adequately, and especially to protect their women from rape or abuse without forfeiting their own lives, has merely served as the logical end of an emasculating process.

The remarkable ascendancy of Booker T. Washington after the post-Reconstruction reaction must be understood against this background. We need especially to ac-

[10] Wiley, *Southern Negroes*, p. 107.

[11] Manigault, Charles, "Souvenirs of Our Ancestors & of My Immediate Family," ca. 1873. Ms. in the Manigault Papers, University of North Carolina.

count for his enormous influence over the black Nationalists who came after him. Washington tried to meet the
legacy of slavery on its own terms. He knew that slavery
had ill-prepared his people for political leadership; he
therefore retreated from political demands. He knew that
slavery had rendered manual labor degrading; he therefore preached the gospel of hard work. He knew that
slavery had undermined the family and elementary moral
standards; he therefore preached the whole gamut of
middle-class virtues and manners. He knew his people had
never stood on their own feet and faced the whites as
equals; he therefore preached self-reliance and self-help.
Unhappily, apart from other ideological sins, he saw no
way to establish self-reliance and self-respect except under
the financial and social hegemony of the white upper
classes. Somehow he meant to destroy the effects of paternalism in the long run by strengthening paternalism
in the short run. It would be easy to say that he failed
because of this tactic, but there is no way to be sure that
the tactic was wrong in principle. He failed for other
reasons, one of which was his reliance on the paternalistic,
conservative classes at a time when they were rapidly
losing power in the South to racist agrarian demagogues.

Washington's rivals did not, in this respect, do much
better. The leaders of the NAACP repeatedly returned
to a fundamental reliance on white leadership and money.
Even Du Bois, in his classic critique of Washington
argued:

> While it is a great truth to say that the Negro must strive and
> strive mightly to help himself, it is equally true that unless
> his striving be not simply seconded, but rather aroused and
> encouraged by the initiative of the richer and wiser environ-
> ing group, he cannot hope for great success.[12]

The differences between these militants and Washington's
conservatives concerned emphases, tactics and public

[12] Du Bois, W. E. Burghardt, *The Soul of Black Folk* (New York, 1964;
first pub. 1903), p. 53.

stance much more than ideological fundamentals. The differences were important, but their modest extent was no less so. The juxtaposition of the two tendencies reveals how little could be done even by the most militant without white encouragement and support. The wonder is that black Americans survived the ghastly years between 1890 and 1920 at all. Survival—and more impressive, growing resistance to oppression—came at the price of continuing many phases of a paternalistic tradition that had already sapped the strength of the masses.

The conflict between Washington and Du Bois recalled many earlier battles between two tendencies that are still with us. The first has accepted segregation at least temporarily, has stressed the economic development of the black community and has advocated self-selp. This tendency generally prevailed during periods of retrogression in race relations until the upsurge of Nationalism in our own day. Washington was its prophet; black Nationalism has been its outcome. The second has demanded integration, has stressed political action and has demanded that whites recognize their primary responsibility. Frederick Douglass was its prophet; the civil rights movement has been its outcome. Yet, the lines have generally been blurred. Du Bois often sounded like a Nationalist, and Washington probably would have thought Malcolm X a madman.[13] This blurring reflects the dilemma of the black community as a whole and of its bourgeoisie in particular: How do you integrate into a nation that does not want you? How do you separate from a nation that finds you too profitable to release?

To probe the relationship between this past and the recent upsurge of the black masses requires more speculation and tentative judgment than one would like, but they cannot be avoided. Let us, at the risk of being schematic

---

[13] For the period 1890-1915 see August Meier's careful and illuminating *Negro Thought in America: Racial Ideologies in the Age of Booker T. Washington* (New York, 1964).

and one-sided, select several features of the developments of the last few decades and especially of the recent crisis for such analysis. In doing so let us bear in mind that the majority of blacks today live outside the South; that they are primarily urban, not rural, in all parts of the country; that whole cities are on the way to becoming black enclaves; that the problem increasingly centers on the urban North and West.[14] Let us bear in mind also that the only large-scale, organized black mass movements until recently have been Nationalist. Garvey commanded an organization of hundreds of thousands; the Muslims have tens of thousands and influence many more. No integrationist organization has ever acquired such numerical strength; none has ever struck such deep roots in the black ghettoes.

Garvey's movement emphasized blackness as a thing of beauty, and struggled to convince the black masses to repudiate white leadership and paternalism. The pompous titles, offices, uniforms and parades did and do evoke ridicule, but their importance lay, as Edmund David Cronon says, "in restoring the all but shattered Negro self-confidence." There was enormous ideological significance in Garvey's delightful description of a light-skinned mulatto opponent as "a white man passing for Negro."[15]

A decisive break with the white man's church, if not wholly with his religion, has formed a major part of black Nationalist thinking. In view of the central role of anti-

[14] For a perceptive discussion of these trends see Charles E. Silberman, *Crisis in Black and White* (New York, 1964), esp. pp. 7, 29-31.

[15] Cronon, Edmund David, *Black Moses: The Story of Marcus Garvey and the Universal Negro Improvement Association* (Madison, 1955, 1964), p. 174. It was never Garvey's intention to send all blacks back to Africa; he wanted a strong African nation to serve as a protector to blacks everywhere. See esp. the interview with Garvey in James Weinstein, ed., "Black Nationalism: The Early Debate," *Studies on the Left*, IV, no. 3 (1964), pp. 50-58.

The idea of black nationality in America stretches back to the beginnings of the nineteenth century, if not earlier. See esp. Herbert Aptheker, "Consciousness of Negro Nationality to 1900," *Toward Negro Freedom* (New York, 1956), pp. 104-111; also, Benjamin Quarles, *The Negro in the Making of America* (New York, 1964), p. 157.

Christian ideology in the slave risings of Brazil and the Caribbean and the generally accommodationist character of American Christianity, this has been a rational response to a difficult problem. Garvey tried to organize his own African Orthodox Church. The Islamic tendency, including Elijah Muhammed's Nation of Islam, has followed the maxim of Noble Drew Ali's Moorish Science Movement, "Before you can have a God, you must have a nationality." Garvey's Black Jesus and Muhammed's Allah have had many attributes of a tribal deity. Of special importance in Muhammed's teaching is his decidedly un-Islamic denial of an afterlife. In this way Black Muslim eschatology embodies a sharp reaction against accommodationist ideology. The tendency to turn away from the white man's religion has taken many forms, including conversion to Catholicism ostensibly because of its lack of a color line. In Catholic Brazil, on the other hand, an equivalent reason is given by blacks who embrace Protestantism.[16]

Black Protestants in the United States have largely attended self-segregated churches since Reconstruction. With the collapse of Reconstruction these churches, especially in the South, played an increasingly accommodationist role, but they also served as community centers, protective agencies, marriage counseling committees and leadership training schools. As objective conditions changed, so did many ministers, especially the younger ones. One of the great ironies of the current struggle for integration has been the leading role played by ministers whose training and following have been made possible by segregated organizations. The experience of the Protestant churches and their anti-Christian rivals brings us back to slavery's legacy of accommodationist but by no means necessarily treasonable leadership, of an absence of collective effort, of paternalistically-induced depend-

---

[16] Bastide, Roger, and Fernandes, Florestan, *Brancos e negros em Sao Paulo* (2nd ed.; Sao Paulo, 1959), p. 254.

ence and of emasculation. Theoretically, a militant mass
leadership could have arisen from sources other than enforced segregation; historically there seems to have been
no other way.[17]

The first difficulty with the integrationist movement
arises not from its ultimate commitment, which may or
may not be desirable, but from the determined opposition
of the whites, whose hostility to close association with
blacks recedes slowly if at all. Integration may only mean
desegregation, and outstanding black intellectuals like
Killens and Baldwin insist that that is all they want it to
mean; it need not mean assimilation. In fact, however,
the line is difficult to hold, and segregationists probably
do not err in regarding one as the prelude to the other.
In any case, de facto segregation in education and housing
is growing worse, and many of the professed goals of the
civil rights movement look further away than ever. Communities like Harlem face substantially the same social
problems today as they did forty years ago.[18] I need not
dwell on the worsening problem of black unemployment
and its implications.

Even where progress, however defined, occurs, the frustration of the black masses deepens. The prosperity of
recent decades has widened the gap between blacks and

[17] This recent experience, especially of SCLC, reveals the legacy of the
past in other ways as well. Louis E. Lomax has criticized Dr. King for
organizational laxness and has related the problems of the SCLC to the
structure of the Baptist Church, "The Negro Baptist Church is a non-
organization. Not only is each congregation a sovereign body, dictated to
by no one, but it would appear that the members who come together and
form a Baptist Church are held together only by their mutual disdain for
detailed organization and discipline." *The Negro Revolt* (New York, 1962),
p. 86. As a result, according to Lomax, the SCLC is a loose, scattered organization that mobilizes itself only with great difficulty. Lomax makes
good points but fails to note the extent to which this weakness flows from
the entire history of black America and especially the black South. With
justice, one could argue that the remarkable strength of SCLC in the
face of this amorphousness is a singular tribute to Dr. King's political
genius. He has mobilized masses who are ill-prepared for the kind of
puritanical discipline preached by Elijah Muhammed.

[18] Osofsky, Gilbert, *Harlem: The Making of a Ghetto* (New York, 1966),
p. 179.

whites even of the same class. The rise of the African peoples has inspired blacks here but has also threatened to open a gap in political power and dignity between Africans and Afro-Americans.[19]

The resistance of whites and the inflexibility of the social system constitute only half the problem. A. James Gregor, in an article published in *Science & Society* in 1963, analyzes an impressive body of sociological and psychological literature to demonstrate that integration under the disorderly conditions of American capitalist life more often than not undermines the development and dignity of the participating blacks. He shows that the problems of the black masses, in contradistinction to those of the bourgeoisie, become intensified by an integration which, in the nature of things, must pass them by. As Gregor demonstrates, black nationalism has been the political reply of these masses and especially of the working class.[20] Similarly, in his honest and thoughtful book, *Crisis in Black and White,* Charles E. Silberman analyzes cases such as that in New Rochelle, in which poor black and rich children had the wonderful experience of integrating in school. Why should anyone be surprised that the experiment proved a catastrophe for the black children, who promptly lost whatever ambition they might have had.[21]

When liberals and academics speak of a "crisis of identity," they may sometimes merely wish to divert attention from the prior fact of oppression, but, by whatever name, that crisis exists. Slavery and its aftermath emasculated the black masses; they are today profoundly sick and shak-

[19] See the perceptive remarks on these two kinds of gaps in Oscar Handlin, *Fire-Bell in the Night: The Crisis in Civil Rights* (Boston, 1964), pp. 21-22, 53; C. Eric Lincoln, *The Black Muslims in America* (Boston, 1961), p. 45; and James Baldwin, *The Fire Next Time* (New York, 1964), pp. 105-106.

[20] Gregor, A. James, "Black Nationalism: A Preliminary Analysis of Negro Radicalism," *Science & Society,* XXVII (Fall 1963), 415-432.

[21] Silberman, *Crisis in Black and White,* p. 298. Even under more favorable conditions, as John Oliver Killens has noted, black children in the South often have a feeling of belonging that is undermined when they move north. *Black Man's Burden* (New York, 1965), pp. 84-85.

ing with convulsions. It does us no good to observe, with
Kardiner and Ovesey, that a psychology of oppression can
only disappear when the oppression has disappeared.[22] It
does us no good to admit that the sickness of white racism
is more dangerous than the sickness it has engendered.
We face an aroused, militant black community that has
no intention of waiting for others to heal themselves.
Those who believe that emasculation is the figment of the
liberal imagination ought to read the words of any militant leader from David Walker to W. E. B. Du Bois, from
Frederick Douglass to Martin Luther King, from Robert
F. Williams to Malcolm X. The cry has been to assert
manhood and renounce servility. Every outstanding black
intellectual today—Killens, Baldwin, Ellison—makes the
point in one way or another. Let me quote only one,
Ossie Davis on the death of Malcolm X:

> [Negroes knew] that Malcolm—whatever else he was or was
> not—*Malcolm was a man!*
> White folks do not need anybody to remind them that they
> are men. We do! This was his one incontrovertible benefit to
> his people. Protocol and common sense require that Negroes
> stand back and let the white man speak up for us, defend us,
> and lead us from behind the scene in our fight. This is the
> essence of Negro politics. But Malcolm said to hell with that!
> Get up off your knees and fight your own battles. That's the
> way to win back your self-respect. That's the way to make the
> white man respect you. And if he won't let you live like a
> man, he certainly can't keep you from dying like one.[23]

Is it any wonder, then, that Dr. King could write, almost
as a matter of course, that the blacks of Birmingham during the summer of 1963 shook off three hundred years of
psychological slavery and found out their own worth?[24]

[22] Kardiner, Abram, and Ovesey, Lionel, *The Mark of Oppression:
Explorations in the Personality of the American Negro* (New York, 1951,
1962), p. 387.

[23] Davis, Ossie, "On Malcolm X," in *The Autobiography of Malcolm X*
(New York, 1965), p. 453.

[24] King, Martin Luther, Jr., *Why We Can't Wait* (New York, 1964),
p. 111.

It is no less instructive that his aide, the Reverend Wyatt
T. Walker, denounced as "hoodlums" and "winos" those
who responded to the attempt on King's life by attacking
the white racists. King himself put it bluntly when he
pleaded that the black militant be allowed to march and
sit-in, "If his repressed emotions do not come out in these
nonviolent ways, they will come out in ominous expressions of violence." [25]

King and his followers apparently believe that concerted
action for integration can cure the ills engendered by
slavery and subsequent oppression and break down discrimination at the same time. In one sense they are right.
Their greatest achievement has been to bring order and
collective effort to a people who had learned little of the
necessity for either. But King must deliver victory or face
grave consequences. As we have seen, not all slaves and
freedmen yielded meekly to the oppressor. Many fought,
sometimes with great ferocity, but they generally fought
by lashing out rather than by organizing revolutionary
effort. It would be the crowning irony if the civil rights
movement has taught just enough of the lesson of collective effort to guarantee greater and more widespread
nihilism in the wake of its inability to realize its program.

More and more young black radicals are currently
poring over Frantz Fanon's psychopathic panegyric to violence. Fanon argues that violence frees the oppressor from
his inferiority complex and restores his self-respect.[26]
Perhaps, but it is also the worst way to do either. Black
Americans, like colonials, have always resorted to violence
without accomplishing those goals. A slave who killed his
overseer did not establish his manhood thereby—any wild
animal can kill—he merely denied his docility. Violence
can serve Fanon's purpose only when it is collective and

---

[25] Silberman, *Crisis in Black and White*, pp. 122, 199.
[26] Fanon, Frantz, *The Wretched of the Earth* (New York, 1965). But see
also two good critiques in *Studies on the Left*, VI, no. 3 (May-June, 1966):
Samuel Rohdie, "Liberation and Violence in Algeria," pp. 83-89, and esp.
A. Norman Klein, "On Revolutionary Violence," pp. 62-82.

disciplined—that is, political—but then it is precisely the collective effort, not the violence, that does the healing.[27]

The legend of black docility threatens to betray those who perpetuate it. They are ill-prepared for the yielding of one side of the slave tradition—accommodation and servility—to the other side—antisocial and nihilistic action. The failure of integration and the lawlessness to which the blacks have for so long been subjected and subject combine to produce that result. James Baldwin and Malcolm X, especially in his remarks on the prestige of the ghetto hustler, have each warned of this danger.[28] Bayard Rustin has made a similar point with gentle irony:

> From the point of view of motivation, some of the healthiest Negro youngsters I know are juvenile delinquents: vigorously pursuing the American Dream of material acquisition and status, yet finding the conventional means of attaining it blocked off, they do not yield to defeatism but resort to illegal (and sometimes ingenious) methods. They are not alien to American culture.[29]

Those historians who so uncritically admire the stealing of hogs and smashing of plows by slaves might consider its modern equivalent. In the words of Silberman:

> There are other means of protest, of course: misbehaving in school, or dropping out of school altogether; not showing up for work on time, or not showing up at all (and lying about the reason); breaking school windows or ripping telephone receivers out of outdoor phone booths; or the oldest form of

----

[27] The warning of so humane and sensitive a man as Killens on this matter is worth quoting:

> The advocates of absolute non-violence have reckoned without the psychological needs of Black America. Let me state it plainly: There is in many Negroes a deep need to practice violence against their white tormentors. *Black Man's Burden,* p. 113.

The Muslims understand this very well, as does Dr. King; then try to substitute internal discipline and collective effort for the violence itself.

[28] Baldwin, *The Fire Next Time,* pp. 35-37; *The Autobiography of Malcolm X,* pp. 315-316.

[29] Rustin, Bayard, "From Protest to Politics: The Future of the Civil Rights Movement," in F. L. Broderick and A. Meier, eds., *Negro Protest Thought in the Twentieth Century* (Indianapolis, 1965), p. 410.

protest of all, apathy—a flat refusal to cooperate with the oppressor or to accept his moral code.[30]

Black nationalism, in its various manifestations, constitutes a necessary response on the part of the black masses. The Muslims, for example, have understood the inner needs of the working class blacks who have filled their ranks and have understood the futility—for these people at least—of integrationist hopes. Their insistence on the forcible assertion of a dignified, disciplined, collectively responsible black community represents a rational response to a harsh reality.[31] We need not dwell on what is unrealistic, romantic or even reactionary in the Nation of Islam or other nationalist groups; they are easy to see. Ralph Bunche, in his radical days, Gunnar Myrdal and many others have for years pointed out that the idea of a separate black economy is a will-o'-the-wisp and that the idea of a separate territory is less than that. Yet I am not sure how to answer Marc Schleifer who in 1963 asked whether these goals were less realistic than those of equality under capitalism or a socialist revolution in the forseeable future.[32] I am not sure, either, that Malcolm X, Harold W. Cruse, and Stokely Carmichael have not been wiser than their Marxist critics in demanding black ownership of everything in Harlem.[33] Such ownership will do little toward the creation of a black economy, but many of its advocates are easily bright enough to know as much.

[30] Silberman, *Crisis in Black and White*, pp. 47-48.

[31] The best study of the Muslims is E. U. Essien-Udom, *Black Nationalism: A Search for Identity in America* (New York, 1964). Elijah Muhammed has demonstrated remarkable awareness of the persistence of the slave tradition, even in its most elusive forms. His denunciation of black conspicuous consumption, for example, correctly views it as essentially a reflection of the mores of the slaveholders and counterposes to it standards that recall those of revolutionary petty-bourgeois puritanism.

[32] Schleifer, Marc, "Socialism and the Negro Movement," *Monthly Review*, XV (Sept. 1963), pp. 225-228.

[33] For a suggestive theoretical defense of such a demand see Harold W. Cruse, "Revolutionary Nationalism and the Afro-American," *Studies on the Left*, II, no. 3 (1962), 12-25; and his subsequent communication in III, no. 1 (1962), esp. p. 70. See also *The Autobiography of Malcolm X*, p. 318.

The point is that it may, as Malcolm X suggested, play a decisive role in the establishment of community stability and self-respect.

The black struggle for equality in America has always had two tendencies—integrationist and separatist—and it is likely to retain both. Since a separate economy and national territory are not serious possibilities, the struggle for economic integration will undoubtedly be pressed forward. For this reason alone some degree of unity between the civil rights and nationalist tendencies may be expected. The black bourgeoisie and its allied stratum of skilled and government clerical workers will certainly continue its fight for integration, but the interest of the black workers in this fight is, at bottom, even greater. At the same time there will clearly be serious defeats, as well as some victories, and the slogan "Freedom Now!" may soon turn to ashes.

The cumulative problems of past and present nonetheless demand urgent action. The assertion of black hegemony in specific cities and districts—Nationalism if you will—offers the only politically realistic hope of transcending the slave heritage. First, it seems the only way for black communities to police themselves, to curb antisocial elements and to enforce adequate health and housing standards, and yet break with paternalism and instill pride and a sense of worth. Second, it seems the best way to build a position of strength from which to fight for a proper share of jobs and federal funds as a matter of right not privilege. Black Nationalism may yet prove to be the only force capable of restraining the impulse to violence, of disciplining black rebelliousness and of absorbing the nihilistic tradition into a socially constructive movement. If this seems like a conservative rendering of an ostensibly revolutionary movement, I can only answer that there are no ingredients for a successful, independent black revolution, and that Black Nationalism can ultimately go only a few steps further to the left than the white masses. The rise of specifically black cities, counties and districts with high quality black schools, well paid teachers, as well as political leaders, churches and community centers, could and should uproot the slave tradition once and for all, could and should act as a powerful lever for structural reform of the American economy and society.

I do not offer these remarks as a program for a black movement, for the time is past when white men can offer programs to black militants. They are, happily, no longer listening. But I do submit that they are relevant to the formation of a program for ourselves—for the American left. If this analysis has merit, the demands of the black community will increasingly swing away from the traditional appeal to federal power and toward the assertion of local and regional autonomy. Even now Bayard Rustin and others warn that federal troops can only preserve the status quo. I should observe, further, that the appeals to Washington reflect the convergence of two powerful and debilitating traditions: slave-engendered paternalistic dependence and the growing state paternalism of white America. Let us admit that the naïve fascination of leftists for centralized power has, since the 1930's, greatly strengthened this tendency. With such labels as "progressive" and even "socialist," corporate liberalism has been building what William Appleman Williams has aptly called a nonterroristic totalitarian society. Yet American socialism has never even posed a theoretical alternative. When Professor Williams called for a program of regional and local reassertion and opposition to centralization, he was dismissed by most radicals as a utopian of doubtful mental competence. We may now rephrase his question: How do we propose to support an increasingly nationalistic black radicalism, with its demands for local hegemony, unless we have an ideology and program of opposition to the centralization of state power?

The possible courses for the black liberation movement include a total defeat in an orgy of violence (we ought to remember that there is nothing inevitable in its or our victory), a compromise with imperialism in return for some degree of local rule or the integration of its bourgeois strata, and the establishment of black power on the basis of a developing opposition to American capitalism. Since its future depends to a great extent on the progress of its integrationist struggle for a place in the economy, the black community must for a while remain well to the left of the current liberal consensus by its demands for public works and structural reform. But reform could occur under the auspices of an expansion rather than a contraction of state centralization, and the most militant of the black leaders may have to settle for jobs and local political control in return for allegiance to a consolidating national and international empire. The final result will be decided by the struggle within white America, with the blacks playing the role of an increasingly independent ally for one or another tendency. Notwithstanding some offensive and pretentious rhetoric, the advocates of black power have judged their position correctly. They are determined to win control of the ghettoes, and we would be foolish not to bet on them. The use to which they put that power, depends not on our good wishes or on their good intentions, but on what they are offered as a *quid pro quo*. For American socialism the black revolt opens an opportunity for relevance that has been missing for decades. What we do with that opportunity, as the leaders of SNCC have rather rudely reminded us, is our problem, not theirs.

PART IV

JEWISH
IDENTITY

Arendt's Eichmann
and Jewish Identity

BY *Norman Fruchter*

Volume V, No. 2
Winter 1965

Norman Fruchter is the author of Coat Upon a Stick *(1963).
He wrote frequently for* Studies *while he was an editor, both
on literary subjects and on developments in the student and
civil rights movements. This essay on Jewish identity caused
a minor furor among old leftists, particularly those involved
in the work of various left wing Jewish groups, and articulates
a cultural break of the New Left from the old.*

I

A number of the bearded, black-garbed Jews who help to
make the Lower East Side "picturesque" are slumlords.
The aging buildings they scraped to mortgage or lease,
and now cannot afford to repair, are the locus of rent
strikes staged by Negro and Puerto Rican tenants who see
the old-country Jews (and the several slumlord rabbis)
as greedy, shrewd, Jewish exploiters—the traditional anti-
Semitic stereotype—rather than as bent, suffering Jewish
believers—the traditional Semitic stereotype. A friend of
mine, fluent in Yiddish and Spanish, but swarthy enough
to pass for Italian and somewhat implausibly, on the
Lower East Side, for Hispano-American, accompanied a
Puerto Rican grandmother to the office of her *Chasidic*
landlords, to help her complain about some undated rent
receipts. He listened to the bearded *Chasids* chatting in
Yiddish about the woman's complaint, and heard himself

and the grandmother defined, contemptuously, as no better than *schwartzes*. After the landlords unwillingly corrected their mistake, and my friend assured the grandmother, in Spanish, that her receipts now affirmed what
she had known all along, that she had paid each month's
rent on time, my friend wished the two *Chasidim* good
health and a long life, in Yiddish, and said good-by.

When I heard that story I suggested, with some venom,
that had the *Chasidim* also been Zionists, they might have
used *cushi* instead of *schwartze*, for *cushi* is the Israeli word
for nigger and is used by those Israelis who consider themselves Anglo-Saxon, to define those non-European Jews
(Yemenites, Berbers, Cochinese) who find an ambiguous
refuge at the bottom of the Israeli social structure. I tell
that story now because it suggests the conflicts which
Hannah Arendt's *Eichmann in Jerusalem* presented to
American Jews. Her book aroused fierce controversy in
this country because it questioned the myth of the victim
which Jews tend to substitute for their history, and suggested that the performance of the State of Israel, in the
Eichmann trials, was no better than that of most nation-
states. The Jew is assimilating into America with a success
no other Jewish community has managed, and only the
myth of his separateness as a member of the tribe marked
for eternal suffering as victim, and the reverence for the
State of Israel as a realization of refuge, revenge, and the
age-old prophecies, can help to differentiate him from
other Americans. The drive toward assimilation has
eroded Jewish religion of its remaining spiritual value,
has made impossible, for most Jews, the traditional ob-
servances of the *Kashruth*, the Sabbath, the holidays, and
even the ordinary forms of worship. The secular values
once endemic in Jewish communal tradition—the rever-
ance for social justice, the use of intellect, the pursuit of
knowledge—were similarly displaced by the pressures of
Americanization. Today the Jew shares with most middle-
class Americans a barren but inflated religiosity, a binding

set of material imperatives, an increasing inability to see himself as a social individual with communal as well as personal responsibilities, and a consequent increase in loneliness, despair, and the forms of mental illness characteristic of social atomization. Most important, the Jew increasingly fails to utilize his traditional values and his religious heritage to define his meaning, or his life's project, in any way that differentiates him from his surrounding countrymen. The history of Jewish (and every other culture's) assimilation has been a dynamic of gradual loss of once-orienting traditions and extended entry into the nightmare of inadequate identity which faces most Americans. Jews currently exist within the polarities of a traditional European Judaism and a totally secular, bankrupt Americanism. The only vibrancies within those polarities are the victim myth of the Jewish past, which suggests an unending, dangerous uniqueness, and the State of Israel, which offers both refuge and at least a partial conclusion to the epochs of Jewish suffering.

The victim myth of the Jewish past replaces the continuities of political and economic conflict which form the history of most cultures. It dictates that until the time when the Messiah manifests God's justice, the Jewish people face endless misery, for they will continually encounter the implacable hostility of the Gentile world, and suffer repeated persecution. But their role is to endure, as the Chosen People, until the end of time.

This myth guarantees a unified identity only to the communities of orthodox Jews separate from whatever national community within which they temporarily reside. For a Jew attempting to assimilate, into Germany or America, the myth creates several problems. How does the new life he is accepting, which involves the abandonment of traditional Jewish practices, fulfill the traditional role of witness? If he accepts the myth of unending Gentile hostility, how much can he value his chances for complete assimilation? If, however, the possibilities for assimilation seem unending, perhaps the victim myth needs to be discarded. In that case, who is the Jew?

The establishment of the State of Israel added another complexity for the American Jew. Diaspora Jews flocked to Israel, and many now see the country as the fulfillment of the Biblical prophecy to re-establish the Promised Land, and end the epochs of Jewish suffering. But American Jews have always nourished a curious ambivalence towards Israel; they grant it continuous emotional, political, and financial support, but they steadfastly refuse to emigrate. Ben Gurion's call, a few years ago, for all Diaspora Jews to return to Israel, received hostility and protest from the American Jewish community.

American Jewish identity faces all these pressures: the demands of the old myth, which dictates traditionalism and denigrates the chances for assimilation; the appeal and advantages of assimilation into America, which suggest that the myth must be discarded, but offer no replacement; the State of Israel, which defines itself as the culmination of the victim myth, and offers refuge should that myth become reality in the United States. Identity, for the American Jew, lies in an individual resolution of these three pressures, in which one is usually clearly dominant. But the pressures themselves are inescapable. Hannah Arendt's book caused such controversy because she suggested new definitions for all three pressures. She interprets the man Jews have defined, since 1945, as a monster epitomizing fanatic anti-Semitism as a banal functionary. She analyzes the causes and operation of the Nazi attempt to exterminate the Jews, and finds them far more complex than merely the most vicious example of Gentile hatred and persecution. She assesses the role of the Jews in their extermination, and finds, not the martyrdom of the eternal victim, but cooperation of the Jews with their exterminators. Finally, her evaluation of the conduct of the Israeli trial of Eichmann suggests that Israel is predominantly a national state, involved in the same competitive policies, international duplicity, war-

fare, and atrocities which characterize the behavior of most
national states. Because it offered all these reinterpretations of conventional myths necessary to the tenuous identity of the American Jew, *Eichmann in Jerusalem* was
vociferously attacked, in this country, by Jews.

II

The response to *Eichmann in Jerusalem* started with the
publication of Arendt's first trial report in *The New
Yorker,* but because that magazine prints no readers'
comments or letters to the editor, the public controversy
started with the publication of the Viking Press edition,
expanded and altered, in the spring of 1963. The favorable
responses, in the Sunday book sections of major newspapers, the weeklies and monthlies with space for serious
reviews, and the quarterly journals, were written by both
Jews and non-Jews. The hostile responses, in those same
Sunday book sections (and even in reviews in many daily
newspapers), weeklies, monthlies, and quarterlies, were all
written by Jews, with one exception (Justice Michael A.
Musmanno of the Pennsylvania Supreme Court, in the
Times Book Section). The local Jewish press was unanimously hostile, and often vicious, and the quality Jewish
press, although more restrained in tone, was almost equally
hostile (Jacob Robinson in *Fact* and *Hadassah,* Marie
Syrkin in *Jewish Frontier,* Norman Podhoretz in *Commentary*). Only Konrad Kellen's provoking article in
Midstream managed an original, dissenting interpretation
of the Jewish role in The Final Solution, and a disagreement with Arendt argued with grace and without rancor.

The unanimous hostility of the reviewers of the traditional left press is more surprising than the response of
the Jewish press. Lionel Abel's frank polemic in *Partisan
Review* was one of the most passionate, and least intelligent attacks (though it is doubtful that *PR* should be cited
as a journal of the left). But consider Gertrude Ezorsky,

in *New Politics,* Marie Syrkin in *Dissent,* Morris Schappes in two issues of *Jewish Currents,* Louis Harap in *Science and Society,* Charles Humboldt in the *National Guardian* —all defined as left, all Jewish, all hostile. And those reviewers, with one exception, wrote as Jews rather than as Socialists; only Gertrude Ezorsky challenged the reading of history, and the theories of politics, she felt were implicit in *Eichmann in Jerusalem.*

But to suggest, as Mary McCarthy does in a defense of Arendt's book in *Partisan Review,* that the controversy amounted to "a division between Jew and Gentile," is to oversimplify the response. Bruno Bettelheim wrote the most sympathetic and comprehensive appreciation of *Eichmann in Jerusalem* in *The New Republic*; many other Jews (Hans Morgenthau, Loren Baritz, Harry Golden) praised the book and accepted its conclusions. A third group of reviewers, including both Jews and Gentiles, examined the book dispassionately, disagreeing, evaluating, offering new suggestions. (Daniel Bell in *Partisan Review,* Oscar Handlin in *The New Leader,* E. V. Rostow in the *New York Herald-Tribune Book Section,* Hugh Trevor-Roper in the *London Sunday Times,* John Gross in *Encounter,* and George Mosse in *The Progressive.*) So the attempt to see the controversy as a simple Jew versus non-Jew split is inaccurate. One of the crucial divisions may be between those Jews whose ethnicity is part of their identity, but whose concerns, work, direction, and commitment transcends their Jewishness and relates them to a wider community of purpose and value, and those Jews who tend to maintain the traditional myths of Jewish identity, are more closely connected to Jewish organizations, and seem more rooted in a Jewish ambiance.

If this division between Jew and Jew has any validity, it suggests a further complexity. Arendt's book, as Bettelheim and many others have pointed out, is directly relevant to our American situation. For we also legitimate and participate in the maintenance of a totalitarian state, because we allow and support our government's treatment of individuals as things, not only in Hiroshima and Naga-saki, Vietnam, the Congo, and Cuba, but in all those countries whose inhabitants we see as ciphers in a political confrontation, and whose lives we threaten with nuclear annihilation. The implicit support, through inaction and the refusal to confront the racism interlaced throughout our own society, which we grant to our overt racists and the systems of inequality we perpetuate, increases the extent of a flaccid but pervasive American totalitarianism. The ability to confront that totalitarianism, as Bettelheim does, may possibly depend not only on assimilation, but on the ability to emancipate oneself from both ethnic and national myths. There may be some correlations between traditionalist responses to Jewish realities and traditionalist responses to American realities. What does seem evident, if the previous linkages I posited proved valid, is that participation in the organized American Jewish community involves a static and uncritical acceptance of contemporary American society, since none of the hostile Jewish critics even considered the relevance of Arendt's book to the spread of totalitarianism in America. (Though it is arguable that if critics disagreed with Arendt's theses as they applied to The Final Solution, they would necessarily disagree with the relevance of Arendt's basic theses about totalitarianism. Podhoretz and Ezorsky do this explicitly, and Abel attempts to.) Finally, most of the Jewish critics of the traditional left failed to mention the implications of Arendt's work for the drift of American society. Their failure reinforces their accommodation to American society; they responded to Arendt's book as American Jews rather than as Jewish radicals.

III

Four main foci emerge from the hostile Jewish critics' attacks on Arendt's book: her scholarship; her strictures on the trial; her judgments about the extent and result of Jewish cooperation; her portrait of Eichmann. The charges about the inaccuracies, distortions, and cavalier treatment of fact leveled against her scholarship are similar to the charges raised against her other books. Part of the trouble is the scope Arendt habitually takes on; she offers theses ordering vast periods of history, into which mistakes inevitably creep. But she seems also to be somewhat careless of fact, which may again be the inevitable result of writing her variety of history. But the charges of bad scholarship leveled against *Eichmann in Jerusalem* were seriously out of proportion to the mistakes discovered. A curious log-rolling quality marked the adverse Jewish criticism; one critic discovered a supposed mistake, and subsequent critics, whether or not they agreed with his general attitude toward the book, added that mistake to their listing. As more hostile critics wrote, the indictment grew, until Louis Harap, writing in *Science and Society* a year after the controversy started, could flatly declare that Arendt's theses had been destroyed by her numerous errors, and then simply list all the errors previous critics had discovered.

But very few of those critics stock-piling the errors were historians, or, indeed, had any sophistication about what constitutes historical fact, hypothesis, and error. Many of the "errors" they discovered were caused by mis-reading —the distortions of Arendt's arguments and positions were so widespread and severe, by supposedly intelligent critics, that many "neutral" observers decried the abandonment of usual intellectual standards. Many of the supposed errors discovered were actually the result of false notions about history held by the critics, like the myth that Stalin had destroyed Jewish organization in Russia which I shall examine later. But most of Arendt's errors were actually her reinterpretations of events and persons which the hostile Jewish critics had ordered into a species of historical "fact" both intransigent and immutable.

The two authorities cited by many hostile critics were

both named Robinson. Dr. Jacob Robinson is defined by *Facts*, the bulletin of the Anti-Defamation League of B'nai B'rith, as "an authority on international law and contemporary Jewish history . . . a special consultant to Justice Jackson at Nuremburg and to the prosecution at the Eichmann trial." His article in *Hadassah* magazine, and his report, published as an entire issue of *Facts*, sub-titled "A Report on the Evil of Banality," provided a supposedly firm basis for the charges of inaccuracy and distortion.

But Dr. Robinson forfeits his claim to authority, and indeed, to any respect for his scholarship, in his opening paragraphs. Though he commits himself only to demonstrating "the inaccuracies, fallacies, and misjudgments" of Arendt's book, he begins his article by attacking a category of books, including Arendt's and Bruno Bettelheim's *The Informed Heart,* which do a "disservice to the real story of the Jews under Hitler." Robinson accuses Bettelheim of holding a "death-wish" responsible for Anne Frank's family's failure to survive the Nazis, and then continues to disasterously misread Bettelheim's argument about why the Frank family was not able to face the Nazi danger realistically enough to protect itself. The mis-reading suggests serious limits to Robinson's intelligence, as well as to his ability to control his bias, but the misquotation is deliberate distortion, since Robinson attributes "death-wish" to Bettelheim by using the phrase three times in quotation marks. I have carefully checked all the passages about the Frank family in *The Informed Heart*: Bettelheim never uses the phrase. (I suspect it never occurs in the entire book.)

After this speciousness, Robinson's authoritative stance, as well as his numerous attempts at correction, seem somewhat dubious. He does point out several clear mistakes, which are perhaps more glaring than one expects to find in an authoritative history. (Arendt's book was written as journalism, a running trial commentary, and then rewritten for publication.) But the lapses, inaccuracies, and mistakes Robinson cites are all minor, and corrections would not shake Arendt's theses. Robinson actually set out to challenge those theses, and not merely to point out inaccuracies, but his limitation (aside from his dishonesty), is his inability to understand that historical hypotheses are dislodged by opposed hypotheses which offer more convincing orderings of evidence, rather than by isolated corrections.

Nehemiah Robinson, the director of the Institute of Jewish Affairs of the World Jewish Congress, also published a review and a report, distributed by the World Jewish Congress and cited by other critics. Robinson offers detailed corrections of Arendt's judgments about the extent of Nazi persecution of Jews before 1939, and objects to one of her most bizarre speculations, that both Heydrich and Frank were part, or full-Jews. But most of his other objections are based on mis-readings. He questions Arendt's argument that the law Israel should have used to try Eichmann was the Genocide Convention (pointing out, as J. Robinson does, Arendt's ignorance of the Israeli adoption of that Convention in 1950), and charges that Arendt never considers the problem of retro-activity involved in the use of that Convention, drafted in 1948, to try crimes committed before 1945. But Arendt treats the problem of retroactivity which both the Nuremberg Trials and the Eichmann trial faced, just a few pages before she considers the use of the Genocide Convention; only a singularly obtuse reader would demand that the discussion be repeated. Most suspicious, given the tone of Nehemiah Robinson's attacks on Arendt for her errors and her pretensions to *any* scholarly status, are the similarities between his report and Jacob Robinson's. Whole paragraphs repeat, word for word, the arguments Jacob Robinson made; only an occasional phrase is altered. Reading the reports side by side, it becomes obvious that large sections of one are copied, almost verbatim from the other. Which is the original seems impossible to discern. But what conclusions can one draw about the supposedly crippling inaccuracies of Arendt's book, and the flawed nature of her scholarship, when one of the two chief Jewish authorities attempting to question that scholarship is forced to copy from the other?

The attacks on Arendt's evaluation of the Israeli trial of Eichmann suffered from similar mis-readings and distortions. One would expect that Dr. Jacob Robinson, as assistant to the Israeli prosecutor, would correctly summarize Arendt's objections to the trial, especially since she succinctly stated them: "the failure of the Jerusalem court consisted in its not coming to grips with three fundamental issues . . . : the problems of impaired justice in the court of the victors; a valid definition of the 'crime against humanity'; and a clear recognition of the new criminal who commits this crime." (p. 251)[1] Robinson distorts her first charge to read "non-admission of witnesses for defense," which is only one of the failures Arendt locates within the major problem of impaired justice in the court of the victors. Robinson argues that Arendt is wrong to accuse the Israeli court of non-admission of defense witnesses, and charges her with not knowing, or never stating, that sixteen witnesses from abroad were interrogated by courts of law in Germany, Austria, and Italy. But Arendt does consider the nature of the examination accorded those sixteen witnesses, and their resulting testimony; she finds these inadequate for the defense (see pp. 126, 129, 200, 259). Moreover, her charge is not that no witnesses for the defense offered evidence, but that the Israeli prosecutor retracted his pledge to allow defense witnesses immunity from Israeli prosecution so that they might testify in court. Arendt's charge

---

[1] All pages, except when followed by a cited text, refer to *Eichmann in Jerusalem*, Viking Press, 1963. A paper edition recently published by Compass carries the same pagination.

against the Israeli court is not limited to the court's attitude toward possible defense witnesses. She stresses the more complex problem of impaired justice. She analyzes the inadequate nature of the documents available to the defense, since all the material was compiled by hostile researchers and prosecutors. She considers the kind of research an adequate defense would have to undertake, and the amount of recorded testimony which would have to be challenged, and perhaps excluded. She considers that the problem of impaired justice involves the question of the limits of the Israeli judges' impartiality. Finally, Arendt sees that the entire kidnapping and trial procedure makes Israel vulnerable, as the Allies were at Nuremberg, to the *tu-quoque* argument; could not several Israelis be kidnapped and tried, in Egyptian or Syrian courts, on charges of "crime against humanity," citing the Eichmann trial as a precedent?

For all these reasons, Arendt argues that the Israeli court never adequately faced the problem of victor's justice, and that only two solutions—a trial under the Genocide Convention, or a trial by international tribunal —were possible. By not facing all Arendt's analyses of the problem of impaired justice, but instead distorting the charge into a simpler failure to admit defense witnesses, Dr. Robinson rebuts it and absolves the court, but evades, as the court evaded, the major problems. One of the ironies involved in the attack on Arendt's evaluation of the Israeli trial was that none of the critics understood that in attempting to define a legitimate and valid method under which to try Eichmann (the Genocide Convention), Arendt offered defenses of the trial which answer most of the objections raised by jurists and legal observers. She defends the trial against the charge that Israel lacked previous territorial jurisdiction, arguing that since the Jews were exterminated as Jews, no matter where they were found, the Jewish state, as the political manifestation of that Jewish community which was murdered, had the right to try Eichmann even though no state existed when Eichmann arranged the transportation of the victims. She also defends the trial against the charges of inevitable partiality, arguing that elementary principles of justice as well as the previous trials of war criminals indicate that judges can successfully separate their legal functions from their passions. But Arendt insists that the Israelis imposed limitations on the defense *more serious* than those imposed at Nuremberg, and that these limitations resulted in a seriously impaired justice.

Few of Arendt's critics faced her arguments. Instead, Jacob Robinson and Schappes introduce testimonials to the trial's fairness written by international jurists and legal experts, as if anyone even vaguely familiar with the issue was not aware that there is a continuing controversy, in all legal circles, about the precedents for the Nuremberg Trials, the validity of both the Nuremberg and the Eichmann trials, and the contribution of both to the development of international law. Abel misunderstands her objections to the Israeli trial so completely that he judges them quibbles about "legal niceties." Schappes perceives that Arendt questions the validity of the Nuremberg Trials, but simply asserts that, in spite of Arendt, the Nuremberg Trials "constitute a landmark in the development of international law—and the Eichmann trial, following in its wake, will take its honored place in that development." Both Schappes and Syrkin disagree with the distinction Arendt offers between what Eichmann *did* and what the Jews *suffered,* and Syrkin is particularly pointed in accusing Arendt of callousness toward the expressions of emotion and suffering which the Jewish survivors offered the court. But Arendt argues that justice must only be concerned with what Eichmann *did,* and that no court can evaluate the amount of suffering any man, or any crime, causes another. And Arendt's objection to the parade of the sufferings-of-the-Jewish-people witnesses, *as the prosecutor styled them,* was not simply that they were irrelevant to what Eichmann did, and therefore not necessary to the process of justice. After listening to the first background witness, Zindel Grynszpan, (the father of the Herschel Grynszpan whose assassination of the German third secretary to its Paris embassy, Ernst vom Rath, triggered the *Kristallnacht*) Arendt "thought, foolishly: Everyone, everyone should have his day in court. Only to find out . . . how difficult it was to tell the story, that—at least outside the transforming realm of poetry—it needed a purity of soul, an unmirrored, reflected innocence of heart and mind that only the righteous possess. No one either before or after was to equal the shining honesty of Zindel Grynszpan." (p. 209)

Rather than callousness, what this indicates is Arendt's compassion for the truth of human suffering, and her sense that few individual sufferers are able to maintain that truth in a court of law, fifteen years after the event. Moreover, what Syrkin and Schappes failed to read, when they charged Arendt with a meaningless distinction between what Eichmann did and what the Jews suffered, was that Arendt had pointed out that the District Court judges echoed Arendt's distinction in their written judgment; they held that the sufferings transcended normal human understanding, were perhaps accessible to the realm of art, but did not belong in the courtroom (see p. 193).

Both Dr. Robinson and Schappes dispute Arendt's second charge against the Israeli court (that it failed to achieve a valid definition of the "crime against humanity") by arguing that it was clear from the statutes the court applied that a "crime against humanity" was also a crime against the international order. But Arendt argues that the Nuremberg Charter, and all the trials which were legitimated by it, never adequately defined the "crime against humanity," and confused definitions further by also prosecuting "crimes against peace" and "war crimes," both vulnerable to the *tu-quoque* argument. Therefore the Israeli court had an opportunity to establish a new international precedent, either by re-defining the "crime against humanity" or by trying Eichmann under the Genocide Convention.

Instead, the Israelis tried Eichmann under The Nazis and Nazi Collaborators Law of 1950, which is based on Article 6 of the Nuremberg Charter, and defines the "crime against humanity" as: "any of the following acts: murder, extermination, enslavement, *starvation or* deportation and other inhumane acts committed against any civilian population, and persecution on *national,* racial, religious or political grounds." (From Schappes, who quoted from *6,000,000 Accusers,* Appendix, p. 309. The italicized words were added by the Israelis.) This definition, Arendt argues, is too broad to apply to the unique genocide the Nazis attempted, for enslavement, deportation, and persecution of religious and political groups have always been practiced by nation-states. Though the Jerusalem court managed to separate the systematic crimes against the Jews from the far more inconclusive categories prosecuted at Nuremberg, it failed to understand the necessity to separate genocide from the other charges of persecution and deportation, and to prosecute genocide as a unique crime which threatened the basic fabric of international order.

This distinction is crucial to Arendt's argument, for she sees the emergence of the Nazi totalitarian movement, and its practice of genocide, as an entirely new and dangerous phenomena, necessitating a new international order and a new and effective international penal code to prevent its re-emergence. To argue that genocide is merely a continuation of conventional warfare or the latest form of Gentile anti-Semitism is, to Arendt, to misunderstand the meaning of the Third Reich, and to surrender whatever initiative we still possess to shore up our civilization against another collapse into the barbarity of Nazism, and to progress to an international order which might prevent

another attempt at genocide. Whether or not one accepts
Arendt's interpretation of the causes and mechanisms of
totalitarianism, it is clear that the social conditions favorable to the emergence of a totalitarian movement existed
in post-World War I Germany. That movement emerged,
and attempted to exterminate some eleven million people.
Arendt argues that the enormity of that attempt so violates
the basic assumptions of nations, and so threatens our international order, that new precedents are necessary to
prosecute, and punish the perpetrators, and to insure
against repetition. The Israeli court, Arendt argues, had
the opportunity to try Eichmann under the Genocide
Convention; she outlines the argument the court could
have used to meet the territorial objections. But the court
chose to follow the limiting and questionable precedents
of the Nuremberg Charter and Trials, dispensed a more
flawed justice, and most important, failed to advance the
development of that international order and law Arendt
thinks is crucial to our communal survival. One can easily
quarrel with the utopian and apolitical nature of Arendt's
imperatives for international development, but none of
the hostile critics did. Instead, they defended the Israeli
trial by distorting and evading Arendt's arguments.

The failure of all the hostile critics to see that new
definitions of both the "crime against humanity" and the
criminal who commits those crimes were necessary for the
Eichmann trial was linked to their anger at Arendt's interpretation of Eichmann. Robinson, Syrkin, Podhoretz,
and Schappes question Arendt's facts, accuse her of per-
versity and distortion, and deny her portrait of Eichmann
any validity, but do not explicitly argue that Eichmann
was aware of his criminality and therefore a monster.
Abel and Ezorsky explicitly make this link, and try to
argue that historic, psychologic, and moral evidence proves
Eichmann's monstrosity. Central to both positions is a
curious insistence on the intransigence and immutability

of "facts" which the critics possess. But "facts" never exist in isolation. The evidence necessary to disprove a historical thesis consists of a series of facts unified into a counter-hypothesis, or a more consistent interpretation of the same series of facts.

If these critics were quarreling with an economic and political history, their tendency to insist, as Ezorsky does, that Arendt exhibits "indifference to living fact" might be less embarrassing. (How can Ezorsky, herself a teacher of philosophy, indulge in the naïveté of asserting the existence, let alone the vitality, of facts apart from the interpretative contexts of historians?) But Arendt's book is a clearly speculative attempt at interpretive biography, and the "facts" here are historical fragments, scraps of conversation, perceptions recorded by men whose views can no longer be analyzed, judgments offered by unknown witnesses. Rather than a concrete order of historical fact, Arendt uses the most elusive evidence for her material. Yet all her critics accuse her of ignoring the "facts" of Eichmann's consciousness, behavior, beliefs, and personality as if these "facts" were clearly inscribed in some eternal, monolithic history.

Arendt's attempt to interpret Eichmann could easily be attacked for its folly, given the paucity and flimsiness of the available evidence, the absence of any non-partisan research, the difficulties inherent in any attempt at evaluation. But none of Arendt's critics make this point. Instead, Jacob Robinson sees Arendt's attempt to analyze Eichmann's crisis of conscience as "astonishing and reached in ways contrary to usual methods of scientific research." Do methods of scientific research exist for analyzing conscience? Robinson, Syrkin, Ezorsky, Abel, and Podhoretz charge that Arendt accepted Eichmann's own evaluation of himself and his role, but a careful reading of the text will indicate that Arendt constantly juxtaposes Eichmann's testimony with the evidence she has collated from other sources, in order to demonstrate Eichmann's bad faith, bad memory, distortions, ambitions, inability to use anything but the *Amtssprache* (officialese) of cliches, and his failure to think.

Many of the critics distorted Arendt's portrayal. Nehemiah Robinson finds Arendt's Eichmann "a quite likeable chap," while Schappes concludes that Arendt has made Eichmann "Everyman." For Abel, Eichmann "comes off so much better in her book than do his victims." At stake here is the refusal of these Jewish critics to believe that the man who administered the machinery which sent millions of Jews to their deaths could be more human than monster. Ezorsky's treatment of the Veesenmayer telegram is a valuable corrective to Arendt's presentation, but the conclusions Ezorsky draws are revealingly distorted. The telegram defines Eichmann's protest against both Himmler's and Hitler's decision to allow the emigration of the remaining Hungarian Jews. Eichmann wanted to continue the deportation, and though Arendt argued that Eichmann intended to set his obedience to Hitler's *Fuhrer order* (to exterminate the Jews) against Himmler's political decision to allow the Hungarian Jews to emigrate, Ezorsky's use of the telegram shows clearly that Eichmann was prepared to seek a new decision even from Hitler. But Ezorsky concludes, from this obdurance, that these "facts exhibit not Eichmann's conscience or his obedience to Hitler's orders but his fanatical hatred for Jews." The words of the Veesenmayer telegram indicate only that Eichmann felt that the decision to allow emigration was not wise, that Himmler had not really agreed to it, and that "the Jews concerned were all biologically valuable material." (If the phrase about the Jews, attributed to Eichmann by Veesenmayer, was actually used by Eichmann, it indicates the repetitions of a bureaucrat rather than the implacable hatred of a fanatic anti-Semite. It is possible to argue that though Eichmann used *Amtssprache* throughout his official life, the Nazi *newspeak* only camouflaged his hatred for Jews, but evidence is re-

quired for such a statement, not merely the repeated assertions that Eichmann was a fanatic anti-Semite.) Consider
these judgments, and the relevance they exhibit to any
order of historical fact: "But the real Eichmann was a
killer, ready to take the initiative even against Hitler's
orders, so that no Jew should live." "How could the man
not have been morally monstrous? And all the more a
monster if he did not know that he was one!"

Ezorsky made the first statement. The second, by Abel,
indicates both the impassioned nature of his polemic and
the failure to face the problem of intent, which he shares
with Ezorsky, the District Court, and all those Jews who
believe that Eichmann was indeed a monster. If Eichmann
was clearly aware of his criminality, then we can judge
him monster. But if Eichmann performed his murderous
duties within a criminal state which so transformed conscience, value, and judgment that he had no sense of his
evil, how then shall we judge him?

In spite of all the mis-readings, the real quarrel Jewish
critics have with Arendt is not about Eichmann's role,
but about the extent of his awareness. We know from
sources independent of the present controversy that Eichmann's role in The Final Solution was exaggerated by
the defendants at Nuremberg; that he was never an originator of policy but rather a high-level functionary, carrying out comprehensive orders which left him a comfortable latitude for organizational originality and initiative.
(See Gerald Reitlinger, *The Final Solution*, Vallentine,
Mitchell and Co., Ltd., London, 1953.) Within those
bounds, Arendt constructs her portrait. She is always careful to insist that Eichmann's responsibility was major,
although she has been distorted to argue that he was a
tiny cog in an infernal machine. Arendt attempted to
define, precisely, the limits of Eichmann's responsibility
because the Israeli prosecutor and the Appeal Court
judges found Eichmann totally responsible for The Final
Solution. Arendt (and the District Court judges) see

Eichmann not as the architect, but as the chief of transportation arrangements for The Final Solution.

The quarrel, then, is not about what Eichmann did,
but how he did it; about the nature of his conscience
and consciousness as he performed his role. Arendt ex-
pends her major effort on both a speculative exploration
of Eichmann's psyche, and a more concrete description of
the criminal state within which Eichmann performed his
duties. She discovers in Eichmann a new form of criminal,
a man who abets mass murder without the awareness that
he is transgressing. Her critics disagree, asserting that
Eichmann committed his evil in full awareness. But they
never face the central problem: how is normal conscience
and normal morality sustained in a criminal state? To
argue, as Abel does, that the Greek view of morality still
relevant to our values damns Eichmann as a monster, is
only to reassert *our* means of judging Eichmann; that
argument still evades the problem of how we can evaluate
Eichmann's own awareness of what he did. Charles Humboldt, in his *National Guardian* review, attempts to ab-
solve the German people, and to judge Eichmann, by
offering a distinction between those "ordinary men who
can be deceived, persuaded, or forced to do evil to their
fellow men, and those who deceive, persuade, and force
them." But this is both an irrelevant and a dangerous argument. Irrelevant, because it obscures the discussion as to
whether Eichmann was a persuader or, as Arendt argues,
one of those who was persuaded. Dangerous because it
implies that only those men with sufficient power are
responsible. Ezorsky evades the problem of awareness by
a sophism: "That situation (Eichmann's role as a lowly
bureaucrat in the thirties) did not bring out—what *must*
have been there already—a capacity for mass murder.
That capacity was realized in his crime. It was Eichmann
the *man* who became a mass murderer." (Emphasis added.)
Eichmann was not a mass murderer; he had no capacity
to participate in mass murder—the two executions he

witnessed made him violently ill. His capacity was for
the efficient and assiduous performance of the manifold
administrative tasks which made mass murder possible.
The question is whether he was aware of the monstrous
evil he was abetting, and the answer is not tautologies
which argue that the *essential man* always possessed the
capacities for mass murder, no matter what situation he
found himself in.

The critics who refuse to face the problem of Eichmann's conscience and awareness imply, when they do not
directly assert, that what we take to be normal consciousness of good and evil was operative within Eichmann,
and that he acted in full cognizance of the evil he was
aiding. But since they refuse to face the operations of a
criminal state which seeks to transform and replace conventional morality, they must also conclude that the
myriad Germans who participated *directly* in some form
of the round-ups, deportations, transportations, and mass
executions (the number exceeds a million, and might
even exceed the number of Jews murdered) also acted
with full awareness of their evil, and were therefore monsters like Eichmann. The inevitable question suggests
itself: how is it possible for a supposedly civilized nation
to turn itself into a collectivity of murdering monsters?
Arendt answers this question in both *The Origins of
Totalitarianism* and *Eichmann in Jerusalem,* by developing a complex model and analysis of the operations of
the totalitarian *movement* and its transformation of individual consciousness. But those Jewish critics who attack
Arendt's analysis have no answer to the *fact* that a civilized
nation sanctioned and participated in the deliberate and
systematic murder of perhaps six million Jews. They refuse
even to think about causes, development, process, individual involvement. Arendt's hostile critics insisted, repeatedly, that *there was nothing to learn from The Final
Solution.* What these hostile critics are asserting, in their
intransigent insistence that Eichmann was not a dull man

transformed into an administrator of murder by the Nazi movement, but the latest incarnation of the eternal anti-Semitic fanatic, is the hoary monster myth which substitutes for Jewish history. Eichmann was a monster like the rest of the murdering *goyim,* and the list is both particular and endless. All the Germans were monsters. The Jews have always been persecuted and murdered by monsters. The entire Gentile world is potentially monstrous. And so the myth, the emotions, and the argument proliferate; Arendt's attempt to portray the petty, distorted, and finally horrible humanity of Eichmann, encounters the skein of centuries-old Jewish myth; the thread of Jewish uniqueness unwinds into the frightening tangles of universal Jewish paranoia. And perhaps some of the reviewers were particularly hostile because Arendt herself is Jewish; several of the smaller Jewish newspapers I read accused her of betraying her people.

The hostile Jewish critics expended most of their energy and emotions on Arendt's charges against the European Jews, although the few sections and scattered pages of *Eichmann in Jerusalem* which examine the Jewish role in The Final Solution take up less than a tenth of the book. The attacks on Arendt's general attitude to the Zionist movement, and her characterizations of Zionist movements and leaders within Nazi Europe, I think have some validity. Though Arendt was attempting to suggest the common ground between the aims of the pre-Final Solution Zionist movement and the Nazis, she distorts, as Syrkin clearly points out, the role of the several Zionist organizations after the policy of extermination became clear. Neither Syrkin nor Ezorsky challenge Arendt's judgments about the early Zionist collaboration with Nazism, but they point out her misrepresentation of the Zionist movement once The Final Solution began.

But the main attack was against Arendt's charges of Jewish complicity. The two passages which state Arendt's position require quotation, because they are so often distorted:

> Of course, he (Eichmann) did not expect the Jews to share the general enthusiasm over their destruction, but he did expect more than compliance, he expected — and received, to a truly extraordinary degree — their cooperation (p. 103-4).

> But the whole truth was that there existed Jewish community organizations and Jewish party and welfare organizations on both the local and the international level. Wherever Jews lived, there were recognized Jewish leaders, and this leadership, almost without exaggeration, cooperated in one way or another, for one reason or another, with the Nazis. The whole truth was that if the Jewish leadership had really been unorganized and leaderless, there would have been chaos and plenty of misery but the total number of victims would hardly have been between four and a half and six million people (p. 111).

The general point that these two paragraphs make is the same point that Raul Hilberg exhaustively documented in his massive study, *The Destruction of European Jewry*. The only quarrel Jewish authorities had with the Hilberg book was his use of German sources, and his consequent neglect of the Jewish response to Nazism. No critic seriously quarrels with Hilberg's judgments. Arendt repeats those judgments, perhaps exaggerating them by the qualifications she introduces, and is vehemently attacked. Moreover, she is not attacked simply for her qualifications, for exaggerating the extent and effect of Jewish cooperation. Her position is first distorted into a wholesale indictment: a "picture of Jewish leaders eager to annihilate their own people," (Nehemiah Robinson); "all the brave, heart-rending efforts (at resistance), slight as they were against the Nazi machine, added to the disaster," (Marie Syrkin); "recognized Jewish leaders, 'almost without exception' served in the murder of their fellow Jews," (Ezorsky). Then this position is attacked, first by arguing that chaos and leaderlessness would not have saved the Jews, then by defending the Jewish leader-

ship. Critics like Podhoretz are capable of pointing out
that nothing Arendt tells us about the nature and extent
of Jewish cooperation is new, and then denying the validity of Arendt's judgment.

Part of the trouble lies in the conclusion of that second
statement, for Arendt offers a hyperbole instead of a judgment, to emphasize her point about the extent of Jewish
cooperation. Arendt obviously understands that no people
can ever exist unorganized and without leaders; she has
introduced this impossible supposition to indicate how
seriously she views the scale and damage of Jewish cooperation. Yet Podhoretz, Nehemiah Robinson, and
Schappes laboriously point out that the condition Arendt
postulates is an impossible one within human society.
Worse, Podhoretz, Nehemiah Robinson, Jacob Robinson,
Abel, Ezorsky and Harap seize what they understand
to be the Russian example to disprove Arendt's judgment.

The Russian argument asserts the *Einsatzgruppen* (the
action groups of the Security Police and the SD) murdered close to a million Jews (the number is disputed)
behind the German lines in Soviet Russia. Everyone
knows that the Russian Jewish community was totally
leaderless and disorganized (because Stalin had completely decimated the Jewish leadership). Therefore
Arendt is totally wrong in her assertion that Jewish leadership and organization was crucial to Jewish extermination,
and that chaos would have saved Jewish lives. But the
assertion that Stalin decimated the Jewish leadership in
the Baltic States, White Russia, the Ukraine, and South
Russia (the four areas where the *Einsatzgruppen* mas-
sacred) is a thirties' myth. A glance at the relevant pages
in Reitlinger's *The Final Solution* will reveal that Stalin
destroyed the leadership of the Jewish political and Zionist
organizations, and severely limited the educational and
religious ones, but that intricate welfare, religious, and
communal organizations survived to carry out the tradi-

tional registering and selection of German victims *only five months after the Germans attacked Russia.*

In July, 1941, ghetto organization began in Kovno, Vilna, Libau, and Dwinsk; by September the whole machinery of Jewish badges and *Ausweise,* or employment certificates, was in force throughout the Baltic States; by October, 1941, only four months after the German invasion, Jakob Gens had personally delivered a group of Vilna Jews to be executed by the *Einsatzgruppen* in the pits at Ponary. Throughout the six months that Abel, Ezorsky, and most critics cite, from November, 1941, to June, 1942, when more than a half-million Russian Jews were killed in the Ukraine by the *Einsatzgruppen,* the ghettos functioned as collecting and registering depots for Jewish victims. The massacres at Kiev were initiated by an order to the Kiev Jews to assemble for resettlement; according to Reitlinger the Germans were astonished when thirty thousand Jews assembled. On September 29th and 30th, at the Babi Yar ravine Yevtushenko's poem commemorates, 33,771 Jews, by *Einsatzgruppen* records, were shot to death and then buried. We will probably never learn enough about the role of leadership within the innumerable hierarchies which allowed 33,771 Jews to assemble for 'resettlement' after the news of the massacres in the Baltic States had been disseminated through all the ghettos by the courageous Jewish messengers Ezorsky cites. But can anyone doubt that in one of the largest Jewish ghettos in all Europe, let alone the Ukraine, the operation, advice, and organization of that Jewish leadership was not involved in the submission to massacre of so many people?

What complexities are involved in the acceptance, by so many supposedly intelligent Jewish critics, that the Russian Jews were unorganized and leaderless, and that the *Einsatzgruppen* murdered hundreds of thousands by executing in a chaos? How could the same critics who lectured Arendt about the impossibility of her hyperbole of social disorganization then conceive of a people, numbering over two million, living in towns and villages from the Baltic to the Caspian, without the intricate relationships, communal patterns, religious traditions, and social divisions that result in organization and leadership?

The attempt to defend the European Jews from Arendt's charges of complicity never transcends this level of mulishness, except in parts of Syrkin and Ezorsky's articles. They suggest the complexity of Jewish response, the manifold and varying organizations, the development of different qualities of Jewish leadership, the effect of the selective process the Nazis instituted, the extent of the resistance movements, and the lack of alternatives available to almost all of the leadership. The question of alternatives is complex, and most critics have misunderstood Arendt's arguments. She states clearly that when the bulk of the Jewish population are confronted with deportation to the death camps, and the S.S. men armed to conduct them aboard the "resettlement trains," it is too late for a resistance which has probably become psychologically impossible anyway. She criticizes the Israeli prosecutor for constantly asking the ordinary Jewish witness at Jerusalem, "Why didn't you resist?" The question is futile.

But to conclude from that position, as Syrkin and Podhoretz do, that the Jewish leadership had no alternative to its cooperation, is to distort and simplify Arendt's argument. For what she implies in *Eichmann in Jerusalem,* and has stated clearly in *Origins* and in interviews, is that the Jewish leadership had alternatves, especially in the early stages of the Nazi organization. That leadership ought to have evaluated and understood the German menace (especially after the first news about the extermination camps was received in the ghettos); it ought to have realized that the Nazis were dedicated, as they repeatedly proclaimed, to Jewish extermination; it ought to have warned each Jewish constituency that the Germans meant murder, and that they must prepare for covert and overt resistance on a total scale. That leader ship ought to have understood that its own functions, and the daily communal life of the ghetto and the *stetl*, could not continue; that normal rituals, worship, and cultural and social events obscured the danger and reduced the ability of Jews to prepare to fight desperately for their survival. (The literature describing the social and cultural life within the ghettos facing extermination is terrifying. Approving critics cite scores of examples of *courageous* Jews carrying on with life as usual: worshiping, disputing, holding literary meetings, even dances during the worst periods of Nazi extermination. What is heroic about continuing life as usual when facing extermination?)

It is obvious that an entire people could not have gone underground. It is also obvious that, had the attempt been made, the Nazis would have been forced to expend an enormously increased number of men and materials to accomplish The Final Solution. They might have succeeded, though the evidence Arendt cites about Nazi experience when meeting intransigent moral resistance suggests some qualifications. But it is false to argue, as Abel, Robinson, Ezorsky, and Podhoretz do, that the Nazi will to murder was so extreme that no commitment of resources would have been considered too great to insure Jewish destruction. The Nazis were certainly not rational, and their war effort suffered considerably from their intransigent commitment to murder. But that will was *not* total, and it was constantly inhibited by rational considerations. Reitlinger's *The Final Solution* is full of examples of extermination proceedings shut off because of higher military priorities, and of considerable numbers of Jews kept alive for military, political, and especially economic reasons. Moreover, the comparative success of those small bands of Jews who went underground, printed their own passes, killed Nazis to get uniforms and weapons, and survived to join partisan units, begins to indicate what wholesale Jewish resistance might have accomplished. (It is true that partisans frequently murdered those Jews who sought to join them; it is also true that those Jews who escaped to join the partisans survived in much higher percentages than those Jews who remained in the ghettos and waited for resettlement.)

Hilberg argued that the only chance for Jewish survival was total resistance, the transformation of the Jewish people into a revolutionary movement. He also developed the reason why the various Jewish communities were unprepared for total resistance, a universal underground, and a constant, determined attempt to insure their own survival. The genocide the Nazis contemplated was so unprecedented that not only the Jews found it difficult to accept. Most of the Western world has still neither accepted nor understood that the Nazis intended, and almost managed, to destroy the European existence of one of the peoples of the world. Moreover, the non-assimilated Jews of East Europe were isolated from their national communities, spoke Yiddish rather than the national language, read only their own newspapers, ignored the dominant politics, concentrated on the intricacies of their own communities and relationships. These communities had also evolved traditional methods for responding to Gentile threats; they ceded responsibility for their well-being to their leaders, who went as emissaries to the hostile powers, to discover the price for peace. The traditions of accommodation, by the leadership to the outside power, and by the local inhabitants to their leadership, began in the Middle Ages, but led to the gas chambers. Similar patterned responses, developed through the centuries, resulted in an incapacity for sustained resistance throughout most of the East European Jewish community, until almost the end, when even the most passive could see that death was approaching, and that the traditional defenses would not avail. And even then . . .

In the meshing of all these traditions and social arrangements endemic to European Judaism lies the tragedy of both the Jewish leadership and the Jewish people. For that leadership shared those traditions, just as it shared a class position which would make the abandonment of a still-recognizable reality, and the leap into active resistance, difficult. Once all those social and traditional patterns are evaluated, and weighed within the prevailing definitions of Gentile persecution which tended to see the Nazis as the most gigantic of historic *pogroms,* the choice which the leadership might have exercised seems exceedingly difficult. But that leadership consistently made the accommodating, destructive choices, and Arendt insists on their responsibility.

To refuse to admit that the Jews contributed to their own destruction because they were Jews, particular rather than abstract eternal victims, is to forfeit the ability to learn anything from The Final Solution. "Murderers with the power to murder descended upon a defenseless people and murdered a large part of it," Norman Podhoretz declares. "What else is there to say?" To confront the Nazi extermination of the European Jews with this abstraction is to deny any meaning to the most destructive events in recent world history, to evade all questions of morality and responsibility, and to refuse to consider the human action which might prevent a repercussion. Most important, for American Jews, is the refusal to confront the changing realities and pressures involved in achieving a viable identity, and the insistence that the Jew is eternally and unchangeably—the victim.

If the Jewish critics' hostility to Arendt's book reflects anything of the attitudes of the American Jewish community, Jewish identity in this country is both severely threatened and intransigent. Consider the performance of the Jewish critics. Arendt attacked the conduct of the Israeli trial, argued that the Israelis could have transcended both national and tribal considerations, prosecuted Eichmann under the Genocide Convention, and established a valuable international precedent which might take us one step closer to an eventual, and inevitable, world order. The Jewish critics were unable to transcend their commitment to Israel's national policy; they were also unable to comprehend the force of Arendt's universalist vision, which once distinguished that secular international community of Jewish intellectuals. Instead, a far narrower parochialism muddled the issues or treated them as "legalistic." Arendt offered an interpretation of Eichmann as a banal functionary of mass murder; with all its flaws, the effort suggests an analysis necessary to understand the social and political situation we all begin to face as the pressures which post-industrial society mounts distort traditional morality and normal consciousness. But even those critics not prepared to argue that Eichmann was a monster refused to credit Arendt's analysis of the forces which had transformed his consciousness and secured his participation in mass murder. Arendt suggested that the leadership of the European Jewish community cooperated with the perpetrators of The Final Solution, and increased the toll of Jewish destruction. The critics defended the leadership and insisted that nothing could have altered the tragedy of Jewish extermination.

Why should American Jews exhibit this moral intransigence and insist on a theory of immutable personality, even under totalitarian stress? Why should American Jews find it necessary to refuse to confront the complexity of Jewish tradition which encouraged accommodation, complicity, and submission far more than resistance? Why should it be necessary for predominantly secular, assimilated American Jews to reassert the most primitive myths about Jewish innocence and the hostile nature of the Gentile world?

The answers I have suggested are too simple. It is not enough to argue that without the bonds of religion, custom, or succoring community, the Jew is almost as rootless as most Americans. Sartre, in *Anti-Semite and Jew,* suggests that the root of Jewish identity is the experience of being defined as different by the other. No matter what extremes of non-differentiation Jewish assimilation in America reaches, a Jew will probably have some sense that he is "different." The Gentile world provides that definition, and the Nazis demonstrated its conclusion. The concentration camps provide, for the American Jew, the dangerous guarantee of his uniqueness, the surety that his difference will be maintained, no matter what he chooses. That consciousness of uniqueness is now an asset, for it defines no limits, in America, and suggests only a vague warning. More important, it grants the Jew a separateness, even an elevation, from his fellows, through his identification with a tragic ritual which transcends secular existence. Moreover, the danger which is the logical outcome of Jewish difference is counteracted by the existence of Israel, the answer to the nagging question, What will you do if it happens here?

Sustaining those pressures, the American Jew can continue to participate in the current American celebration, convinced that he is different from, and secretly, perhaps, superior to, most Americans. His attitudes to Jewish religion, traditional patterns of belief and communal response, the meaning of his European heritage, and the current existence and policies of the State of Israel, are necessarily complex, and not rigidly circumscribed. For there are bloody realities conveniently explained by the Jewish myth. The civilized nations of the Western world would have allowed the Nazis to destroy what they could reach of the European Jewish community, provided certain national boundaries were respected. And after all the atrocities and the butchery, no nation moved to accept the Jewish refugees; had the Zionists not fought for Israel, the remnants of European Jewry would have rotted in the DP camps.

But Arendt's book challenges all American Jews who have accepted a definition as "different" by the other, and have attempted to construct an identity from the remaining fragments of Jewish tradition. To those whose Jewish "differentness" means an identification with the millions of innocent European Jews murdered by the Nazis, she suggests that innocence and guilt must be re-defined; to those whose "differentness" means an identification with the aims of Zionism and the establishment and present policies of the State of Israel, she suggests that nationalism may well transform the Jew from victim to agent of evil. The American Jew who accepts some definition of his difference is further challenged by *Eichmann in Jerusalem* because Arendt develops a concept of the citizen responsibility necessary in every modern state to prevent the re-emergence of the totalitarian movement which ravaged Germany. But once a Jew accepts his definition, by the other, as "different," he seeks an identity commensurate with that definition which places him somewhat outside the bounds of his normal society. To the extent that the American Jew achieves that different identity, whether through a valuation of the Jewish past, particular Jewish traditions, or the current Jewish state, he diminishes his responsibility for events within America. Arendt's book not only questioned basic assumptions about the Jewish past and the State of Israel which are necessary to American Jews who must achieve a Jewish identity without religious, spiritual, or communal values. She also suggested that Jews are not exempt from the responsibility to confront their society, to maintain its freedom, and to combat any drift toward totalitarianism. To ask the American Jewish community, whose accommodation has been so swift and comprehensive, to conform, and to attempt to change, the society they have so thoroughly accepted, proved an enraging demand.

Index

Abbott, Charles F., 177
Abel, Lionel, 427, 435, 439, 440, 442, 446-47, 449
Acheson, Dean, 97n
Advanced industrial capitalism, 21
  See also Corporate elite
Agriculture, 44, 144
  Hoover's policies on, 168-69
  New Deal and, 179
Amalgamated Clothing Workers, 138-42, 227
American black slavery
  Black nationalism and, 418-19
  lack of revolutionary tradition under, 394-409
  Negro docility and, 397-408
American Communist Party, 190-92, 308, 385
  banquet followers of, 212-13
  Cold War and, 213-14
  crisis in, 3, 5
  early development of, 211-12, 223, 245-52
  historical works on, 221-24
  limited accomplishments of, 4-5
  McCarthyism and, see McCarthy, Joseph R.
  Negroes and, 349-50, 354, 355-56, 359, 360, 370, 374
  popular front strategy of, 15
  roots of, 236-45
  Russian influence on, 322
  trade unions and, 184, 188
  in Wisconsin, 185, 186, 190-93
  See also Red-baiting
American Federation of Labor (AFL)
  complaints of workers in, 156
  corporatist outlook in, 127-34, 139
  leaders of, see Labor leaders
  New Deal and, 148-54
  public works, demands of, 165
  Socialists and, 103, 113-14, 118-20, 124, 205, 226-29
American Jews
  assimilation of, 424-25
  attitude toward Israel, 426
  Eichmann in Jerusalem and, 451-54
American Socialism
  Cold War and, 216-19

failure of, 198, 217-18
  parties, see American Communist Party; American Socialist Party; New Left
  prospects of, see Socialist perspective
  totalitarianism and, 215-16
American Socialist Party
  decline of, 210-12
  diverse tendencies in, 111-12, 204, 224-27, 236-37, 241-47
  early campaigns against, 110, 206-7
  election successes of, 229-31, 234-35
  evolution of, 204-10, 224-47
  historical works on, 221-22, 224
  immigrants and, 112, 119, 206, 244, 246
  innocence of, 207
  liberal coalition policy of, 15
  membership of, 124, 206, 229-31, 236, 239
  Negroes and, 111, 113, 119, 205-6, 228-29
  organization of, 124, 205
  publishing activity of, 233-34, 244
  Russian Revolution and, 239-40, 245-47
  syndicalist issue in, 225-27
  in thirties, 232
  trade unions and, 103, 113-14, 118-20, 124, 205, 226-29
  vote for, 121, 225, 238
  wartime split in, 236-37, 241-43
  women and, 111, 112, 119, 228, 239
American trade unions
  Catholic Church and, 103
  collaboration with corporate elite, 15, 102, 115, 121, 126-52, 159, 209-10, 340
  Communist Party and, 3, 184, 188
  Hoover supported by, 131, 143, 165, 170-71
  labor leaders in, see Labor leaders
  membership of, 108-9, 160
  militant struggles of, 153, 157
  open-shop drives against, 116-18
  Socialist Party and, 103, 113-14, 118-20, 124, 205, 226-29